New
Essays
in
Metaphysics

D1453419

SUNY Series in Systematic Philosophy
Robert C. Neville, Editor

Whether systematic philosophies are intended as true pictures of the world, as hypotheses, as the dialectic of history, or as heuristic devices for relating rationally to a multitude of things, they each constitute articulated ways by which experience can be ordered, and as such they are contributions to culture. One does not have to choose between Plato and Aristotle to appreciate that Western civilization is enriched by the Platonic as well as Aristotelian ways of seeing things.

The term "systematic philosophy" can be applied to any philosophical enterprise that functions with a perspective from which an attempt to spell out the basic features of things in a system. Other times it means the examination of a limited subject from the many angles of a context formed by a systematic perspective. In either case systematic philosophy takes explicit or implicit responsibility for the assessment of its unifying perspective and for what is seen from it. The styles of philosophy according to which systematic philosophy can be practiced are as diverse as the achievements of the great philsophers in history, and doubtless new styles are needed for our time.

Yet systematic philosophy has not been a popular approach during this century of philosophical professionalism. It is the purpose of this series to stimulate and publish new systematic works employing the techniques and advances in philosophical reflection made during this century. The series is committed to no philosophical school or doctrine, nor to any limited style of systematic thinking. Whether the systematic achievements of previous centuries can be equalled in the 20th depends on the emergence of forms of systematic philsophy appropriate to our times. The current resurgence of interest in the project deserves the cultivation it may receive from the SUNY Series in Systematic Philosophy.

New Essays in Metaphysics

Edited by

Robert C. Neville

STATE UNIVERSITY OF NEW YORK PRESS

Published by
State University of New York Press, Albany

© 1987 State University of New York

For information, address State University of New York
Press, State University Plaza, Albany, N.Y., 12246

Library of Congress Cataloging-in-Publication Data

New essays in metaphysics.

   (SUNY series in systematic philosophy)
   Bibliography: p.
   Includes index.
   1. Metaphysics.   I. Neville, Robert C.   II. Series.
BD111.N48   1987   110   86-30011
ISBN 0-88706-357-8
ISBN 0-88706-358-6 (pbk.)

10 9 8 7 6 5 4 3 2 1

Contents

Editor's Introduction

The first third of the twentieth century saw a great flowering of philosophy in the grand tradition. In America, Europe, and Japan, philosophers understood themselves to be carrying on or providing alternatives to the master works of Plato, Aristotle, Thomas, Scotus, the great modern rationalists and empiricists, and Kant and Hegel. One thinks of Alexander, Bergson, Bosanquet, Bradley, Croce, Dewey, Heidegger, Husserl, James, Marcel, Nishida, Peirce, Royce, Russell, Santayana, Whitehead, and Wittgenstein, to recite the more influential figures. These writers took up various stances toward the tradition – defending, rejecting, or reforming it. But most were historically learned and developed systematic stances toward philosophy in the grand tradition, embodying it in one way or another as they created contemporary philosophic positions.

Philosophy in the second third of this century was overwhelmed by war, by the geographical dislocation of centers of philosophic discussion, and by panic about what philosophy is not supposed to be able to do. Thinkers in phenomenological, positivistic, and analytical modes pushed concerns for methodology to the point of delegitimating philosophies that had other methods or little concern for method – not refuting them but claiming that they lacked a philosophic status worth refuting. In many respects, these movements in philosophy were analogous to contemporaneous modernist movements in literature, drama, art, and architecture. Philosophy in America became narrowly academic and attempted to justify itself as a profession with an identifying method. No matter that the continental and analytical methods delegitimated each other; both agreed that the grand tradition, now identified with "metaphysics," had been overcome. Historical erudition languished and philosophers came more and more to write for one another; in fact, for a select few of their colleagues. Both analytic philosophy and continental philosophy turned their backs on the grand tradition by launching an attack, usually epistemological, on metaphysics.

During this middle period, Charles Hartshorne at the University of Chicago (later at Emory and The University of Texas), Paul Weiss and

Brand Blanshard at Yale, John Findlay at London and then Boston University, and Justus Buchler at Columbia and then Stony Brook struggled to keep metaphysics in the grand tradition alive, drawing on the heritage of the British idealists, Peirce, Royce, Dewey, and Whitehead. In the very early 1950s, Weiss founded the Metaphysical Society of America and *The Review of Metaphysics*, and drew many scholastic, neoscholastic, and post-scholastic Roman Catholic thinkers into the American philosophic scene. Many of the philosophers he convened and published have produced works of enduring value, some with full-scale systematic development. But their achievements were pushed more and more to the margins by the dominant philosophical styles. By the 1960s, all the major graduate schools in philosophy were hostile to metaphysics in the grand tradition save for Yale, where John E. Smith led a protracted defense of the tradition through many pitched battles lasting into the 1980s.

Now in the last third of the century, there is a recovery of interest in metaphysics. Partly this is due to fatigue in the antimetaphysical programs, a searching for new directions. But in large part it is due to an accumulating body of work by a new generation of philosophers, much of which is being published by The State University of New York Press under the leadership of its Director, William Eastman. These younger philosophers have joined Hartshorne, Weiss, Blanshard, Findlay, and Buchler, who themselves may have retired, or thought about it, but have not ceased participating in the discussion. The justification and explanation of the recovery of metaphysics must lie ultimately in the quality of philosophy that results. The purpose of these *New Essays in Metaphysics* is to display both the diversity of the new approaches to metaphysics and its many kinds of high quality.

"Metaphysics" is a word on whose precise definition no two of the contributors to this volume would agree. In soliciting contributions, I asked only that the essays be "metaphysical" and that historical criticism be suppressed in favor of an expression of the author's own views. Early reviewers of the collection have pointed out the diversity of responses, obvious enough, and it is worthwhile to comment, contrariwise, on the shared convictions about metaphysics. First is the conviction that the most basic structures of the universe constitute an important philosophic problem. The emphasis is on the problematic character of the topic: the relation of structure to nonstructure, the locus of structure in things, in mind, in culture, the knowability of structure. Diverse answers are given to these issues, but there is practical agreement on their legitimacy, and this is what makes the authors here metaphysicians in contrast to philosophers whose methods deny meaning to the topic or appropriate power to philosophic reflection. Second is the pragmatic conviction that addressing the "basic structures" question has something to do with systematic thinking. Only a few of the contributors have "systems"; most deal systematically with certain basic issues, e.g., freedom, possibility, norms, the future, God, truth, or relations. Some of the authors argue for limitations on the use of systems relative to basic structures. But there is a common recognition that the metaphysical scope of basic structures constitutes a problem for systematic thinking able to respond to that scope. Third is a conviction that metaphysical thinking as defined in the first two points is interesting and culturally valuable. Another way of expressing this conviction pertains to philosophical responses to the de facto limits of any given thought. Whereas many philosophers think it properly humble to accept those limits and work within them at something that can be known to be well done, the contributors here respond to limits as an occasion for wider reflection. "Wider reflection" might mean expanding the system, objectifying system as such, or consideration of the cultural implications of the limitations; but in all cases it stands opposed to the scruples about conventions or "data" that feed the antimetaphysical biases of modernist philosophies.

Since the authors in this collection were invited to contribute, it should be no surprise that we share a common discussion. The group was not chosen by a panel of experts in a blind reading of an impartially selected set of journal articles. Rather, taking myself to be a metaphysician of the right age, I asked for contributions from friends and colleagues with whom I have had serious metaphysical discussions; all of the contributors know at least some of the authors besides myself. Philosophers other than these were invited to contribute to the volume but declined for one reason or another. A great many other philosophers could have been invited had space been greater.

A word needs to be said about a specific lacuna in the list of contributors. For purposes of scale and historical limitation, I set the upper limit of this "new generation" at those whose graduate work in philosophy took place in the late 1950s and early 1960s. This eliminates a generation of extraordinary metaphysical philosophers, many of whom were our teachers; people such as William Barrett, Robert Brumbaugh, John Cobb, Edward Pols, and John E. Smith, as well as those mentioned earlier. My only justification for finding principles of exclusion in terms of a generation is that these philosophers have already been recognized in their metaphysical identity.

Few generalizations can be made about the fourteen essays that follow. Perhaps one is that cultural awareness, even philosophy of culture, has taken the place of epistemology as the axle round which metaphysics turns. Each of the contributors is self-conscious about the peculiar historical position of metaphysics today, and even when the essay's topic has nothing to do with metaphysics today, that is a sub-theme; the first three and last two essays make it a major theme. More than metaphysicians of the middle third of the century, the contributors here emphasize diversity, plurality, and sometimes even incommensurability. David Hall's lead article is the strongest statement of the case. All of us take very seriously the view that thinking is interpretation and respond to both the continental hermeneutical and the American pragmatic understanding of this. Patrick Heelan here argues that even perception is interpretive, and David Weissman's concluding essay, "The Spiral of Reflection," treats metaphysical systems as beginning, if not ending, in a hermeneutical status. There is little unanimity about God, Freedom, Goodness, or Science.

The first three essays focus on the nature and task of metaphysics, and argue for specific metaphysical views. David Hall, Professor and Chair of Philosophy at the University of Texas at El Paso, claims in the first that speculative philosophy limited itself arbitrarily and unnecessarily when it moved from mythos to logos, construing the latter as univocal order. Nietzsche saw this, and attempted to counter with a philosophy of chaos over against order, but was frustrated in assuming an identity over against ironic Socrates. The essay is a straight forward introduction to Hall's own philosophy as set out in *Eros and Irony* (Albany: State University of New York Press, 1982). He is also author of *The Civilization of Experience* and *The Uncertain Phoenix*, both from Fordham University Press, 1973 and 1982, respectively.

The second essay, by George Allan, Dean of the College and Professor of Philosophy at Dickinson College in Carlisle, Pennsylvania, gives Hall's point about order a cosmological turn. He contrasts philosophies that emphasize "eternal" kinds of things with philosophies that emphasize passages and changes. The latter deal with the real issues of the "mesocosm" of experience and find their dialectical foil in rejecting divinity, the source of eternity. He then sketches a view of the mesocosm in relation to micro- and macrocosmic concerns. This essay is an introduction to the third volume of Allan's projected metaphysics, the first volume of which, *The Importances of the Past*, will have come forth from State University of New York Press before the present volume reaches print.

Nicholas Capaldi, in the third essay, defines metaphysics as "the study of primordial reality." He contrasts the "old" metaphysics with the "new," as the belief in primordial structures independent of human reality versus the belief that "primordial reality is man's relation with the world." The "new," "Copernican," metaphysics, first understood by Hume and

Kant, thus insists that culture mediate any claims about primordial reality. Capaldi elaborates the role of culture in metaphysics and criticizes positions that seek to transcend it. The essay is especially keen in its critique of the standard philosophy of science which seeks to transcend culture, a theme taken up again by Patrick Heelan. Capaldi is Professor of Philosophy at Queens College in the City University of New York and the author of *David Hume* (Boston: Twayne Publishers, 1975).

The fourth essay, by Patrick Heelan, presents a technical argument that perception involves interpretation, precisely defined by Heelan's extensions of the German and French hermeneutical tradition, with attention paid to Peirce. The essay responds to criticisms of this view from the analytic philosophy of culture-transcending science attacked by Capaldi and presents a sophisticated introduction to Heelan's major book, *Space-Perception and the Philosophy of Science* (Berkeley: University of California Press, 1983). Heelan is Professor of Philosophy at the State University of New York at Stony Brook.

Charles Sherover, in the fifth essay, presents a variation on Capaldi's theme of the culture-boundedness of knowledge, emphasizing not just culture but the very structure of subjective human time. The analysis of time shows human freedom to be constitutive of experience, not merely a lucky (or fateful) achievement. Professor of Philosophy at Hunter College of The City University of New York, Sherover is the author of *Heidegger, Kant and Time* (Bloomington: Indiana University Press, 1971) and *The Human Experience of Time* (New York: New York University Press, 1975).

In the sixth essay, "Possibilities and Constraints," Jay Schulkin returns to the theme of freedom and choice, naturalizing the transcendental context of Sherover's argument and showing in the world of neurobiology how freedom is pervasive within the limits of innate constraints. Schulkin presents a metaphysical scheme within which neurobiology and cognitive science need not be deterministic, pushing "naturalized epistemology" back toward the field of everyday life. After graduate work in philosophy at the University of Pennsylvania, Schulkin took a Ph.D. in anatomy; he has published extensively in the field of neuroscience and is a Fellow of the Institute of Neurological Sciences at the University of Pennsylvania.

George Lucas, in the seventh essay, continues the discussion of free agency but interprets moral constraints not as the limitations of possible actions but as the limitations of what is normative. With a sophisticated (rhetorically Kantian) review of current moral theory, he relates normativeness to order and concludes that "it is thus the (apparently) paradoxical task of metaphysics to admit a notion of order which allows for pluralism without caving in to relativism." (Hall wagers it can't be done; I think it can.) Lucas is Visiting Associate Professor of Philosophy at Emory University in Atlanta, Georgia, and the author of *The Genesis of Modern Process Thought* (Metuchen, N.J.: Scarecrow Press, 1983). He is editor of *Hegel and Whitehead: Contemporary Perspectives on Systematic Philosophy* (Albany: State University of New York Press, 1986).

William Sullivan moves from moral theory to metaphysics applied to practical morals, in the eighth essay. He raises the problem of individualism and entrepreneurship in light of the anti-atomistic principles of Whitehead and Dewey, arguing that the current revival of entrepreneurship marks the end of the technicist paradigm, which opens the possibility of a recovery of the aims of earlier American philosophy. Professor of Philosophy at LaSalle University in Philadelphia, Sullivan is author of *Reconstructing Public Philosophy* (Berkeley: University of California Press, 1982) and *Habits of the Heart: Individualism and Commitment in American Life,* with Robert N. Bellah, Richard Madsen, Ann Swidler, and Stephen M. Tipton (Berkeley: University of California Press, 1985).

The ninth essay, by Antonio de Nicolás, describes "The First Metaphysics" as the metaphysics of imagining, both interpreting Plato's work as a founding metaphysics of imagination and defending a theory of imagination as such. De Nicolás has developed the theme of imagination in many writings, including *Meditations on the Rig Veda* (New York: Nicolas Hays, 1976), *Avatara: The Humanization of Philosophy through the Bhagavad Gita* (New York: Nicolas Hays, 1976), and, most recently, *The Powers of Imagining: Ignatius de Loyola* (Albany: State University of New York Press, 1985). He is Professor of Philosophy at the State University of New York at Stony Brook.

With Lewis Ford's "Creativity in a Future Key," the collection moves to direct, pure metaphysical issues. Known as an interpreter of Whitehead, Ford presents his own philosophical theology in the tenth essay, arguing that God is neither an actual entity (Whitehead) nor a society (Hartshorne) but rather the future as the activity that empowers present actual occasions to create themselves out of their inherited past. God as future utterly transcends the present yet is purely temporal. This is a conception of God quite different from "the source of eternity" Allan rejects. Most recently the author of *The Emergence of Whitehead's Metaphysics: 1925–1929* (Albany: State University of New York Press, 1984), Ford earlier wrote *The Lure of God* (Philadelphia: Fortress Press, 1978) and has edited *Process Studies* since 1971. He coedited (with George L. Kline) *Explorations in Whitehead's Philosophy* (New York: Fordham University Press, 1983).

In the eleventh essay, Elizabeth Kraus's "God the Savior" presents yet another original development out of Whitehead's scheme, closely related to Ford's but focusing less on the nature of God and more on divine action in the world. Generalizing the Christian theological categories of "sin and death" to a cosmological level, she shows how sin and death are intrinsically necessary to a process in which individuals aim at self-value. She then analyzes what God must do if there is to be a cosmologically general equivalent of redemption. This essay continues her discussion in *The Metaphysics of Experience* (New York: Fordham University Press, 1979). Kraus is Professor of Philosophy at Fordham University in New York City.

Carl Vaught, in the twelfth essay, addresses the nature of truth, examining pragmatic, coherence, and correspondence conceptions. He derives from these theories requirements for openness and otherness, and then develops a subtle theory of metaphoric/analogic truth that satisfies these requirements. His theory, crudely stated, is that truth is an analogy between metaphoric relations in the object and metaphoric relations in the subject. Vaught is Professor and Head of Philosophy at The Pennsylvania State University and is author of *The Quest for Wholeness* (Albany: State University of New York Press, 1982) and *The Sermon on the Mount: A Theological Interpretation* (Albany: State University of New York Press, 1987).

Whereas Vaught appeals to the notion of indeterminacy in explicating his conception of metaphoric truth, Brian Martine in the thirteenth essay focuses upon it directly in explicating a theory of relations and individuals. His theory recalls many of the points about interpretation raised by Capaldi and Heelan, but is an original construction and differs from Capaldi and Heelan in its naturalism. Martine is author of *Individuals and Individuality* (Albany: State University of New York Press, 1984) and is Associate Professor of Philosophy at the University of Alabama at Huntsville.

In the fourteenth essay, I take the opportunity to follow the advice of Paul Weiss, who said "Why don't you just sit down and write out what you believe is true." So I sketch the lineaments of the systematic conceptions guiding my philosophy: harmony, essential and conditional features, the one and the many, order, chaos, mixtures, normativeness and value, vagueness, triviality, narrowness, breadth, personal structure, and social analysis. My first book was *God the Creator* (Chicago: University of Chicago Press, 1968), and the last two, *Reconstruction of Thinking* and *The Tao and the Daimon*, were published by State University of New York Press in 1981 and 1982, respectively. I am Professor of Philosophy and Religious Studies at the State University of New York at Stony Brook.

David Weissman, in the final essay, presents a system grander than any other in this volume, preceded by a subtle and far-ranging critique of unrecognized and (in his view) unfortunate principles in modern philosophy that may lie at the heart of everyone else's position. The "spiral of reflection" is a dialectical ladder leading from common confusions through science to a positive content for metaphysics. His ringing conclusion is a fitting end to our volume. Professor of Philosophy at City College of the City University of New York, Weissman is the author of *Dispositional Properties* and *Eternal Possibilities*, both from University of Southern Illinois University Press, 1965 and 1977, respectively, and *Intuition* and *Ideality* from the State University of New York Press in 1987.

David L. Hall

Logos, Mythos, Chaos: Metaphysics as the Quest for Diversity

The history of metaphysical speculation is replete with ironies and indignities that bespeak the exotic character of the enterprise. Not the least of the ironies lies in the fact that the speculative philosopher has often been betrayed by his own insights. Pythagoras, whose faith in rational harmony led him to choose a voiceless mysticism rather than to confess the truth of incommensurability, is certainly a case in point. Or, consider Parmenides who waved the wand of truth over the world only to see most of it disappear. As often, the betrayal has come at the hands of pupils and colleagues: Socrates called philosophy down from its heights of metaphysical romance into the concreteness of ethical inquiry, urging patience upon the speculative thinkers until such time as we might first come to know ourselves. But his clarion call was immediately muffled by his prize pupil who thematized the message and attempted to harmonize it with his own more systematic ambitions.

Even the scholars and historians of speculative philosophy have not always served it well. Certainly the most singular instance of such disservice is that of the first century shepherd of the Aristotelian corpus who willed to future generations the embarrassing confusion as to whether the name of philosophy's most (and least) vaunted discipline had an ontological or merely an editorial reference.

Can anything good come from such beginnings? From the strictly historical perspective that is a most impertinent question, for philosophies, even metaphysical philosophies, are justifiable by recourse to time, place and circumstance that together provide the context within which judgments of relevance may be made. Yet, there is this undeniable fact to contend with: speculative philosophers have claimed a broader, deeper and more lasting value for their reflections and constructions than could be satisfied by mere contemporary cultural relevance. Indeed, no philosopher of record has been permanently consigned to the status of possessing "merely historical interest." One of the essential features of speculative visions, it seems, is their incorrigibility. Philosophies are precisely those enterprises to which we must have recurrent access, those constructions from which various new beginnings may be launched.

The persistence of philosophical doctrines seems, by all accounts, to ally philosophy with art and literature, and to cancel its presumed kinship with programmatic science whose truths are thought expendable. Yet it is precisely the intrinsic connection of philosophy to science that has permitted it to question so successfully the latter's progressiveness. Cosmological doctrines shape scientific disciplines sufficiently to infect the scientific interest with the relativity of philosophic speculation. Caretakers of the intellectual enterprises have been forced to realize that progress in thinking – scientific or philosophic – cannot plausibly be characterized by a progressive approximation of Truth or even by an increasing enlargement of the understanding.

Intellectual progress (viewed in detachment from the technologies that shape and are shaped by the intellect) is progress in the elaboration and ramification of classical intuitions into articulated philosophic paradigms, a process that has finally resulted in the recent widespread capitulation to the notion of theoretical incommensurability. Thus, philosophic progress consists either in the refinement of theories housed within established traditions or in the refinement of schemes that classify and organize these traditions. Presently, we have phenomenologists, analysts, Marxists and speculative philosophers who claim privileged perspectives on the world and one another; and we have taxonomists who would bracket the question of "the World" and remain content with promoting a theoretical schema for the organization of theories. Between the uneasy slumber of the doctrinal thinkers and the frenetic insomnia of the metaphilosophers falls the shadow of philosophic culture. Remaining alert in the shadows, yielding to neither extreme, philosophers may seek renewal.

The commonly exercised recourse when philosophy has fallen into such a dilemma is a retreat to the Socratic mode of speculation, which requires that inquiry, not system, be the aim of philosophic activity; or at the very least, that system must give way to inquiry until such time as consensus may be achieved. Unfortunately, this position does not seem nearly as promising as once was the case. Overtaken as we are by a burgeoning metamentality, it is increasingly difficult to believe that inquiry will lead us anywhere but into the preciously landscaped avenues long since charted by the taxonomists.

At the end of the nineteenth century, when the philosophic enterprise was being tossed about between the extremes of programmatic science and the literary imagination, it was the sardonic guidance of Friedrich Nietzsche that proved most fateful. Recognizing as unavoidable the choice between the Scyllan rock of system and science on the one hand and the Charybdian vortex of philosophic relativity on the other, Nietzsche forwarded not one but two strategies, each a form of the *amor fati*.

The morale of systematic thinkers could be maintained if they conspired to engage in an "active forgetting" that would free them from an "excess of history." By abandoning historical reference, at least the psychological consequences of relativity could be avoided. Taking their cue from the classical beginnings of scientific rationalism, dogmatists could proceed by canceling history, by refusing to open their speculations to historical reduction, sublation or dialectical articulation. Presently, reconstructive efforts in philosophy that hope to reground the discipline – whether they be found among analysts, phenomenologists or speculative thinkers – have taken the route of active forgetting. The sense of novelty and the hope of systematic certainty are much easier to sustain if one is freed from the debilitating effects of perfect historical recall.

Active forgetting was not to be Nietzsche's way of yielding to destiny. He chose the vortex, and his harsher fate called forth intenser love. Unburdened by the numbing comforts of active forgetting, Nietzsche was opened to an insight that positioned him beyond the system-inquiry dialectic and thus beyond philosophic consciousness itself. This insight was to satisfy Nietzsche's *hybris* (the *déformation professionnelle* of this all-to-human philosopher) by justifying his claim to a unique place in the history of philosophy.

Nietzsche recognized that philosophic culture had permitted the full benefits of immortality to but a single individual. Other philosophers live on through their epigoni – there are Platonists and Aristotelians, Cartesians and Hegelians. There is, however, only one Socrates. In his untoward ambition to displace Socrates in the history of thought, Nietzsche realized the philosophic strategem that has come to provide the major impetus for recent activity in both the scientific and literary areas of philosophy.

Socrates' place in history was guaranteed by his ironic openness. As the original *eiron*, Socrates would never be without an *alazon* to show up. The list of Socratic fall guys is impressive, containing practically every important thinker in the history of philosophy. From Plato the present, there has always been a new crop of know-it-alls waiting to be brought low by the corroding influences of continued inquiry. Nietzsche's fear of being considered a buffoon and his vigorous attempts to cast Socrates as such demonstrate his recognition of the sort of struggle imposed by the Socratic presence. It was Greek comedy that was played out in the contest between Nietzsche and Socrates; but this time, so Nietzsche believed, he would turn the tables on the "fencing master of Athens" and make of Socrates the same sort of fool that Socrates had made of others.

The scale of Nietzsche's ambitions may be appreciated by reflecting upon the history of philosophic culture, which advertises the collapse of one system after another consequent upon the compulsive search for consensus. The history of philosophy is a Greek comedy authored by the ironic Socrates who, in Nietzsche's words, "discovered a new kind of *agon*." Philosophy's history can be read as a series of contests between the openness of Socratic method and the systematic, dogmatic, approach of those who fervidly demand consensus. So read, it is clear who is the buffoon, the *alazon*, and who the heroic *eiron*. Socrates is the fencing master of our entire philosophic culture.

In his contest with his dizygotic twin, Nietzsche confronted the problem of how to philosophize in spite of the full recognition of the futility of constructive thought. Nietzsche had to exclude the Socratic solution of open inquiry, which lays no systematic claim to truth. Had he chosen such a path he would have not been Nietzsche, but Socrates *redivivus*. Beyond the dogmatic claims to have "gotten it right" echoed in the works of Descartes, Spinoza, Kant, Hegel, etc., and beyond the Socratic counter-claim that open inquiry must suffice until true consensus is gained, Nietzsche offered a new philosophic program: truth is found neither in system nor inquiry, but in the summative act of the "mosaicist."

The truth of things for Nietzsche is that "a thing would be defined once all creatures had asked 'What is that?' and had answered their question."[1] "The World" is a *mélange* of interpretations, a congeries. Interpretations need not possess mutual consistency. There is conflict, contradiction − chaos. Within this morass, the only metaphysical truth is that the totality of interpretations constitutes that which is. Added up, gathered together, interpretative perspectives provide truth. *Everything,* in the summative sense, is true.

Appealing to Nietzsche to establish this or that philosophical point has become not only fashionable of late but downright clichéd. The truth that grounds the clichés is that Nietzsche was prophet and pioneer of this new age of fragmented self-consciousness, the very symbol and symptom of the failure of Hegel's program. The Absolute fell to earth and was shattered into myriad hologrammatic pieces, each one as conscious of the whole as of its own fragmentation. Nietzsche was an avatar of this fractured Absolute. It was he who returned to the murky ground of philosophic speculation, the origin that lies beyond the comforts of *mythos* and twice removed from the even more comfortable environs established by *logos*.

Recognizing the tense relationship of the philosophic impulse to the literary and scientific pursuits that each in its own way sought to replace it in the wake of Hegel's cultural apotheosis, speculative philosophers today find themselves caught between the claims of rhetoric and of reference in every act of philosophic construction. Some are willing to retrace the path taken by Nietzsche at the end of the last century. If they do, they will find what Nietzsche found, what finally drew him beyond the realm of acceptable discourse: that Chaos against which Western culture had set its face "from the beginning." The source of original speculation may be found only at the origins. There we encounter the original *Arche*, the source of the myriad perspectives that have come to form our intellectual culture: the sum of all orders, Chaos-Itself.

This is not the path of the nihilist. Accepting everything — the gathering of all perspectives — as true leads to a position precisely antithetical to skepticism and nihilism. Nor is it a path congenial to the taxonomist who is, in fact, no more than a systematic dogmatist raised to the second power. The position cannot be understood in terms of the interpretative categories presently available to us. There is very little in our received tradition that disposes us toward the acceptance of the omnicredulity resulting from such a position. To accept the sum of all perspectives as true is tantamount to the acceptance of Chaos as the only truth. How would one come to offer such a claim?

Essential to the task of defending the mosaicist's vision is some demonstration of the strict arbitrariness of reason and reasoning, the essential interdependence or *ratio* and *arbitrium*. The claim that reason is rooted in arbitrariness has haunted Western philosophy since at least the Sophistic period.

Plato's *Phaedrus* raises this issue with regard to the relations of *mythos* and *logos*. Phaedrus inquires of Socrates whether he accepts the Sophists' method of "allegorical" interpretation, which permitted the naturalistic explication of mythical themes. Socrates replies that he has no opinon to offer on that question, that he must first examine and come to know himself: ". . . to be curious about that which is not my concern, while I am still in ignorance of my own self, would be ridiculous."[2] Apparently, Socrates did not believe that he had to have recourse to mythical themes to come to know himself. By attempting to ground philosophic speculation upon self-analysis, Socrates thought he had avoided the consequences of seeking the origins of *logos* in *mythos*.[3]

While the Socratic defense of the independence of *logos* should not be undervalued, in itself it would not have been sufficient to establish the separability of *mythos* and *logos*. Not only *psyche* but *physis* had to be freed from the power of myth. Philosophy, therefore, had to be allied with rational science. Plato's account of the four levels of the clarity of knowledge and Aristotle's explicit contrast of the *philosophos* and the *philomythos* in his adumbrations of the methods of programmatic science did just this.[4]

The claim that philosophy and mythology are discontinuous has been made on behalf of both the pre-Socratic search for *physis* and the Socratic search for an articulated *psyche*. Both Self and World are protected from the power of *mythos* at the very beginnings of our philosophic tradition. Without this defense of reason, philosophy would never have developed as a rational discipline. For had not the influence of myth been successfully denied, philosophers would never have thought themselves freed from the essentially nonrational beginnings associated with cosmogonic myths. This insight of our first philosophers was, I believe, quite sound. The defenses of the autonomy of reason, however, are questionably so.

For those who have not already acceded to the device of "active forgetting," it has become increasingly difficult to maintain a belief in the separate origins of *mythos* and *logos*. The closer we look at the relations of myth and culture in our classical and preclassical periods, the more we begin to realize that both the meanings of the self and the methods of programmatic science are sufficiently imaged in our myths of origins as to raise serious questions about their "logical" character.[5]

Mythos provides a sensuous articulation of our origins. Myths are etiological tales. The *logos* of a thing is its essence or essential meaning. Both *logos* and *mythos* are accounts; the former is an account of what something is, the latter tells the story of its coming into being. The dominance of *logos* in philosophic speculation has precluded our richest understandings of myths by impelling us to seek a rational understanding of them. The *logos* of *mythos* expresses principles extracted from the myths and posited as grounds for reasonings. Henceforth, what is grasped is not the Chaos of beginnings but the principles themselves. Only by active forgetting have we been persuaded of the relative independence of *logos* and *mythos*. But ours is an increasingly self-conscious age; there are indications that this expedient will not serve us much longer.

Two great shocks in the Modern period occasioned a return to the recognition of the continuity of *mythos* and *logos*. The first was the influence of Hume's skeptical claim concerning reason, namely, that it "is and ought only to be the slave of the passions and can never pretend to any other office than to serve and obey them."[6] That one of the principal passions served by reason is that of "belief" offers grounds for the troubling suggestion that *logos* may indeed have its origins beyond custom and social praxis, in *mythos* itself.

The second shock went unrecorded for several generations, for the intent of its author was to calm the troubled waters stirred by Humean skepticism. Ironically enough, it is the form of Kant's defense of reason which, viewed dispassionately, provides the most graphic retelling of the story of the dependence of *logos* upon *mythos*.

In *The Critique of Pure Reason*, Kant sought to distinguish the faculty whereby we grasp first principles from the power whereby we come to be possessed of them. The faculty is reason; the power, understanding. "Understanding . . . secures the unity of appearances by means of rules . . . and reason secures the unity of rules of the understanding under principles."[7] From the perspective of the contemporary *philomythos*, an appropriate translation of the above might be: *Mythos* secures a single ordered cosmos from primordial Chaos through cosmogonic construction, while *logos* articulates the lineaments of that ordered world. *Logos* reaches only so far as the ordered beginnings arbitrarily established by *mythos*. The possibility of rational inquiry is insured by the cosmogonic construal, which provides the source of rational principles.

Kant saw, as clearly as any philosopher has ever seen, that reason could be defended only if the means of grasping first principles could be made categorially distinct from the means whereby we come to possess them. By claiming that the categories of the understanding were necessary conditions for any scientific knowledge, Kant sought to describe the essential and universal character of the process of coming to know. In fact, he performed an act of *mythopoesis* consisting in the construal of order from sensible chaos. Subsequent to this mythopoetic act, he found the *logos* of *mythos* articulatable in terms of the means whereby reason secures the unity of the rules of the understanding under principles. It is the essential arbitrariness involved in positing the categories of the understanding that leads one to the conclusion that Kant was, as essentially all rational thinkers must be, first a *philomythos* and only later a *philosophos*.

The cosmogonic tradition that reason serves contains not only the *Genesis* myth telling of an ordered world coming into being from an act

of the Divine Will, but also draws upon the Orphic cosmogonies illustra-
ted by Hesiod's myth of the creative power of Eros, which overcomes the
yawning gap separating Heaven and Earth. The myth of the *Timaeus*,
which celebrates the rational ordering of brute necessity, is yet a third
influential model of the beginnings. In these cosmogonic myths, we have
not only alternative accounts of the beginnings of our World, we have
primordial explications of the functions of the three principal elements
of the modern *psyche*: will, passion, and reason. Thus, both Self and
World have mythical foundations.[8]

Are we really justified in separating *logos* and *mythos*, except that in
that manner we are able to save the rationality of philosophic construction and inquiry? The consistent theme celebrated throughout the cosmogonic myths is the necessity to bring order from Chaos. The science
of metaphysics is a science of order. Its analyses of the principles of self
and world cannot ignore myth, for neither in the pre-Socratic investigation of *physis* nor in the Socratic analysis of *psyche* – nor in the
philosophic traditions emergent from each – is there evidence of a significant break with the mythological underpinnings of thinking.

Quite apart from these reflections on the original relations of *logos*
and *mythos*, there is a growing tendency to accept the arbitrary and pro-
vincial nature of metaphysical speculation because of at least two recent
insights into the status of Western metaphysics. First, there is some
transcultural evidence that supports the arbitrariness of the purported
need to appeal to transcendent or absolute principles to perform the
most general sorts of philosophic speculation. In classical China, for
example, there was no developed cosmogonic tradition that could have
determined philosophic thinking in accordance with the Chaos-Cosmos
problematic. Thus, neither in classical Taoism nor Confucianism will one
find recourse to theoretical principles or categories such as "pure possibilities," "the principle of sufficient reason," "God," and so forth. The order
of things may be accounted for in terms that are not categorically distinct
from the things themselves.

A second reason for believing that our traditional metaphysics lacks
the generality it has claimed for itself is in fact but an alternative rendering of the first. Beginning, perhaps, with the speculative philosophy of
A. N. Whitehead, there has emerged a relatively novel conception of
"order" that provides a significant alternative to that which has dominated our received tradition The connection between these two
challenges to the dominant metaphysical tradition lies in the fact that the
classical Chinese thinkers grounded their philosophic speculations in the
novel understanding of order that has only recently emerged into consciousness among Western thinkers.[9]

The very status of metaphysical thinking is at issue. The mythical tradition determines that philosophical problematics will be shaped by the questions of the origin and character of order. Metaphysics, both as *ontologia generalis* and as *scientia universalis*, seeks to account for the existence of order. The former pursues the meaning of order by recourse to the ontological question, the latter by asking the cosmological question. Metaphysical accounts seek principles, *archai*, as transcendent determining sources of order; and they do so in accordance with the pattern of speculation begun by the cosmogonic tradition.

The ontological question "Why is there something rather than nothing at all?" is generally thought to provide a more radical beginning for metaphysical speculation than the cosmological question "What kinds of things are there?" Thus, Martin Heidegger has been considered a more radical thinker than A. N. Whitehead, who (at least according to received interpretations) remained content with the strictly cosmological concern.

As traditionally interpreted, both the cosmological and ontological questions presuppose an *ordered ground*. But the truly radical question is, in fact, the cosmological one, since it may receive the Nietzschean answer: There are only interpretations, perspectives, the sum of which is Truth, the sum of which is Chaos.

The radical character of the cosmological question is rooted in the insight that one cannot pursue the ontological concern without thereby meaning to ask why order rather than disorder, or why *this* order rather than some other. The cosmological question, however, can certainly mean "What kinds of orders are there?" And this can mean, with Democritus and others, "How many and what kinds of *kosmoi* are there?" As most often understood, the ontological question is thought to mean "Why Cosmos rather than Chaos?" The question could, of course, be brought into line with the more radical concern by being inverted in this manner: "Why Chaos (*kosmoi*) rather than Cosmos?" But here we see that such a formulation depends on the cosmological concern for the nature, character and kinds of orders (*kosmoi*). It is the cosmological question that is the more radical, for it is, as I shall now attempt to demonstrate, predicated upon a profounder understanding of the meaning of order.[10]

I was first set to wondering about the ambiguity of the notion of order when I encountered the following words of C. S. Peirce:

> [T]he great characteristic of nature is its diversity. For every uniformity known, there would be no difficulty in pointing out thousands of non-uniformities; but the diversities are usually of small use to us and attract the attention of poets mainly, while the uniformities are the very staff of life.[11]

Orderedness is characterized by something more than uniformity, of course. This must be so if we are to save ourselves from the embarrassing implication that the absolute uniformity of the items forming physical nature, a condition which would entail the state of maximum entropy, expresses the highest degree of order. The majority of our thinkers have not been troubled overmuch by this implication and have tended to discuss the meaning of order in terms of pattern regularity. Such a bias may largely be a consequence of our theological heritage, which has conditioned us to consider the concept of order from the perspective of the Mind (but not the Heart) of God.

To understand the order of things we must imitate not only God's entertainment of essences and formal relations, but must, along with Him, "count the fall of the sparrow." It is, after all, not merely an instance of sparrowness, a member of the family *frangillidae* or *ploceidae*, that falls, but an irreplaceable being, one that shares with others of its kind the characteristics of uniqueness and diversity – the very uniqueness and diversity that poets must continually celebrate lest taxonomists inherit the earth.

Fundamentally, there are two perspectives one may assume with respect to the subject matter given in experience: One perspective leads to the appreciation of the manner in which the experienced items instantiate a given pattern or set of formal relations; alternatively, one may celebrate the manner in which just those items constitute themselves and their relations one to another in such a way as to permit of no substitutions. Each perspective involves abstraction. The first abstracts from actuality, the second from possibility. The first observation is governed by the aims of logical consistency; the second by the claims of inconsistency. In the first, a member of the family *frangillidae* or *ploceidae* falls; in the second, this unrepeatable, irreplaceable being is lost.

In the so-called "world of concrete experience" the extreme of selective abstraction obtains when any item except one fails to meet the conditions for the order or harmony in question. At the other extreme, that of the primary instance of logical or rational order, pure uniformity is guaranteed by the condition of absolute substitutability. Those who would realize a balance between the claims of logical and aesthetic orderedness are involved in the decidedly challenging task of attempting to balance the recourse to formal and selective abstraction.

Metaphysics, presumed to be the science of order, has most often advertised itself as the science of uniformities. Both as *scientia universalis* and as *ontologia generalis*, metaphysics has sought to articulate those characteristics or relationships that allow us access to the uniformities of existence and experience. As "universal science," metaphysical speculation has uncovered those principles of order that together permit the organization and classification of the elements of the World and our experience of them. The "general ontologist" searches for the meaning of the *being* of beings – that is, the set of uniform relations that qualify everything that is.

There is an alternative notion of orderedness celebrated by many poets and some few philosophers, a notion emergent from the appreciation of diversities. When Aristotle said "science is concerned with what happens always, or for the most part"[12] he pegged the scientific interest quite well. The aesthetic thinker, however, is concerned with what happens only sometimes (the spontaneous, uncontrolled act of creation) or but once (the unique product of such creative acts).

It is simply not the case that uniquenesses establish no orders. The composition of a work of art is, of course, abstractable from the unique items that compose it, but its greatness lies in large measure with the comprehension of just those particular items comprising the work. Although our enjoyment of the harmony of a work of art is both aesthetic and logical – that is, based on an appreciation of the uniformities (the compositional elements) as well as the diversities (the irreplaceably unique characteristics that constitute the work) – we find it difficult to discover a coherent notion of orderedness that can account for this fact.

The apparent inability to provide an adequate account of both types of order within a single theory is, oddly enough, one of the principal grounds for that singularly important division in our intellectual culture between the claims of reference and those of rhetoric – that is, between the attempt to reference the World and the relations of the items that comprise it, and the attempt to untie our imaginations, to develop free constructions of images and ideas unfettered by objective reference. Rational understandings of order are grounded in what we shall have occasion to see is a rather narrow meaning of reference. Rhetorical thought, on the other hand, is associated with the imaginative origins of thinking.

Images are intentionally nonreferential. That is to say, the imagination is exercised when objective reference could only be indirect (as would be so with an absent object) or when such reference would be presumed impossible (as with a putatively nonexistent object). In both cases, the aim of imaging is based on a recognition of the futility of referencing. Thus, the imagination is both a *terminous a quo* and *terminous ad quem* of the image. If it is insisted that reference is always present in any act of intending, then one is forced to admit that images are self-referenced – an admission to which we shall return later.

The imagination serves only as the *terminus a quo* of the presentation of a concept. The requirement that concepts be internally consistent establishes the basis for the contrast between image and concept. The "noisy rhombus" is an image; the "isosceles triangle" a concept. The former is rhetorical, the latter referential. Concepts, at most, begin in the imagination; images have the imagination as their source and end.

The image-concept contrast raises the subject of the distinction between logical and aesthetic consistency. Images are aesthetically consistent if the constituted image serves its contextual function – as an element in a painting, poem, and so forth. Logical or rational consistency is rule-bound, subject to the principles of identity and contradiction. Metaphyscial speculation, as a supposedly rational discipline, must find aesthetic orderedness to be a special case of logical orderedness if it is to account for the aesthetic dimensions of existence and experience. For the dominant strain of metaphysical speculation in the West has proceeded in accordance with the assumption that the World is one – that is to say, that there is a single ordered Cosmos. This assumption necessitates the affirmation of rational order as the primary meaning of order and the search for uniformities that articulate that order as the primary task of the metaphysician.

If speculative philosophers are in truth concerned to envision things from the most general perspective possible, then they must begin with the notion of aesthetic order. For the understanding of orders as functions of the particular, idiosyncratic items which in fact comprise them provides a much richer conception of order. Aesthetic consistency is not bound by putative reference. The orders established by images include those selected orders which will in fact meet the demands of logical consistency, but they also include myriad others which will not. Logical or rational order is the sort of order grounding the search for those uniformities in nature which are of particular interest to individuals constituted by compatible sorts of uniformities.

The disconcerting truth of the matter is that what we call logical or rational order could as appropriately be termed *moral* order. We are speculative thinkers largely because the sorts of beings we presume ourselves to be provide us relatively rich and complex perspectives that lead us into asking questions concerning the order(s) of things that would account for and sustain these sorts of beings. Diverse philosophies exist, most believe, because we cannot agree about the sorts of beings we are. Actually, the most fundamental reason for the diversity lies in the fact that we are not, primarily, *sorts* of beings. We are particular individuals constituted by our diversities. The disposition to ignore such diversities in the development of metaphysical theories is determined by the fact that, at the very least, physiological and linquistic uniformities are presupposed as grounds of order ensuring the successful uncovering of interesting uniformities in the world beyond the self.

Here we find the reason for the rather narrow sense of reference operative in our tradition. Reference is initially made to sorts of things whose characters are guaranteed by the background uniformities that a single ordered world provides. For metaphysics to develop from the alternative ground of aesthetic order, the meaning of reference must be enlarged so as to permit its initial exercises to be performed with respect to diversities, not uniformities.

The cultural interest of morality is primarily concerned with the recognition of uniformities that, appropriately exploited, would serve to promote the viability of the sorts of beings (*human beings*) served by those uniformities. Both aesthetic and mystical interests maintain an ontological reference not present to the moral interest. The aesthetic interest primarily considers the value an item has for itself; the mystical interest is concerned with the value possessed by an item with respect to the Totality of items construed as complete context.

Tensions between the aesthetic and mystical interests as they translate into conflicts between art and religion are symptoms of the failure to balance the value a thing has for itself with the value claimed for it by recourse to the consideration of the total context of experiencing. Conflicts between aesthetic and moral interests are more likely, however, since the moral context is in principle no broader than that established by the uniformities associated with the sorts of beings human beings are thought to be. In practice, of course, moral theory promotes the viability of a relatively small selection of those beings (the male, the educated, the powerful, the wealthy, and so forth). Alternatively, theories may be developed that attempt to broaden the application of moral principles beyond the sphere of the merely human. These latter efforts, when they constitute more than conceptions of ecological *noblesse oblige*, are informed by at least some appreciation of aesthetic understandings of order.

Metaphysics is thought to be the most general science of order. This claim turns out to be a sham, however, once the implications of the traditional search for order are grasped. The sorts of beings we conceive ourselves to be search out the uniformities that sustain us. Metaphysics, as traditionally constituted, is a moral discipline. Such metaphysics can combine both aesthetic and logical dimensions of order only if it argues that the value a thing has for itself is in principle always determined by its value for its environing others, be they constituents of a finite moral context or the indefinite totality that establishes the context of mystical experience. Such an argument is, at best, pernicious.

Order is bifocal, stereoptic. It has the character of a gestalt in which the shift between figure and ground is an alternation between logical and aesthetic orderedness. That order presupposing the priority of uniformities is, practically speaking, the most important conception of order; the most relevant to the sorts of beings we conceive ourselves to be. Theoretically, it is aesthetic orderedness that demands the greater concern, for one of the primary aims of speculative philosophy must be that of testing the viability of our habitual assumptions about the sorts of beings we are and the kind of ambiance that would appropriately sustain us. This can be done by resort to a metaphysical perspective enjoining a balanced appreciation of rational and aesthetic understandings of order. Such a perspective must provide the means of shifting figure and ground in any given consideration of order, structure and harmony.

Orderedness is an ambiguous notion because it presupposes what for most of us is a disturbing double vision that we can avoid only by the expedient of closing one eye. It may not be possible as yet to so coordinate our abilities as to correct the myopic and astigmatic character of our vision, but we can at least learn to open each eye in turn. Happily, there is some evidence that we have awakened from our Newtonian slumber and have begun to realize that he who can see with both eyes in the kingdom of the single-sighted at least ought to be king.

The problem for the metaphysician is to demonstrate how the alternative conceptions of order can receive balanced recognition in the articulation of a speculative vision. Plato's dialectical movement from many to one; Aristotle's coordination of the ends in nature by recourse to a *primum mobile* (as well as the coordination of the pursuit of those ends guaranteed by the classification of the ways of knowing into theoretical, practical and productive endeavors); Leibniz's *more calculi*, sandwiched between the *more geometricae* of Descartes and Spinoza; Kant's architectonic; Hegel's dialectically articulated Absolute − all these symptomize the dominance of the logical over the aesthetic understandings of order. This dominance is a function of our tendency to seek unitive rather than associative solutions to the problem of the One and the Many. That is to say, forced to presuppose something in our endeavors, we presume that unity is prior to plurality and tacitly shape our metaphysical endeavors in unitive terms.

Our unitive bias has been with us almost, but not quite, from the beginnings of our philosophic tradition. With Aristotle, and the major strand of Plato's thought, we defend the intuition that there is a single ordered cosmos. The World is one. The intuition of other of the early Greek thinkers, namely, that there are many worlds, is largely ignored. What I have termed Second Problematic Thinking, which was born out of the great syntheses created by Plato and Aristotle and which requires that only one actual world exist, has usurped the authority of the older, less articulated vision of the First Problematic – the view that there are many *kosmoi*.[13] The First Problematic challenges the concern for uniformities that so characterizes the majority of our thinkers. First Problematic thinking dwells on the diversities. It is the vision of the disenfranchised poet. The reenfranchisement of the aesthetic vision is the burden of the contemporary metaphysician.

It would be all too easy to underestimate the difficulty of this task if we did not reflect on the contemporary efforts to articulate a coherent vision of aesthetic orderedness. The language permitting aesthetic constructions has yet to be developed. Heidegger's tedious obscurity, particularly toward the end of his career, well illustrates the problem. The slightly less obscure Whiteheadian vision attains its (relative) clarity through a capitulation to the morphological bias entailed by the doctrine of the primordial nature of God. Poststructuralist thinking runs aground on the anthropocentric danger: Man is the measure of linguistic virtuosity (or is it vice-versa?). Dewey and Mead, whose appreciation of the aesthetic intensities of experience could provide substantial support for a truer understanding of pluralism than may easily be found in the classical tradition, were unable to follow the course of their thinking to its aesthetic extreme. Each finally invoked the methods of programmatic science as a consensual background for his pluralistic theories.

Seeds and soil are present. Cultivation of the aesthetic turn in metaphysical speculation requires the rooting out of perhaps the most pernicious of the unannounced assumptions of our speculative thinkers – namely, the belief, tacit but firm, that speculative philosophy serves primarily to justify morality. This would require turning away from uniformities and toward diversities. But what would become of the philosophic spirit were it fully to engage diversity? Would that require the abandonment of philosophy and the substitution of the poetic stance? Martin Heidegger and his French epigoni have provided the most recent context for addressing this question.

Heidegger's extremely limited success is certainly occasion enough for the aesthetically oriented philosopher to feel chastened. Heidegger recognized that philosophical thinking could not survive unless disciplined by the claims of reference. It was this recognition that ulitmately make a bad poet of a great philosopher. The poststructuralist abandonment of reference has certainly purified the Heideggerian program, and the deconstructionists in particular have been able to avoid the "fall" into poetry, but only at the great price of having yielded to the sophistic virtuosity that provides the only classical alternative.

We must find a stance beyond dialectic and critique. Even Nietzsche's (and to a lesser extent Heidegger's) attempt to sound the original note that occasioned the philosophic variations patterning intellectual culture was too much engaged by a critique of the excesses of metaphysical thinking. The only pristine source of diversity, one shared by both the scientific and literary dimensions of philosophy, is that of the "imagination" conceived as the *terminus a quo* of thinking.

Imagination is the *fons et origo* of culture, society and personality. Imagination is the only unchallengeable authority, for it is the sole *arche* which, answering to no strictures without ceasing thereby to be imagination, is (at least formally) beyond critique. Critique is an act of construal that in its primordial form brings rational order from the amorphous imagination. The authority of the imagination as the source of aesthetic order is, therefore, self-referentially secure.

Two problems immediately plague the enterprise of imaginative thinking. The first concerns the act of naming; the second, the activity of relating name to name. The first is a question of referentiality; the second, a question of rhetoric. Critique is the process of getting past the name, either in order to rename or in order to recover primordial, prenominal, experience. The first process leads to metaphysics; the second, to mysticism. As traditionally exercised, tropological thinking stands at the other extreme from imagination. Thus, rhetoric is made to function in a postcritical fashion. It is thought necessary only when referential language fails.

What I am calling the imagination is prior to both appearance and reality. There is no direct route from imagining to sensing or perceiving. The capitulation to language as a play of signifiers is rooted in linguistic phenomenalism. At the same time, the surrender entails the most sophisticated form of cultural positivism in that the structure of language – i.e , the putatively common structure across languages – is taken as a paradigm of consensual meaning. Language is cosmos; *texts* constitute culture.

There is surely some truth to this position, for language is the most precise expression of the form of our embodiment. We speak to others of our kind, and they understand because they are *our kind*. The sorts of beings we are can communicate with the sorts of beings we are.

While it is doubtless true that shared meanings underlie any expressive act, the focus of expression, and thus of communication as well, is otherness, difference. Communication is the articulation of differences. The act of communication, therefore, presupposes thinking in a way that communal sharing does not. For thinking requires that one express "on the contrary" or, at the very least, "on the other hand." Thinking and communication do not necessitate foreground commonality, but exactly the opposite. One does not seek to communicate what another clearly knows. An obvious comparison may be made between the intellectual impasse of our present age and that of the fifth and fourth centuries occasioned by Parmenides and Zeno. The use of dialectic as both a positive and negative tool – that is, both to support the claim that being is and to refute the possibility of thinking change or motion – occasioned the severest of reactions on the part of those Sophists who otherwise seemed to share the same sort of methodology. "Only Being Is; Not-Being is Not" is not only the primary expression of the form of the dialectic itself, but it establishes the fact that the victory of the same (the identity of "is," the self-identity of "being") is essential to the dialectic as so construed. The weighting of dialectical thinking on the side of being over not-being, of the oneness of being over the chaotic plurality or openness of not-being, uproots thinking from its imaginative ground.

On these terms it is clear that the act of thinking per se is undervalued in Plato. It is a means to knowledge but cannot provide knowledge directly. For if knowing is remembering, then thinking is an act of uncovering preexistent knowledge, and the attempts on the part of a knower to express that knowledge can only be based on the assumption that communication is fundamentally a communal endeavor. In such case, dialectic (the presumed paradigm of "on the contrary" or "on the other hand") is made to serve the ends of communion. The irony of dialectic argumentation is that it does not presume real differences; and this is not so only in the hands of Socrates, Plato, Hegel or Marx. It is the essence of dialectical thinking that it express the victory of the same.

Dialectic is necessarily in service to the communal function. Plato's four levels of the clarity of knowledge culminating in the form of the Good, establishes the formal, and historical, ground of dialectical thinking. Hegel's Absolute and Marx's *eschaton* provide the alternate *teloi* of such dialectical analyses. Understandably, dialectical argumentation has come to be assaulted most heavily in a period such as ours when both formal and teleological categories have become unfashionable.

The search for metaphysical principles is an attempt to engage the uniformities of existence and experience. The diverse metaphysical principles and categories in our philosophic inventory are, at least since the classical period, a function of the successive critiques of one thinker by another. Distinctly different metaphysical systems are constructed as much by critique of other systems as by attempting to look again at the data available for speculation. Critical dialectics give the metaphysical enterprise the shape of metacritique.

Unquestionably, dialectic is essential to the performance of certain sorts of communicative enterprise. Dialogical and dialectical encounters presuppose, as background, a common language of discourse, and thus dialectic is a most appropriate intrasystematic or intratheoretical tool. *Inter*theoretical uses of dialectic are, however, merely disguised sophistries. The embarrassing implications of theoretical incommensurability have raised serious doubts about the ability of one systematic thinker to communicate with another intertheoretically. This is a fortiori true of metaphysical theories which, as the putatively most general sorts of theories, must entail context-dependent languages affording no point by point translation into alternative metaphysical schemes.

The aporetic dialectic used by Socrates may have been an acceptable means of engagement. The systematic employment of dialectic in Plato's more constructive endeavors, and the final parody of dialectics in Hegel and Marx, however, illustrate the shady implications of that method. Its aim is consensus; and such an aim is, in principle, destructive of diversity. The only diversity that remains after the dialectical engagements of the sort that pattern our intellectual history is that guaranteed by the small family of classical traditions – idealism, naturalism, volitionalism, materialism, and so forth. These traditions primarily serve as grist for the taxonomists' mill.

Metaphysics, speculative philosophy, has lost much of its prestige in contemporary culture principally because the doctrines of theoretical relativity and incommensurability have had such widespread influence. The persuasiveness of these doctrines has been fatal to metaphysical ambitions insofar as they are motivated by the desire to guide the movement from Chaos through *mythos* to *logos*.

The reference-rhetoric imbalance has shaped philosophic activity from the beginning of its classical development. The rhetorical dimension of philosophy, disciplined by the claims of reference, has been permitted to serve merely as a source of metaphorical accoutrements meant to ease the tedium of highly serious speculation or, at the extrasystematic level, as the means of winning commitment to a philosophical position. "Principles" as sources of rational order, as grounds of order, and as theoretical ordering agencies, transcend the Cosmos they create, sustain and explicate. The contrasts of Being and Not-Being, of One and Many, of Reality and Appearance, of God and the World, etc., have therefore been shaped hierarchically. Cosmogony, the name of the specific set of strategems that chart the transition from Chaos to *mythos* to *logos*, has determined the fate of metaphysical speculation in the West.

"Originality is a return to the origins." True enough. But which origins? The metaphysician cannot be content simply with a return to *our* origins, since "we" are, at least in part, products of the very acts of speculative philosophy that must be circumvented if we are to realize the putative aim of the metaphysical thinkers. It is *the* origins we seek. But where are they to be found? Should we return to the blind, reckless confusion, the empty void, the yawning gap that is our Chaos? That is still not far enough; for we must get beyond even the subjective form of feeling that leads us to grasp our beginnings as nihility and negativity, and that thereby necessitates a capitulation to the dialectic of Is and Is-Not.

The origin we seek is the Vast Indifference of Chaos as the source of all orderedness. If we can leave open the question as to whether order is uncovered or construed, then we can take up our stance prior to that point at which rhetoric and reference, *mythos* and *logos*, diverged. Then we would stand at the first fork in the road. Looking forward, philosophers would see the diverging paths of our cultural tradition; the one path well-worn and familiar; the other, a narrower way, traveled by the poets.

But it is a backward glance that we want to take. If we did, what would we see? Is there a story to be told before the tales told by *mythos* and *logos*? Or is *historia*, the weaving together of *logos* and *mythos*, the tale of two tales, the only means of accommodating both?

The two paths that lead from the Vast Indifference that is the inchoation of poetry and philosophy, the paths we later name reference and rhetoric, require that we twice bridge the stream of history. The *historia* of our culture is a twice-told tale. We shall lend fresh interest to it only if we can discover something novel in the account.

The *mythos* of *logos* is presumed to be a proper subject of poetry. Like the logistical perspective, however, there is something derivative here. The poet is trapped by the presumption of a transcendent *logos*, just as the philosopher is hamstrung by the acceptance of a single *mythos*. Neither *mythos* nor *logos* may be encountered apart from *historia*. We have attempted to demythologize our intellectual tradition by appeal to logical and rational methods that are themselves unaccountable except by recourse to the cosmogonic myths that ground our *historia*. Moreover, the remythologizing of *logos* by Jewish and Christian *philomythoi* has led to the notion of a transcendent *logos* in large measure characterized by qualities that are born out of Greek *mythos*. The shadow of that transcendent *logos* falls across even the most secular of our philosophies.

As postmoderns, we look to poetry today as once we looked to programmatic science. Lacking novel speculative resources, philosophers have become taxonomists or dogmatists by default. But poets suffer a complementary disease. The myths and metaphors metered by poets are already infected by the rationality of tradition, already disciplined by the claims of reference. Culture has closed upon itself.

The return to the origins can be effectively original only if we find our way back to that Chaos that is neither hostile nor accommodating only of our specific human needs. Chaos as the sum of all orders is a Vast Indifference when assessed from the perspective of a class of uniform existences, established orders, or selective criteria. As such, it is passive to an indefinite number of aims, ends and aspirations, and it sustains an indefinite number of "sorts" of things, providing privileged status to no single set of uniformities. The diverse particulars comprising the Vast Indifference that is original Chaos each establishes its own perspective on all others. At one end of the spectrum of existences, these particulars constitute the chaos of imagination; at the other end, they comprise the sum of all world-orders.

Here we confront the original situation of thinking; thinking before there was a World, before there was a substantial focused Self. Thinking prior to embodiment is original in both effective senses: it is novel and originating. The thinking of the philosopher and of the poet are at this very place, and perhaps at no other place, identical. The two specific diremptive actions that gave rise to the distinction between the poet and the philosopher were largely responsible for casting the form of our intellectual culture.

As the story is often told, it was the rational philosopher who set out on a new path, breaking away from the poetic ground of our culture. This is the account traditionally given by the majority of both poets and philosophers. In fact, there were two quite distinct diremptions, one from the side of the would-be poets, another from that of the potential philosophers. The prephilosophical act was the original act of naming, which gave birth to reference. Original referencing constituted the act of self-reference that, we must presume, was identical with the emergence of self-consciousness. The alternative diremption involved the allusive "referencing" of one word by another, which is the rhetorical move. In this peculiar sense, then, reference preceded rhetoric – a claim that seems to challenge received accounts of the relations of *mythos* and *logos*. However, neither poetry nor philosophy, strictly as human potentialities, could be said to have preceded the other. The grounds for each were jointly constituted and their distinctiveness guaranteed by the tensions between rhetoric and reference.

Original thinking can be nothing more than thinking prior to the diremption of rhetoric and reference. This is protometaphysical speculation. The return to that pristine form of thinking may be taken along two distinctive routes. The poets have one way home, the philosophers another. I will feign no wisdom on behalf of the poets; it is the philosophical itinerary I wish to rehearse.

Self-reference is the source of both reference and rhetoric. This is the first philosophical truth. Self-reference entails referral conditioned by otherness; however, that referral is not to some *thing* constituting an aspect of a World, but is a referencing of the very act of referral. The recognition that all reference is grounded by self-reference is the source of the ironic gesture. Irony establishes the place of beginning for philosophical speculation. For the Greeks, philosophy began in Wonder, for the scholastics in Faith; Doubt was the origin of philosophical thinking for the Moderns. We postmoderns, we who are as yet without a legitimate name, must take up the ironic stance.

Wonder, Faith, Doubt – and the gesture of Irony: Each of these "moods" anticipates the character of a World that will be discovered through its employment. Wonder is the passive openness to experience in all of its vastness and complexity; it is the wide-eyed openness to truths encountered for the first time, truths that ground the historical beginnings of thinking. Faith posits a given and articulates its character and consequences. Wonder opens its eyes and receives a World as yet unknowable; Faith knows in advance all that is essential. Doubt is the coarse-meshed sieve through which passes most of the finely articulated wisdom of the past; it is the winnower whose dessicating currents turn the wheat to chaff.

The culmination of each philosophical epoch is realized through the self-consciousness of its beginning. The wondering of the first thinkers of ancient Greece was thematized in the Platonic vision of the Good and the Aristotelian doctrine of self-reflective thinking. The articulated concepts defending the philosophic significance of faith and its relations to reason developed by Scotus and Occam played the final variations on the Augustinian *fides quarens intelligam*. Although the doubt celebrated by Descartes was self-consciously entertained, at least as a programmatic notion, the substantive consequences of that notion were hardly understood until regrounded in Hume's retreat from pyrrhonian skepticism and Kant's uneasy synthesis of phenomenal certainty and metaphysical skepticism, which inverted the poles of the Cartesian system. In fact, the fading echoes of thematized doubt may still be heard, even by postmodern ears.

The Age of Irony begins with Hegel, though it is a dramatic irony which Hegel himself was unable to enjoy. The self-articulation of the Absolute is the paradigm of the ironic gesture, the recognition of self-reference. If we look for the constitutive irony that ushers in the age in its fully conscious manner, we must cast our eyes again in the direction of Nietzsche, whose irony, though reluctant, was fully conscious. Having returned to Nietzsche, our argument has turned back upon itself, and we are faced once more with the two escape routes previously offered us: An active forgetting that cancels history and with it the historical consciousness that grounds the ironic gesture, or the full recognition that neither system nor inquiry may prevail, and that Wonder, Faith and Doubt have run their course. Either way irony prevails – in the former case as merely dramatic; in the latter, as constitutive of thinking in its most rigorous form.

Irony is the sole philosophic attitude that can survive full self-consciousness. This is so, of course, because irony is itself a consequence of reflexive consciousness. Much of the confusion of this philosophic epoch is occasioned by the fact that we are "between the times," and our ending and beginning seem so similar. We are wringing the last droplets of meaning from the Age of Doubt. The extreme responses of the skeptics and the taxonomists to the conditions of theoretical relativity and incommensurability are activities associated with the self-consciousness of doubt. The emerging ironic epoch, contrary to that of preceding philosophic periods, *begins* in self-consciousness, in consciousness as paradigmatic self-reference.

Thus, postmodern culture insists on turning back upon itself and advertising reflexivity in its purest form because its "beginning" presumes the culmination of the entire history of our metaphysical speculations insofar as they have been grounded in the notion of rational order. The tradition coming to its close is one defined by the quest, not for certainty, but for uniformities. The uniformities encountered, discovered, construed and created by speculative philosophers since our time of beginnings have been the result of understanding order in rational, logical terms. With the exhaustion of the viable uniformities discoverable by the sorts of beings we have deemed ourselves to be, we have no choice but to begin our speculations from an alternative conception of order.

Philosophy may not abandon reference and go whoring after the pleasures of rhetorical excess. But self-reference is still reference and it seems most certainly to be the major concern, if not the most creative discovery, of the postmodern period. The first approach to diversity must be through the recognition of the aesthetic meaning of the coexistence of a number of diverse speculative theories.

The burden of the contemporary speculative philosopher is to account for the existence of theoretical diversity on other than rational grounds. The appeal to notions of order that anticipate antecedent uniformities permits the classification of schemes of thought but does not provide an account of the positive value of the diversity. The most "reasonable" explanation of theoretical diversity within the philosophic discipline is that most views are wrong-headed and the remainder express varying degrees of truth. Understanding such diversity in aesthetic terms, however, leads to the insight that each has a value for itself within the context constituted by the alternatives.

Philosophy truly references itself not through the activity of the taxonomist but in the form of the mosaicist. The same insight that permits an aesthetic ordering of theories requires an aesthetic appreciation of the order(s) of things. It is this insight that leads us to ask: Freed from the debilitating effects of almost two and one-half millennia of intellectual inertia, wouldn't the obvious conclusion one might draw from the plurality of speculative theories be that there are a plurality of ways things are? Of course, the difficulty most of us have in coming to that conclusion is due to the fact that its corollary is that we ourselves must potentially be a number of ways.

Metaphysics is the science of order. As long as order is interpreted solely in rational terms, the moral interest cannot but truncate the metaphysical enterprise. But aesthetic order provides an alternative speculative model, one that has been slighted overmuch in the tradition that we serve. The revitalization of speculative philosophy awaits the emergence of articulated understandings of the enriching diversities celebrated by recourse to aesthetic ordering.

The minimal requisite for beginning this "quest for diversity"[14] is acceptance of the First Problematic with its implications of the primacy of aesthetic ordering and of self-reference as the ground of the ironic gesture. Productive ventures in metaphysics will come not from philosophic reconstructions shaped by *scientia universalis* or *ontologia generalis*, but from attempts to speculate in the mode of *ars contextualis*.

NOTES

1. Nietzsche, Friedrich *The Will to Power*, trans. Walter Kaufmann and R. J. Hollingdale (New York: Vintage Books, 1968), Section 556.
2. *The Dialogues of Plato*, vol. I, trans. Benjamin Jowett (New York: Random House, 1920), pp. 235–36.
3. For an important discussion of the Socratic separation of the aims of *mythos* and philosophic speculation, see Ernst Cassirer's *The Myth of the State* (Garden City, New Jersey: Doubleday, 1955).
4. John Burnet's *Greek Philosophy: Thales to Plato* (New York: St. Martin's, 1964) provides a classic discussion of the history of ancient philosophy grounded in the assumption that philosophy and rational science must be totally distinct from mythical thinking.

5. I have devoted a book to the defense of precisely this claim. See *The Uncertain Phoenix* (New York: Fordham Press, 1982).

.6 Hume, David *A Treatise on Human Nature*, ed. L. Selby-Bigge (Oxford: Clarendon Press, 1960), p. 415.

7. Kant, Immanuel *The Critique of Pure Reason* trans. N. K. Smith (London: Macmillan, 1956), p. 303, B359.

8. For an elaboration of this point, see *The Uncertain Phoenix*, Chapter Two, "Disciplining Chaos."

9. This claim underlies a recent book by Professor Roger Ames and me: *Thinking Through Confucius* (Albany: State University of New York Press, 1986).

10. It would certainly be possible to interpret Whitehead along more radical lines if one were willing to accept the most fundamental consequences of his notion of "cosmic epochs." See Whitehead's *Process and Reality* (New York: Macmillan, 1929). However, most Whiteheadians have not been disposed to follow this line of interpretation.

11. Cited in ed. Justus Buchler, *Philosophical Writings of Peirce* (New York: Dover Press, 1955), p. 221.

12. *Metaphysics*, VI, Chapter Two, 1027a 19-21.

13. For a discussion of what I am calling First and Second Problematic Thinking, see my *Eros and Irony* (Albany: State University of New York Press, 1982), Chapter Four, "The Ambiguity of Order."

14. "The quest for diversity" is the theme of my forthcoming work, *The Diachronous Web: History, Culture and The Quest for Diversity.*

George Allan

The Primacy of the Mesocosm

Our primary convictions about the world originate in the pervasive pungency of molar experience. This is the mesocosm: a world proportional to human dimensions in its size and duration, a world of moderate length and breadth, as old as memory and as potent as the reach of practical aspiration. It is our home and thus the yardstick by which we measure truth. Its familiar content is one of impermanent complex unities. Everywhere around us, catching us up into their reality, we experience finite orderings that emerge, struggle to persist, and eventually pass over into new orderings. All that we know is in some way an aspect of this continual process, this endless making and unmaking of meaningful totalities.

Speculative philosophers, since their mandate is to save the appearances by means of a coherent and adequate interpretation of mesocosmic experience, should therefore be busy constructing various versions of a metaphysics of passage. But the history of Western thought testifies to the persistent occlusion of such thinking by a metaphysics of eternity. This popular approach is grounded in concepts at the extreme, antimesonic notions regarding what is foundational or ultimate, originative or summative. Its attention is riveted on things that transcend the molar realities that comprise whatever is humanly comprehensible. The various metaphysics of eternity include all the forms of traditional substance ontology, with their claims regarding the really real, things in themselves, and timeless divinity. But they also include most of the more recent systems of process philosophy which, despite their rhetoric, end up by giving primacy to permanence. Every metaphysics based on the extreme, whatever its ontological priorities, turns out to be a celebration of transcendence; of some god's aims and saving acts, of values that lie beyond the vertigo of temporal change.

In this essay, I will therefore argue on behalf of what might well be called metaphysical godlessness. I will begin by indicating why notions

at the extreme intrude into our philosophies despite the obviously contrary evidence. Then I will attempt to characterize the middling world
in which we live as providing a sounder basis for understanding and for
action than the old metaphysics provides. My purpose is therefore normative. By insisting on the primacy of the mesocosm, I will argue, philosophy can be returned to its proper moral function as archivist, guide, and
critic of the human effort to fashion the communities of meaning that are
our only hallmark of reality.

I

Everyday experience is overwhelmingly an experience of change, of
complexly ordered realities coming to be, suffering and causing alteration, and eventually passing away by decay and by integration into other
complexities. Our body goes through constant transformations as it
develops from zygote to fetus to human child to mature adult to old age
to death. Our families and communities gain new members and lose old,
with the structures of our relationships to one another, and to former and
prospective members, shifting as those developmental transformations
change who we are. We know that the subsystems and even the cells of
our body have some degree of self-functioning integrity, and that at the
same time we are participating members of a generous range of wider
societies, some of them so fundamental to who we are that analogies to
our body seem quite appropriate.

Yet as we push toward the extremes of size and duration in a metaphysical attempt to comprehend and encompass the full range of actual
and possible experience, this willingness to give primacy to changing
complexity dwindles and finally disappears in a flurry of assertions
regarding the extramundane requirements of whatever is first or last,
foundational or universal. However much the world may appear to be
transitory, and in significant ways is acknowledged as actually being so,
we nonetheless insist that there must be a sustaining receptical within
which all that flux goes on, an origin or end that lies beyond its
tremulous proceedings, a truth that escapes its ever-shifting relativities.
Understanding, meaning, and purpose cannot function for us in the
absence of some reality that transcends the pervasive experience of temporal passage. We insist that there must be something beyond the becoming, a god to save us from our enveloping contingencies.

This line of reasoning has no metaphysical justification, however.
The assertion of something at the extremes of experience that is of a different sort than what constitutes the heart of experience is no more than

a failure of nerve, a flight from reality into comforting illusion. Found order is the idol of eternity metaphysics, an attempt to substitute necessity for the all-pervasive contingency of invented order. That we should offer incense to such a god is a demand steadfastly to be refused.

The baal of eternity has many persona. The first appears, at the microcosmic level, in the guise of simplicity. The traditional metaphysical beliefs in such entities as simple ideas, windowless monads, and indivisible atoms are attempts to extrapolate from the unsettling relativity of ever-shifting structures to a foundation for flux and for its ordering that is not itself a product of that process. Without such a transition to things that are basic and permanent, it is argued, action cannot be effective nor understanding accurate.

This line of reasoning is compellingly attractive. Whatever is compound can be understood by knowing its components and the specific ways in which they are interrelated. If the entities of experience are complex, then for purposes of comprehension and control they must be analyzed into their less complex constituents, and this process should then be repeated until we arrive eventually at what is no longer complex and so incapable of further analysis. Such simple foundational entities are claimed to be either brute facts immediately given to experience or the endpoints of a logically necessary extrapolation from experience. They are, being simple, unchangingly just what they are, the building blocks required in the construction of any and every complexity. They are required to make sense out of other things but are themselves not to be made sense of. They are required, that is, in order to bring the passage from more complicated to less complicated realities to a halt. For only if we arrive at unanalyzable simples, it is argued, does it become possible to build back synthetically to a comprehension of every possible complexity and to the predictions requisite for effective action.

If space and time possess extension, they must be divisible; but lest such division generate an infinite regress, there must be something that is constitutive of extension but not itself extensive. Thus, for instance, Leibniz's monads are posited: timeless, punctilinear, relationless entities out of which time, space, and relationship are somehow constituted. The monads are taken as a requirement of rationality even though they are themselves irrational, are of a kind and nature radically different from the familiar entities they make possible. The actual occasions of Whitehead's cosmology are neither more nor less complex than these monads, for the unique determinateness of each is a direct and irreducible function of its perspective on the universe, its situational context, as ordered by a principle. An actual occasion's subjective aim is probabilistic with respect to its articulation within that context, whereas a monad's *conatus* is necessary; but in both instances the defining principle is itself not further analyzable. It is bestowed by God, which is to say that it is an expression of what is its own sufficient reason. There is no going behind the plurality of individuating principles except by reference to a divine purpose aiming at universal good. But this merely links the extreme of simplicity to the other metaphysical extremes of traditional thought. This we all call God.

In contrast to these claims, a metaphysics of passage must insist that monads, actual occasions or any other fundamental entities can be construed in no other way than as complex totalities, that the foundation of things must be of a piece with that which is dependent upon it. There can be no experience of the absolutely least or simplest, because such an entity would be at an immensely indefinite remove in magnitude from whatever the direct instruments of knowledge could ever record. Nor can reason intelligibly hypothesize what is beyond experience except by analogy to the experienced. Hence, any attempt to articulate a microcosmic base that grounds the mesocosm by virture of its differences from it is merely a form of special pleading. The foundation for complexity can only be other complexities; the conditions of flux must be themselves in flux.

At the macrocosmic level, a second idol of eternity makes its appearance, robed in the garments of universal necessity. Complexity can be grasped not only in terms of its components but also by reference to the more general patterns it exemplifies. In traditional metaphysics, geometric, logical, or aesthetic relationships are identified and recurrent elements in the successively emergent patterns of achievement taken as fundamental. In this way, the repetitive aspects of change serve to aggregate individuals into kinds or sets, and these into kinds of kinds and sets of sets, species into genera, phyla into kingdoms, systems into metasystems. But, it is argued, this cannot go on to infinity, and so at the extreme we must come at last to some structure that is not expressive of any still more encompassing structure. The very universality that such a principle of order possesses is able to rescue it from change, for it is the system without which no altering of lesser systems can occur. This pattern for all patternings, the Unhypothesized One of Platonic speculation, is the repeated condition for repetition and thus for change, the receptacle within which all spatio-temporal passage takes place. Its recurrence is therefore inevitable; universality necessarily entails necessity.

Whitehead's philosophy of organism is little different from these traditional assertions about universal invarience. Every actual occasion has the same necessary structure, exhibiting a pre-given form of becoming within which the upswelling of creativity must work its magic. The particular achievements of concrescence have their fleeting moment and are gone, the eternal objects are instantiated in that moment or excluded. Such matters are impermanent, to some degree unpredictable, in some sense irrepeatable. But the structure itself, the phases of concrescence from initial aim to final satisfaction, are invariant. They are norms for the becoming of determinateness, and, therefore, whatever emerges into time and space must conform to them.

Consequently, insofar as *Process* and *Reality* is taken as providing the description of a template for becoming, Whitehead can be legitimately accused of having succumbed to the fallacy of misplaced concreteness he warns against. A metaphysics of passage, in contrast, must insist that every structure of concrescence or transition is an abstraction that reflects but does not determine the way by which concreteness and complexity are born from the mix of fact and possibility. As cosmic habits change so do all the generalizations. A natural law – just like a civil law – is a guide to behavior, coercive only by virtue of its persuasive capacities and the actions on its behalf contributed by predecessors and contemporaries. What is repeated need not have been, and, no matter how general and enduring the repetition, it always implies alternatives realized elsewhere and potentially to be realized here as well.

When the metaphysical focus is protocosmic, the eternity demon masquerades in a third way, this time as creative purpose. The tradition argues that persistent transformation can be meaningful only if its overwhelming variety can be said to arise from a single source and be governed by appropriate kenotic reasons. This notion would seem at first to be a legitimate speculative attempt to paint human purposing onto the wider cosmic canvas. Intentionality creates a unifying structure by assigning otherwise independent events or entities a function, a role within a sequence of instrumentalities culminating in an outcome. The initial situation, and each subsequent moment in the process of realization, includes an ideal, whether grasped vaguely or precisely, against which all functionally intermediate achievements and the final result can be assessed. This dialectic of ideal and actual within a finite temporal framework, one with a beginning and an end, means that purposive processes serve as powerfully integrative structures of meaningfulness. They tell a story, which is to say that the principle of order at work in them is necessarily coherent. The relata are not only compatable with each other but are so in virtue of their mutual interdependence.

But story-like orderings are unavoidably finite. They require the contrast of a resistant environment over against which the pursuit of a possibility for realization must be undertaken. Realization by fiat and *ex nihilo*, however, tells no tale, because there are no intermediate relevances, no strategies to articulate the readjustment of one configuration of things into an alternative. Necessary realization has nothing to recount, because whatever might intervene between start and finish will be irrelevant to it. So purposes entail freedom and opposition, possibilities at risk and an adventure essaying their instantiation. Yet the whole of reality, the cosmos as absolute totality, can have no such contrasts. A purpose logically or temporally prior to every contrast between actual and potential can be conceived of only by redefining it as a purpose essentially different from human purposings. A primordial and necessary purpose is consequently no purpose at all, even though it be proclaimed the source for every subsequent purpose.

Whitehead's principle of creativity is such a notion, posited at the extreme to give unity to what would otherwise appear as only a meander of local orders endlessly emerging and perishing, born and reborn. But the principle of creativity is energy without specific aim, and so there is no end that can be anticipated by making reference to its power, only the assertion of cosmic continuity, the claim that the future like the past will be a process from the collapse of accomplishment to the emergence of successor accomplishments. Whitehead requires a primordial occasion, a first purposiveness, to provide creativity with focus, to convert energy into direction, to make the meander into a story. But this begs the question. Like the scientific principle of induction, Whitehead's principle of creativity unavoidably presupposes what it is designed to establish. Only an initial and unswerving purpose can provide the unassailable unity required as the foundation for both the fluctuations and the permanences that comprise the experienced universe. The Taoist's chaos and the German romanticist's Ground of Being are similar metaphysical contradictions. They can encompass the whole of reality only by being purposeless receptacles for change, but they can provide meaningful structure to that whole only by rising purposefully against a reality other than themselves. Alas, both are not possible at once. The Tao is not yin nor is it yang, and the Ground of Being is not a being. An absolute teleological source for the cosmos is an impossibility.

The fourth and last mask worn by eternity is eschatocosmic. It is the persona of preservation, the traditional conviction that, however problematic the cosmos might be, however fragile and unpredictable the concrete realizations comprising temporal reality, what is of worth in the universe will not perish from it. If order is an achievement and if whatever value there is in the world is a function of such achievement, then there must be some sense in which values realized are retained for their own intrinsic sake as well as for their relevance to other realizations. If whatever is excellent is also difficult to attain, then without the assurance that this effort if successful will be rewarded, the urge toward such ends becomes crippled and atrophies. Worth that is merely fleeting is not worth at all.

This concern lies behind Kant's arguments for God and personal immortality, for the claim that moral duty has no sense unless in some ultimate reckoning of good and evil the good will prove triumphant. Whitehead's notion of God as having a consequent nature is the same argument in only slightly altered form. The reward for accomplishment – for realizing some aesthetically intense integrative harmony of component elements, or for instantiating some universal moral principle of freely chosen integrative harmony, or for serving instrumentally to help realize some integration of component purposes into a wider end – is the rescue of its meaning from a fate that would be indistinguishable from simply the absence of such accomplishment. If effort and non-effort come to the same, the difference, it is argued, has no significance. So preservation of value beyond the perishings of time is a precondition for voluntary accomplishment. If all were necessary, there would be no value since no effort would be required; but without a framework of meaningfulness, no value can be evoked. It follows that achievement not immortalized entails the collapse of achievement and so of cosmos. Eschatology is the necessary precondition for temporal duration.

But here once again we have a notion posited at the extreme of experience that attempts to overcome the deliverances of that experience by insisting that it be grounded in something other than itself. The result is to undermine what was to be affirmed. Thus, Whitehead's God gives objective immortality to the efforts of the creatures by treasuring up in divine remembrance every worthwhile aspect of determinateness, everything capable of being woven into the single concrescing unity that is the progress of God's immediacy toward full and final determinateness. At that final omega point, God will be all. But this means that the temporal passage toward divine realization is without intrinsic value, its worth solely a function of the outcome it serves. What would be true at that final endtime is also true now: the birth and perishing of actual occasions, and the physical and cultural orderings they collectively fashion, are meaningful because they are retained in the ever-enriched life of God's concrete experience. The world continually perishes that God might become more fully God.

The antidote to all four of these metaphysical forms of idolatry is a metaphysics that is insistently godless. A metaphysics truly rooted in the dynamic cosmos that we encounter everywhere in experience must be silent regarding divinity. I say this because the traditional notions of divinity advocated within Western culture, as well as those more recently proferred by process thinkers, all exemplify the four versions of eternity I have been discussing. For substance theologians and for process theologians, God is irreducibly and primordially one, unchangingly characterizable as requiring and exemplifying universal principles of order and virtue, the single source of the cosmos and its unfolding history, the redeemer who salvages the good of the world forevermore.

The idea of God is thus a compilation of claims regarding the nature of cosmic extremities. In the direction of the microcosm, complexity must finally give way to a foundationally simple unity that God is or exemplifies. Macrocosmic aggregation of ever more inclusive orderings must finally culminate in a universal first principle that is God or by reference to which divine activity proceeds. There must be a protocosmic ground that provides the conditions for temporal direction and meaningful activity, and these require also eschatocosmic preservation as the promise motivating the struggle of creatures toward the appropriate realization of primordial purpose. God as alpha and omega, our creator and our redeemer, lord of history and sovereign of nature – such a God, according to the various metaphysics of the extreme, is the exception to experience in order to be its basis and its explanation.

But we human beings inhabit a middle realm, a mesocosm far removed from these supposed metaphysical compass points, and nothing in our experience gives us license to claim that the extremes of the cosmos are fundamentally different from that with which we are familiar. Kant's discussion of the antinomies generated by such attempts at overrunning the human world should still regulate our metaphysical speculations. We have been driven by our fear of temporality and its perishings to devise a metaphysics of eternity and by its means to posit a God at the extreme who, in the spirit of Aristotle's four causes, is ground, principle, source, and end of our fleeting activities. The radical reformulations promised by process philosophy, pragmatism, and phenomenology in this century have unfortunately betrayed their mandate. For each of them have in one way or another also made appeal to the same four versions of eternity that are our legacy from classical thought.

The secularization of metaphysics is long overdue. The claim that becoming and perishing are the locus of all reality needs at long last to be stalwartly affirmed. The God of eternity is a false god, an idol for the worshippers of transcendence to adore. Even when imbedded in time and endowed with the capacity to change, it is a god hypothesized and not experienced, an escape from truth and not its highest expression. Until there can arise a notion of God stripped of the four extremist affirmations that are exceptions to the metaphysical categories appropriate to mesocosmic experience, our philosophies must be silent regarding divinity. There remains work enough to do in understanding the flux of things and figuring out how best to act within that flux for the sake of our deepest values.

II

Agree, then, to set aside a theological inquiry into the nature of God or the meaning of language about God. Set aside as well an investigation of fundamental particles or an analysis of possibilities for a unified field theory in the natural sciences. Such matters deserve philosophical investigation, but they should not be taken as the starting point for metaphysics nor the source of basic presuppositions, axioms, and other dogmatic foundations. I will begin with the mesocosm, our environment for experience and action. To find metaphysical foundations at the far extremes from such familiarities is to court all the errors typical of strangers to a foreign land. So I will seek to find a foundation in the middle kingdom where humanity is normal sized, its knowing and its deeds routine examples of truth and accomplishment. What I find there is the reality of process, omnipresently transformative.

The epistemology of passage concerns itself with interpretive orderings. From the endless fluidity of our encounter with the world, we fashion the persistent structures that give meaning and importance to our lives. I will attempt to sketch some of the conditions that make this making possible.

For experience to be denotatively characterized, its content must include regions of order that possess boundary, capacity, and trajectory. We impute individuality to such regions; they are the objects of experience that we name and categorize, the things of our world with which we interact. A region of order has boundary if under some criterion of relevance a demarcation can be made between an inside of relatively interdependent elements and an outside of other elements relatively independent of those comprising the inside. This bounded order, this totality, has capacity if there is a set of powers, of potential or realized behaviors, that it will distinctively, perhaps even predictively, display under specifiable conditions. Such an entity has trajectory if a career is traceable wherein those capacities are sequentially realized while preserving continuity in regard to boundary.

The experienced world has no indivisible atoms, monads, or actual occasions in its population. There are no objectively given boundaries separating its membership, no roster of predetermined capacities, no inevitable trajectories. For the everyday entities of experience, the boundary that individuates them must be determined rather than found. To select out a single entity from the welter of experience, a criterion of relevance is required, a decision regarding how most appropriately to assess whatever opportunities there are for resolving the inherent ambiguity and vagueness of what is encountered. Likewise the capacities and trajectories of things require judgment. The conditions for displaying capacities must be specified, the pathways of a trajectory defined, the conditions for continuity made clear. Mesocosmic things arrive at our door like unassembled merchandise, but with the necessary instructions conveniently enclosed.

Such instructions are primarily cultural. The human organism interacts with its environment by means of behaviors that are biological only at a generalized level. These generic response mechanisms are then made specific by training. A unique way of characterizing experience, and a distinctive manner of behaving in response to that information, are taught and retaught by agents of the culture until these become habitual, become for all practical purposes instinctual, for the infant or cultural neophyte. We are human because of an environing culture that molds our protean animality into distinctively procrustean practices. Our culture defines for us the acceptable range of kinds of boundary that a totality can have and still be called a real thing, the proper repertoire of possible capacities it can exhibit, the plausible shapes of its trajectories, and the behaviors available to us for dealing with the presence of whatever exhibits any appropriate set of these individuating conditions.

Thus, I am able to build a rude shelter in the forest as protection from the rain and cold because I distinguish myself from my environment. I take for granted certain assumptions about the differing capacities of each, of my body and of the weather, and how changes in the trajectories of both, due in part to their interaction, will affect my continued well-being. I have a similar grab bag of beliefs regarding saplings, mature trees, and leafy branches, and how each responds to specific kinds of stress. I possess a lore of construction techniques, some – but by no means all – of which can be articulated, combined with habits of their exercise and expectations concerning the likelihood of their success under assumed conditions.

These behaviors are arbitrary in their detail although it is biologically necessary that there be detail of some sort. Our species survives not because I use my hatchet to fashion a Boy Scout lean-to while praying to a favorite saint for protection, but because my capacity to foresee danger, perceive the utility of things, and alter my situation accordingly has been instantiated, in my case in terms of merit badges and Sunday School. The cultural specificity could have been quite different, but without it there would have been no response at all and so no survival.

What is true of the participant in any such enterprise is also true of another who views it externally. Someone is able to see my efforts as the attempt to fashion a temporary shelter against the impending storm, and to judge those efforts as effective or silly, because that person reads experience by means of previously inculcated beliefs regarding the natures of things. If the observer's habits and mine have no commonality, it is more than likely that he or she will not understand my actions, will therefore not be able to assess their value, and may not even recognize them as human activity. To understand another's world is to have become aware of the specifying conditions that constitute it that world of totalities and not another.

We must acknowledge, therefore, that experience is necessarily ordered by means of such primary categories as boundary, capacity, and trajectory. Yet we must also realize that the orderings themselves are contingent. They are not arbitrary, for they can be objectively assessed with respect to worth. But they are invented, not discovered. The passage of things has a human shape because culture rather than nature determines the meaning of a passage and the means by which there can be things that pass. Nature structured by cultural beliefs and practices yields the world and its objective content of totalities, including the very distinction between nature and culture that was the precondition for such a claim.

To assert that the boundary of a thing is contingent is to deny that the thing is simple. If there is more than one possible tracing of a boundary, then the individual so identified must have components, aspects, or substructures which need not have been gathered within its circumference but nonetheless for some reason were. Different boundaries imply different capacities or trajectories, and vice versa. A thing is uniquely specified by indicating the manner in which its constituents are arrayed so as to comprise a complex but determinate totality. The justification for any such specification is contextual, with the fundamental condition being that the order among the components be such that the relational pattern is definitionally essential and the relata distinguishable but not separable. The mode of order may be logical, aesthetic, and/or ethical. It may have a spatial, temporal, and/or intentional axis of connection. Any one of the nine orderings defined by a specific combination of mode and axis can be loose or tight, imposed or extruded, rigid or flexible, dynamic or static. But whatever the order, it is this which, relative to some context, gives distinctiveness to the relata as so related. The boundary, capacities, and trajectory of an entity are the way in which its ordered components are exemplified.

Totalities so construed are achievements. An ordering of components into a whole requires effort. Either the constituents themselves or some entity external to them must introduce novelty into a given situation. The spectrum of realized and unrealized capacities among the constituents must be somehow redistributed, various trajectories redirected, sub-boundaries refashioned, existing modes of order replaced by other modes or their axes reoriented, degrees of fit altered. This requires effort: the work of overcoming the resistance inherent in the momentum of established processes. A similar effort is required to sustain the resulting achievement in the face of other creativities and other established processes.

This means that the process of realizing some specific totalization is risk-filled. It is vulnerable to error, misjudgment, and the force of circumstance. Over time a particular accomplishment will, and indeed must, suffer constant reinterpretation and reformulation. That is, its unity will be modulated by thought or by action, and most likely by a complicated interplay of both.

Sartre's philosophy, for instance, recognizes the restless transformations in the meaning of self that are at the heart of its reality. A human self alters as the *pour-soi* of its intentions shifts, as the *en-soi* of its accomplishments accumulates, as the look of another or its own slide into bad faith redefines its self-understanding, as its death hands the meaning of its existence over to others, as its totalizing praxis is detotalized by another or by the *pratico-inerte*, as this evokes for it a group-reality and offers it the possibility of transindividual meaning. Depending on the double perspectives of actor and observer, the pattern of relationship among the components of Sartrean selfhood constantly shift. An individual is constituted now this way, now that, as thought and deed continually transform the conditions for self-identity appropriate to the context at hand. When Sartre says that freedom is the nonfoundational foundation for human being, he is claiming that persons must invent themselves, and should. I need only add that we are also invented by our cultural environment, and that humans are in no sense unique for this being so of them.

If individuation is thus a matter of delineating a relationship more primary than its relata, and if this structure is contingently effected and therefore constantly in flux, then passasge through time must involve not only the building up of more complicated unities out of lesser, but also the breaking down of the former into the latter. The fluctuating structures of the world are each themselves composed of fluctuating structures from which they ceasely emerge as new totalizing achievements and into which they regularly decay as that totalization fails. The process is both diachronic and synchronic. Any particular individual is an ordered unity the relata of which are in some definable sense individuals of lesser scope. But that totalized individual is also a relatum for some more broadly defined relationship. Passage is into and out of these lesser and greater orderings, and at any given moment it exemplifies some instance of each.

Any reality we confront, interact with, are concerned about or for, will turn out to be comprised of components and to be a component, to have arisen from constituting predecessors and to be contributing to constituted successors. From the small to the great, from the ancient to the anticipated, complex unities in transition are all we will find. This uniform extrapolation away from the direct experience of ourselves and our immediate world rests on the claim that the character of primary experience is typical. The mesocosm is everywhere experienced as being the same elsewhere.

As mesocosm gives way to microcosm and macrocosm, complexity remains central. The molar object turns out to have parts, the parts are found to be composed of molecules, the molecules are shown to have atomic constituents, and the atoms dissolve into subatomic particles that in turn are found to be probability distributions at a moment. Ourselves and the things around us turn out to be part of an environment that belongs to a planetary ecosystem, which is discovered to be part of a solar system contained within a galaxy, and the galaxies comprise a universe that may in no way be unique. Similarly, creation of the protocosm presumes an antecedent complexity of creator and creative possibility, and the eschatological day of cosmic judgment is said to usher in yet another heaven and another earth.

Nor should it be surprising that these fluctuating structures of fluctuating structures pursue us even as we move toward the extremes of the spectra involved. For since mesocosmic experience has one primary characteristic, that of complex unities in transition, it follows that the mental and physical attempt to push against the conditions of that experience will succeed only by utilizing the instrumentalities provided by and within those conditions. We find more of the same wherever we look because what we see is a function of how we look, and the how of our seeing is culturally. At the metaphysical extremities of experience we encounter not God but ourselves. As William James so aptly put it, the trail of the human serpent is everywhere.

III

Of particular interest as well as importance are the mesocosmic structures comprising human culture: the beliefs, practices, and institutional
inventions characteristic of the social world of human interactions.
These historical entities are especially normative for metaphysics
because they are the most visible and accessible of all the kinds of order
that surround us. They are ourselves writ large, our universe brought
down to human scale. The family is the eldest and most central of these
structures, based on ties of blood and nurture as well as cooperation and
subjugation. As the procreative conditions of social order fade in significance and ones based on choice or will are augmented, family order
becomes tribal and then political. Over the whole spectrum from family
to polis, to the even more complex orderings of the modern nation-state,
the twentieth century's increasingly global communities, and the even-
tual possibility of interstellar civilizations, the essential feature of
historical passage is that of totalities emerging and then giving way to
other totalities.

One distinctive feature of these historical artifacts is that they are
self-fashioning unities. Their order is the result of achievements rooted
in the agency of the relata. These achievements are always dependent
upon previous structures that the agencies in question set about altering
in either intended or unintended ways. Whatever we might decide to
designate as the first human familial order, we would discover that it was
a modification of some previously existing form of socialization that we
are reluctant for some reason to define as truly a family or as fully
human. In every instance of social formation, previous structures are
cannibalized, rearticulated, eradicated, along the road toward fashioning
a newly emergent reality. Social orders endure only by continually
renewing their prior achievement in the face of contending alternatives
from the outside and nagging inadequacies from within.

Historical structures are therefore always in passage toward new
structure. That passage may be smooth or abrupt. The continuities
among certain phases of a passage may be sufficient to justify their being
treated within a given cultural perspective as though they were one
enduring structure, or the phases may involve such radical reformulations of the inherited order that earlier and later must be distinguished
as an individual and its distinct successor. But in either case, passages
from one configuration to another are everywhere going on and will
always be going on, making and remaking the character of the world.

What, after all, defines the boundary of a particular family? A male
and female have offspring who in their turn mate and produce further

progeny. It requires an awesomely complicated set of cultural interpretations and ritual practices to define an appropriate perimeter to the results of such iterative behavior. Marriage rites may serve to separate familial from extrafamilial procreative activities, with only the former being the source of children accepted as members of the extending family. Custom will decide how offspring after they marry should continue their association, and the resulting patrilinear or matrilinear orderings will then give a distinctive shape to the behaviors of wide ranges of other people. A role for parents beyond their productive years will be assigned, as well as the proper practices for unmarried adult offspring and for the still-dependent young. The precise conditions under which two sons or daughters are taken as defining two new families rather than continuing to be direct explications of the parental family will vary not only among cultures but from family to family, and even within a single patrimony one child may seek independence while another sibling prefers subservience.

In precisely similar fashion the boundaries between family and tribe, gens and polis, metropole and nation, culture and civilization, are always in flux and the lines of separation glimpsed only through a strongly interpretive lens. Did the Roman Empire complete its fall in the fifth century A.D. and a new civilization then slowly emerge out of the resulting chaos? Or is the Graeco-Western world one civilization and the turmoils of that time best explained as an incisive shift in its political elites from Mediterranean to Nordic tribes, with resultant alterations in the predominant style, structure, and intentionality of the civilization, but with significant underlying continuities in fundamental beliefs and institutional practices?

It might seem that questions concerning magnitudes in space and time of such vast civilizational proportion are inherently imprecise because arbitrary, whereas individuating queries about persons or families have a more clearly natural and therefore objective foundation. But this is not at all the case. Freud, Darwin, and contemporary genetics blur the lines that would unambiguously separate one human being from another, and if the width of the separation line is made proportional to the size of what is to be divided, then the empire of Romulus Augustulus and that of Charlemagne are about as different or undifferent as a mother is different from her child — a child she grew within her, then birthed, and them helped nurture into relative independence.

If ambiguity is one distinctive feature of the flux of social order, another is the instability of that order. The totalities that emerge do not long endure. The primary reason why families come apart is also the reason why both empires and republics fail to sustain themselves in history for more than a season. A structure with human beings as the relata is confronted continuously by a problem of plenitude. Each new situation must come to terms with a heritage of ordered possibilities and demands that are in excess of what can be readily woven into a workable social order. There are more values competing for realization at any given moment than can possibly be supported. The facile capacity of human imagination to frame goals that can focus individual and collective energies into powerful instruments for social change, or in resistance to such change, is everywhere the cause of an embarrassment of riches. Exclusion, or some milder equivalent such as subordination or epitomization, is the necessary condition for continuance. The plenitude comprising any given societal situation must be dealt with by decisions that bring relative harmony out of cacophony, and at whatever price might be required.

A people arises into history under the impetus of unifying powers that are both ideal and practical. There are widely shared visions of possible futures that serve as guiding norms and provide unquestioned assumptions for action, creating parallelism even where coordination and control are not feasible. These ideal ends are also able to harbor less noble purposes, serving as opportunities for narrow-visioned agencies to further their parochial ends by cooperating at least for the moment with their competitors and enemies. Egoist and altruist are both transformed by this surprisingly symbiotic enterprise, and a novel form of order emerges that seems an improvement to everyone involved. The problems of a prior plenitude have been woven into a new kind of totality, marked by the elimination or muting of former difficulties and by the enhancement of fortunate threads of reconciliation or indifference.

But to resolve a problem of plenitude is to increase the subsequent plenitude and so to set further tasks for the fashioners of the new order. They are not as well prepared for these new tasks, however, as they were for the old. These new problems were unknown to the leaders of this new order at the time when they were preparing for the labors that have brought them glory and success. New ideal visions thus wink into life as the new age is born and therefore as new ranges of private purposing are stirred. But these are ideals and purposes for which that age is not prepared because their realization will be, in some way or another, at the expense of the very achievements that have made the world possible.

The available options are obvious: deal with these buddings either by nipping them off or by encompassing them within some new dialectical adventure into the unknown. The former method preserves the old accomplishments, themselves barely realized and still threatened by the yet more ancient accomplishments they have supplanted. It does so by reaffirming the judgments that were the source of its success. The latter method requires new imaginings, new politiking, new fashionings – ones not ready-at-hand because not needed or even thought of until now. It is small wonder that the usual response, therefore, is to clip off the bud for the sake of the blooming rose, out of fear that both bud and rose would be lost were the confusing surfeit of novelties to continue unabated.

The tendency within a culture, within any historical community, is therefore toward rigidity. When successful invention spawns the need for further and ever more demanding invention, a reasonable solution is to insist that minor regions of activity be stabilized so that attention can be focused on the creative requirements of what is clearly more significant. So these lesser regions employ strategies of repetition, which means eliminating novelty and shoring up familiar patterns of accommodation. Any particular ordering of a region thus becomes increasingly dependent on these subordinate regional regularities, which after a time take their habitual behaviors and necessities, define their traditional roles a proper privileges, their liberties as rights. This makes it more and more difficult for the wider harmonies to handle their upswelling of abundances, with which they must contend by working out novel reconcilings that entail adjustments at the lesser levels. The older interests have been vested in their various authors, and as a consequence those responsible for the whole find themselves increasingly without the capacity to effect change in those severally responsible for the parts. The authority of creative imagination that was once the key to communal leadership gives way to authority arising from the sheer power to coerce begrudging change on the part of subordinates. Or the leadership comes to reflect passively at the level of the totality the same repetitions it finds everywhere at the regional levels.

Thus the risk of failure grows. The originality needed to cope with the new kinds of problem that an excess of possibilities breeds is less and less in evidence. Old methods are increasingly applied in an attempt to solve problems with which they were not designed to cope. As a result, the problems do not get solved and stultification ensues; the totality allows the newly emerging realities that surround it to go unrecognized and unincorporated. The whole permits its other to arise and eventually to become its nemesis. This new center of order is a threat to the old because it lacks the burden of a past to weigh down its imaginings and so can find a form and a trajectory that is more responsive to actual conditions than that of its competitor. It is therefore more successful. The old ways are crowded over or crowded out. Under such pressures, the old will likely perish and itself become salvage for its successors to make of what they wish.

What is true of civilizations is true throughout the whole range of creative agency. The emergence of various degrees of organic hierarchy is the story of effective control being exercised over ever more complex structurings of the agencies of which each is composed. Energy is atomized, atoms combined into molecules and eventually into prokaryotic organisms, and these in their turn are melded into single complex cells as the various symbiotic purposes of the different prokaryotes take on structural necessity. These nucleated cells then achieve structural differentiation and culminate in structures exhibiting neurological order, this in turn allowing for the emergence of consciousness, selfconsciousness, and finally the communication networkings that comprise a culture's symbiotic unities. But at each level of complexity the problems to be solved eventually outrun the capacities of that order to control them. The order then collapses into suborderings: a given civilization into its component cultures, a polis into its tribes, a tribe into families, a family into individuals, persons into their organic residue, cells into molecules, the atoms themselves into dissipated energy. Such is the way achievements emerge, compound their success, exhaust themselves, and are finally overtaken by entropy.

The primary strategy against the hubris of creative power would seem to be stabilization at some specific and still controllable level of social achievement. The keystone for such an enduring artifact would need to be a method by which the relative autonomy of the supporting substructures in a totality can be responsive to change while remaining essentially repetitive. The middle levels of an ordered hierarchy can provide refreshment to the whole by exhibiting reasonable flexibility within the boundary of essential continuity. This requires perishing, the constantly repeated death of the constituents of middling accomplishment, but in proportions that at any given moment are few in comparison to the whole. If one of the middle regions should be forced to deal with the novelties that arise from the ashes of prior perishings, it must have the capacity to do this without suffering radical alterations in its distinctive totality, without threatening the familiar functions that that middle region performs and for which it exists. The greater totality should have to attend to such transformations only at the margin, only on those occasions when accumulated modulations of this sort across a number of regions require some kind of reconciling adjustment at the higher level. In this way there is the emergence of novelty in the components, altered but not wholly new patterns that – because of their newness – evoke the need for alterations at the next more complex level, but which – because of their continuities – do not require fundamentally destabilizing change.

Throughout the meaningful universe each order has a higher level that it serves through its relative autonomy and lesser levels with a dynamic it must always be adjusting and adjusting to. Refreshment at the intermediate levels gives suppleness to the higher level, and this is accomplished by perishing at the lower levels. The higher unity is able in this way to replicate itself in part but not in full, and so remains, perhaps despite itself, flexible enough to suffer the partial changes required for survival but rigid enough to sustain the heritage of subordinated quasi-autonomous orderings without which the environment needed for complex adjustment would not be possible.

A nation endures when its citizens are free to pursue their own ends, but only in ways that are socially functional; when the death or defeat of a leader can be the opportunity at once to consolidate old achievement and anticipate the unsettling influence of new leadership, and when this is true throughout the society – from shifts in a family's responsibility structures to the appearance and demise of voluntary organizations and special interest groups, from the way children play to the way a people handles the transfer of power from one head of state to the next.

Such ideals are difficult to realize. But their occasional manifestations in history comprise the roster of excellences to which we defer and for the sake of which we live and work and die. Change is at the heart of the enduring civilized values that give life its meaning. Being and perishing are thus the essential instrumentalities of all mesocosmic accomplishment. To denigrate passage in the name of timeless permanence is treason to life, to history, and to the cosmos itself.

The failure to solve the problem posed to inventiveness by self-feeding patterns of plenitude is why human history, and the history of the whole cosmos, is a tragic story of suffering and irredeemable loss. But this story is a noble tale for our telling, because the struggle with such problems is self-justifying. It is reason enough to have lived if life means to be able to become one among the creatures of passage, to be able to work with them at the invention of meaningful order, to be able to die so that such inventiveness might be sustained. Such is our dignity as human beings as well as our destiny.

Nicholas Capaldi

Copernican Metaphysics

I. Classical Metaphysics

Every new metaphysics begins with a critique of the old metaphysics. Our outline of "the" new metaphysics will be no exception. We will commence with what we take to be the errors or error of the old metaphysics in all of its varieties. The identification of these errors is made from a standpoint; and when we become self-conscious of this standpoint, we can articulate the new metaphysics. Taking this approach is neither just a tradition nor a mere convenience. As we will show, it is integral to the discipline of metaphysics itself. In calling this standpoint "the" new metaphysics and not "a" new metaphysics, we will do several things. We deny that metaphysics can or does advance by substituting one new intellectual fad for another, and we deny that this new metaphysics is the product or insight or property of a single individual.

Before we get on with the articulation of the new metaphysics, we must first identify the old metaphysics; and before we can identify the old metaphysics, we must define what metaphysics is and in such a way that we preserve a meaningful continuity between the new and the old. *Metaphysics is the study of primordial reality*; it is the belief that there is a primordial reality, that the primordial reality is meaningful, and that man is capable of grasping that meaning.

The most prevalent variety of old metaphysics may be dubbed Aristotelian. It asserts that the familiar world of everyday experience has a structure that constitutes primordial reality. Man is himself a natural part of that structure. In the seventeenth century, Christian Wolff called this structure ontology. Since the eighteenth century rise of science to prominence, specifically the view that science is the whole truth about everything, the most fashionable version of Aristotelianism in metaphysics has been called the philosophy of science. So closely is the term metaphysics associated with Aristotelianism, that some

Aristotelians find unimagineable the possibility that there can be any other kind.

The major antagonist to the Aristotelian tradition in metaphysics has been Platonism. Platonists also believe in a primordial reality with an objective structure, but they deny that any such meaningful structure can be found in the world of everyday experience. On the contrary, that structure is more akin to a logical construct. In accord with this, primordial reality is modelled along the lines of the mind of man rather than external physical objects or processes.

It is not our purpose here to discuss the relative merits or the indigenous difficulties of Aristotelianism or Platonism. What is important for our purposes is that both major varieties believe in a structure independent of man. Even when such a structure is inclusive of man, any structure to or by man is derivative from the more inclusive structure. God, the Forms, even electrons, for example, would continue to function or to exhibit meaningful structure even if there were no man.

The primary error of all classical metaphysics is the belief in a meaningful structure independent of man. The new or modern metaphysics begins with a denial that there is such an independent meaningful structure. It denies that such a structure could exist without man. It denies that our fundamental categories can be explained by extraconceptual reference.

II. The New Metaphysics

Having stated what the new metaphysics rejects in the old metaphysics, we can proceed to state what the new metaphysics asserts positively: *Primordial reality is man's relation with the world.* Primordial reality is not an object; it is not a physical object; it is not a mental process. It is a relation. The relation is meaningful, but neither man nor the world is meaningful apart from the relation.

If that relation is meaningful, how are we to understand it? The relation cannot be understood as a mechanical system (spatial, atemporal structure), not can it be understood as a purely organic system. Although organic systems of explanation are preferable to mechanical ones, no organic system, and therefore no teleological system, can ever be adequate to the job. The relation can be understood only culturally. By *culture*, I understand the conjunction of the social and the historical.

The obvious question to be raised here is the extent to which this shifts the emphasis to man and away from the world. In an important sense the shift is clear enough. But what we must remember is that man is not to be understood as an object, and most certainly not an object with a fixed structure. Although the focus is shifted to man, man himself cannot be understood independent of his relation to the world. Moreover, man's relation to the world is mediated by culture.

Man and world are both abstractions from the primordial relation. The primordial relation is mediated by culture. But culture is not an object with a fixed structure either, so we must avoid hypostatizing it as well.

So far, we have defined metaphysics as the study of primordial reality; we have identified the primordial reality as the interface of man and world; we have asserted that there is an order to that interface; we have denied that the order is either logical, mechanical, or organic; we have instead opted for understanding that order as cultural. If that order is cultural, how are we to understand or interpret it?

The following are the possible perspectives from which cultural order can be understood:

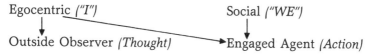

There are, therefore, four possible combinations. Classical metaphysics can be characterized as adopting the perspective of the egocentric ("I") outside observer (applied to order as logical, mechanical, or organic — but not to cultural order). The new metaphysics has adopted the perspective of the agent, the engaged participant. But, by and large, the agent has been viewed as an egocentric one.[1] The most notable shortcoming of the new metaphysics has been the failure so far to give a sustained account of the social exchanges that constitute cultural order. It is implicit in much of the new metaphysics, but in an undeveloped form.[2]

If the new metaphysics is ever to succeed in accounting for ultimate reality and itself, it must embrace the social ("we") perspective of engaged agents or participants. Once again we must avoid the temptation of turning the "we" into an object with a fixed structure, that is, of hypostatization. "We" is here understood as shorthand for "you and I." Here again the question will be raised as to the extent to which this shifts the emphasis even more to man. Clearly it does, but since neither "you" nor "I" is a mere object in space, there are no mere facts about man that in any way explain his origin and destiny. It is not empirical research that can help here. Rather, what metaphysics does is to explicate the concepts of ourselves already implicit in our everyday practices.

By starting with what we (you and I) do, we accomplish a number of things. There is nothing we do that does not flow from previous human action and reflection on that action. That is, the historical dimension of ultimate reality emerges as the second ingredient along with the social to define cultural order. Next, by rooting ultimate reality in practice, in action, and refusing to divorce reflection from action, we prevent thought from degenerating into intellectual narcissism, i.e., mindless modelling.

The new metaphysics is to be called *Copernican* in deference to the Copernican Revolution originally explicated by Hume and Kant. It was Hume and then Kant who first saw the philosophical significance of Copernican astronomy – namely that we are not mere egocentric observers of a process totally independent of ourselves. We are part of, in fact participants within, the process. Hence, no explanation is adequate that does not incorporate the mutual inclusivity of the object of explanation and the perspective of the explainer.

To sum up, the new metaphysics involves two key points, one negative and one One positive. Negatively, the new metaphysics denies that it is meaningful to talk about the "external" world as meaningful, structured, or the extralinguistic referent of truth. Positively, the new metaphysics locates primordial reality, and therefore fundamental meaning and truth, within cultural order.

III. The Historical Dimension of the New Metaphysics

Primordial reality is the interface of man and the world as mediated by culture. Cultural order is to be understood by explicating what you and I do. Here it should be clear that the *order of the primordial reality and the perspective from which we study it are mutually inclusive.* Philosophical and metaphysical reflection are thus necessarily enclosed in culture. As such, philosophy cannot get outside of itself and examine itself as an object. But this is just to say in another way that man cannot examine himself apart from his relation to the world. Understanding has to be internal to the relation. The relation is discovered retrospectively through time. Metaphysical thinking is therefore historical.

Metaphysical thinking is not historical in the sense of being anti-quarian. It is self-consciously historical. To think historically in meta-physics is to explicate the norms of previous practice and how they have been continuously reapplied to new situations. It is to see which possibilities have been developed and which discarded, to compare what we are to what we have been. The most important events in this history have been changes in our understanding of our relation to the world.

The illusion in classical metaphysics has been the hope of finding meaning, order, and guidance in some sphere independent of man (e.g., in the Forms, in Nature, in God, in the 'selfish' gene, etc.). But all we have found is a distorted reflection of ourselves. The important moments in modern metaphysics have been those occasions from Descartes to Nietzsche on which the illusion has been exposed. Recognizing this illusion does not lead to nihilism except in those who refuse to believe that order and meaning can have another locus. Nor does this liberation from past illusion lead to the transcendence of culture.[3] We can never transcend culture. Every critique of culture is a critique from within, a recognition of and a choice to develop some but not all implicit possibilities.

The belief that it is possible to transcend culture is largely the result of taking the observer's perspective (even a "we" think perspective) as opposed to the perspective of the agent (what "we" do). A disengaged and alienated observer or group of observers can always opt to give the kaleidoscope one more turn, but an engaged group of agents who have not lost sight of their own immersion in the world face no such temptation. The demands of responsible action force us to embody some norm.

The new metaphysics, by being historical, is also *conservative*.[4] To say that it is conservative is simply to say that it is forever required to work from the cultural order. That cultural order is not itself a structure independent of man, it is not ordained by God, it does not reflect eternal Forms, it has no inner teleology of either the cyclical or the progressive variety. The great danger here is the temptation to "rationalize" the cultural order by likening it to some other kind of structure. On the contrary, all other structures are only intelligible by reference to it.

One could say that the cultural order evolves so as not to confuse it with something teleological. But the concept of 'evolution' is merely organic and does not quite capture what is unique about man who lacks a species specific nature. Moreover, culture does not as a whole undergo social evolution. It would be more accurate to say that cultural order is historical. To say that it is historical is to say that we work from intersubjectively shared understandings continuously emerging from mutual dialogue about what we are doing. The term "historicist" is inappropriate because it attributes to culture a frozen structure it simply does not have.

In order to clarify explication, we shall contrast it with exploration and replacement. If metaphysics and philosophy were a form of exploration, then we should be following out the implications of some hypothetical model in order to realize its possibilities. If metaphysics were a form of replacement, we would be substituting new ideas for our everyday ideas. Reductionism is a form of replacement. Both exploration and replacement rely on imaginative theoretical constructions and ask the question "What is possible if...?"

If metaphysics is the *explication* of meaning, what we seek to do is to extract from our previous practice a theory of that practice, a theory that may be reflectively applied in deciding what to do next. Such a "theory" is unusual in that it makes norms fundamental. Explication is the serious attempt to clarify an intuition – the sense we have of ourselves as we act.

Cultural order is not a set of timeless axioms but immemorial accretions of rules of thumb. We discover such rules only in retrospect. They are a kind of center about which we always seem to circle, and it is our circling them that makes them the "center."

Metaphysical reasoning as explication does not lead to totally novel conclusions. Instead we are led to understand in a new way what we already understood in a different way. We do expose the errors of the past, but only in order to articulate the principles presupposed in the critical process. The critical process is thus itself a part of the tradition. It is not possible to engage in meaningful critique without restating in a fresh way the whole of the previous tradition. Philosophical critique is not a matter of refutation but of dialogue. It is hermeneutical, dialectical. It is self-critical.

The great philosophers of the past always formed their positions by a critique of their predecessors. Without some understanding of the predecessors we cannot grasp what the critic is saying. The original theorists, of course, were not criticizing a text but a practice. In a logical sense, current theorists are also critiquing practices, not just texts. Rooting theory in past practice, not just past texts, exercises a kind of limit on what would otherwise degenerate into mere kaleidoscopy. At the same time, we must gauge the extent to which current practice reflects the influence of past texts (as scripts).

In examining philosophy's past there is always the temptation to give a formal analysis of what a philosopher says by focusing on his words, as if words were the symbols of thoughts and thoughts intelligible in their own right. What we should be doing is examining the practice (style, for example) of a philosopher and the practice to which he was turning our attention. Try appreciating Aristotle's wisdom without some knowledge of the polis.

Let me offer two brief examples of how metaphysics is a kind of self-clarification. It has been traditionally held that the emergence of philosophy in ancient Greece was accomplished in part with the liberation from anthropomorphism. Whereas mythopoeic thought tended to attribute human characteristics to inanimate objects and to natural processes, the Greeks, it is alleged, avoided anthropomorphism by distinguishing clearly between the subjective and the objective. Allow me to suggest that the Greeks did not go far enough and that one of the consequences of that incomplete break is that we continue to attribute meaning, truth, significance, etc., to entities that do not possess them. The world, for example, has no meaning. It neither possesses meaning nor acquires it by reflection from Forms or from being part of a teleological chain. I suspect that Plato and Aristotle themselves understood this in an important sense. Meaning is something human and cultural. Hence, they found it necessary to postulate a demiurge, unmoved movers, and subsequent philosophers continue with God or the Absolute.

Modern science is not in a better position. Seemingly, such science denies "meaning" to the world, but it nevertheless asserts that the world has a structure that can be discovered and articulated. Having said this much, the articulators of science are in the awkward position of having to deal with the why and the wherefore of this particular structure. It has no serious answer. Instead, the articulators of the activity of science either sophistically or polemically deny the question, or they remain in ostrich-like silence even about science's own intelligibility, or they opt for a bizarre technological solution. What is that solution? It is the science fiction hope that space travel will lead us to an *extraterrestrial* intelligence who will explain the whole story to us.

What this sophisticated anthropomorphism shows us is that we really cannot comprehend meaning that is not of the order of a human social intelligence.[5] Put positively, we have come to see at last how meaning is only a property of a cultural order. That cultural order is the product of the interface of man and the world. The order, the meaning, does not exist apart from the relation. That is why the primordial reality is that relation. Moreover, any attempt to explain that meaning, the cultural order, in terms other than the cultural order, is doomed to incoherence.

The last and most powerful illusion about the transcendence of cultural order is modern science. Curiously, one finds this illusion more persistently among so-called philosophers of science than among scientists. The dream of unified science is of a science that explains the whole of nature – man, as a part of that nature. It would even at some point explain scientifically the activity of explaining. Critics of this illusion have been content so far with explaining the failure of such a dream to date or have charged it with an inadequate conception of natural order. When successful, the critic even succeeds in pushing the naturalist back into the direction of teleologizing nature once more. Witness the lack of clarity in attempts even to define how "life" could arise from inorganic elements.

The critics are correct to stress the inadequacy, nay, the incoherence, of such scientism (i.e., the belief that science is the whole truth about everything). But they have not gone far enough. What we need is a better understanding of the activity or practice of science, especially in a culture like our own that has made science into a sacred cow. Philosophy of science as practiced by analytic philosophers (overtly or covertly committed to the dogma of scientism) has focused on one of the products of science, namely formulas (texts of a sort). It then seeks to understand (or to reduce) the activity as if it were designed to produce one such product. This reduction of a process to a product is precisely what Dewey warns us against. It is just the sort of product that would appear intelligible to theorists whose perspective is that of the egocentric observer.

What would an alternative philosophy of science be like, especially one that saw physical science as one way but not the only way in which man relates to the world? To begin with, theoretical physical science cannot be divorced from technological manipulation of the world. Experimental science is aimed at giving us control over nature, not the grasping of a meaning. Any nonideological history of science would show this. More important, try imagining what science is like without the conducting of an experiment. Further, try to understand the performance of a scientific experiment without employing the distinction between intentional human activity and what happens when no intentional human activity is present. Without the presence of the agent, physical scientific inquiries could not get off the ground. If it is asserted in response that someday these intentional human acts will themselves be explained by the nonintentional, then one would still have to back up the validity of this claim with other experiments. These other experiments would require an agent who was able to recognize the consequences of his own action. There can be no explanation that does not finally come to rest upon the action of an agent conforming to some social (communal) notion of how to act in conformity to some model.

It is not science that can succeed in explaining man or culture, or even the modest aim of explaining the act of explaining. On the contrary, science is itself unintelligible unless it is seen as a subordinate part of culture, as just one of the many ways in which man relates to the world. The historical bent of the new metaphysics makes *time* the most fundamental category. The new Copernican metaphysics began to develop in Hume and Kant in the late eighteenth century at about the same time that history as temporal was beginning to be taken seriously. It is not a coincidence that Hume, for example, combined two careers: one as philosopher and one as historian. Prior to the eighteenth century, time was largely ignored. The ancients, at best, had worked out a cyclical conception of time that denied any real change or development through time. Even Aristotle, despite his intense interest in biology, made change of location fundamental to all other kinds of change. Even during the scientific revolution of the sixteenth and seventeenth centuries, theorists attempted to reduce time to space. The calculus is a measurement of movement through time, but not the study of real temporal change. Mechanical technology views the world as exclusively spatial: a world whose parts can be rearranged at will and in which the rearrangements themselves are temporally irrelevant. It was Kant who objected to this spatialization and who insisted that time was, on the contrary, more fundamental than space even to the intelligibility of science as an enterprise.

The recent trend among some scientists and philosophers of science to organicize nature (for example in process philosophy) is not a return to teleological cycles but the recognition that time is crucial, that organic systems interact with their environment and are what they are because of the past. It is to recognize the possibility of irreversible qualitative changes. It would be impossible to capture the logic of structural transformations by using a logic of momentary spatial relations. That is why mathematical logic, which is inherently spatial, cannot make sense of time. The tense logics that have been modelled on spatial logics are futile and bizarre attempts once more to reduce time to space by adding a new operator in space.

Given the irreducibility of time to space, it is no wonder that Descartes is led explicitly to separate the mental (temporal) from the physical (spatial). He thereby bequeathed to metaphysicians the intractable mind-body problem. As long as we continue to assert the existence of an ultimate reality that is timelessly external to man and culture, we either have to ignore the mind-body dichotomy by ingenious subterfuges or have to pay court to idealism. If, however, in the light of the new Copernican metaphysics we take cultural order, which is inherently historical, as the ultimate reality, we will have neither a naive mechanical view of the world of physical nature nor a reductionist view of mind. Mind is a function of time, it is locatable in the shared public and historical domain of culture. Our thoughts and beliefs begin in a public context, and this original public context remains temporally a permanent part of their meaning. It is only later, and with much effort and artifice, that we learn how to keep our thoughts and feelings private.

IV. Some Misunderstandings

The first and most crucial misunderstanding is the folly of denying metaphysics, i.e., denying that there is metaphysics in general or in one's own views. It is worth repeating that reports about the death of metaphysics are not just premature but that the obituaries are themselves metaphysical. All such denials (whether sceptical, positivistic, analytical, or deconstructionist) harbor in the form of a covert dogmatism positive views about intelligibility and method. Such dogmas are concealed and immunized from criticism but at the cost of consistency, as critics of such criticism never tire of reminding us. Such dogmas invariably cause us to speculate about the motives and intellectual integrity of their practitioners.

The second misunderstanding, and the one of longest duration, is the belief that the world outside of and independent of man has a meaningful order. The belief in such a wholly exterior meaning is a form of anthropomorphism, quite understandable in retrospect given the practical importance of astronomy for agriculture and agriculture for civilization. We no longer look to the heavens for guidance, except for those who seek E.T. The most that is possible is to understand the world as it relates to man. What must be avoided is making any statement about the extra-human world that does not implicitly relate to man. We must resist the temptation to state what the world is like or must be like in order to make culture possible. Such statements would place culture in a larger envelope of intelligibility, but by our account that is not possible.

Here we must be on guard against individuals who have so closely identified metaphysics with their version of it. (the Aristotelian-external enveloping structure) that they cannot separate our rejection of their view from a rejection of metaphysics. Aristotelians must sometimes be reminded that they do not have a proprietary interest in the concept of 'metaphysics.' It is not practical to anticipate every variant of the question, but Aristotelians usually like to ask if the new metaphysics is true? That is, what is the larger envelope that contains cultural order? Even when they are told that such a question is not meaningful within the new metaphysics, they persist in asking some version of the question, often

without realizing that the question merely reflects their frame of reference. On the contrary, the new Copernicans are in a position, because
order and the perspective from which we study it are mutually inclusive,
to understand the Aristotelian question in its context. The Aristotelians
often fail to understand what the Copernicans are doing.

The third significant misunderstanding is the obverse of the second.
Starting with the correct perception that understanding, truth, meaning,
etc., must ultimately be analyzed in human terms, theorists from Plato
to Plotinus to the idealists have tried to make man-in-himself (apart from
the world) the locus of order. But hypostatizing man or some part of him
is the same kind of error as hypostatizing nature. Such a narrow focus
either turns man into a concept or into a collection of categories. This is
the result of taking man to be identified with his thought or thoughts, the
inevitable consequence of taking the perspective of the egocentric observer. If man in some personalist sense were the primordial reality, and if
man were nothing other than his thought, then metaphysics could aim
at presenting a conceptual analysis of the unity of thought.

Contrary to idealism, an understanding of man requires us to try to
grasp the unity of thought and action, not the unity of thought alone. The
latter does not exist. The former, the unity of thought and action, is
impossible to grasp apart from man's relation to the world. Moreover, the
unity of thought and action cannot be grasped by conceptualization, if
by conceptualization we mean a purely logical structure. The coherence
of thought and action is temporal and therefore not purely spatial. The
actual intuition of unity is grasped in action, not in thought. Any
understanding we have of this unity becomes a part of it, or, more accurately, flows from it and into it. Hence, we see again the importance of
explication and the rejection of exploration as the primary mode of
metaphysical discourse.

What would grasping or understanding this unity be like? It would
not be a theory about thought, and it would not be a theory about action.
It would be a "theory" about the unity of thought and action. It is not a
theory in the traditional sense. Such a "theory" would have to "fit" what
has been done (descriptive) and indicate what should be done (prescriptive), but the prescription would have to "flow" from the description. This
is the inherent conservatism of metaphysics.

As we have already indicated, this is not a theory in the usual rationalist sense. It could only be a kind of *analogical* thinking. Moreover, the
analogues would have to be historical, not spatial, in keeping with the
temporal dimension of the primordial reality. In this way, we can come
to perceive a kind of historical coherence not a timeless spatial identity.

Many theorists would grant that you cannot conceive of the unity of thought and action in a mechanical or spatial sense. But once more there will be an attempt to envelope this unity in a larger teleological process. Of course, these theorists are correct in stressing that this unity is in a sense organic, that is, that the unity of thought and action can only be construed as existing in an interaction with the physical environment; that within the interaction the unity transforms itself in such a way that later configurations of the unity are dependent upon earlier configurations. The unity is qualitatively transformed through time (Dewey's constant theme). Nevertheless, the objection to settling for organic order is that unless we proceed to the level of cultural order, we shall not be able to do justice to the historical dimension. We shall be tempted to think in terms of adaptation to the environment (evolutionary epistemology), and such adaptation will be limited to individuals or viewed socially as a form of progressive social evolution. The real historical development is much more precarious and in no sense unilinear. It evolves but it does not progress to an endpoint. The teleological envelope over-rationalizes and at the expense of historical truth.

We suggest that all of these misunderstandings are related to the adoption of the viewpoint of the disengaged egocentric observer. It is such an observer seeking outside of himself for order who fails to find it (skepticism); or who keeps postponing metaphysics in the interest of epistemology – discussing the search for external order comes to displace any discussion of what we are searching for; or a retreat into mysticism. Carried over into public and social life, the perspective of the disengaged egocentric observer degenerates into the language of criticism that fails to recognize its own sources. All social and political speculation to such an observer will soon appear as illusion and ideology.

V. Consequences of the New Metaphysics

The *first* consequence of the new metaphysics is that philosophy in general and metaphysics in particular can defend the traditional claim of being the fundamental intellectual discipline. Philosophy is not a secondary discipline that services others such as theology, science, linguistics, or politics. Metaphysics (philosophy) is the fundamental intellectual discipline because its focus is on and its concern is for the primordial reality. *Primordial* reality is not a thing or entity, but a process; yet the process is not merely natural nor supernatural. It is social, historical, and first in the logical sense that although initially indeterminate, all subsequent differentiations are intelligible only by reference to it. All explanation and all understanding must, if pressed to the ultimate, come to rest in the cultural order. The cultural order is *ultimate* in the sense that it is what encompasses everything. By encompassing everything, it encompasses itself. The self-encompassing quality is a virtue of this view, and we have expressed it previously by noting that the order within the primordial reality and the perspective from which we study it are mutually inclusive. It is not a hypostatized mind (idealism) that encompasses the physical world; rather what we have are human beings jointly reflecting on what they have done and are doing and how the reflective process itself emerges from the previous activity. The reflection independent of that activity is meaningless.

There is no other system of metaphysics that has ever been able to account for the self-explanatory dimension required by any primordial reality. To cite but a few major examples: 1. Plato never explains how the articulation of all possible hypotheses reveals first principles – even in mathematics we cannot conceive of how this is possible (Godel); 2. neither Aristotle nor his successors have ever indicated how making referential language primary ever eventuates in self-explanation; neither the mind of God nor the mind of the Absolute is comprehensible to us; 3. scientism makes a mockery of the whole question. Searching for meaning in scientism is like looking for a mirror in the reflection of another mirror.

The *second* consequence of the new metaphysics flows from the first. If metaphysics (philosophy) is fundamental, then philosophy has a *unity*. The privilege of metaphysics is to speak fundamentally about primordial and ultimate reality. However, if reality is exclusively extraconceptual and extralinguistic, and if all thought and discourse are themselves to be explained by reference and denotation, then the unity of thought is either abandoned or disappears into myth. This problem has become especially acute in the contemporary world with the advent of scientism and its claim to pass judgment on all referential language. This would relegate philosophy to speaking only secondarily, to being a kind of secondary metalinguistics. The dominance of this view in the profession at the moment reduces philosophy to an aggregate of specialized subdisciplines lacking all coherence. On the contrary, the new metaphysics, by making cultural order and the perspective of the engaged social agent mutually inclusive, provides for a unity we can begin to explicate.

The *third* consequence follows from the second. If philosophical reflection is unified, then all of the usual dualisms and bifurcations can be obviated. Specifically, the *distinction between knowledge and value can be rejected*. Cultural order is inherently normative, so that any attempt to understand an activity must look for the norms integral to that activity. Notice once again that what we try to understand is an activity, not another thought process divorced from action. This point applies, quite obviously, to metaphysical speculation itself.

Try to imagine, for example, ethics as a purely descriptive discipline. As such it would be indistinguishable from anthropology, or even worse, journalism. Now imagine ethics as a purely normative discipline, that is, imagine that philosophers just tell people what they ought to do, including other philosophers. As the latter it would be pretentious, arrogant, and intolerable. On the contrary, if we view ethics as an explicatory activity, ethics could attempt to extract the norms already inherent in any context. The Anglo-Saxon common law tradition would be a near perfect analogy.

Suppose someone were to object that cultural order might not be good. If he did, then he would be asserting the existence of a set of standards and meaning external to the cultural order. Such an assertion presupposes an alternative metaphysics of the "old" variety. There is no point in repeating what has already been said against such metaphysics. It would be useful to add, however, that traditional notions of value-free, externally referential, and extraconceptual reality usually involve covert assumptions that once such reality is discovered we are to conform to it. Its model is something like the relationship between the calendar (astronomy) and agriculture. When translated into other and more serious moral issues, we invariably are faced with irreconcilable gaps between "is" and "ought" or endless variations on this theme. The is-ought gap is not a profound moral philosophical issue, but the symptom of the inadequacy of the "old" metaphysics.

Similar points can be made about *logic*. Logic must be understood as a form of explication, not a form of exploration. As a form of explication it is both descriptive and prescriptive. If logic is prescriptive, then its insights cannot be conveyed by hypothetical if-then statements. Trying to capture logic by hypotheses and exploration would mean that logic could never account for its own status but would at best be able to present a theory ("if-then") about itself. For logic to be unsure of itself is the ultimate absurdity. For example, we continue to use the law of the excluded middle while at the same time being unable to explain its status, although the literature that ponders its status ponders it by means of the law of the excluded middle. Finally, logic can never be captured by mathematics, for the latter is hypothetical and a form of exploration. That is, in mathematics we frame hypotheses and then examine the consequences. This is not a criticism of mathematics but of the failure to see logic as a form of explication.

Let us return now to one of the points made two paragraphs earlier, namely, the example about how "old" metaphysics can be viewed as tied to metaphors like astronomy-agriculture. This example shows how philosophy is both continuous with and how it uses and understands its own past. From our point of view, philosophy has always tried to make sense of practice, but it has done so by reference to "seemingly" external standards. Yet, I would argue, that the standards were derived from a metaphysics that was itself an anthropomorphic projection of one or more successful practices. For example, the Greeks gave ontological status to the circle-cycle (geometry-astronomy). So rather than declaring what earlier philosophers said to be as false, meaningless, or irrelevant, we can interpret what they "did" as well as what they "said" in a way that makes them continuously relevant for what we do. In short, the emphasis on explication 1. avoids irreconcilable dichotomies such as descriptive-normative, theory versus practice; and 2. stresses the historical continuity in philosophy between past and present in a way that demeans neither. The past is *not* a storehouse of hypotheses but an integral part of the present.

The *fourth* consequence, and the final one we will mention, is that the new metaphysics provides us with a *new research program*.

Philosophers in general and metaphysicians in particular are no longer to be confused with artists or scientists or dentists. In art (including some forms of technology) we witness the creation and exploration of new imagery, or what we have previously identified as theory replacement and theiry exploration. In science we witness theory exploration of the consequences of novel hypotheses. But in philosophy and metaphysics we are not concerned with replacement and exploration. Rather, we are concerned with the explication of norms inherent in *any* given cultural activity. That is why there can be the philosophy of science (although not what usually passes for such) and the philosophy of art, but not the art or science of philosophy. The explication that is involved is not mere description, for the very process of revealing the norms opens up the possibility of responsible criticism, re-presentation, and reconstruction. Metaphysics is that dimension of philosophy that tries to encompass all of these explications as a whole (as a plurality not as a monism) and includes itself – it is the "criticism of criticism." Yet that criticism must not lose touch with the myriad activities (actions) on which the original criticism is based, otherwise it degenerates into a pedantic scholasticism. Any partial explication is always subject to challenge by reference both to the activity itself and the relation of that activity to others. Every explication is subject to modification in the light of evolving action. There is no final and definitive explication.

Those who undertake explication, in partial or in grand form, must be individuals with a special sense or grasp of our activities. This special sense is not to be confused with the talents or skills of artistic creation or scientific thinking. This kind of thinking is not likely to be evident in young people without much experience of life and culture (the opposite of what is usually found in science). It is also the most demanding kind of thinking, involving an unusual combination of depth and breadth. To engage in it requires humility and presumptuousness at the same time. You cannot train someone to do this sort of thing, for it is not a collection of techniques. You can only do what in fact has usually been done – expose novices to the whole past and ongoing activity of explication and hope that some of them will "get the hang of it." In short, you cannot teach *how to* explicate, but you can explicate and show the work of past and present explicators. The history of metaphysics, then, is not a museum of changing styles but the study of how our predecessors tried to carry over what they thought important into newly emerging contexts.

NOTES

1. The stress in Dewey is always on man as an organism, an embodied agent. Dewey also recognizes the social perspective with regard to thought. What is lacking is a well worked out theory of the social world. Dewey was much more at home as a psychologist. Perhaps this is also why so much of the literature of pragmatism sounds like unfocused methodology.
2. Two exceptions to this charge are the works of H. G. Gadamer, *Philosophical Hermeneutics* (Berkeley: University of California Press, 1976); and Charles Sherover, "The Temporality of the Common Good," in the *Review of Metaphysics* (1984).
3. See John D. Caputo, "Hermeneutics as the Recovery of Man," in *Man and World* (1982): "*in Derrida the critique of presence tends to pass over surreptitiously into a critique of retrieval itself. And that is what I deny.*" (p. 363).
4. This is a remarkable naivete about the nature and variety of conservatisms. This is not the place for an exposition, but we note that conservatism is not to be confused with a defense of the status quo.
5. "*. . . the cause or causes of order in the universe probably bear some remote analogy to human intelligence.*" David Hume, *Dialogues Concerning Natural Religion*, Part XII.

Patrick A. Heelan

Perceived Worlds
Are Interpreted Worlds

Phenomenology studies what is directly given to perception, and as such is often contrasted with theoretical science – the objects of which, it is said, are imperceptible and only inferred. In *Space-Perception and the Philosophy of Science*, I argue that the objects of theoretical science can be given directly in perception and that scientific inquiry should be (and often is) from the start ordered to the goal of making at least some of its theoretical objects perceptible.

Perception is analysed within the context of a hermeneutical phenomenology. *Hermeneutical* phenomenology is a development of the phenomenological tradition characterized by the basic principle that all human understanding – and perception is included in this – is existentially and methodologically interpretative.[1] I claim that by looking at the philosophy of science from the perspective of a hermeneutical phenomenology, some of its current most difficult and recalcitrant problems undergo a remarkable transformation under which they become amenable to solution.[2] The twin foci of perception and interpretation can be found in many authors other than those in the continental tradition. One is reminded especially of the later work of C. S. Peirce. However, the total picture that emerges from this study is unique.[3]

Two main principles are used in this analysis: 1. the principle that perception is an interpretative or hermeneutical activity[4] and 2. the principle of the primacy of perception that says that the possible kinds of

The original version of this paper was read at a symposium on my book *Space-Perception and the Philosophy of Science* (Berkeley: University of California Press, 1983) – hereafter *Space-Perception* – held during the APA (Eastern Division) meeting in New York on 28 December 1984. The paper is my response to Professor Lawrence Sklar's "Perceived Worlds, Inferred Worlds, The World" (*Journal of Philosophy*, LXXXI [November, 1984], pp. 693–706). An abstract of my paper under the current title appeared in the same issue of the *Journal of Philosophy*, pp. 707–708.

reality are determined by the possibilities of perception.[5] Before addressing the three principal challenges a critic can make to the conclusions of my book, I will discuss the semantic, epistemic, and ontological burdens that the two principles given above must bear if they are to transform successfully our understanding of science. For this purpose, I will use as illustration the variety of visual spaces experienced historically in our culture.

There is much evidence, mostly informal but quite persuasive, that suggests that the geometrical structure of the real life visual environment is often not Euclidean. An environmental space has a geometry if and only if both the things in it and the empty intervening spaces between them obey the same set of geometrical laws. I surmise that the structures exhibited by the real life visual environment can be characterized by the family of finite hyperbolic Riemannian 3D geometries. This was a hypothesis originally made by Rudolf Luneburg[6] but it was made within the context of a purely causal "frameless" theory of perception and was abandoned because it failed to satisfy the experimental criteria of a causal theory. I have now proposed it within the context of a contextual and interpretative theory of perception. Aspects of this study will be summarized below.

The study assumes that physical space is Euclidean or, to speak more precisely, that as far as cultural interest goes in the measurable mesostructure of the human environment, that this follows the model of Euclidean geometry. When such mathematical models are used descriptively of the empirical world, they function semantically like descriptive metaphors — the empirical world is not composed of mathematical objects, mathematical models serve as descriptive metaphors for the empirical world. Visual space is related to physical space by a point for point nonconformal mapping between their respective models. Ordinarily it is the case that the geometrical model for visual space is, like the geometrical model for physical space, Euclidean. However, I claim that this is a contingent cultural matter, and that visual space also follows an older and more primitive set of geometric models: the two-parameter family of those hyperbolic non-Euclidean 3D spaces that have a finite diameter; that is, in which the infinity of the Euclidean model is mapped on the inside of a finite sphere having the observer at its center.

Let me try to convey to you an intuition of how such a visual world appears. Imagine it is night and you are outside looking up at the stars and planets. There are some galaxies also visible. You see them all imbedded in the celestial sphere. The Euclidean infinity of physical space is the celestial sphere that you see, and the whole of physical space is inside this visual sphere. There is no outside to it. Aristotle and the ancients sensed this, for they held that Archytas of Tarentum's question about space beyond the celestial sphere was no more than a nonsense question, for real space was finite – in our terms, non-Euclidean. In such a space, railway tracks curve upwards and meet at eye level at a finite distance. Distant objects look both larger and nearer than we believe they should be; objects quite nearby are smaller and more distant than we believe they should be. These aberrations generate for us a variety of visual illusions, the Moon Illusion and the Müller-Lyer Illusion. Strange inside effects are noticed, for example, inside a church or temple; the columns that flank the nave appear to grow smaller and converge on a point behind the altar or in the apse, while at the same time, as Rudolf Arnheim points out,[7] they appear to be of equal size and parallel. Such inside spaces can give a sense of a totally enfolding closure, sometimes claustrophobic, sometimes warm, protective, and womb-like, such as Vincent van Gogh's bedroom at Arles.[8] These are I claim, the residues of a visual world that our culture has lost, together with the semantics that go with it. How long ago? Not very long ago. In fact, in the early fourteen hundreds.[9]

How does one characterize this primitive visual world? One characterizes this world by studying the mathematical model it is presumed to follow. Such a model divides the world into two qualitatively different regions, *near* and *far*. Of these two zones, only the near zone, which is directly in front of the viewer, is fully and clearly three-dimensional; the far zone is a progressively shallow three-dimensional shell of finite depth where objects sufficiently distant from the viewer are stacked like painted images on an all-enclosing spherical backdrop. Nearby things would suffer certain kinds of deformations; distant things would suffer other kinds of deformations; only in a limited zone directly in front of the perceiver would things appear in their customary physical size and shape. Such a world in which near and far are qualitatively different has distinct advantages for a human community in early stages of cultural development, where the source of manipulable evolutionary pressures and opportunities is principally nearby.

Styles of philosophical inquiry differ notably among themselves. Some have a predilection for the formal mode where questions arise out of the language used by philosophers, scientists, and others, and are resolved in a transformed and clarified semantics. For a hermeneutical phenomenology, however, questions arise out of experience and are resolved in a transformed experience. Experience, of course, comes already equipped with a semantics, but merely transforming the semantics does not guarantee its truth. There must also be a transformed understanding of experience, that is, a transformation of the truth domain. Methodologically, the semantics should be transformed through a better interpretation or hermeneutic of the experience that serves as its material mode. It is by working on the latter that the former is corrected or transformed.

Returning to the primary illustration about visual spaces, we ask the following questions: 1. What is the *descriptive semantics* of a perceptual world such as this one? 2. What *epistemic* validity has it? 3. What, if any, is its *ontology*?

1. Semantics of a perceptual world.

We have lost that part of our natural language that speaks of this primitive world of hyperbolic space. Old words have changed their meanings and have been appropriated by the Euclidean language we now speak. To recover the semantics of this world, we need to enlarge our use of spatial terms so as to include visual hyperbolic shapes and visual hyperbolic relations. Given that we are no longer primitives, this requires a deliberate and planned effort on our part, starting from a geometrical model such as Luneburg's and learning to apply it within the realm of our experience. In this way, we hope to reconstruct the framework of the primitive experience of space.

2. Epistemic validity.

What epistemic validity has the new semantics? Its epistemic validity will stand or fall on the basis of two kinds of tests. *First* and evidently, tests that use the new semantics to describe the recovered phenomeno-logical world of hyperbolic first-person perception. I point to evidence for this world in everyday life, among visual illusions, and in the history of art, architecture, and human cultures. *Second,* tests that study the mediations of signs that affect how we see. For in any interpretative theory of perception, what we perceive − the object considered as *perceptual horizon* − has a Thirdness about it (to use Peirce's term); what we perceive is the outcome of having responded to a sign, and we perceivers are a community of skilled interpreters − the interpretant (in Peirce's terminology). Such signs have text-like qualities, and I will call them texts or (if you wish) "texts." This line of inquiry leads us in a threefold direction: a. What is the text to which the perceiver is respond-ing? This is a paradigmatically scientific inquiry leading into, among other things, neurophysiological networks, instruments, and readable technologies. b. Who are the interpreters; meaning, what kind of interpreters are they, how are they embodied, e.g., what instruments do they use to perceive, what are their cultural interests? This is a predominantly cultural and anthropological inquiry. c. A normative inquiry: Within the new semantics, should such a text yield on interpretation the kinds of perceptual horizons that such interpretants claim to perceive? This is the hermeneutical question. It links the possibility of perception, first, to its quasi-textual preconditions in the world, and second, to the semantic forestructures of understanding seeking fulfillment in the world.

Occurrences of hyperbolic vision do not exclude the capacity to enjoy Euclidean vision. The two forms of vision, however, are attached to separate codes that are present like alternative texts in the environment. Hyperbolic vision is attached to a set of three angles in the surrounding optical field; Euclidean vision is attached to the artifacts of the carpentered environment, such as the architectural modules that spell out the units of length, width, and depth, and so make visible the spatial frame of reference. Vision interprets these codes. They play the role not of causes of vision but of systems of signs or "texts" to be interpreted or "read" by vision.

Like a child learning language, the perceiver may not know what a perceptual text is or what perceptual text he or she is responding to while striving to understand perceptually what it stands for. Perceiving is a skill; it is not a species of deductive or inductive inference but an interpretative skill.[10] C. S. Peirce gave it a special name, "abduction." It does not belong to the categories of induction or deduction, nor is it just another term for hypothetico-deductive method. Its goal is not explanation but vision – or more generally, *perception* – and it heralds a perceptual revolution. Perception in this sense is historical, cultural, and hermeneutical. Failing to recognize this is a source of many of those recalcitrant problems in the philosophy of science that seem to have no solution within the predominant traditions.

3. Ontology of a perceptual world.

What, if any, is the ontology of a world – of this world? Such a question can be understood in two ways: What *kinds* of things are real? Or what *individuals* of what kinds exist in reality? I take reality to belong to perceptible individuals. I take kinds to be defined by *perceptual horizons*; these are possible invariants of systems of perceptual appearances of profiles. Perceptual horizons are structures in the life world of perceivers. Hence, the kinds of realities are defined by the life world –

or life worlds – of perceivers. Perceivers themselves, of course, constitute perceptible horizons for other perceivers, and so they too are real.

It remains, then, to analyse the perceptual relationships between perceptual subjects and perceptual horizons. These relationships can be *active* or *passive*: that is, the same perceptual horizon can be defined by the activity or motions of the object that preserve its horizon intact while showing successively a variety of its profiles, or by the activity or motions of the subject that leave the horizon of the object intact while actively sampling its profiles. In the first case, the invariance is the horizonal structure of a real system (called by Husserl the "noema"); in the latter case the invariance is the representation in the subject of the horizonal structure of the real system (related to what Husserl calls the "noesis").[11] The character of such a representation need not be formally known by the perceiver; it is sufficient that it be antecedently had or possessed by the perceiver – it is a *Vorhabe* in Heidegger's terminology[12] – since it is a necessary condition in the subject for the recognition of the kind of object so represented. Such a reciprocity between subject and object defines the horizonal structures of the world. It follows from this that the bodily structures of perceivers – their capacity for having or making representations of horizonal structures – is crucial for an ontology under the principle of the primacy of perception. The capacities in question are those of the sensory, motor, and neurological representational systems of the human body as directed by or responding to the conceptual or semantic systems we use.

Consider now what would follow from adopting the common view that perception is limited to the unaided capacities of our sensory organs. If this were so, then the ontology accessible to humans would be limited to what a body endowed in this limited way could touch or interact with. The space of such primitive evolutionary horizons, I claim, would be hyperbolic, since artifacts of the carpentered environment are necessary intermediaries for perception in Euclidean space. The entities of such a primitive Manifest Image are just those invariants definable by human action in such hyperbolic spaces. The passage to scientific physical space requires a certain kind of technological transformation of the environment to (what has been called) a carpentered environment that functions as a readable technology. It is this that has extended our perceptual powers to perceptual horizons – for example, to scientific physical horizons – beyond those of primitive cultures.

Three powerful challenges have been made against the account that has been just presented.

First, it has been charged that the phenomenological tradition cannot do what I want it to do; it cannot, for example, discover in the spark chamber the phenomenon of the hyperon of strangeness +1. My answer is that the phenomenological tradition is broader and deeper than such a critic knows. Just as empiricism is broader than Hume and Carnap, rationalism broader than Descartes and Rescher, so phenomenology is broader than the *Ideas* of Husserl and Merleau-Ponty's *Phenomenology of Perception*.[13] The thesis regarding the phenomenology of instrumental use, that instruments can serve as "detachable [sense] organs" – Merleau-Ponty's words![14] – making visible (or, more correctly, *perceptible*) new phenomena as perceptual horizons not attainable with the unaided senses, is already suggested by the later works of Husserl and is there full-blown in Merleau-Ponty's later works.[15] The phenomenological tradition does indeed recognize the fact that powers of perception can be extended through the functional use of (what I call) readable technologies. The new phenomena have horizonal structures like other directly perceived entities. They show an entity "dressed," as it were, by its standard instruments, its appearances or profiles defined with reference to the standard line of manufactured instruments. Such entities also belong to the perceived world.

Neither Husserl nor Merleau-Ponty, however, made the move to give an interpretative account of perception. Interpretation or hermeneutics was reserved for literature, art, and social sciences. The discovery that interpretation played a key role in perception came later in the tradition. The thesis was first adumbrated by Heidegger in *Being and Time*. But the first full-length phenomenological studies of the constituting role of interpretation within acts of perception (such as, Edward Ballard's *Principles of Interpretation*, Graeme Nicolson's *Seeing and Reading*, and my book[16]) are recent. The theme of Nicholson's book, for example, is that seeing is analogous to the paradigmatically interpretative process of reading a literary text.

But what does perception read? What is its text? It seems to me that unless this question is answered satisfactorily there is danger of arriving at some unacceptable conclusions. First, there is danger that interpretation could be taken in a merely metaphorical way when applied to perception – for who is to say that interpretation is not just another name for organizing differently a given sensory field, in one of the many ways familiar to empiricists, conventionalists, Neokantians, and others? Second, there is danger that, unless the underlying text is discerned, there can be no public control over what perception can claim as evident; such a weakness would undermine the authority of perception as precisely the place where we verify our reality claims. Third, because of the inherent indeterminacy of hermeneutical processes, there is danger that, unless the underlying text can be discerned, no limits can be set to the cultural and historical changes in perception that underlie, among other things, scientific revolutions. After all, while we admit that there can be many different ways of reading a literary text, the legitimacy of any reading must be established. It is not the case that the art of reading a literary work is altogether arbitrary. A reading is justified with reference to the *text as a whole* and to the *context* of interpretation.[17] Hence the importance in the case of perception of establishing the whole text that in any instance the perceiver is responding to, and the context or interests of *intentionality* that guide the act of perceiving.

Let me say that the major obstacle toward establishing that there is a text for perception is the belief that what we perceive is just an organization of sensory data. It is possible that the Husserl of the early *Ideas* held this view, but it gradually became clear to him that this was not the way the perceptual object was to be analyzed. No introspective analysis of the perceptual object by the first-person perceiver yields a content of sensory data. To expect so is to believe the Myth of the Given, namely, (a) that there is a foundational level of sensory objects given apart from antecedent linguistically defined network relations and (b) that these are the content of more complex perceptual objects. Whatever the text is that perception reads, it is not then composed of this sort of sensory data. Instead, we have to admit that the text that a perceiver S1 is responding to is not part of S1's perceptual field. The text belongs to the latent conditions of perception – latent, that is, to S1. That among such structures are neurological networks belonging to the central nervous system is axiomatic among neurophysiologists and many psychologists. Moreover, as for example in Marr's computational model of vision, terms for such structures, such as the neurophysiological "vocabulary" of the brain, often suggest the textlike character of such representations.[18] Such structures are accessible only to third person scientific researchers – call them S3 – who study the processes and conditions of S1's act of perceiving. (Note: The first person S1 perceives an object O, while the third person S3 studies S1's act of perceiving O.) S1 and S3 are complementary knowers. Both they and the perceptual horizons they respond to exhibit a certain kind of mutual incompatibility or complementarity. Let me explain by some examples. If S1 perceives what is depicted in a photograph, then S3 perceives the grey patches on the surface of the photographic representation; if S1 perceives the strange hyperon, then S3 perceives the spark in the spark chamber; pictorial object and picturing surface, strange hyperon and spark in spark chamber are complementary pairs of horizons. I believe a historical study of what Bohr and Heisenberg felt in their time to be at issue in quantum mechanics would justify the claim that incompatibility of this kind – which they called "complementarity" – is characteristic of quantum mechanics.[19]

The second challenge to the position outlined in the first part of this paper is a criticism for excessive ontological "liberality" – for being ready to accept both of Eddington's tables, the one we see in ordinary life (the ordinary table) and the one made up of molecules (the scientific table). The reason I opt for the reality of both ordinary and scientific worlds is that in my view both are – or aim to be – perceptual worlds. A world is a system of perceptual horizons accessible to a skilled group of perceivers; it is characterized by (a) a set of community interests that define the aims of perceiving; we interrogate sensory experience and the answer is given through perception; interrogation presumes antecedent interests; (b) a semantics that incorporate these interests; and (c) physical mediations that join the perceiving subject to the perceived object; such mediations produce or themselves constitute the text that is read by perception; such a text existentially unites subject and object in perception; in Heidegger's phenomenological language, it is *Vorhabe*. It is not surprising then that there are a variety of worlds, defined by group interests, by the semantics that articulate these interests, and by the texts one has to turn to in order to find one's interests fulfilled in the world. The texts are existential structures produced by mediating processes that unite subject and object while completing the specification of the bodily reality of the perceiver and of the reality of the object as a perceptual horizon.

Where are the texts to be found that make scientific worlds visible – or more correctly, perceptible? They are not the mathematical models of scientific theory; they are not perceptible. Scientific worlds show their reality through transformations of perception mediated by standard instruments used as readable technologies. Mathematical models are the descriptive metaphors that guide the construction of conditions under which the entities of the theory appear "dressed" for participation in human life.[20] Most important among such conditions is the design of a new family of readable technologies.

Side by side with simple sensory horizons of the world – the only ones recognized by such critics – are then other horizons made accessible by the use of readable technologies; for example, *thermometer-viewing* horizons, *rule-and-clock-viewing* horizons and, in general, *instrument-X-viewing* horizons, where X is some appropriate readable technology. Only such theoretical entities for which readable technologies can be constructed belong to the real world; others merely play a mathematical role in the theory. All these multiple complementary perceptual viewpoints, *together with the perceivers who possess them,* constitute horizons of the *Lebenswelt,* and therefore of reality. Though complementary, they are not contradictory, since they relate to different semantical spaces as appropriated by differently – incompatibly – embodied perceivers. For example, besides primitive hyperbolic viewing, there are at least three forms of ruler-and-clock-viewing that give three different physical space/time horizons. As long as our perceptual interests lie within those satisfied by the technologies of classical physics, we have access to flat Euclidean horizons; but when these interests are not satisfied, we can use relativistic or quantum mechanical ruler-and-clock technologies that give us different curved or "granular" space/time horizons. All are real, because all are equally perceptual horizons of real – though differently embodied – perceivers. My point of view is then naturalistic, pragmaticist, and pluralist; the knower does not "look into" the world from outside, the knower is part of the world – and a variable part at that!

Because of this existential dependence of perception on texts, it is reasonable to suppose that the same individual cannot at a same time and place use all readable technologies – and none. Would each perceptual world seem to be disjoint from the others, like different Gestalts read from the same text? Note that, unlike the case of different Gestalts, the texts for two worlds are in general different. (Arnheim's example of seeing the interior of a church as simultaneously presented in two visual spaces may indicate that it is humanly possible for individuals to read at least two perceptual texts simultaneously.) In chapters thirteen and fifteen of my book, I resolve the problem of multiplicity of worlds by arguing that all of these worlds are partially ordered and share – at least, in principle – a common upper bound. They would constitute a nondistributive or quantum lattice, not of sentences, but of descriptive frameworks or languages. Let me call the common upper bound "The World." The World must be the common, anonymous, never perfectly realized possession of the human race. But it is not "out there" in the sense in which many philosophers of science today use that term, for to be "out there" supposes one is looking through the eyes of an uninvolved, disembodied, disinterested spectator of an already defined – by what? or by whom? – reality.

Let me add here for those who have a theological interest (a) that the reality I am speaking about is that of *res,* the material thing comprising what the medievals called "the proportionate object" of the human intellect and (b) that the demand for "out there"ness as a necessary character of reality is an uncritical theological residue stemming from a common belief in the divine ideas as the Logos of creaturely being, a Logos that was of course conceived to be independent of human culture, history, and group interests; such, I claim, is not the Logos *for us* of *res*.

But let me return to the two tables. Many philosophers of science speak of two tables: an everyday table and a scientific table. Such a duality in opposition of ordinary and scientific worlds is, I believe, a philosophical artifact of the empiricist and rationalist traditions. There are not two tables. There is in fact only one table, that of ordinary life. Go to any dictionary, you will find no mention of molecular arrays in the definition of a table. A table is something that serves a specific set of everyday interests that do not involve scientific apparatus; its profiles are its appearances in this ordinary world. Moreover, replace all the molecules in the table one by one with similar molecules and you have not changed the table one bit from what it was before; it will look the same, it will serve the same functions in the same way, and more importantly it will be the same in possessing continuity with its predecessor in the space and time of ordinary life and of communal history. The new table is the same identical individual in the ordinary world that it was before the molecules were replaced. The scientific table is not, strictly speaking, a table at all; it is the set of molecular arrays or other scientific entities or relationships that can be got by performing scientific measurements on the everyday table. The scientific profiles, say, of a molecular array, are organized by the instruments we use to study it. Perhaps, you say, the individual scientific table is just the set of such individual molecular arrays. But not so! For each individual molecular array can be moved from everyday structure to everyday structure, from table to chair, without losing its individual identity as a scientific reality. The individual everyday table could not then be identical with the scientific table taken as the set of its individual molecular arrays, for the individualizing and identity conditions for its scientific components are different from the individualizing and identity conditions of the everyday table. *The relation of identity then that constitutes the conditions for individuality is world (or horizon) specific.*

In more technical language, the real table is an invariant among a set of profiles defined by certain everyday uses of ordinary perceivers; scientific components or structures are invariants among sets of profiles defined for scientific perceivers by the use of appropriate standard scientific instruments. What unifies these two worlds is that both include the human subject, though under varying embodiments; that is, as responding to a variety of natural or artifactual perceptual texts. Within an interpretative account of perception, there is, as we have seen, a certain complementarity between the perceptual text and the perceptual object. The perceptual text does not lie within the perceptual horizon it offers to perception, it is rather a "window" to that horizon. No text then is part of the world that is revealed through it.

Taking a world to be the sum of all the perceptual horizons compatible with one form of human embodiment, it now becomes possible to state the kinds of relationships that exist between different worlds. Events in one world are "windows" into horizons of another world; they become *signs* for *objects (signified objects)* in another world. We pass easily from seeing events within one world to "reading" such events as "speaking" about events in another world. Let these world3 be the world of strange hyperons, world2 the world of electromagnetic discharges in spark chambers, and world1 the world of flashes of light in natural (unaided) perception. Then the standard texts for horizons of world3 – in this case, for strange hyperons – are sign-events in world2 – i.e., electromagnetic discharges in spark chambers; the standard texts for horizons of world2 – in this case, electromagnetic discharges in spark chambers – are sign-events in world1 – of sparks in general, and so on. Moreover, the order between worlds can be reversed relative to sign and object. A light flash in world1 can be a reading of a particular kind of text – that of spark chamber electromagnetic discharges – in world2, and a spark chamber electromagnetic discharge in world2 can be a reading of a strange hyperon event in world3. Without world1, world2 and world3 cannot exist; without world1 and world2, world3 cannot exist. Each is necessary to the knowledge and reality of the other. They are connected to each other through the human community of variously embodied perceptual knowers. Whatever is, as Peirce says, has Thirdness, the Thirdness of interpretant, sign, and object.[21]

What is The World in which all the partial worlds are united? It contains the human community together with the material and cultural environments that respond to the interests of its various worlds; its dynamic of growth is in its power to discern and even to fashion signs as texts for the interpretative powers of perception; and it contains in latency, elective goals for human history and cultural development. Such a hermeneutic structure ensures that perceptual horizons are never unique or infallible, and change historically. It is always possible to address the same perceptual field with new questions, and so to find new answers even in old signs. What does it all add up to? It is what I describe in chapters ten, thirteen and fifteen of my book as the logical sum (in the lattice) of possible worlds. Where does one go from there? Probably on – or back – to a postmodernist version of Hegel, but that is a project for another time.[22]

The third challenge is to lay out more clearly what the structure of *scientific explanation* is in my account, and to try to be more persuasive in getting it across. Clearly, I repudiate all the standard inductive, deductive, and hypothetico-deductive accounts of scientific explanation, since all of these fail to take account of the transformation of the observational field by theory.

One often hears it said that all observation is "theory-laden," that is, that it involves systematic connections with things not given in observation but implied by the semantic network of the language. From this, it is inferred that natural language is a theory about the world. But this is an erroneous conclusion. Natural language is not a theory about the world. A theory always implies a move beyond natural perception; it attempts to give an explicit account of what underlies and makes possible a range of human experience. Whether this turns out to be, as I claim, a new form of instrumentally aided perception, or something less, can be disputed; but a theory is not just the name for the semantic network we are using, it is (at least) a move beyond the semantic network of natural (that is, unaided) perception.

Nor is theory just something like a mathematical model that has technical applications; a scientific theory is a *means of seeing* – more correctly, of *perceiving* – by constructing readable technologies that serve as detachable sensory organs tuned to (a set of) the theory's explanatory entities. Natural perception uses standard instruments too; they are not artifacts, they are the sensory organs given to it through the developmental processes of evolution and ontogeny; but how and why they operate as they do – that is, the theory of their operation – is not part of what is given to the perceiver within the semantic network of natural perception.

Scientific observations, as I have said, use a theory-laden semantics. But an act of semantic description is not necessarily a perceptual act, for a perceptual act comes to recognize and name its object only through the reading of an appropriate existential text, and in the case of scientific observation, this is usually provided by some piece of specialized apparatus. The problem of the theory-ladenness of scientific observation is not whether one uses a semantic network in making an observation – for that one always does – nor whether the semantic network one uses is a scientific one, but whether in the making of a scientific observation, the mediation of instruments is compatible with a direct act of perception. To this question I have already answered, Yes! On the one hand, the phenomenology and semantics of scientific observation give support to this view, and on the other hand, the interpretative character of perception explains how this is possible, and provides criteria – among them, hermeneutical criteria – for the testing of disputed claims.

In giving an account of scientific explanation, one has then to distinguish carefully among the following. First, there is (a) that aspect of explanation that is causal or nomological from its hermeneutical aspect; the former is the production or recognition of that which is taken as the sign, the latter involves the interpretation of the sign. In the vocabulary of Paul Ricoeur, Karl-Otto Apel, and other continental philosophers, only the causal or nomological are called "explanation" and it alone is taken to be characteristic of the natural sciences, while the hermeneutical is called "understanding" and this is taken to be characteristic of the human sciences. It is clear that a fuller account of the notion of explanation in the natural sciences employs both of these activities. In addition, one would have to distinguish (b) between semantic and perceptual contexts, (c) between the perceptual contexts of everyday world horizons and those of scientific world horizons in which readable technologies are used, and (d) among the respective communities of inquirers involved in the different phases of the inquiry, each in relation to perception with its different mode of embodiment and different interpretative or hermeneutical interests. If the concept of explanation were to be so enlarged, it would be necessary to go beyond the semantics of naive truth-functional discourse to the pragmaticist dimension of discourse, and consequently to distinguish (e) between truth-functional sentential logic and a lattice logic of the perceptual contexts of discourse.

Where does this leave the account of explanation in the natural sciences? It shows that if explanation is taken to be exactly causal or nomological, then the same categories must be used in the *explanans* and in the *explanandum*, and these categories are observational (or perceptual). But if the notion of explanation is enlarged to include connections between everyday states and their scientific conditions, then explanation is no longer just the making of a syllogism, or the completion of an induction, but it is a historical, social, and hermeneutical act involving a plurality of complementary worlds partially ordered in a lattice.

NOTES

1. For a review of the tradition of hermeneutical phenomenology, see J. Bleicher, *Contemporary Hermeneutics: Hermeneutics as Method, Philosophy, and Critique* (London and Boston: Routledge and Kegan Paul, 1980). The major figures of this tradition are Emilio Betti, Martin Heidegger, Hans-Georg Gadamer, Paul Ricoeur, Karl-Otto Apel, and Jürgen Habermas.

2. The most recalcitrant problems in the philosophy of science arise out of the historical studies made by T. S. Kuhn and the new culturally oriented

historians of science; by philosophers of the history of science such as members of the Popperian School, among whom are I. Lakatos, P. Feyerabend, and L. Laudan; by sociologists of science such as D. Bloor, H. Collins, B. Latour, and S. Woolgar; and by a group of philosophers critical of the existing tradition, among them M. Hesse, H. Putnam, I. Hacking, and N. Cartwright.

3. My book is a contribution to the current effort of many on this side of the Atlantic – such as R. Bernstein, H. Dreyfus, J. Margolis, R. Rorty, J. Searle, and S. Toulmin, to mention a few – to bring about a *rapprochement* between the continental traditions of phenomenology, hermeneutics, structuralism, and poststructuralism on the one hand, and the analytic and pragmatic traditions of Anglo-American philosophy on the other. See the forthcoming proceedings of the research conference *Continental and Anglo-American Philosophy: A New Relationship*, organized by S. Toulmin and P. Ricoeur, at the University of Chicago, May 11–13, 1984, and my paper, "Issues in the Philosophy of the Natural Sciences: Continental and Anglo-American Philosophy," read at that conference.

4. See this writer's "Perception as a hermeneutical act," *Review of Metaphysics*, XXXVII (September, 1983), pp. 61–75; also see Graeme Nicholson's excellent book, *Seeing and Reading* (Atlantic Highlands, N.J.: Humanities Press, 1984).

5. For the primacy of perception, see Maurice Merleau-Ponty, *The Primacy of Perception and Other Essays* (Evanston, Ill.: Northwestern University Press, 1964), and his *The Visible and the Invisible* (Evanston, Ill.: Northwestern University Press, 1968).

6. For references to the literature, see *Space-Perception*, Appendix.

7. Rudolph Arnheim, *Art and Visual Perception* (Berkeley: University of California Press, 1954), p. 266.

8. See Heelan, *Space-Perception*, pp. 114–128.

9. See my paper, "Is Visual Space Euclidean? A Study in the Hermeneutics of Perception," in *Mind, Language, and Society*, ed. Otto Neumaier (Vienna: VWGÖ, 1984), pp. 1–12.

10. Cf. Ian Hacking's *Representing and Intervening* (Cambridge and New York: Cambridge University Press, 1983), where it is argued that a significant component of scientific research is the creation of new scientific perceptual "phenomena" through the operation of largely theory-independent instrumental traditions; also see Joseph Margolis's "Pragmatism without Foundations," *American Philosophical Quarterly*, XXI, No. 1 (1984), pp. 69–80.

11. Cf. Eugene Wigner's *Symmetries and Reflections* (Bloomington: Indiana University Press, 1967), Part I, where, following David Hilbert, the reciprocity of active and passive space-time transformation groups and their invariants is shown to be at the basis of modern physics.

12. See Martin Heidegger, *Being and Time*, trans. J. Macquarrie and E. Robinson (New York: Harper and Row, 1962), p. 164.

13. Edmund Husserl, *Ideas: A General Introduction to Pure Phenomenology*, trans. W. R. Boyce Gibson (London: Allen and Unwin, 1931); M. Merleau-Ponty,

The Phenomenology of Perception, trans. Colin Smith (London: Routledge and Kegan Paul, 1962). Note: Husserl's *Ideen I, Ideen II,* and Ideen III belong to his later and more mature works.

14. M. Merleau-Ponty, "Eye and Mind" in *Primacy of Perception*, p. 178.
15. See, for example, E. Husserl, *Crisis of European Sciences and Transcendental Phenomenology*, trans. D. Carr (Evanston, Ill.: Northwestern University Press, 1970), and M. Merleau-Ponty, *The Visible and the Invisible.*
16. See also the work of Don Ihde; for example, his *Technics and Praxis* (Dordrecht and Boston: Reidel, 1979).
17. See Paul Ricoeur, *Hermeneutics and the Human Sciences*, trans. J. B. Thomson (Cambridge and New York: Cambridge University Press, 1981), pp. 145–164.
18. See my paper, "Machine Perception," forthcoming in *Philosophy and Technology II: Information Technology and Computers in Theory and Practice*, ed. C. Mitcham (Dordrecht and Boston: Reidel, 1985).
19. See *Space-Perception*, chap. 10.
20. In Hacking's account, and in Nancy Cartwright's – e.g. in her *How the Laws of Physics Lie* (Oxford and New York: Clarendon and Oxford University Press, 1983) – theoretical models either have no truth value or they "lie." For an account of mathematical models as *metaphors*, see Mary Hesse, *Revolutions and Reconstructions in the Philosophy of Science* (Bloomington: University of Indiana Press, 1980), chaps. 4 and 5, and my paper "Natural Science as a Hermeneutic of Instrumentation, "*Philosophy of Science*, L (June, 1983), pp. 181–204.
21. See *Collected Papers of Charles Sanders Peirce*, ed. Charles Hartshorne and Paul Weiss, Vols., 1–6 (Cambridge, Mass.: Harvard University Press, 1931–1958), Vol. 1, 1.300–1.353; also Vol. 2, 2.228–2.308; for the interpretative character of perception, see Vol. 5, 5.182–5.184.
22. Such flexibility defines the *post-modernist* attitude; cf. Jean-Francois Lyotard, *The Post-Modernist Condition: A Report on Knowledge*, trans. G. Bennington and B. Massumi (Minneapolis: University of Minnesota Press, 1983), pp. xxiii–xxv.

Charles M. Sherover

Toward Experiential Metaphysics: Radical Temporalism

Dismissing all "metaphysicians from Descartes to Hume," and defending the thrust of the Kantian rejoinder, Peirce explicitly gave voice to the essential Kantian orientation by explaining "we can never attain a knowledge of things as they are. We can only know their human aspect. But that is all the universe is for us."[1] As Kant consistently urged, we can only speak cognitively from within the scope of human thinking, from within the structure of the human mode of looking out onto the world within which we find ourselves.

Our mode of "looking out"[2] constitutes our attempts to understand both the functioning of the natural order in which we participate as we find ourselves apprehending it *and* also our ways of participating in it. But we can only do this by means of the free decisions we make concerning our ways of studying it and using it for the ends we find ourselves setting for ourselves. Our ways of looking, directing and using the structure of our human outlook combine to constitute the particular perspective we bring to bear on whatever attracts our operating concern.

I. The Primacy of Perspective

In order to comprehend our way of looking out, we first have to "look in" so as to discover the structure of that outlook we bring with us in every attempt to understand and understandably deal with the aspects of the world in which we find ourselves functioning. If every species is, as Leibniz repeatedly urged, to be defined by its mode of representation, then this peculiar outlook on the way in which humans look out upon the world defines in advance of any empirical particularity the essential common nature of the human species, the parameters within which, and by means of which, we humans may justifiably claim cognitive insights into the nature of the world in which we exercise the activity of living.

Before any speculation concerning the nature of that supervening reality that transcends and undergirds our particular experiences can be justifiable, it must explicate and accept the enabling-and-limiting structuring parameters of the human outlook from which it emerges. Accepting both its own finite capability and reach at the outset, it can then seek to go beyond what has been established with some degree of cognitive certainty to those rational beliefs that human reason's self-understanding cannot demonstrate but nevertheless sees as implicitly coherent with what it already claims to know.

A systematic metaphysic has then a two-fold task. It needs to delineate, first, the categories of thought by which it functions and, second, the situational parameters which it necessarily takes up into that thinking. Taken together, these set out in advance the specific ontological characteristics it is able to discern in any object or entity that comes within its ken. Its first task is then to become self-conscious about the peculiarities of the particular selective perspective it brings along: For it can only justify its particular questions, and thereby evaluate the answers it discerns, by first making explicit the point-of-view or concern by means of which its inquiries are generated. Only after this can it properly turn to that more exciting realm of rational speculation concerning the cosmology within which it sees itself as functioning – by an imaginative extension of its grounded cognitive claims to the ultimate nature and structure of the things of the world and the world itself as one whole.

Systematic metaphysics is then from the outset bound by its own interpretative categories. It cannot be reduced to intellectual reporting; it cannot claim to provide particular factual truths describing specifics of the world. In its speculative reach it is an interpretive, not a cognitive, discipline. It offers canons of interpretation for the comprehension of particular kinds of experiences within a unificatory outlook that is ultimately more concerned to discern meaning than fact. As such, it is a necessary human activity. Although it often yields answers that cannot be demonstrated, these answers respond to questions that we have to ask – questions concerning the essential meanings that undergird the cognitions we have succeeded in establishing. The answers we develop serve as guidelines for using the degrees of knowledge attained to resolve the problems that define the actions marking our lives. The legitimacy of both the questions we ask and the answers we develop are grounded in the nature of the human inquirer; our understanding of our questions and our answers must take into account the structure of the human perspective and the role that that perspective seems to play in the world, the ultimate nature or meaning of which is being interrogated by our activity of thinking.

Aristotle had argued that insofar as thinking is deliberative it is not about the past or immediate present but about the future, which is yet open to some degree of determination by what we decide to do (cf. e.g., *Nicomachean Ethics*, Bk. VI, Ch. 2, 1139); the function of our speculative beliefs is then to guide us beyond the limits of presumably established certainties into that future that we necessarily take to be somewhat open and thereby in its specificity presently unknown. Part of the limiting bias of our speculative thought then is not so much to understand the world as it, in a Parmenidean sense, "really *is*," but rather how it can be rationally seen as coherent with the situations out of which our quests arise. Although all speculations do not appear to be equally justifiable, alternate frameworks for speculative insights appear to be defensible. The validation of conflicting speculative beliefs would then seem to require at least a correlation with, and reasonable extension of, what already seems evident about ourselves as we find ourselves functioning in our world.

Each of us is then thrust back into himself as he finds himself in the world as he sees it functioning about him. How do I find my world – not only in what the current authority of the sciences tells us, but in the ways in which I develop and experience those sciences themselves; my own encounters with our fellows; with my own self? What characteristics, norms, categories, structures, do I find animating me in interpreting my world as it presents itself to me? How do I define the ways in which I experience the experiences that are mine? In being thus thrust back on myself, I am not thereby thrust back alone – for each of us is essentially enmeshed in a network of relationships that helps us to define ourselves to ourselves.

As we meet ourselves only in meeting our fellows (from whom we progressively differentiate our separate individual selves), we seem to discover common facets of our outlooks and concerns, seemingly universal ingredients of human experience we share together that suggest something of the nature of the world in which human experience itself is taken as the prime experiential reality. If human experiences are themselves real, their structural ingredients suggest something of the nature of the world of which they are a part and which, in their ultimate wholeness, must somehow coordinate with that experiential reality which we, as humans, each experience as our own. If rational speculation is to be not individually or culturally bound, but justifiably giving expression to the universality of its human ground, its final test must be its ability to account for the origin of the viewpoint being expressed. For that viewpoint, however faithful or erroneous, is itself a part of the world-order that is to be understood and explained. Any comprehensive speculative portrait of the order of the world needs to account for the perspective within the world from which it arises.

This world-order can only be seen and understood by us from a human vantage point – employing the particular enabling and limiting factors built into human sensibility, understanding, and judgment. Any interpretative attempt to comprehend the world in which we find ourselves is thus biased in advance by the particular characteristics of the form of the outlook with which we see it. Each of us, then, starts from the peculiarities of his own thinking – those characteristics he shares with others, those idiosyncracies that distinguish him from them – and these peculiarities of outlook are themselves constituent components of the world-order, the understanding of which is being sought.

II. The Particularity of Experiencing

This may seem to suggest a resuscitation of the Cartesian *cogito*. Even Sartre found himself defending this as basic.[3] But, as even he recognized, no man can ever experience his own thinking in isolation as a somehow disembodied spirit looking out onto a world intrinsically separate from him. I am, from the first, in a world of other persons and of things that are developmentally interrelated; I only find my own self in a contextually developing differentiation from them.

If I am to follow modern precedent and seek a first principle for my own thinking that is modeled on the Cartesian *cogito* while yet remaining true to my own experiential reality, it would seem immediately apparent that such a principle must differ from the Cartesian original in at least two ways. It must recognize that all thinking is temporally structured in specific historic situations that entail a continuing dynamic of all components comprising an experiential situation in continuously changing relations with each other. In addition, it must equally acknowledge the thinking act to be a social activity that continually engages with others – by virtue of the language, concerns, dependencies, involvements, and privacies that mark out the living of my life.

Yet, just because all experiential reality is what is experienced in some level of consciousness, Descartes's general notion of the *cogito* is a defensible starting point: for however explained, recognized, or defined, my experiences, separately or together, appear to me as the object of the verb "I think," even if he did not pause to examine the dynamic nature of the 'I think' itself. If the 'I think', the *cogito* or *'je pense'*, must be the starting point of my own metaphysical reflection, however, it differs radically from the one Descartes proposed in at least two ways:

1. The *cogito*, the *je pense*, is itself a temporal activity; as Leibniz said, "to think and to be thinking are the same";[4] it is what Locke had already termed "the constant train – or succession – of *ideas*, in our minds," inherently a temporally structured process.[5] Thinking, on either account, is thereby already engaged in temporally developing situations; as an intrinsically temporally structured activity, it is always 'in time', in temporally defined situations.

2. What is presupposed in every act of consciousness is its intrinsic involvement in and reference to what has variously been termed intersubjectivity or community. No matter how individually idiosyncratic I might be, I presuppose in all my thinking the historically developing language in and with which I think, and the historically developing society out of which I have emerged but still within which I am continuing to do so – as the mores, morals, and evaluatory norms that I accept or reject but which, in either case I carry with me; things of the physical world that I take for granted and frequently use in accord with common understandings; and the particular persons, whether seen as anonymous aggregates or individually discernible personalities, with whom I am (whether agreeably or otherwise) engaged.

A more appropriate formulation (of this second point) might then well read: "We think, therefore, I am." For it is only in the community of our thinking with, or with regard to, each other that each individual becomes aware of himself as an existent center of experience. The converse of this formulation appears to be equally true: "We are, therefore, I think." For the 'we' is already presupposed in the *'je pense'* and thereby in the *'je suis'*: "*Nous sommes, donc je pense, donc je suis.*" The free convertibility of this form of the *cogito* suggests that it points to something more primordial. In addition to Kant's set of categories setting out the universal nature of theoretical human reason we each exemplify, or Heidegger's set of existential categories we each manifest in our round of activities, we then find out that our individual perspectives are also enstructured by the ontological imputations of the particular language we each use to think and communicate, the evaluative judgments we bring into ourselves from our historically developing cultural, religious, and national heritages, the whole set of social outlooks that are built into each one of us from the outset, defining the social parameters within which each one of us finds his own individual self.

It is then the particularity of the 'we' that is primordial; the 'I' – what German Idealism denominated as the 'ego' – is only found as a self-differentiating process within it.[6] From the outset, the 'we', is experienced and understood as made up of individuals, although encountered in collections, groups, aggregates – often perspectively undifferentiated as duplicatable units rather than as discernibly different individual beings. Every existent is seen as a particular, an individual, an entity which, no matter how similar to those others with which it is originally associated, is nevertheless somehow also seen as being somehow distinguishable if not actually distinguished.

But however the objects of our attention may be individualized or grouped, we each seem to exhibit an individual particularity of perspective within whatever encompassing perspectival community is acknowledged. No matter how closely we may share the outlook, evaluations, and judgments of our fellows, we are each aware of individual differentiations within the common judgment. Indeed, it is that which we see in common that points up, wht Royce had often referred as a "contrast effect," the idiosyncratic individual particularities that each of us denominates as "mine."

We each experience our common lived world as one particular organization of extant entities; our experiential world appears to each of us as composed of individual beings sharing attributes of similarity and distinguishing dissimilarities, beings that are – in even a minimal sense – active in their being: each exhibits some quality of temporal lastingness or duration, which may be (partially or wholly) sequentially or simultaneously congruent with other entities, and also occupies at a particular time some spatial area only describable in relation to other existing entities – two ontological attributes any entity must itself manifest and share with the human observer in order to be directly observable.

What has so far been said would seem to be but rudimentary because exception would be difficult to understand. To these must be added two noticeable experiential facts: 1. all of these particular existents appear to us to be somehow coordinate with each other by virtue of appearing to act according to some common laws or rules regulating even their differentiating behaviors, and 2. they seem generally to be divisible into two broad behavioral groupings: a. those that appear to be passive or inanimate, i.e., only moveable (in regard to place or state) by the activity of some entity other than itself, and b. those that seem to be, in some degree at least – and always within the bounds of the physical regulations seemingly covering *all* observable entities including ourselves – self-directing in their activities.

Any human speculation about the nature of the world we inhabit would seem tied to such elemental observations. To the extent that a speculative outlook is to be rationally coherent, it will bring them together with related aspects of human experiencing into a unified "picture" of the structure of reality that offers instructive explanation of how particular aspects of individual experiences are related to each other and to the structure the experiencer finds himself using in trying to make sense of the experiencing that is his conscious life.

However far one's speculative reach may extend from within his own experience, it must be his. It must start from the presumption that the individual experiencing is real; that it is somehow truly a coherently explicable constituent of the world that is being experienced. It must also be able to account for the elemental characteristics of the human perspective. An acceptable speculative metaphysic must be able to account for both the sociality and individuality of particulars, as experienced and as experiential centers; of their developmental flow and spatial involvement; of the common patterns of dynamic stability in both perceiver and perceived, and yet the continual changing patterns of each and their continuing dynamic interplay with each other.

Whatever may be said about individual experiences – singular, plural, or universal – human experience is our only intelligible point of departure. If such experience is to be regarded as genuine, its own attributes must be attributes of and thereby in functional harmony with the reality it seeks to comprehend. For the reality of this particular world, whatever it may ultimately be discerned as being, includes within its scope the multitude of particular human experiences and perspectives that seek to discern at least aspects of its nature and thereby its meanings, so that the individual experiencer may function as he does within it.

But however comprehensively conceived, we cannot hope to transcend a human point of view, a particular selective perspective that inherently carries its own capabilities, limitations, and interests with it. That human viewpoint is with*in* the world and its time. It is *internal* to the world, is thereby bound to some theory of internal relations, and cannot hope to see the world as one whole from some external perspective, as it may conceivably be perceived in itself.

III The Temporality of Decision

The central strand of any individual experience appears to be its temporal structuring. Temporal factors denominate our self-awareness, our perceptions of the physical environment, the activity of seeking out and interpreting the meaning of what we see, and the ideas we have and use in all experiences (and that cannot be reduced to spatial "thingness"). The objects we see in the surrounding environment, as the content of self-consciousness, display a continuity of both lastingness and change. However different we may conceive ourselves to be from the inanimate things of nature, predicates of temporal structuring seem to be common to both. As James and Royce argued: After all the differences between the living and the non-living, the mental and the physical, the mutuality of temporal structuring is the one common tie we each have to the things we think about and the ideas that constitute our thoughts.[7]

We each seem to have at least three somewhat distinguishable kinds of temporal experiences. 1. Our appreciative acts appear as a spread of *present* enjoyment or satisfaction, in which lastingness is the prime temporal mode; that appreciative present itself takes up an acknowledged continuity out of past moments (or more) as it looks to its continuity into the at least proximate future. 2. Our acts of reminiscence focus on events recalled from the past and contemplate either mere acceptance, satisfaction, or sorrow that they did or did not have a greater future continuity. 3. Most of our present acts are concerned neither with the past (except as a source of lessons to retrieve for present use) nor with the immediate present — except as presenting problems to be faced, tasks yet to be done, decisions or commitments yet to be made: Any temporally present situation does indeed present us with the need for deliberate decision about what is yet to be done. If all deliberative thinking is concerned with what is not yet, with a future understood to be somewhat open and dependent in some degree on what is in the power of the deliberator, then all deliberative thinking is, as Aristotle pointed out, future oriented.

The need for deliberative thinking is itself forced by the temporal flow of things and events. In any situation, not to decide between available options is itself a decision. Forced by time, any decision is a decision into the unknown concerning the use of future time. Futurity, as Heidegger suggested, carries with it the full force of the German *Zukunft*, that which is coming at us. We have no choice except to meet it by deliberately "wading" into it or else trying to stand still and then being overwhelmed by it.

Such decisions can concern trivial acts, which are often made without conscious deliberation; most of our daily routines, encrusted by developed habits, are made in this way and are dependent for explanation on earlier adoptions of behavioral habits. Indeed, it has been argued that one specific human attribute is the ability to economize on deliberative thinking by *not* having to rethink a specific kind of problematic situation each time it occurs, i.e., the ability to depend, when nothing unexpected is offered, on earlier decisions embodied into an habitual mode of conduct.[8] We thus find ourselves "going about our business," implicitly making innumerable actional decisions, without any conscious deliberative effort. This may be as true of the scientist in his laboratory pursuing a methodological procedure as of the man in the street buying his newspaper before getting onto the train or bus.

But conscious deliberation is a different kind of experience. It depends on an assessment of the options with which we see ourselves presented and also the capabilities we see ourselves as carrying into the situation. Intelligent decision confines itself within the open area their integration appears to permit. Intelligent decision distinguishes those possibilities for future development that are genuine from those that are merely desired; it confines its discriminatory consideration to those alternative possibilities that are judged to be not illusory but from among which a future actualization can be regarded as feasible. Any such assessment also considers the capabilities, the power to effect decision, the potencies or potentialities one carries along. To write a symphony is a genuine possibility only for one who has the musical competency to do so; to discover a new facet of a law of nature is a genuine possiblity only for the trained scientist in the field; to rectify a moral dilemma is a genuine possibility only for one who has some control or power of "input" into the moral situation. Any act exemplifies not only the Kantian principle that "ought implies can," but a broader one that "does implies can."

This is to suggest that, on one level at least, the old ambiguity between potentiality and possibility[9] may well rest on a lack of discernment of temporal modes. In any lived situation, possibility seems to mean the alternative viable offerings for the future that the present appears to hold open, while potentiality would seem to mean the defining capabilities or powers – which we bring with us out of our historical development and which have thus become descriptive predicates out of the developed past of our present being. Any temporal juncture of decisional action is then something of a synthesizing of inherent or defining potentiality brought out of the totality of past experience with the situational possibilities discerned as offerings of futurity that are seen as presented to us in the temporal present.

In a basic sense, this seems to be true on nonhuman levels of existence as well: A particular oak tree, at any stage of its life, carries with it developmental potentialities that depend for their realization on the environmental presentation of genuine possibilities for incorporation into its perduring being; at any stage of its life that oak tree embodies a living integration of its own perduring nature, its individual history, and the proximate future that it is, as a living entity, continually incorporating into itself. As with the oak tree, so with man; to live means the continual appropriation of as-yet unrealized possibilities – but with one crucial difference: Although a particular individual person may find himself accepting into himself much that seems "destined," he also experiences himself as making *some* decisions about alternatives – passively accepting some presented possibilities while deliberately selecting some and denying others.

Potentialities then, *at any given temporal juncture*, must be regarded as given: Although one may act into the future, by deliberation or habitual conduct, to develop some potentialities or leave others moribund, he must start with what has been developed so far *and* with what is presently discerned. The mere assessment of one's potentialities, the becoming aware of one's present capabilities and limitations, thus involves discernment but in itself no selectivity. How specific potentialities may be sorted out and developed is continually dependent on possibilities that are situationally presented, not as immediate actualities, but as options for future development that are selectively separated into those that are accepted as action commitments and those that are left by the wayside. As such, they orient one not to the past or the immediate present but to what is not yet but yet may be, to the future that is within grasp and can be developed. By accepting into one's present activity some particular possibilities instead of others, one is bringing into his activity of being a particular commitment to a chosen future state that he is attempting to actualize. Insofar as viable alternatives appear, within the range of what is presented, their discrimination, appropriation, and incorporation into one's ongoing being depends on a process of conscious or subconscious selectivity.

Temporal experience is then a process of bringing potentialities along and determining which to develop in the light of proffered possibilities, while accepting those conditioning limitations that appear to be beyond present control. Lived temporal experience is the experience of a continuity of selectivity of possible alternative future states. In order for me to appraise apparent alternatives,, interpret their meanings, set priorities, select some while dismissing others, and commit myself to a course of action into the future as I anticipate a particular transformation of possibility into actuality, I must be able to do so. But this is what is meant by freedom. Lived temporal experience is the continual experiencing of limited options: bound by potentialities generated from the past and possibilities appearing as offerings of the future, living is the continual experience, within these limits, of the exercise of freedom.

IV. The Necessity of Freedom

However the standard arguments about determinism, chance, and freedom as the capacity for rational or deliberate choice may go, there seems little doubt that we experience ourselves as free beings who are continually faced by the necessity of selecting a particular focus, deliberation concerning alternative actions in both thought and deed, and commitment to decisions concerning actional commitments. Even so trivial a decision as whether to take a bus or a train provides an existential demonstration. Even if intellectually convinced that we have been fully programmed and are now merely acting out a preordained role, such a conviction does not set aside the *necessity* of appearing to ourselves as being involved in a continuity of possibility-selection and decision-making.

In this light, many contemporary defenses of determinism take on a somewhat ludicrous note: How does one explain in a conceivably fully determinist world the continuing *appearance* of freedom?[10] Indeed, if full determinism were true, what would be the point of advocating its recognition? By his own premises, the author of an argument for determinism, on his own principles, can rightfully claim to be doing no more than playing out a predetermined role. So why should we attend to his argument instead of his role? Further, why should he attempt to convince his doubtful reader? For the reader too, on his premise, whether accepting or rejecting his argument, is making no real decision, but merely playing out, as on a phonograph record, what was previously destined to be played.

However explained or explained away by speculative thought, the experience of freedom is at least part of the essence of what it means to have a human experience and thereby to be human. The philosophic roots of this contention, with all the ambiguities attendant on it, can be traced at least as far back as Augustine. Any intellectualist attempt to call a fundamental experiential fact of human experience into question should itself first be called into question: "Instead of saying that we are free only in appearance in a way sufficient for practical life," we might well heed Leibniz' admonition that "we should rather say that we are determined only in appearance but that in strict metaphysical language we are perfectly independent relatively to the influence of all other creatures."[11]

The issue of freedom is usually depicted in contemporary discussions as concerned with external choices and actional dilemmas. But

Descartes has already given it a more fundamental ground: In the Fourth Meditation, in tracing out the sources of error, he effectively argued that freedom to control one's own thinking is requisite to the attainment of any cognition. Freedom is intrinsic to thinking, to seeking out the questions to be answered, the conceptual connections to be used, the evidence to be admitted, the obligation to pursue lines of inquiry, the laws of nature and of thought that one accepts as binding, the test of conclusiveness that one finally chooses to accept. Arguably, all living is not reducible to thinking, as the Cartesian argument has been construed to suggest, but all thinking, as an exemplification of living, would seem to explicate that freedom that is intrinsic to conscious living activity.

If what this Cartesian argument suggests has any validity, then freedom is an enabling condition, not only of all morality as Kant had originally urged, but of any kind of rational activity as well. Indeed Kant, in his later works, came to this. For even cognitive thinking, the attainment of those kinds of cognitive assurances his First Critique was designed to delineate, Kant finally rooted along with morality in freedom as their common enabling condition.[12] The rationale of such a move is clearly evident in any problematic situation. Whether the problem is moral, methodological, cognitive, or even aesthetic, one faces, in any situation demanding deliberation or decision, one fundamental question: "What should I do?" The "should" is inherently future-oriented to what is not-yet but yet may-be or can-be within the range of possibilities presented and potentialities carried toward meeting it. The entire question of any "should" presupposes the capability of freedom − for if this were not so, the question of "What should I do?" on whatever level, would be meaningless.

Freedom, as Heidegger has argued, is thus the basis of all rational activity; for both "obligation and being governed by laws, in themselves, presuppose freedom as the basis for their possibility. Only what exists as a free being could be at all bound by an obligatory lawfulness." The ground-problem of thinking, of logic, as of any sense of obligation or responsibility "reveals itself to be a problem of existence in its ground, the problem of freedom."[13] To live is to exercise finite freedom, the selective appropriation of presented possibilities for the actualization of potentialities carried along as essential elements of one's individual being. To live is to be within a situational context that is historical in development, bound by incontrovertible necessities, a finite range of options or opportunities dependent for their ongoing development on the choice that the controlling individual makes. To live is then to re-form one's world and irrevocably alter, in at least that respect, its ongoing development − by closing off some paths and opening up others in the multitude of

either/or choices one makes (whether by habit, predisposition or conscious deliberation) along one's way.

One's present is then (not a point) but a field of focus, deliberation,
action that is constituted "at any point" by the conjunction of potentialities, brought with one as essentials of his being out of his own
historic development, and those possibilities that are situationally
presented. But, again, possibilities, if they are truly genuine are not
merely future actualities — the next few grooves on a phonograph record
to be played out — but *alternative* courses of development, which are
finite in number but in their finiteness constitute the specific options one
faces. Living a life is experienced as a continuity of deciding between
available options; lived life presents no alternative but the continuity of
doing so. Whether to drift, which is inherently a decision, or to resolve
to follow one path instead of another, is not a decision one can abjure.
For the oncomingness of time is the oncomingness of options: At any
temporal juncture, one faces the necessity of selectively focusing attention, discriminating between what is deemed important and what is not,
discerning one's options, and committing one's course of action to one of
them.

Freedom is then not itself free; it is itself not a free option the exercise of which can be abjured. To-be is to-be-necessarily-free within
definable limits. Every choice of alternative decision cannot be avoided
and also has its price — always at least that of the excluded options; to-be-
free is to be compelled to face specific limited options. No one of us is
truly granted the option of whether to-be-free or not. We have no possible "escape from freedom." To-be is to-have-to-make-decisions — of
selectivity, interpretation, emphasis, alternatives — in thinking as in
active involvement with the environmental world and the continuing
formation of one's own self. To-be-free is to be bound by the necessity
of the continuity of judgment; and whatever else judgment may entail,
it does entail the continual necessity of evaluating, of deciding.

The context for such deciding, the necessity for doing so, does not
come out of some abstraction. It comes out of the specific societal situations within which we find ourselves — our comport with family,
friends, colleagues, associates, acquaintances, and encounters with other
persons who are anonymous to us (if not to themselves); the organized
society that provides for us the prime environment in which we find
ourselves functioning; and the physical accoutrements that demark the
geography in which we exercise the time of our being. On multifarious
levels, these contextual aspects of our lives continually present us with
objects of selective attention, provocations for habitual responses, the
basis of justifiable claims we have upon others,[14] trivial choices hardly

noticed as such in passing, and deliberative decisions we often struggle to make. On whatever level, each is made in response to the question, often not even consciously asked (but explicable if pressed): "In this situation, what should I do?" Each is made then in response to a living concern about facing the oncoming future that is delineated in any present perspective by means of possibilities – whether they are merely accepted as "obvious," discerned as posing a question, or discriminated as presenting "hard" decisions that one feels oneself called upon to make.

Freedom is no real option. It is *essentially* ingredient to the fabric of living. It is the continuing necessity to interpret the meaning of the lived present by means of discerned possibilities of futurity on levels both trivial and profound. *Freedom is not merely an open option to make choices; freedom is the continuing necessity to make interpretive decisions* – decisions based on an assessment of possibilities for continuing development along selected lines, decisions concerned with what is to be done, whether denominated on an intellectual or actional plane.

Lived freedom takes us beyond the bounds of any empirical knowledge. It takes us beyond the reports of the five senses, which can only really tell us about what has *already transpired*.[15] The necessity of freedom is not concerned about the past; its concern is with what can yet be done, with what is not yet actual, with that from which we cannot conceivably have any present sensory knowledge, with what can yet-be but is literally not-yet, with the future options the consideration of which constitutes our living present. The necessity of freedom is to live into what is, in the most literal sense, presently unknown. The necessity of freedom is the necessity of commitment beyond what can now be confirmed. The necessity of freedom is the necessity of *now* moving on into "mere" possibility, into that which is not now actual but rather some kind of "no-thing" reality; it is the necessity to re-form the ongoing structure of the world in that area of its progression in which we exercise some degree of influence or control. The necessity of freedom is the necessity to make a difference, however picayune or grandiose that difference might be. For if freedom enters into the reality of a dynamic world, every decision – trivial or profound – changes the world's future *total* description, changes what Leibniz would have termed the *complete* list of its future descriptive predicates. The necessity of freedom would then seem to be the necessity to make a difference, by diffidence or decision on a thousand different levels, in the ongoing history of this one actual world in which we dwell and of which we are a part – and whose ongoing being is constituted by a genuine continuity of becoming, of changing possibilities, some of which will be discarded and some of which will be, by decisions of choice or chance, incorporated into the actuality of its ongoing history.

V. Real Being as Becoming

That the experience of freedom can, in principle, not be explained in terms of the categorial constructs needed for the scientific understanding of natural phenomena is a prime thesis of the Critical philosophy. Indeed, the formal presentation of the Critical enterprise ends with the assertion that freedom as "a matter of fact"[16] not only grounds the "actual actions [constituting] . . . experience" but opens the way for the extension of human reason "beyond the bounds to which every natural or theoretical conception must remain hopelessly restricted."[17] (As requisite to our exercise of obligatory judgments, as of all cognitive activity and speculative thought, freedom then appears to be the root "category" of all human activity and thought, what Kant has called man's "supersensible faculty.")[18] What Kant seems to have been urging is that theoretical understanding of the necessary processes of nature as an efficaciously determining causal system is not adequate to insight into the nature of our world; at the very least, such efficaciously causal determinism cannot explain the fact of our experience of it and involvement in its development.

Freedom is not a speculative assessment of something external to us. It is our active involvement in our world and thereby gives us a kind of insight into the nature of our functioning world, which must be somehow primordially constituted so as to require its continuing appropriation of our true interpretations and decisions, which we see in its continuing accomodations to our decisions concerning its ongoing development.

Any real comprehension of natural processes comes by way of dealing with them directly – by the interpretations, decisions and choices that one makes in doing so. Freedom is not a speculative attempt to look at the world as though we were somehow outside of it and unaffected by it. Freedom is the direct encountering involvement with a developing world *in which* we participate and which we are continually altering as we are continually affected by its ongoing dynamic development. Freedom is our continuing necessity to respond to the continuity of change in our own selves and in the environment in which we find ourselves by broadening interpretational and actional decisions.

Our experiential involvements usually lead us to seek an ex post facto theoretical interpretive understanding in terms of fixed laws of nature that explain its regularities and that we then often seek to use as a guide to future dealings on the ground that such understandings have more than a strictly empiric force. In the end, however, it may be questionable whether human attempts to discover unalterable laws of nature can possibly be successful. For, if man is an historical being – biologically as well as socially – in an historically developing world, human questions are being asked from a perhaps gradually but nevertheless continuously changing interpretive perspective, just as the world itself would appear to be a dynamic system in which changing is inherent even if with a perhaps continuing developmental direction.

However this in itself may be, the basic thesis of the priority of human freedom is to argue the priority of practice. [19] For practice looks to a future that cannot be seen but can only be passively expected or actively anticipated. Our pragmatic encounters tell us, on a first-hand basis, just how we may understand nature – that nature that includes our activity of being, which is a continuity of ordered becoming – and its encompassing reality, beyond the recollection of the relevant past and the immediacy of any present moment. Our plans and anticipations for dealing with those aspects of the world that provoke our responses tell us something of the nature of the reality within which we find ourselves that theoretical understanding can only retrospectively seek to explain. It is necessary for us to accept this, for the human investigations of the nature of this, our world, are themselves transforming the nature of the world we are investigating – and also ourselves.[20]

The systematic human attempts to comprehend the underlying laws of nature's developmental being, which we understand as science, cohere with the futural orientation of the human temporal perspective. For science's method of testing its own hypotheses is by means of practical involvements with that particular selected aspect of the environment it is concerned to explain; and its prime test of truth is no mere logical consistency but a future-oriented predictability of particular occurrences. The laws of nature turn out to be not pure platonistic forms but norms for correlation of particular behavioral patterns. What is sought is not some law of pure chance, as both Aristotle and Peirce allowed, but "some principle of reason sufficient" to explain not only the general conformity of particular occurrences to general rules but also the particular deviations from them.

Whether we approach the world of nature in strictly scientific terms or in terms more explicitly commensurate with the subjective biases and outlooks of particular human experiences, we find essentially similar and compatible principles of the human outlook operating. The test of the scientist as of the craftsman is workability, and that workability is taken as showing us aspects of the reality within which we find ourselves functioning as somewhat free interpretive agents who are intrinsically involved with that with which we are working.[21]

The reality of the world in which we find ourselves functioning as finitely free causative agents appears in human experience as an interrelated dynamic process that cannot be reduced to its material components locked together by a completely determining efficacious causal sequence. If that were indeed so, the present state would be completely reducible to a temporally first cause that governs all details and allows neither any contingency nor the efficacy of temporal process in nature, much less in man; possibility would then mean not open options but merely future as yet unrolled actuality. But we do not experience our world in this way. We do experience our world as continually setting forth new tasks to be undertaken, new choices to be made, as continually demanding new interpretive understandings that are requisite for any deliberate time-situated action, and therefore the use of reason or intelligence in deciding upon action. We experience the world by means of ideas and principles, hopes and fears, which move us to seek out areas of control and redirection; the free use of intelligence penetrates into and thereby changes the developing character of physical nature itself and our own selves, as well as our growing experience of successes and failures, of mistaken judgments, fortuitous guesses, and insightful discernments.

The form of time that encompasses and structures our experience of our own selves and of our world suggests that it is in some sense an inherent aspect of the reality with which we continuously deal. The form of enveloping time seems to be somehow manifest as that Logos, that developmental rational order of our world, to which Heraclitus had originally pointed. The inherent temporality of our experience does not appear to be a closely knit set of Cartesian moments. Rather, it presents to us the dual aspects of continuity and change. This continuity of change would itself be impossible if continuity itself was not itself developmental. If human experience has any reality to it, then that continuity is not merely the motive power of originary efficacious causes and unalterable potentialities; human experience depends for its being on the genuineness of possibilities, of options not yet resolved, of alternatives not yet decided, of a futurity that presents itself as open to the contingencies of innumerable decisions – and of a perdurance that is not itself "permanent" but is a continuity of dynamic becoming, the driving principle of which might, as Heraclitus once obliquely suggested, itself be conceivably changing as it continues its continually operative force. [22]

Human experience may indeed be an experience of illusions or illusionary appearances, as some philosophers seem to have argued. But if human experience is not itself an illusion, then the reality of perduring time, as the reality of genuine possibility, also constitutes a real aspect of our experiencing – and thereby of the real world in which the reality of our real experiencing transpires. Genuine possibility depends for its being on the omnipresence of time so that discerned possibilities may be sorted out – some passing into the realm of first present actuality and then remaining as the actual retrievable inheritance of what has been.

If we are to seek for some ground principles by which we can come to a fuller comprehension of the human experience of the world, it would then seem that the reality of time, freedom, and possibility must be understood as joined together as the enabling, and thereby defining ground of experience. In something of a Kantian sense, they must be understood as somehow noumenal, as characters of that ultimate reality with which we are always working and which, in our more speculative moments, we seek to comprehend.[23]

But to pass from a careful delineation of the kinds of ontological characterizations we project from our own way of seeing onto the world *in* which we are and we seek to comprehend, we must be careful. Our own ways of looking out, as social beings who function by means of synthesizing potentiality and possibility in time-bound situations that are themselves defined out of specific historically developing concerns, exclude in advance any possibility of achieving in speculative thought any assured insight into the ultimate nature of the things of the world, or of the world itself as one integrated whole, as they may be "in and of themselves." The ontology of our own structured outlook thus forecloses at the outset the possibility of any final "cosmology" of the things and systems of order that constitute our world. On this level, then, our speculative thought may attain degrees of coherence and insight but cannot attain to any final truth.

If this is so, then we cannot hope for any "final" metaphysic. For if time, freedom, and possibility are somehow or somewhat real, then the world is in some degree open-ended. New interpretive understandings emerge as the range of human experience widens and grows. There cannot then be, as Heidegger (among others) suggests, any "end of philosophy"; for the "love of" or "quest for" that wisdom – which is based on knowledge but seeks to go beyond knowledge – is a continuing attempt to comprehend the growing wholeness of the world within which the growing human perspective functions.

Each of us brings to bear an at least unspoken metaphysical assessment of what constitutes reality and illusion when we face the vicissitudes of our daily living. If any defensible metaphysical outlook; or way of seeing and comprehending our world, is indeed the intellectual understanding of what the content of the human perspective indicates, we explicitly need to accept as fact that it operates from within the world as a part of the world, that it can only recognize partial aspects of that world in terms of the ontological characteristics its own cognitive and existential "categories" permit as the delineation of its outlook, and it does so to use whatever insights it gains in order to continue its free use of intelligence to enhance its level of being in the harmony of the developing whole.

In seeking out clues to what Heraclitus had once termed "the hidden harmony" within or behind the whole, we might face the question that he implicitly raised but neglected to answer. The notion of harmony is itself borrowed from musical experience, in which the particular harmonic relation of the notes in a song or symphony is itself changing as their relations change while the piece is being performed.[24] Harmony is then a dynamic concept that transcends the particularity of any specific notes by binding them together into an integrative system that is itself never quite the same but is a continuing dynamic mode of creative developmental unification. If "the hidden harmony" is itself the Logos of the world-order, then perhaps it too is changing. For time, as the continuity of change, appears to be the encompassing form within which we necessarily understand our own selves as participating in the ongoing becoming of the world. However there may seem to be a continuity of principles behind nature and man, their exemplifications and thereby their meanings are continually, if imperceptibly and gradually, changing for us.

What we call "abiding principles" may indeed be truly transtemporal, but we have no philosophic right to term them "eternal."[25] But we should be especially careful in making even this limited claim. For changing continuity and the continuity of change mark the structure of our experiential world — as we are able to see and comprehend those aspects of the world with which we deal by the use of freedom in the employment of intelligence, which operates by taking possibility as well as potentiality seriously, and necessarily presumes that time, as their enabling and defining form or conditon, is real.

If there is any truth to the ancient maxim of Empedocles that "like knows like," or that of Anaxagoras that "like produces like" — "Like" does not imply identity; it merely asserts essential similarity — we would seem to have a presumptive right, if not a necessary mandate, to presuppose that the prime characteristics of our experiential activity, out of which decision and knowledge and understanding arise, tell us something of the nature of the world in which we find ourselves and within which we function as effecting members.[26]

Different as we may be from other constituents of our world, we find that (1) possibility seems to be genuine just because we cannot function without that presumption, (2) freedom seems to be real because without it none of our experiences seem to be intelligible, (3) futurity appears to us as finitely open just because, within given limits, deliberate choices by beavers as by men seem to determine what a future actuality can be, and (4) time seems to be a fundament of both ourselves and the other entities with which we deal just because it appears to envelop us all as the encompassing form of freedom, of possibility, of our being that is a becoming insofar as it appears within our ken.

To the extent that a metaphysical framework for understanding our world is not only comprehensive but is also projective of our ways of understanding, its success in explanation will be marked by its correlation of the world – whether taken as physical, biological, historical, sociological, or moral – within which we find ourselves functioning with the ways of functioning we find ourselves able to utilize. Such a comprehensive understanding is no mere intellectual exercise. It too has a function. An understanding of the world to which we belong has much to say, in a normative way, to the ways in which we should conduct ourselves, the ways in which we should organize our moral conduct and social practices, the ways in which we may integrate our religious commitments,[27] the ways in which we may justifiably interpret the cognitive claims of our sciences. A speculative use of reason to comprehend the world, as human reason is able to take it all in, is itself a guide to how reason may finally come to guide that chief business of men that Dewey always pointed to, the organization of solving the multifarious "problems of men." To what extent any particular metaphysic may be finally "true" (aside from the coherence of workability), we really have no way of knowing; but to the extent that a metaphysic is essentially useful and rationally necessary in guiding the rational development of human concerns, it is itself functioning as if it is true. Perhaps, beyond all dreams of a Cartesian-like certainty, that is the best for which we may hope.

Emerson once said that the fins of a fish tell us about water as the wings of an eagle tell us about air. An experiential metaphysic will then take the essential structures of human experience – the only experience, let us never forget, that we may directly know – as somehow indicative of aspects of the nature of the world in which it functions. The attempt of reason to achieve a speculative comprehension of the world in which we find ourselves can be both intelligible and useful only to the degree that it encourages us to explore it by means of structures commensurate with the structures of human experience – within which possibility functions as genuine invitation, freedom functions as enabling the use of intelligence, and time is recognized as grounding both the experiential reality of the world in which we function and of our own selves as inherently creative beings in a world open to creative development.

NOTES

1. "Letters to Lady Welby," [May 20, 1911], *Values in a Universe of Chance: Selected Writings of Charles S. Peirce,* ed. P. Wiener (Garden City: Doubleday Anchor Books, 1958), p. 426.

2. *N.B.* Kant's word was *Anschauung,* usually translated as "intuition," and was argued by him to be the determining frame of all the specific content of empirical knowledge.

3. See Jean-Paul Sartre, "Existentialism is a Humanism," reprinted in many collections.

4. *New Essays on the Human Understanding,* IV, vii, 7; *Leibniz Selections,* ed. P. Wiener (New York: Charles Scribners' Sons, 1951), p. 295.

5. *Essay Concerning the Human Understanding,* ed. A. C. Fraser (Oxford: Oxford University Press, 1894; New York: Dover, 1959), II, xiv, 4. 16.

6. This would seem to be a prime point of Rousseau's *Of the Social Contract,* considered as a phenomenological description of the human condition even if expressed as the metaphysics of a justifiable democratic politics. e.g., cf. *Of the Social Contract,* ed. C. Sherover (New York: Harper & Row, 1984), p. xxv and Par. 55–57, 79–86.

7. See, e.g., Josiah Royce, *The World and the Individual,* (New York: The Macmillan Company, 1904), II. V.

8. See, e.g., Donald R. Griffin, *Animal Thinking,* (Cambridge: Harvard University Press, 1984).

9. Aristotle, in Book Delta (the 'Lexicon' of the *Metaphysics*), offered what James had called "his most revolutionary stroke," the notion of potentiality; but Aristotle certainly left the distinction between potentiality and possibility anything but clear.

10. If the appearance of freedom is so radically discordant from the presumptive determinist reality, if our experiences of free decision are not real but discordantly illusionary, they are, by definition, cognitively irrelevant. If our own experience of free decision is hopelessly illusionary, how can we seriously attend to what appears within its outlook? A complete determinism poses an unbridgeable gulf between our own experience of intellectual freedom and an allegedly complete determinist world in which it claims to function. As such, any doctrine of complete denial of free thinking and decision can only yield a cognitive skepticism that, in principle, cannot be transcended by free human thought.

11. "New System of Nature," 16, in Wiener, Leibniz, p. 116. *N. B.* This, indeed, seems to have been Kant's point in removing Freedom from the realm of phenomenal appearance to that of the noumenally real. On this ground, all the standard determinist arguments are, in principle, illegitimate. Because of this sweeping claim, it would seem methodologically incumbent for the determinist to show that this separation should be ruled out before he asks us to attend seriously to his arguments, which only function within what

the Kantian regards as the phenomenal realm in which efficacious causal explanation is but a necessary interpretive procedure.

12. See, e.g., *Critique of Practical Reason and Other Writings in Moral Philosophy*, ed. L. W. Beck (Chicago: University of Chicago Press, 1949), pp. 118, 153, and 224–25. For a crucial extension of this, see note #14 below.

13. Martin Heidegger, *The Metaphysical Foundations of Logic*, trans. Michael Heim (Bloomington: Indiana University Press, 1984), pp. 19–20.

14. See Kant's *The Metaphysical Elements of Justice [Part I of The Metaphysic of Morals]* (trans. J. Ladd, Indianapolis: Bobbs-Merrill Co., 1965, p. 56) for a crucial statement about the concrete knowledge, out of freedom, of physical (proprietary) things not subject to the stringencies of the First Critique: "... if there is to be anything externally yours or mine [that is, any property], we must assume that intelligible possession (*possessio noumenon*) is possible. Thus, empirical possession is only possession in appearance (*possessio phaenomenon*), although in this connection the object that I possess is not regarded as an appearance, as it was in the Transcendental Analytic [of the *Critique of Pure Reason*], but as a thing-in-itself. That work was concerned with reason as it relates to theoretical knowledge of the nature of things and with how far it extends. Here, on the other hand, we are concerned with reason as it relates to the practical determination of the will in accordance with laws of freedom, and its object may be known either through the senses or merely through pure reason."

15. *N. B.* If we take modern physics seriously in its assertion that both light and sound "take time" to travel (i.e., manifest durational reality), we can only see and hear what is, in the most literal sense, already in the past by the time we are conscious of being aware of what these senses claim to tell us in the momentary present. Were classical English empiricism correct in its claim that our abstract or general ideas are only generalizations out of past sensory reports, then the ideas of which we are conscious could only be generalizations about the past, about what is over and done with – already reduced to historic actuality. Without some kind of – in the most literal sense – a priori knowledge, we then have no rational basis for projecting such generalizations into the immediate present, much less the future. As such they may indeed provide grounds for historical understanding but no ground whatsoever for deliberation or decision. It is for this reason that the "empirical" tradition so easily comes to terms with a determinist metaphysic, whether on an efficaciously causal or logical plane: its epistemology, being entirely genetic, can do more than trace the present as an extension of the determinate past by efficacious sequence; and its methodology, bound by what is already given, can do no more than trace the logical implications of its accepted premises; on neither level can it transcend the actual given and face within its own terms, contingency, chance, or real possibility – which is to say, futurity – with any philosophic seriousness.

16. Immanuel Kant, *Critique of Judgment*, trans. Meredith (Oxford: Clarendon Press, 1928), p. 141 Hereafter cited as *CJ*.

17. *CJ*, p. 149.

18. *CJ,* p. 99.
19. In this regard, Peirce may well have been true to the underlying spirit (if not all the letters) of the Critical Philosophy by merging Kant's distinction between the pragmatic and the practical into the pragmatical. (See *Critique of Pure Reason,* A800 = 828).
20. One has merely to consider what human industry has already done to the enveloping atmosphere of the earth. While it has transformed the level of human living upon the earth, it has orbited a 'junkyard in the sky', consisting of the debris of investigatory projectiles. The changes in the human organism (so far) result less from deliberate intrusions onto genetic inheritance than from the effects of man-made environmental changes intruding upon us as environmental inhabitants.
21. In contrast to a naive pragmatism, workability is not then the nature of truth; but workability is surely, as Royce had urged, at least one essential criterion of truth: for any statement about workability implicitly says not only that any truth must harmonize with the world but also that "the world *is such* that within it this procedure works to produce that result."
22. See. e.g., Fragment #67.
23. As but one of Kant's intimations of this, see the closing passage of *CJ,* p. 149: "Freedom is the one and only conception of the supersensible which (owing to the causality implied in it) proves its objective reality in nature . . . Consequently the conception of freedom, as the root-conception of all unconditionally-practical laws, can extend reason beyond the bounds to which every natural, or theoretical, conception must remain hopelessly restricted."
24. See Heraclitis's Fragment #54; cf., Aristotle, *Ethica Eudemia,* 125a, 25.
25. Just because human experience cannot attain to any insight into eternity – whether it be construed with Aristotle as "all unending time" or with Plato as literally devoid of the temporal – we have no way of knowing what such "principles," or their ontological ground, might be beyond the horizon of possible temporally formed human experience. To say that they are "transtemporal" is a more limited claim, i.e., that they appear to function in any temporal juncture, at any "moment" of our experiential time.
26. Is this not this the at least implicit meaning of Kant's "Highest Principle of Synthetic Judgements"? Its key sentence reads: "The conditions of the *possibility of experience* in general are at the same time the conditions of the *possibility of the objects of experience."* Critique of Pure Reason, A158 = B197.
27. The ultimate object of that speculative thought in what I term a philosophical "cosmology" that seeks rational insight into transcendent beings, is, of course, God. That such belief can only properly emerge from a "moral teleology" was argued by Kant (see *CJ,* p. 144ff.); but Kant argued that our conception of God must necessarily accord with the temporality of the human outlook even though that conception can not be taken as truly descriptive (see *Kritik der praktischen Vernunft,* ed. J. Kopper, (Stuttgard: Phillipp Reclam, 1966), pp. 217–18). Quite independently, Heidegger urges a similar outlook: "If God's eternity may be 'construed' philosophically, then

it only can be understood as a primal and unending temporality" (with the explicit consequent that the tradition of negative theology is thereby reopened.) See, *Sein und Zeit* (8th ed., Tubingen: Max Niemeyer Verlag, 1957, p. 427, n.1.

Jay Schulkin

Possibilities and Constraints

Introduction

I sit here imagining a range of possibilities. Possibilities abound – exist – and yet they seem ephemeral. In what sense do they exist? That they exist as possible states of affairs, as future occasions for actuality, is a natural answer. But it is a bit like saying that the difference between a possible and an actual state of affairs is that one is possible while the other is actual.

Whatever their reality, possibilities are nonetheless grasped, but certainly not all of them are; only some of them are expressed and become actual. In part, our cultural practices limit the kinds of possibilities considered. In part, the way our brains have evolved also limits the kinds of possibilities open to us. I will mainly be talking about the kinds of possibilities our mind-brain imposes on us. These possibilities allow us to have a world in which to function; they constitute and regulate. When speaking of such possibilities, one is referring to the design of the mind-brain, which will become clearer as we go along.

Possibilities are not just nominal; they are not just fabrics of the mind. Nominalism is an impoverished philosophical presupposition. We have all had the experience of discovering that reality rejected some ideas in a rather brute manner. The world matters; the world sets the stage for what is possible and for what is actual. We need a conception of the world, of reality. It is highly entrenched, with good reason, in our epistemological stances. I posit the real as a warranted hypothesis, one entrenched in a framework, though not free from skeptical concern.

I want to begin by suggesting that the imaginative is the intermediate link between the possible and the actual. In many instances a possibility is imagined. It may later turn out to be so – to be made actual. Without imaginative leaps there is little hope for change and resurrection. One imagines what a just order would be like, and then one discourses about it. In this case it is a probable state of affairs, under some historical condition.

The imagination is important in coming to know another being. To some extent the mental "resonates" with the real, in the biological capacity to recognize the experiences of conspecifics and at times other animals. We imagine what the other is like. The actuality of the other may be grasped. Defining characteristics are hypothesized.

The imagination often gets things off the ground. Desire can "stretch" and help form new possibilities. This is one way that the imagination influences the possible. By imagining possibilities, resources are provided for determining real actualities. The richness of the imagination provides the search for some of the resources, but not all. That's why its cultivation is important. Imaginative moments are not degraded forms of thought. But while the mind's capacity to imagine is essential, one should remember that the world is also an important factor in that it provides some of the resources for one to imagine possibilities and then instantiate them in actualities. Losing the world is falling into idiocy.

Possibilities, in the present context, are not ideals in Aristotle's sense but rather basic mental forms.[1] The imagination works within these mental forms, creatively using them as resources. The desire to reach perfection which Aristotle recognized, is real – a basic natural drive. But the focus here is on creatively using mental resources that are imaginatively tested against a world that initially selected for them in the evolutionary process. Our notion of freedom suggests that we creatively employ what we have, and not that we blindly try to reach some set determination of perfection. Having introduced possibilities as mental forms, let us turn now to metaphysics.

Consider a dog named Chester. Chester, like most of us, has a set of behaviors (and experiences) that are to an extent always ready to go, ready to be triggered into action. They are mediated by representations in the mind and they stand as possibilities in the repertoire of expressions of Chester. I come along to pet and play with Chester pretty regularly. I know Chester fairly well. I know how to trigger much of Chester's repertoire. It is not difficult to discern his possibilities or to make them actual. Psychobiologists can uncover the design and engineering principles presupposed in order for Chester to express what he does. What I want to suggest is that the behavior is sometimes triggered because of a decisive factor embedded in Chester's mind-brain; Chester is not always tropically oriented. In so far as one believes that freedom is a natural biological property that speaks of degrees, one is inclined to attribute to Chester some freedom. Our human biology, though more evolved, is related to Chester's as is our freedom. The difference between dogs and people is that people have more choice, more freedom – at least some do. We have more choice because of our mental resources. The behaviors are organized by possibilities of the mind, for which there is finally a decisive factor before action – someone decides, at least some of the time. It is the issue of choice that is the essential factor of possibilities being expressed in actualities.

The metaphysical hypothesis is that Chester selects from possibilities. In doing so, he achieves a unified sense of being. He becomes substantive. This is in contrast to being a set of aggregate parts (design principles or habits) with no unified sense.[2] When one speaks of Chester making a choice among the possibilities he has open to him, one speaks of his being an organism. An organism here means something like the ability to unify – to pull together into a one. Being a one is being decisive and active. Epistemologically (in intelligent action), the creative moment is in choosing and using the resources. Because Chester's repertoire is limited, so is his creativity. This is because Chester does not have much to choose from or be creative with. Still there are imaginative components to Chester's life; and they are expressed in his creative use of his strategies or forms of behaviors. The imaginative links the actual with the possible, in a sense analogous to the way the imaginative is the intermediary in Kant between "sense" and the rules of thought, the schema or connective thread.[3]

I assume, with some warrant, that choices are made among possibilities or else why speak of choice? The decision unifies the aggregates; possibilities are actualized. They become embodied. The actuality is real and substantial. Insofar as one emerges from nature, freedom is to be construed (as I've indicated) as a matter of degree – not all or none, which is the traditional characterization in Kant or Sartre.[4] Despite this freedom, Chester is often only an aggregate of parts, without a unified choice and sense of action – without freedom. The display is blind and tropic. But when Chester decides, which he does on occasion, he achieves unity; he selects among the possible.

There are varying degrees of this phenomenon that reflect evolutionary ascent and descent. Like Chester the dog, humans are often aggregates; no unity dominates us, no choice and creative event that integrates can be spoken about. One envisions dead habits instead. The person is lost in the habit, asleep. When one submerges oneself in habit one is more likely to be triggered like a tropic factor. Responsibility as an ontological human factor is lost. Pushes and pulls predominate. But when persons creatively select from the possible, something very different emerges. Nausea is what some experience, awe is found by others, and depletion emerges for others. Some experience none of this, and some have a good time of it. Chester has none of this. Ultimate moments for humans are about choice and the creative. The rudiments of choice are tied to our biology, and animal life more generally.

The metaphysical point here is this: Decisions unify and overarching decisions unify or integrate into a one. This is where the possible and the actual meet in the life of animal organisms; some sort of creative synthesis takes place. In contrast to the Aristotelian who posits form as actual and matter as potential, form is potential and the real is actual. What is posited as the possible, in the present context, is the mental fabric presupposed; the actual is the real world that selects the mental fabric. The biological foundation posited is not one of fulfilling a form, but of creatively using forms. It corresponds more to our sense of life.

In this essay, I sketch some thoughts on possibilities as mental constraints. There is the metaphysical point running throughout each section that has just been loosely adumbrated and will be made clearer as we go along. By metaphysics I mean the study of the most generally pervasive characteristics of being. By epistemology I mean the study of what we can know, and the means by which knowledge is made possible. In the present context the metaphysical and epistemological claims overlap one another.

Form and Knowledge

To be is to be embedded in some form, to have shape. That is, in knowing being, one knows its form. The structure itself expresses a natural harmony. An understanding of form is at times represented mathematically, a mathematics embedded in physics; the mathematical-physics is itself related to the laws of logic though not reducible to it as we have learned in this century. Inquiry is itself possible because of logic; thinking is possible because of logic. This is the logic of what Peirce called "abduction,"[5] the logic of the genesis of ideas.

Knowing is always embedded in some form. The formal properties of mind set the possibilities for knowing. The mind "constitutes," or imposes order; it is the condition for there being an intelligible order. The mind's categories are necessary in having a world at all. Idealism and realism meet through real worlds being embedded in ideal minds that reach agreement through convergent tests about existence, despite the fact that agreements are never picture perfect and inquiry itself may never fully terminate.

Intelligibility is itself an adaptive achievement of the mind. Possibilities are tied to such capacities. This is the sense that possibilities are presupposed mental functions. The question for the epistemologist is, what kinds of mental competence does the creature presuppose in order to display the actualities it does?

The world matters in the formation of such minds. Nature has limited, or constrained, the kinds of ideas that we can generate. Here one looks to the ecological conditions that minds adapt to for guidance. Nature has also insured that we can hit on the right ideas very often. Ideas are then not arbitrary. They are adaptive; they guide behavior. If the ideas are bad, they are rejected. The constraints on our hypotheses are tied to our creative potential. The abductive and the creative are intimately linked: Abductive moments are the prototypical mental event – creatively generating ideas and then testing them against the world.

In more contemporary terms, we speak in the following manner; no mental life imposed, no intelligibility to be found. We talk about the constraints of cognitive organs, the way the beast is wired up, the limits of what it can do, how it operates, the strategies or hypotheses it employs. But also we just don't consider the animal's mind, but the world's impositions. The ecological niche of the animal is uncovered in the context of determining the behavioral options, or strategies, that the animal can possibly employ. Without the notion of a world, the mind's possibilities lose all sensibility (e.g. light-dark-circadian cycles). The possibilities are often shared properties with humans and other animals in the world. The animal can only exist as embedded in a world. In some contexts, the mind's possibilities can meet the actualities of nature's design. Their evolution in some fundamental fashion speaks of a joint effort.

Hypothesis Testing

A general feature of organisms that learn is that of being a hypothesis tester. In this view, children, rats, or amoebas are all little scientists. They discern first what it is they are faced with and then decide what is the appropriate response. They hypothesize and test. They alter their beliefs and actions if need be – at least ideally. The phenomenon is one of degrees. The amoeba tests very little, the rat tests more, primates do the most. Genesis and feedback are pervasive and constantly overlie one another. Adaptation and success are features of the survivor. Approach and avoidance mechanisms organize the action. The hypotheses that work survive. They resolve problems. If they survive they become the habits for future engagements. As they become entrenched their novelty diminishes. The hypotheses, or beliefs, that orchestrate behavior are not altered until called into doubt, until some breakdown of a habit. Then the animal generates other hypotheses to test; and with success there arrives the emergence of a new habit.[6] The new habit, or entrenched belief, is instantiated in the brain and becomes a possible expression in the animal's repertoire.

Stated in the language of everyday life, at first the behavior feels lively and then it becomes routine. At first one is present; after a while it's hard to say where one is. Again one encounters the useful distinction between being an organism and being an aggregate. The aggregates are the entrenched beliefs, the beliefs through the course of time that have become habitually applied. As a result they have deadened somewhat. The liveliness is gone. But entrenched beliefs that organize behavior are at the basis of organized action. They are part of the "cognitive unconscious." But what is pervasive across all kinds of animal life is the capacity to test and change. The extent of this is contingent on the possibilities of expression open to the animal. When it's an organism, there is some choice and creative use of one's mental resources. There is the enjoyment, or consummation (or not), of a choice in action.

The mental in biological systems has essentially to do with choice and check, with intelligent strategies and successful stays. Most essentially the mental has to do with self-generative behavior and consummatory experience. Animals are essentially active and not passive. The active sense of mind-creating and hypothesizing is a precondition for achieving unity of being. The creative is tied to an active sense of mentation.

There is more than a mouthful here. But I think one can see that the conception adumbrated here of being a biological kind is that of being a mental creature, one which generates decisions or hypothesis that then get tested against reality. If nature does not reject the hypothesis, it becomes a habit, an entrenched hypotheses that eventually loses the essential abductive moment (the act of creating the hypothesis). In other words, the richness of the moment of creation is lost in its continued success. Routine and redundancy follow success. Stability is achieved. But the success is probably at some time challenged; choice and hypothesis testing is renewed. In higher animals like ourselves, this moment is tied to reflection and understanding, and the whole show begins anew with new hypotheses to test. Thus while tropic factors are real, there is nonetheless activity in the animal; again the animal is not just passive, not just habitual. Since choice and check are at the heart of mental life, there is a common principle that can envision persons and ants as being natural elements and related to other biological kinds. Let's consider further the issue of mental constraints in a contemporary contexts.

Language Acquistion

There may be several linguistic constraints that are operative in language acquisition.[7] No language learning is possible without certain linguistic rules. They set the conditions for the child learning the language of his or her culture. They constitute the innate rules. The linguistic rules are presupposed in order for there to be the possibility of a human language user. From a finite set of rules, or constraints, an infinite array of sentences can be generated. The finite set constrains, but richly so, allowing for creative linguistic expression. These linguistic rules are unconscious. We do not have privileged access to them.

Almost all agree that there is no learning without innate rules. The question is one of degree. Empiricists say it's a small degree; rationalists say it's a large degree. Both agree that something innately given to the animal is presupposed. The question then is about the scope of innate knowledge. The job of the inquirer is to uncover them. In the case of language, one could not learn a language without linguistic rules that are presupposed. One is led with good reasons to believe that a language-generating device is operative, that it may develop or mature, as do other biological organs over time, and that this maturation (though influenced by environmental contingencies) has built within it a rhythm of development endogenous to its nature. This also holds true for bird song or cortical development.

The thesis is this: The child acquires the language of his or her culture by generating hypotheses guided by universal syntactical constraints that serve the child in this acquisition. The child's creativity exploits the resources that stand as his or her possibilities. In the case of language, the syntactic constraints and the continuation of successful linguistic strategies are the resources. The question for scientific inquiry is what rules or syntactic constraints or pragmatic strategies make this possible and there one spells out the rules that are presupposed, that are constitutive – that set the possibility of creative language use.

Dietary Strategies

It is well warranted to assert that animals come into nature selectively "prepared" to learn some things quite readily. For example, nature prepares animals to learn relationships between gastrointestinal disturbances and the selection of foods quite easily.[8] This learning is rapid; the animals learn to avoid noxious food quickly; they select one food at a time, and determine the consequences. The learning takes place over a long temporal spread. This mechanism is important to an animal in nature – it is designed to solve food-related problems. This intelligent strategy is a specific adaptation. There are many other examples. Understanding intelligence, then, requires understanding the cognitive machinery that makes it possible – the strategies operative within the animal. The strategies are the possibilities in the having of a world, in there being an actuality in which to be a forager and solve these problems.

For example, when animals are rendered sodium deficient they search for salty sources – salt licks. The knowledge is innate; the first time they are sodium deficient they ingest the salt immediately when exposed to it.[9] They recall where salt can be found when they are sodium deficient, despite the fact that they may have discovered the salt when they were sodium replete. To the sodium deficient animal, salt sources are noted and are searched for. This is specialized knowledge. But the innate knowledge of this one mineral deficiency has been extended to other mineral deficiencies.[10] Potassium and calcium deficient animals will also ingest salty sources. The very possibility of the sodium, potassium, or calcium deficient animal being able to solve its dietary needs requires the opening, or horizon, of salt-related events. The constraints of ingesting salty sources determines the ingestive responses. A "universe(s) of discourse" opens up. The creative use of the innate sodium appetite was extended to other minerals. In the world, salt licks are rich in other minerals besides sodium. But from the one innate appetite for salty tastes that results from sodium deficiency the animal could "hook up" the other related mineral appetites in the strategy to ingest salty sources. It was a creative moment. The constraints made this possible.

The evolution of intelligence on this view is seen as the liberation of these strategies; specific adaptive achievements become more generally applied.[11] The use of these basic strategies in new domains speaks of the creative: the extension of possibilities provided by the animal's innately endowed resources. Possibilities, or mental constraints, are given to the animals by their inherited success.

Inquiry has revealed that the cognitive unconscious is a rich source – the predominant source – of our ideas. The cognitive unconscious is in varying degrees a highly specialized source; so that the rules of linguistic use are distinguishable from those of reasoning about numbers, or visual space perception, or dietary strategies. These "cognitive organs" are often highly modularized, or specialized.[12]

Thinking Brains

The brain is largely designed for performing specific tasks; for example, visual tasks, gustatory tasks, spatial mapping tasks, etc. The design is often one of modularity. Each neural system embodies design principles. The job of the neural scientist is to spell out how the different systems are designed and organized. Wiring diagrams are drawn, physiological and psychological mechanisms are uncovered and the principles of the system are discerned − how it operates, the constraints on the system that make it possible. In thinking of how the system works, the neural scientist often considers the strategies employed by each system, and whether different neural systems gain access to one another or not.

One attributes intelligence to such systems, neural or otherwise, when thinking about information processing, coding, transformations, decision procedures, etc. When constructing the design of the brain, the language of "cognitive devices" is used. (The design is one of centra-fugal control.) The cells in the retina, as well as those in the visual cortex, can be said to serve some function of mental activity. The mental activity is all theory-laden, from what the retina "sees" to what the visual cortices receive. The design is for optimality.

The evolution of nervous systems suggests that increasing accessibility of one system to another may be at the basis of the rise of intelligent action, from specific to more general accessability. [13] The capacity to be responsive in a broad range of domains appears. The animals can then be said to know more and to do more because of such liberation. In some cases they can also be said to experience more. Such intelligent sentience is instantiated in neural design.

There is convergence of the mental and the physical. There is specialization, accessibility in a hierarchy of strategies, where decisive hypothesis testing takes place and where creative new strategies emerge; this is at the heart of animal life. Each neural system creates in a context because of constraints, or possibilities, that provide order. The more evolved, the greater the sense of unity, the greater the capacity for creativity. Thus each neural system decides and acts with varying degrees of freedom on the basis of the constraints, or order, that it works from − from its design. On a continuum of orders, some are more or less constrained. Where decisions are made, creativity is manifest; in form, creativity labors.

The Designer's Stance

In constructing a machine, one adopts the "designer's stance." In the construction of artificial intelligent systems, one is placed in a position of having to design an apparatus to solve a problem, to perform some task. In the design of such systems, one has to think of strategies, or what the system must know in order to solve the problem. One is put in a designer's, or creator's, position.

Our understanding of cognitive mechanisms – e.g., language-generating devices, visual systems, or the strategies of successful food selection – are further substantiated when our own design of an intelligent system can perform these functions. To understand a mental system and to give it psychological reality is, in part, to show that it is constitutive of an intelligent system of our own creation. This is a strong thesis for artificial simulation of cognitive capacities, and it's probably false. Yet it captures an intuition that has appeared in culture for several thousand years: to know something is to create something that displays the knowledge. The phrase "show me" is an old one. Without reducing all aspects of mind to bits of machinery, and so avoiding crude and false scientism, the study of artificial intelligence needs little defense. Simulation does teach us something about the design of systems and possibly the design of our own minds. Our own constructions, perhaps, may become known. So in understanding how knowledge is possible one very important line of inquiry is the construction of intelligent systems. If the system is to perform, stated in this very general and abstract way, the constraints and strategies in terms of determining factors are at the heart of the design of such systems.

But we have not been very successful in producing sophisticated intelligent systems anything like that seen in animal life. This is the so called "frame problem." The "frame problem" is in providing the knowledge requisite for intelligent behavior, so that the thinking system can draw the right inferences in resolving problems in novel situations. Machines have not arrived yet. If a framework anything like our own or other animals' can be designed, then the designer's stance and real mentation would meet. Its possibility is in the distant future.

But if, in simulating the artificial, animal unity is achieved, where a one (a decision) emerges to dominate and take hold of the many (aggregates or basic forms) in a nontropic manner, then an epistemology and a metaphysics meet quite intimately. The epistemology is in uncovering the mental apparatus that organizes behavior, which gives meaning to the world. The metaphysics stipulates that at the heart of life are decisions that unify. Systematic psychobiology, in part, shows the natural relationships between the frameworks that animals work from and the decisions that are at the heart of their organic unity. For now one knows that artificial simulation shares some of the design principles of biological systems; and it is compatible with the metaphysics of choice, action, and being.

Mentalism and Metaphysics

Theories in psychobiology are directed toward uncovering the operations of the mental apparatus in the context of real world selection pressures:

cognition that is adapted to and in resonance, or harmony, with the environment. Conflicts for animals are resolved by intelligent mechanisms. The language of "cognition" is readily and intelligibly extended to biology and artificial "thinking machines." The constrained systems and decisions made through their use constitute mental life.

The metaphysics of animal life is that, at the heart of being, there is a decision of some kind. This has been expressed by Sartre in the analysis of humans, by Whitehead in the analysis of everything.[14] That is, the essential feature of a mental event is a decision about how to be.

This is a metaphysics compatible with the contemporary turn towards cognitive theories, as I've indicated. Decision making is revealed by the creative expression of thinking. The creative is embedded in constraining factors yielding abductive moments of insight during existential decision making.

To be is to be a mind. To be a mind is to be a decision–maker. The degree of unity varies with the subject. As stated at the outset, a distinction between aggregates and organisms emerges. Aggregates do not have a single unified sense. Within aggregates there are collections of little minds. They are subsystems unified for a goal, directed by decision and driven toward satisfaction. But the whole is without unity. There is no overarching mind across the subsystems – no One. The subroutines are operative and cooperative, but not joined together through a unifying connection between them. There is no connective frame. The apparent unity perceived is one of "clockwork," but not a self-made unity achieved by a creative decision and the action to be a one out of the many.

We often refer to the "healthy" person as an integrated individual. The "person" is less in charge when fractionated. Such a person may be an aggregate: a many not a one. An organism contains a many within a one. A cockroach is an organism. So are we. Both cockroaches and people are also often aggregates. Conceptions of the evolution of mind, ontogeny, and maturity become prominent.

Without vector connections there is no unity. Without unity there is no one mind – no being as a single organism. We live with this, accept it. Disparity is predominant. But creative being is the overarching sense of unity across parts. A one emerges from the unification of many, animation exists throughout because of the creative choice, and the many pieces fall into a whole – into an individual, for at least an ephemeral moment. Minds within minds get connected into one mind that binds them, holds them together, providing unification.

The metaphysics goes a bit further. One speaks of determinate features,[15] or constraints or boundary conditions, in epistemological terms that set the possibilities for action. Resources are determinate recurring features, or the background conditions for subsequent occasions. They are connected to the real.

Determinate features can be represented, such as in Whitehead's notion of "coordinate analysis."[16] We map relationships on Cartesian graphs, spelling out the determinate features that are in some order. We then perform various kinds of formal analyses. The determinate features are extended. The world for a mind comes designed in an order of determinate features. These regularities of the past, as they are instantiated in the form of a graph, are "frozen." But without the creative it would all be dead. Mind is absent when inert matter dominates. The regularity continually repeats itself, deadness of habit rather than the achievement of the novel emerges. When alive, sentient, and thoughtful, the creative creature chooses from the past regularities and is geared toward a future of self-expression or decision. This is freedom with bonds, within constraints.

The metaphysics and epistemology is one of process of movement, of action. The events are existential because they require decision; because they are tied to action they require pragmatism and resourcefulness. They are free yet constrained acts of self-determination; they are acts of genesis, of coming into being, which is why they are existential. The essential features are those of activity. At those moments, the past is captured by a decision to be. The creative power to unify into a one is directly related to the place the animal inhabits in the hierarchy of biological being. To a high grade animal, it is possible to achieve unity often.

But this metaphysical position is riddled with paradox. All metaphysical stances seem mysterious. However, if one wants a metaphysics that justifies a conception of freedom as self-determination (or imaginative decision), constrained by determinate factors (for background data), and expressed in acts of genesis, this one has some warrant. The metaphysics is also compatible with an epistemology that envisions mentation as decisions within constraints; mind as the creative tester in many cases producing a brilliant survivor or thriver. Constraints are the determining or limiting factors, as is the world. They set the possibilities. Essential features, in contrast to determinate features, are the acts of creation through decisions to be — those abductive moments of bringing something into being through decision and action. The world is constantly being rejuvenated, through choice.

As knowers, we seek unity. I have sought to bring together some metaphysical beliefs in concert with practices and theories of modern "naturalized" epistemological inquiry. One of the messages of "modernism" is that if the "world(s)" we live in are radically incongruous, are not unifiable, then the endeavor of looking to unify is useless. There is no unity, according to this view. But if one strives to provide some coherence to the many frameworks we inhabit, then vague hypotheses are inevitable, possibly desirable.[17] The advance consists in connecting the disparity or coping with it. Unification of our conceptual world is a basic goal, as well as an advance in our sense of being.

In summary, each epoch in evolution often constitutes some stage in development. The evolution into a higher order is expressed in the propensity for more integration; with more order there is more unity and with more unity there is advancement. The more access to the many, the greater the control, the greater the use, the greater the creative synthesis. In this regard, the evolution of intelligence corresponds in kind with the evolution of order. This evolution of order and integration is instantiated in the hierarchical design of nervous systems. As we ascend the intricacies of neural networks, the degree of integration and overall control increases. In phylogenetically older parts of the brain there is a high degree of specialization. They are modular in design. As one moves up the brain, specialized systems of lower brainstem units are accessed and extended in their use. Metaphysically, when creatures become organisms they start being a one embodying a many. Freedom grows as the accessibility of aggregate parts increases. Decisions expressing unity traverse the variety of aggregates. The decision is a creative essential moment of coming into being. The determinate features stand as possibilities. They constrain and set the order. The essential acts are determined, or confined, within these possibilities. Creation takes place in something; it is not creation ex nihilo. The problem of freedom and determinism is set in the context of being a one unifying a many. Freedom is within form. The form stands as possibilities, as constraints in epistemological terms, or determinate features in metaphysical terms. There are many orders of determinate features. The degree of determinateness is contingent on the range of possibilities and past creative abductive syntheses. The more free, the greater the range. The denial of this in humans is where one can speak of "bad faith,"[18] since freedom and choice are at the heart of being. But the extent to which a person is a one, is an organism, or an aggregate, is always going to be difficult to say. This is the problem of attributing responsibility. But the existentialist's fear, or nausea, is a self-imposed limitation. It results from a conception of radical freedom. Freedom, however, is constrained. This conception corresponds with our sense of things, with our "funded knowledge." In the end, the beliefs adumbrated may necessitate a "will to believe." Metaphysically, being and choice meet; epistemologically, choice and order converge.

114 *Jay Schulkin*

NOTES

1. See Aristotle's *Physics*, trans. Richard Hope (Lincoln, Neb.: University of Nebraska Press, 1961) II. Book Beta.
2. For a recent discussion of these issues, read G. Wolf's "The Place of the Brain in an Ocean of Feelings," *Existence and Actuality: Conversations with Charles Hartshorne*, ed. J. B. Cobb, Jr., and F. I. Gamwell (Chicago: Univ. of Chicago Press, 1984).
3. Kant discusses this in the *Critique of Pure Reason* (orig. printing 1781), trans. N. K. Smith (New York: Macmillan & Co., New York 1929; New York: St. Martin's Press, 1965) Transcendental doctrine of judgement, Ch. 2.
4. Immanuel Kant, *Critique of Practical Reason* (orig. printing 1788), trans. by L. W. Beck (Indianapolis: Bobbs-Merrill Co., 1965) Preface; and J. P. Sartre, *Being and Nothingness*, (orig. printing 1943), trans. H. E. Barnes (New York: Washington Square Press, 1975) part 4, Ch. 1.
5. C. S. Peirce, *Volumes I and II Collected Papers of Charles Sanders Peirce* (orig. printing 1934), ed. C. Hartshorne and P. Weiss, (Cambridge, Mass.: Harvard University Press, 1974) Book II Lecture VII.
6. For an interesting discussion of single cell organisms as hypothesis testers, read H. S. Jennings, *Behavior of the Lower Organisms* (orig. printing 1905) (Bloomington: Indiana University Press, 1967). For discussions of the logic of inquiry see J. Dewey's *Essays in Experimental Logic*, (Chicago: University of Chicago Press, 1916) Ch. 6.
7. N. Chomsky makes this case in a number of places, but see his *Language and Mind*, (New York: Harcourt Brace Jovanovich, 1972).
8. P. Rozin reviews the literature in his "The Selection of foods by rats, humans and other animals," *Advances in the Study of Behaviors*, ed. J. S. Rosenblatt and R. A. Hinde, E. Shaw and Co. Beer, (New York: Academic Press, 1976).
9. D. Denton provides an exhaustive analysis of the salt hungry animal in his *The Hunger for Salt*, (New York: Springer-Verlag, 1982).
10. J. Schulkin, "The Evolution and Expression of Salt Appetite," *The Physiology of Thirst and Sodium Appetite*, ed. A. N. Epstein and G. De Caro (New York: Academic Press, 1986).
11. P. Rozin provides a concise description of this view in his "The Evolution of Intelligence and Access to the Cognitive Unconscious," *Progress in Psychobiology and Physiological Psychology*, ed. J. M. Sprague and A. N. Epstein, (New York: Academic Press, 1976).
12. See J. Fodor's *The Modularity of Mind* (Cambridge, Mass.: MIT Press, 1983).
13. Again, see P. Rozin's "The Evolution of Intelligence."
14. See J. P. Sartre's *Being and Nothingness* and A. N. Whitehead's *Process and Reality* (orig. printing 1929), ed. D. R. Griffen and D. W. Sherburne, (New York: MacMillan, 1979). Part II.
15. See P. Weiss's *Modes of Being*, (Carbondale, Ill.: Southern Illinois Univ. Press, 1958) Ch. 10. Also see R. C. Neville's *The Cosmology of Freedom*, (New Haven: Yale Univesity Press, 1974) for a discussion of determinate and essential features.

16. See A. N. Whitehead's *Process and Reality* (Part IV).

17. For a discussion of "vagueness," see R. C. Neville's *Reconstruction of Thinking* (Albany: State University of New York Press 1981), Ch. 2.

18. J. P. Sartre, *Being and Nothingness* (Part I, Ch 2).

George R. Lucas

Moral Order and the Constraints of Agency: Toward a New Metaphysics of Morals

My own principal interests in systematic metaphysical inquiry lie in the area that Kant first designated, somewhat awkwardly, as "the metaphysics of morals."[1] With this in mind, the question that I will pursue in the following essay may not seem quite so strange. The question is this: Do moral rules or principles have any ontological significance – do they possess any particular status in the "nature of things" that it is the task of metaphysical inquiry to elucidate?

Such a question is quite readily answerable in the affirmative in the traditions of Platonism and of the "natural law" derived by St. Thomas from Aristotle and the "divine logos" formulae of the Stoic philosophers, which together shaped the course of Western philosophical and theological thought well into the modern era. In the present climate of opinion, by contrast, it borders on the nonsensical to attach any "ontological status" or metaphysical significance to moral principles. Such a question, even, is reminiscent of that disciple of the "Blessed One" given to pursuing unwarranted cosmological speculations, whose endless questions Gotama finally dismissed as unanswerable, because they were "not rightly put."[2]

I will assume a rather different perspective in this essay. I will assume (only for the sake of argument, if one wishes) that inquiry into the ontological status or significance of moral principles is not absurd or nonsensical; rather, there is much regarding common moral experience and commonsense undestandings of what morality might be that render this question quite perplexing and important. Furthermore, I claim that the inability to frame a satisfactory answer to this question does *not* simply reflect a misguided preoccupation with speculative questions that are "not rightly put," but reflects rather an inability to provide a distinct *philosophical* justification for morality generally. While it is embarrassing to admit, the fact is that teachers and scholars in the discipline of philosophical ethics cannot come even remotely close to agreement on what a moral rule or principle is, let alone how this or that rule or principle might properly be justified, nor (and I think this is the most interesting puzzle) what if anything would be signified in the event that one or more rules or principles *were* justified or justifiable to all conceivable parties to this dispute.

Ethics is not the only area of philosophy that admits of ambiguity and controversy, of course. But there is no other area of philosophy in which the *degree* of ambiguity, controversy, and general lack of consensus are any more pronounced than in ethics; nor is there any other area of philosophy in which such fundamental confusion has had so great an impact on the broader cultural context within which that philosophical confusion is set.[3] In the past, such widespread disagreements in other fields have resulted from a basic confusion over first principles and fundamental conceptual categories – a confusion that can be remedied only through systematic metaphysical inquiry.

There is an urgent sense, moreover, in which this particular metaphysical task is more than merely another isolated academic exercise. Recent years have witnessed a renewed widespread interest in the historical details and in a moral repudiation of the Holocaust in Germany during World War II, even as our generation has reluctantly witnessed another "holocaust" of a different sort but of similar proportions in Kampuchea. It is nothing short of remarkable the extent to which citizens and governments around the globe can be won to the view that brutal torture as an instrument of political repression is abhorrent and even disfunctional as a means of establishing and maintaining political power – even though Amnesty International annually reports a decided increase in the use of torture as an instrument of political repression by many of the same governments and peoples who would otherwise publicly eschew its moral validity. Since the United Nations Universal Declaration in 1948, and especially since the signing of the Helsinki Accords by the U.S. and the U.S.S.R. in 1975, discussions about fundamental human "rights" and the necessity of meeting basic human needs have enjoyed an unprecedented resurgence of interest and concern, even though the most basic of these needs or rights routinely goes unmet.[4] Finally, over the past two decades there has been a growing awareness of and interest in the sorts of conflicts that arise in the professional practices of medicine, business, law, engineering and journalism – conflicts of a sort that have nothing intrinsically to do with degrees of professional competence in any of these fields.

Such "empirical" matters might seem to fall more within the domain of law and the social sciences. Their citation might not seem to raise any important metaphysical issues or constitute the traditional realm of metaphysical inquiry. Collectively, however, these experiences suggest (even as their analysis seems to require) that moral rules and principles must in some sense possess a determinate status or significance in the nature of things, independent of their particular recognition or application within any particular culture or society. Yet such a claim seems indefensible in the context of current widespread cultural perspectives concerning the nature of morality, linked with the philosophical ambiguity and controversy indicated above in the discipline of ethics generally.

Whitehead defined metaphysics as the "endeavour to frame a coherent, logical, necessary system of general ideas in terms of which every element of our experience can be interpreted."[5] It follows that any system of "general ideas" that lies at the heart of a fundamental component of human experience, but nonetheless seems to ignore or render wholly unintelligible many of the most important dimensions of that experience, is metaphysically inadequate and requires a substantial recasting of its metaphysical foundations.[6] The conflicts and puzzling omissions I have cited indeed point to such a need, for moral experience and the apparent conditions for its possibility are not adequately encompassed by theories that deny in principle what seems evident in fact.

I. Transcendental Aesthetic

It is fair, I think, to characterize the problematic status of moral rules and principles as a thoroughly modern phenomenon. In classical and medieval Western philosophy, the question is not *whether* the moral law enjoys a determinate and independent ontological status but rather *what* rules or principles are to be found on the canonical list. By contrast, the problematic ontological character of moral principles as such emerges with a peculiar urgency in the modern period as a result of a series of aggressive reformulations of the metaphysical foundations of morality generally. Moral principles come to be portrayed either as somewhat arbitrary conventions for the controlled exercise of power (Hobbes), as the outgrowth of natural (but formally arbitrary) psychological tendencies toward sympathy and self interest (Hume, Butler, and to an extent, J. S. Mill), or as manifestations of a deeper ideological defense of historically outmoded forms of cultural order (Marx). The final blow to any meaningful metaphysics of morals comes at the hands of Wittgenstein, for whom any system of rules (moral or otherwise) represents merely a convention for ordering objects and states of affairs around the performance of certain sorts of activities, or later, for establishing procedures for the use of verbal symbols that describe and occasionally prescribe such activities.

The Hobbesian approach treats questions concerning law and morality as on a par with questions concerning physics and mechanics: how to achieve a stable equilibrium among a plurality of centers of force and power. The Humean approach reduces questions about law and morality to questions about human psychology and aesthetics. The Marxist approach treats questions about law and morality as questions about cultural anthropology, and replaces the metaphysics of morals with the (highly speculative) metaphysics of historical progress. The Wittgensteinian approach denies any fundamental connection between regulative principles or rules (the "sense of the world") and the sorts of existent entities (the "world in itself") whose language and behavior may be described by such rules.[7] All of these approaches reflect a thoroughgoing naturalism and reductionism that are among the chief characteristics of modern intellectual life.

The chief resultant of this historical development is an account of moral principles that is wholly consistent with cultural pluralism – the observable diversity of systems of moral principles that has always constituted an irreducible feature of human societies. The chief *problem* with this result, however, is that all of these naturalistic accounts of the foundation of morality have seemed also to entail normative relativism – a position that constitutes a kind of hidden *evaluation* of the ontological status of pluralism. According to this normative position, no reasons can be given to compare or to prefer one rule or system to any other.

R. M. Hare has shown that it is possible to provide some logical norms that imply a qualified degree of intersubjectivity and cross-cultural validity to some instances of prescriptivist statements.[8] Such tendencies toward a defense of the metaethical position of "moral absolutism" during the past two or three decades proceed directly from the common recognition that there do, on occasion, seem to be rules or principles that transcend the particularities of history of culture. Notwithstanding, as G. E. M. Anscombe noted over twenty-five years ago, no purely philosophical justification for this observation, let alone of morality generally as a normative human practice or convention, has proved plausible or viable.[9]

Despite Hare's considerable and sophisticated logical refinement toward universality of what had hitherto been purely subjectivist accounts of moral claims, no explanation seems possible for the agreement or "fit" between cultural mores or individual moral "intuitions" that is quite frequently encountered in human experience, often with respect to issues of fundamental practical concern. For example, torture can be found to be proscribed under a large number of cultural systems, and the literature even of societies in which the practice is common leaves no doubt of widespread personal anguish and disavowal of this practice out of intuitive respect for the principles of fairness and reciprocity. The same sorts of claims hold with regard to the arbitrary destruction for nonmilitary reasons of civilian noncombatants in wartime; the practice is now quite widely condemned in principle, and the literature even of ancient cultures that routinely practiced massive civilian retaliation as a matter of military necessity reveals again a widespread anguish and dissatisfaction with this state of affairs.[10] Is the broad coincidence of such moral intuitions and principles purely accidental, or does that frequent coincidence reveal some fundamental characteristic about the status of some moral principles?

Shorn of the traditional recourse to moral Platonism or natural law theory to account for these observations, contemporary advocates of universalism in morality, including Roderick Firth, Thomas Nagel, and John Rawls, attempt to account for moral universality or universalizability by having recourse to the judgments of a hypothetical "ideal rational observer," a common standpoint of disinterested benevolence, or otherwise by referring to a presumed "archimedian standpoint" from which moral dilemmas may be rationally surveyed and analyzed, a state of "reflective equilibrium" from which common consent upon widely held moral principles may be presumed, or an "original position" from which such basic principles as constitute the institutions of justice may be constructed on the basis of the concept of rational agency.[11] These approaches share the virtue of approaching the "universality-coincidence" question head on, in a manner that is wholly philosophical and entirely consistent with other widespread assumptions about ourselves and our "moral universe." Such approaches, however, do not avoid formulating a fundamental metaphysics of morals.[12] Rather, the problem is more that substantial metaphysical assumptions proceed unexamined and metaphysical positions often remain uncriticized.

The basic positions of Firth, Rawls, and Nagel, for example, entail substantial unexamined metaphysical assumptions about reason and rationality. Judgments proferred from the "original position" or some "archimedian standpoint" presume that individual moral agents are both fully rational and primarily motivated by private self-interest, and that their individuality is logically and ontologically prior to and more significant that their finitude and interdependence in a social matrix. Even if "rationality" for these authors means nothing more than the most fundamental and self-evident sort of autonomous deliberation and action that Kant took to be a basic "fact" regarding agency and practical reasoning, the remaining "self-evident assumptions" and starting points comprise a sweeping metaphysical position in need of some clarification and considerable defense.[13] I am inclined to agree with Kant, as a result of his polemic against Cartesianism, that no clear answers can be given to questions about "fundamental human nature" or the psychological deep-structure of agent intentions, and accordingly that moral theories that rest upon substantive assumptions about "human nature" are bound in principle to prove inconclusive and unsatisfactory.[14]

In a more sinister fashion, moreover, such approaches sometimes seem to confuse "justification" with the history of a decidedly limited cultural consensus. If "ideal observers," or contractualists allegedly blind to their individual cultural interests behind a "veil of ignorance," merely recapitulate the insights of the Western Judeo-Christian tradition of law and morality (for example) at the expense of the insights of *other* cultures and traditions (such as Hinduism or Taoism), one cannot escape a suspicion that such theories constitute merely parochialism and cultural imperialism masquerading as "pure reason."

The question about the metaphysics of morals and the status of moral principles is a demand for a philosophical explanation of the possibility of such principles; it is a demand for a legitimate philosophical justification of morality. The problem encountered in this demand is quite similar to the sort of problem one encounters in attempting to develop a conceptually complete and fundamental justification for mathematics. In both disciplines, one can fairly readily formulate theories and apply them to paradigmatic cases with a high degree of consensus, without at the same time being able to explain fully the origin and foundation of this consensus or what it signifies. Mathematicians simply "get away with" such conceptual incompleteness more readily than do moral theorists; perhaps because that incompleteness at the foundation of things is not nearly so devastating for the usual practice of mathematical sciences either theoretically or in an applied sense as it is for ethicists. We know that human beings can and do "think mathematically" and tend to take this phenomenon as a demonstration or definition of what is meant by intersubjective and cross-cultural rationality. Strictly speaking, however, we do not know *why* human beings are able generally (and in widely varying degrees) to do this or what this feature of their reasoning signifies in any broad sense, let alone whether other creatures might be able to do likewise. Much the same conundrum holds for moral reasoning and moral experience.

II *Transcendental Analytic*

One of the most important and far-reaching investigations of the foundations of morality in a contemporary setting is Alan Donagan's *The Theory of Morality* (1977). In the preface to this important work, Donagan claims that any system of morality necessarily rests upon a double foundation: a theory of practical reason and a theory of the nature of moral agents.[15] While this approach might appear self-evident to many moral theorists, the particular way of defining this issue has had unfortunate consequences. Rationalistic accounts of the foundations of moral theory often seem to critics to have defined the possible domain of deliberation and choice solely in terms of the exercise of calculative rationality, and to have defined the range of moral agents a priori as dependent solely upon the possession of a well-developed and analytical reason. Such restrictions at the outset place indefensible limits on the class of entities that might be due full consideration as genuine moral agents. Critical evaluations of rationalistic nonconsequentialism thus invariably diverge from the main features or merits of the particular version of the theory itself and focus instead upon important but decidedly second-order questions of moral considerability (the class of entities accorded full respect in treatment under the terms of the theory) or upon criticisms of narrowly rationalistic conceptions of "agency" (whether, for example, children, the mentally retarded, or nonhuman animals might conceivably be classified as "agents").

In my own view, "agency" (as distinguished from an account of what sorts of entities might qualify as "agents") is entirely equivalent to a very broadly conceived notion of practical reason*ing* – one that makes "reasoning" more a function of the occurrence of certain activities or events than the possession of fixed and determinate mental states or characteristics. A minimal list of the generic events or activities associated with agency would include the activities of deliberating, evaluating, choosing, and subsequently framing and carrying out strategies of action in response to those determinate choices. The advantage of this approach is that the events in question are real occurrences in a public world associated with determinate entities of a variety of sorts in that world.

The particular motivating mental states of such entities, by contrast, are inferences based on the observer's private experience, and often, even more narrowly, based even on the peculiar biases of a specific disciplinary approach to the topic of morality. By focusing upon the inferred nature of inclinations and motivations, rather than upon the observable events, we risk the covert introduction of a specious requirement for considerability and agency; *viz.*, the possession of something like *our own* peculiar private experiences. Hence, moral theories come to be elaborated more upon the restricted experiences or disciplinary biases of some analytic philosophers (for example) than upon the broader experiences of *persons* as such or *agents* as such.[16] My preference at the outset to base the metaphysics of morals on a minimalist, event-oriented description of behavior, rather than upon a covert Cartesian-rationalistic analysis of inferred mental states and private experiences, is intended to bypass a lengthy diversion into these interesting ancillary issues.

In my view, the neglected area of metaphysical inquiry concerning morality is one that is logically *prior* to the current fascination with moral considerability or the rights of the nonhuman world. These popular debates presuppose both existing communities of moral agents and varieties of theories describing their agency, and then proceed to inquire whether this or that entity is *also* an agent or ought to receive some consideration in the existing moral community. Let us likewise presuppose the evident facts of our common experience: that there seems in some sense to be a community or communities of moral agents, and that the activities and events associated with their agency *do* in fact occur in the world. The first proper metaphysical move is *not* to push these notions forward analytically by asking about requirements for membership and privileges in the community; that refining move will come later! Rather, we must first make the explicitly Kantian regressive or transcendental move of asking *how* these self-evident features of agents and agency are *possible* in the first place. That is to say, the interesting metaphysical question now becomes: Under what sorts of *conditions* is agency *possible*?

Suppose, for example, that the existence of a plurality of agents engaged in the exercise of practical means-ends reasoning, *however* this might be carried out in a context of action, can in some sense be taken for granted. (Kant referred to the existence of autonomous moral actors as a self-evident "fact" of reason.)[17] Suppose further that each such agent was, in principle, capable (by whatever means) of evaluating, deliberating, deciding, choosing, and finally carrying out consequent strategies of action that, while clearly representing the *expressions* of the agency of each, were simultaneously and fundamentally *incompatible* with the expression of a similar agency by all of the other agents in that community. The second supposition is incompatible with the first; the conditions described in the second supposition would render it impossible for the conditions of the first ever to obtain. But since we were invited to take the first supposition for granted and inquire into the grounds of its possibility, the conditions of the second supposition give us, in effect, a negative criterion for that possibility. That is, the sorts of expression of agency suggested in the second supposition turn out to be incompatible with the very possibility of agency. Hence, some highly general conditions or constraints on the exercise of agency seem to constitute a necessary condition for the very possiblity of agency, let alone for the determinate existence and activity of any sorts of entities that might properly be designated "agents."

This result is not surprising: it is the most general formulation possible of the common insight of social contract theory, from Hobbes to Rousseau and Kant, as well as in its recent revival by Rawls. Indiscriminate and wholly unrestrained agency is logically and physically incompatible with the ongoing existence of a plurality or community of agents. The ontological significance or status of moral rules and principles is simply that these are (or normatively, are *intended* to be) at minimum those ordering principles that are the required *constraints* upon agency consistent or compatible with the possibility of agency. In the realm of practical activity, then, moral principles are the *logoi* that inhibit chaos and result instead in the actuality of determinate social orders and structures.

In this vein, we might be led to recast our conventional understanding of certain tests and procedures that, from time to time, have been proposed as formal limitations on the logical consistency of actual moral principles. Kant's famous "second formulation" of the Categorical Imperative – the Formula of the End-In-Itself – for example, would be *misconstrued* as expressing, say, an unarguable preliminary thesis regarding human rights (simply following the lead of the radical reformers, Locke, or Rousseau); it would likewise be wrong to see in this formula merely a restatement of the specific content of other general principles, such as the "Golden Rule." Rather, we would come to understand Kant's categorical imperative as representing a highly generalized, formal constraint upon the forms of order consistent with the exercise of agency. The "second formula" specifically is a requirement for noncontradiction: for agents not to act in ways in which agency is abrogated or rendered otherwise impossible for themselves or other agents, *mutatis mutandis*.[18] Here we have, then, a formal condition of reciprocity that is satisfied to varying degrees by several specific statements of the content of principles of reciprocity, such as the "Golden Rule" and the "Silver Rule." The formal condition also specifies a *procedure* that might be applied or followed to determine the adequacy or legitimacy of any specific proposal regarding reciprocity, or the treatment of agents in action generally.[19]

The point to be noticed here is the high degree of generality or abstraction sought, such that the formal constraints on agency identified can apply as normative standards for *any* entities that answer to the description of "agents" engaged in any sort of activity that might reasonably be described under the categories of practical reasoning, as I have more broadly construed this notion. Kant's concluding chapter of the *Allgemeine Naturgeschichte* (1754), for example – in which he discusses the conceivable moral sensitivities and proclivities of the presumed denizens of Jupiter and Mercury – strikes most modern interpreters merely as an amusing flight of "precritical" speculative philosophical fancy not even worth translating for English readers. When read in the light of the foregoing extraordinary agenda, and compared to his later careful delineation of degrees of rational agency (from homo sapiens through "rational beings as such") in the *Groundwork* (1785), we are led to appreciate this highly unique quest for the most generally applicable principles of generic consistency that would have to be satisfied by any system of moral principles in order to constitute adequate constraints on agency regardless of contextual cultural details.[20]

Moral rules or principles, then, would seem to constitute types of order that embody this logical constraint on agency. Specific systems of rules or principles are the possible "languages" of which this generic logical constraint constitutes the common element of grammar. Moreover, the philosophical understanding and justification of moral principles can proceed only if they are seen as the sorts of ordering of their affairs by agents that are, at minimum, not incompatible with the very possibility of agency.

While my use of the concept of incompatibility in this context may seem clear enough, the continual stress on the notion of "formal impossibility" may seem puzzling, even contradictory. After all, we know full well from experience that there are actual human agents who undertake specific actions and larger-scale action strategies that are "incompatible" with the like agency of other human beings – terrorism, torture, enslavement, and fraud, for example – and who do not thereby cease to exist nor even to have their own agency measurably interrupted. What then can this pivotal notion of "formal impossibility" mean.

By introducing the notion of possibility, I intend to frame the search for minimal constraints on moral agency as a kind of modal argument designed to distinguish those subjective principles of action that are coherent with one another and compatible with the general notions of agency and practical reasoning broadly construed, from *other* principles of action that are clearly *not* either internally coherent or compatible with the notion of agency. Indeed, I understand Kant's third and most fundamental formula of the Categorical Imperative – the "Kingdom of ends" – as representing just such a modal test of agent maxims. The test would operate as follows.

Imagine a society with rules and principles – i.e., existing constraints on agency – roughly identical to one's actual situation. Next, imagine one's own proposed subjective principle of action (or alternatively, the central guiding principle of one's larger proposed action-strategy) as suddenly being factored into the existing structure of principles in this imaginary society, as a general perturbation on the prior existing order. The question then arises: Does this new arrangement – what Rawls has termed this "socially perturbed world" – represent a new stable equilibrium? Is the form of agency being contemplated *possible* in the socially perturbed world?

Systematic deception – lying – as Kant, and more recently Sissela Bok, have noted,[21] constitutes a relatively straightforward example of the sort of subjective principle of action that could not pass this modal test. Under the provisions of this test, as Kant avers, the maxim of lying as an expression of agency, when added as a perturbation to the preexisting social order, creates an unstable situation; this new preturbation is in direct conflict with an already-established principle of fidelity. The latter principle is required as the necessary background of framing the former action-strategy. (Where fidelity is not presumed, lying cannot conceivably work to any advantage and would not likely be proposed). But in the socially perturbed world subsequently envisioned, the two principles cancel one another. Consequently, this proposed expression of agency is literally *impossible* in the resultant socially perturbed world. Any maxim is inconsistent with the generic notion of order and agency if it fails to pass this modal test, and thus renders agency "formally impossible."

It is quite important to notice that such an account of the peculiar form of ordering that systems of moral rules and principles represent is relatively noncommital about the specific form or content of any individual such rule or principle, and does not in any sense rule out the possibility that there might be more than one coherent system of such principles. The Categorical Imperative procedure sketched above, for example, when interpreted as a modal test, does not itself *generate* a complete system of rules and principles. Rather, the CI-procedure functions as a "means test" for those principles of order and forms of agent-constraints that already exist, as well as a procedure for examining the suitability of proposals of action within some prior stable context of order and agency. The features of indeterminacy and nonexclusiveness present in this formulation parallel closely the manner in which highly abstract constraints upon what sets of fundamental axioms qualify as a "geometry" nonetheless do not uniquely specify the particular content of any one such system of geometry nor preclude the possibility that there might be more than one such system. Or even further, in keeping with the linguistic analogy above, the claim that any language necessarily includes some method for expressing activity and distinguishing action from objects and agents likewise says nothing about the number of possible languages that might evolve or be constructed to do this. Hence, the generic claim that any system of moral rules or principles that expresses a cultural ethos must provide for the respect of agency and agents says nothing about how this generic feature might be (or fail to be) actualized in a variety of cultural settings.

This conception of "order" is therefore consistent with the evident experiential features of pluralism, without confusing such pluralism with the total absence of nomative constraints. This feature will prove especially significant below.

III. Transcendental Dialectic

If we agree to consider moral principles under the metaphysical category of "order," then it becomes useful to examine theories or assumptions concerning the sort of status of significance that such forms of order represent, and the sort of metaphysical contradictions to which these theories give rise.

One widely held cultural view regarding the status of moral principles is that of radical subjectivism. Hume, Nietzsche, and Wittgenstein in various senses expounded subjectivist metaphysical theories regarding the status of moral principles, and such views are implicit in emotivist theories, such as those of C. I. Stevenson and A. J. Ayer, that were common coin in the field of metaethics earlier in this century. I am interested primarily in the broad generic features of this view and will not bother with the (sometimes dramatic) differences in its enunciation by the philosophers mentioned above, let alone with the problem of the extent to which their various interpretations have influenced or been accurately appropriated in the cultural views to which I referred earlier.

The relevant generic feature of these theories with respect to the metaphysics of order is that "moral principles" or rules represent types of ordering in regard to agency that are wholly *private* with respect to individuals that are agents. That is, subjectivism allows that the sort of ordering an agent adopts with respect to its agency might well not be duplicated by any other agent, and is, moreover, arbitrary with respect to any community of agents or with respect to "nature" as the realm of entities including but not limited to agents that forms at minimum the necessary broader context of their agency. Alternatively, such forms of order may represent the ordering merely of one community of agents and thus be "private" in Kant's[22] sense of that term; *viz*, arbitrary with respect to other agent-communities and to nature as such.

Any particular ordering of agency that we might be tempted to identify as constituting a moral code, or a system of moral rules and principles, is thus merely one in a nondenumerable infinity of possible such orderings, the particular selection of any one of which is entirely arbitrary and bears no necessary relation to any of the other infinite possible such orderings. There is no ranking or evaluation of the adequacy of alternative orderings possible. Since, in this view, there are no normative constraints on what constitutes the ordering of agency, it follows that no particular form of order can claim a privileged status or special relevance for "persons" as such, or for "agency" as such, let alone in the nature of things as such. This formulation captures the essential features of relativism as a normative theory of ethics, as distinguished from the descriptive factual account of individual-beliefs and cultural pluralism.

In opposition to this view on the status of moral principles stand the older traditions of "moral Platonism" and natural law theory to which I referred at the outset. On the basis of such theories, moral rules or principles constitute "determinate objects" of some sort: They are fixed, definite, timeless and enduring – although they may be "abstract" or deficiently actual in Whitehead's sense[23] in that they may be more or less adequately (or not at all!) actualized or instantiated in individual or community instances of agency or accepted standards for the ordering of agency. The fact that moral principles are determinate objects of some sort, however, permits that they can in principle be known or rendered intelligible in any conceivable situation or circumstance, and that they can be actualized or instantiated in custom or behavior in different historical settings, and, most importantly, that agents or agent-communities are in some sense culpable for any deficiency in the knowledge or practice of such principles. Indeed, it is precisely this privileged ontological status of invariant determinate objectivity that establishes the function of moral principles as standards or norms for the evaluation of determinate forms of individual or cultural ordering of agency and agents in the actual world.[24]

It is well to recall that the widespread cultural acceptance of a sub-jectivist or private ontology regarding the status of moral principles reflects earlier *philosophical* formulations of that position during the early decades of the twentieth century in response to the perceived logical and metaphysical inadequacies of Platonism and natural law theory. Dewey once noted that philosophical positions are never so much refuted as merely *abandoned* as unreasonable or inadequate. This has been the fate of moral Platonism as well as of natural law theory in this century, at least as a metaphysical doctrine, even if scattered stubborn adherents to the latter tradition have been slow to acquiesce to this judg-ment. Both moral Platonism and natural law theory run counter to our contemporary naturalistic sensibilities; both seem to ignore or deny the obvious features of pluralism that attend the ordering of agency and the acceptability of moral customs and practices in widely variant com-munities. Platonism in particular entails a rather strange ontology that is difficult to define or defend outside of an explicitly theistic context.

More significantly, however, the rejection of Platonism and the natural law tradition in favor of varieties of subjectivist theories owed much less to perceived philosophical inadequacies or formal refutation than to the suspicion surrounding the sorts of moral claims and public authority that adherents of both views tended historically to make. The language of both forms of ontological objectivism and universalism as often as not merely masked unwarranted authoritarian generalizations of private practices and beliefs as suitable universal or "public" norms of behavior. Specious universalism and absolutism constitute continual threats to pluralism and to autonomy as regards the constraint of agency and the variety of possible systems of order that may be fully compatible with the ongoing possibility of agency generally. Defenders of subjec-tivism invariably portray moral absolutists or universalists as harbingers of moral imperialism and a new Inquisition, thereby unfortunately accounting in large part for the stubborn immunity to criticism of subjec-tivist ontologies.

Nevertheless, subjectivist theories of either the individualistic or col-lective variety are no more tenable than Platonism or natural law theory, either experientially or metaphysically. On the view that orderings of agency are private and to a large extent infinite in variety and arbitrary in content, there are no intersubjective or cross-cultural grounds for distinguishing between (let alone preferring or recommending) the activ-ities of a prisoner of conscience protesting arbitrary limitations on publication, speech, and assembly, and a brutal rapist-murderer who happens likewise to be imprisoned. There can likewise be no *reasons* or justifications offered (apart from private aesthetic perference of coincidental cultural standard) for ranking the sacrificial act of one lifeboat passenger to save the lives of others over the actions of another passenger undertaken to *preserve* his own life at the *expense* of others. The former act, in this private-subjectivist ontology, appears simply as an arbitrary, odd, and fortuitous accident whose consequence is ultimately to eliminate such sensibilities and considerations from that lifeboat, or from any given society in which the sacrificial and selfless act occurs.[25] Yet agents are generally able to and seem in most cases to distinguish quite readily in *all* of these cases between moral and immoral, principled and wholly unprincipled behavior. Subjectivist theories simple do not account for the weight of evidence in this respect.

It is important to drive home this important experiential point. On the one hand, all persons can and do discriminate and prefer in such cases. They do so, perhaps unreflectively, but on the basis of some intuited perception of the normative status of some forms of order and constraints upon agency over others. Subjectivist theories of all sorts thus deny what the experience of the very agents that hold them affirms, and hence are somehow inadequate to the metaphysical task of framing a coherent set of "general ideas" or categories in terms of which experience may be rendered intelligible. If common moral experience is rendered unintelligible or unaccountable on some theory, then the theory must be defective. Moral principles must enjoy more than merely subjective or private status alone, although they need not and apparently do not answer to the description of platonic forms or immutable natural laws of a specified and determinate form.

The resultant "moral dialectic" is clearly Kantian, rather than Hegelian or Socratic, in that this dialectical tendency in moral argument reveals little, analyzes nothing, and is constructively barren. The dialectic itself turns on a specious opposition of relativism and absolutism, stemming from a deficient understanding of the nature of universalism and the metaphysics of pluralism. One must avoid the deficiencies of subjectivism and relativism by accounting for certain universal and determinate features that moral rules and principles exhibit in human experience. But one must also avoid the sweeping, grandiose, and exclusivist claims of platonism and natural law theory that counter the experience of a viable pluralism. The reformulated metaphysics of morals must account for systems of rules and principles as types of order with a determinate and universal structure – "pockets" of discrete and determinate order, if you will [26] – while admitting there may be a plurality of possible orderings answering to this description. It is thus the (apparently) paradoxical task of metaphysics to admit a notion of order that allows for pluralism without caving in to relativism – a contemporary problem that was simply not central to Kant's earlier formulation.

It seems readily apparent from the historical positions on this question that I have surveyed that some forms of contractarianism have succeeded in attaining the degree of generality required to fulfill these conditions. [27] The notion of a "contract" or covenant admits of an infinite possibility of arrangements, each of which exhibits certain determinate generic features and legitimate claims of universality. Yet contracts are "constructed" in a sense by those agents whose interactions they constrain and prescribe. One can admit that there might be an inherent "logic" to such construction without claiming simultaneously that the constructs themselves are platonic forms, or represent immutable natural laws – let alone claiming that only one "legitimate contract" is possible!

The historical problem with social contact theory, even in its revival by John Rawls and Thomas Scanlon, is that substantive but ultimately conflicting and unsupportable claims are made regarding human nature (i.e., that agents are basically rational and self interested), as well as regarding the ontological priority of individuals over communities. That is to say, actual social contract *theorists* almost always seem to make ad hoc and unwarranted metaphysical assumptions about the nature of agents beyond what is required to establish the notion of a contract per se. Discussion then quickly diverges from the central question of the sorts of order that might be found legitimate within such constraints, to ancillary questions about whether, say, animals or humans deficient in higher reason for a variety of causes are given proper moral consideration under the conditions of this or that particular contract – or even, as with Hegel, whether the model of a "contract" captures the essentials of interrelatedness and organic totality that comprise human social and institutional interaction. Such issues are interesting, but hardly to the point.

We can avoid these sorts of digressions from the central issue by taking as our starting points only the highly general and abstract notions of order and agency. Given the apparent *fact* that there *are* such entities as agents in our actual experience (regardless or whether or not, on some occasions, "agents" comprise certain animal species, extraterrestrials, human beings lacking or having lost certain "normal" capacities, and the like), we would be led to ask not whether there were agents or whether agency is possible but rather what are the *necessary conditions* for this self-evident possibility of agency.

In the modal argument developed in Section II above, I suggested that systems of moral principles are forms of *order* and, further, that the constraint upon types of possible order with respect to moral agents is that each principle of order be such as *not* to be formally inconsistent with the possibility of agency or the activity of agents. It is possible to envision the formal construction from some original position or state of nature – or more realistically, the cultural evolution by trial and error in actual practice – of wide varieties of systems of such principles. Two normative criteria would apply to each such possible system.

First, as implied by the opening sentence of this paragraph, a *negative* criterion of the sort that would rule out such practices as slavery, torture, systematic deception and the like, and would account for why, despite wide historical and cultural separations, individuals and cultures have uniformly been led to disapprove of these practices as formally inconsistent with the possibility of agency.

Second, a positive criterion of consistency and coherence among the individual principles within each such system is evidently required. A principle of total nonintervention and noninterference among agents is wholly consistent with the most impoverished possiblility of agency, but it may nonetheless prove inconsistent with other principles that stress the fullest possibility of agency under reasonably normal circumstances – such as principles that emphasize the importance of the common good, or the cultivation of each agent's talents and abilities, or the importance of care and compassion for the aged, disabled or handicapped. None of these additional principles can in practice be acted on without violating the restrictions against intervention and interference. The practice of refusing to aid the needy may be compatible with a marginal exercise of agency under extreme general conditions of hardship and deprivation in a hostile natural environment, but it is inconsistent with the vastly increased possibilities of agency under more favorable natural conditions. It is thus possible to avoid harsh moral condemnation of societies living at the very margins of subsistence, without simultaneously engaging in the extraordinary fallacy of *recommending* these resultant mores to citizens of an affluent industrialized nation-state! It is likewise possible to learn valuable lessons of ecological interdependence from animal species in a state of nature where survival is a constant struggle, without wrongly inferring that our moral education as agents in rather different material circumstances should somehow proceed on the basis of these examples!

Thus, this "constructivist" approach to the formal (logical) origin and philosophical justification of moral principles is compatible with the fact of pluralism without advocating relativism. Indeed, as Kant himself anticipates the matter: "Multiplicity of rules and unity of principles is a demand of reason."[28] Systems of moral principles can be evaluated for internal consistency and coherence (libertarian individualist moralities do not fare as well as do systems of order that are cognizant of the requisite features of interdependence in a social setting, for example) as well as for the relative exclusion of principles and practices that are fundamentally incompatible with agency in any sense, as is the case with torture, slavery, and systematic deception or coercion generally.

Such normative standards, however, do not covertly produce a linear hierarchy or scale of forms on which our own cultural tradition conveniently is self-justified at the pinnacle: There is no moral "great chain of being." Rather, the possible forms of moral orderings that represent legitimate constraints upon agency may well form a lush and abundant tree with many branches. The relevant point is that, in this rush of tolerant cultural generosity, there are still grounds to detect and condemn (whether from within a society or without) a wolf among the sheep, or a holocaust society among the plausible candidates for a multifarious *koinonia*.

Moral principles themselves thus enjoy *no* ontological status whatever, any more than do triangles or the concept of "triangularity." They are rather, "constructs" in the same sense as are actual triangles or the analytic geometrical equations for triangles – or, more appropriately, in the same sense as detailed features of a specific language could formally be constructed upon the abstract principles of linguistic systems generally.

The ontological burden of proof is thus lifted from specific sets or systems of moral principles and vested elsewhere. Yet the normative status of such systems of principles as an answer to the general constraints is every bit as determinate and "objective" (i.e., intersubjective and cross-cultural) as are individual proven theorems in some coherent and internally consistent algebraic or geometrical system.

The initial question about "ontological status" has thus been pushed back from moral principles and systems of such to the prior feature of these highly generalized "constraints" that they are seen to obey. The difference is that, at this point, questions about the ontology of morality are shown to be of an identical kind to questions about the ontology of generic features of grammar, logic, or of the most fundamental features of mathematics.

There is some comfort, perhaps, at keeping such good company when it finally comes to examining the fundamental nature of things. The generic and foundational features of all four of these areas – morality included – exhibit at this level a high degree of what Goedel termed "irreducible self-reference," or what Heidegger, in quite another sense, termed "thrownness." Both phrases refer to conceptual or explanatory incompleteness; for finally, no reasons can be given internal to nature or history *why* these differing sets of formal conditions or constraints on human or rational activity are what they appear to be. It is possible that these different "senses of the world" do indeed lie outside the world and constitute ultimately a profound mystery. Or, it is equally likely that such foundational conditions and constraints reveal something irreducibly and stubbornly factual about reality itself – "facts" that could conceivably be otherwise but, for whatever reason, *are* as we happen to encounter them.

It is not unwarranted to speculate that the irreducible generic requirements of consistency discerned within otherwise varied systems of moral principles are themselves somehow dependent upon the nature of agents (or perhaps of "pure reason") per se. These generic conditions and constraints on the possibility of agency *could* thus be different if the agents themselves happened to be constituted in some manner other than they are. Indeed, we could possibly *imagine* other sorts of agents than those that we ourselves represent, but this imaginative act would turn out to be relatively devoid of specific content. We might in a similar vein imagine other forms of theoretical as well as practical reasoning, which would accordingly issue in other types of mathematical or logical principles; but we cannot *know* what these might resemble, let alone can we pattern our quantitative, scientific, or moral reasoning after such conjectures, nor still can we abandon conviction in the objective grounding of language or moral reasoning on the basis of such speculative hypotheses.

Are the features of agency and practical reasoning themselves irreducible givens, features of the fundamental nature of things, or are they (or might they be) otherwise? Given that they are what they are, mathematics and morality and systems of language are constrained to be what we encounter and perceive them to be, complete with the ability to distinguish and dismiss the illegitimate and inadequate. Unless we encounter (in sharp contrast with Kant's own amusing speculations) extra-terrestrial beings who can reason theoretically and quantitatively but nonetheless wholly unlike our human version of mathematical and logical reasoning, or who can reason about means and ends and carry out strategies of interactive behavior without constraints against cruelty and torture and injustice, then our confidence in the irreducible character of the foundations of morality must remain vindicated and unshaken. Indeed, in light of the foregoing analysis, it well may be the case that

Plato's confidence in the ultimate comparison between mathematics and the Good can be salvaged and shown to have some fundamental status in "the nature of things," without having to accept the dangerously authoritarian and limited implications of his own metaphysical account.

NOTES

1. My perspective on this problem has been deeply influenced by the recent work of John Rawls ["Kantian Constructivism in Moral Theory: The Dewey Lectures." *Journal of Philosophy*, 77, no. 9 (1980), pp. 515–572; and three unpublished lectures on "The Fact of Reason" in Kant's Second Critique] and of Onora O'Neill [*Acting on Principle* (New York: Columbia University Press, 1975); "Consistency in Action," *New Essays in Ethical Universalizability*, eds. Potter and Timmons (Dordrecht: D. Reidel, 1986); and an unpublished paper, "The Public Use of Reason"]. The present context of discussion (metaphysics) is quite different from, and perhaps alien to, their own interests.

2. *Majjhima-Nikaya*, Sutta 63.

3. For example, it is perhaps fitting irony that contemporary teachers of ethics must endure, as the current unreflective received opinions of their pupils in this subject, views that represented their intellectual predecessors' attempts to divest philosophy once and for all of this embarrassing lacuna by declaring morality equivalent to aesthetics and the question of any further status to moral principles purely nonsensical. It is all the more ironic that, on this one point, the opinions of hostile or indifferent students largely concur with those of professional colleagues in other academic disciplines, as well as with the perspective of the educated public generally. If prevailing cultural views of morality represent the assimilation of the philosophically inadequate metaethics of logical positivism, it is no less true that these cultural views point to the decided failure of John Dewey's ambitious and programmatic attempts earlier in this century to place science and morality on an equivalent footing.

4. For a catalogue of these rights and the recent history of their systematic violation, see Henry Shue, *Basic Rights* (Princeton, N. J.: Princeton University Press, 1980). For a broader summary and philosophical analysis of the foregoing points, see Onora O'Neill, *Faces of Hunger: An Essay on Poverty, Justice and Development* (London: G. Allan & Unwin, 1985).

5. Alfred North Whitehead, *Process and Reality* (New York: Macmillan, 1929), p. 4.

6. Thomas Kuhn identified such a process as the basis for substantial shifts in the prevailing worldviews and disciplinary assumptions that characterize the enterprise of what he terms "normal science." Cf. *The Structure of Scientific Revolutions* (Chicago: University of Chicago Press, 1962).

7. Here I have in mind specifically the following passages from *Tractatus Logico-Philosophicus* (London: Routledge & Kegan Paul, 1922): 6.341, 6.342, and the sections 6.4–6.421.
8. Cf. *The Language of Morals* (Oxford: Oxford University Press, 1952); see also *Freedom and Reason* (Oxford: The Clarendon Press, 1963) and *Applications of Moral Philosophy* (Berkeley: University of California Press, 1973).
9. G. E. M. Anscombe, "Modern Moral Philosophy," *Philosophy*, 33 (1958), pp. 1–19.
10. E.g., the respect for *jus in bello* principles of discrimination between combatants and noncombatants as well as of proportionality regarding the employment of military force by the Persian, as contrasted with the earlier Babylonian and Assyrian empires, seems to have been regarded as a major moral advance (as well as a policy reflecting extraordinary political acumen) by the nation-states and cultures affected by such policies.
11. Cf. Roderick Firth, "Ethical Absolutism and the Ideal Observer," *Philosophy and Phenomenological Research*, 12 (1952), pp. 317–345; and Thomas Nagel, *The Possibility of Altruism* (Oxford: Clarendon Press, 1970). The most far-reaching development of this position is found in John Rawls, *A Theory of Justice* (Cambridge, Ma: Harvard University Press, 1971): See especially pp. 260–263, the whole of Part One, and particularly ch. III on the analysis of the "original position" as a variation of social contract theory.
12. This remains the case, despite John Rawl's own recent disavowal of any metaphysical tendencies or intentions. At issue here are not the alleged psychological dispositions of certain authors but the logical presuppositions and implications of any intersubjective theory of justice. These issues cannot be gainsaid merely by authoritative fiat. Cf. Rawls, "Justice as Fairness: Political, Not Metaphysical," *Philosophy and Public Affairs*, 14, no. 3 (Summer 1985).
13. Nietzsche makes similar but highly tendentious charges against Kant's assumptions regarding "pure reason": cf. *On the Geneology of Morals*, Part I (sec. 13), Part II (sec. 6), and Part III (sec. 6, 11 and 12). Bernard Williams brings his own version of an indictment against the easy and uncritical presuppositions of most moral theory in *Ethics and the Limits of Philosophy* (Cambridge, Ma: Harvard University Press, 1985).
14. On the problematic status of Cartesian psychology, cf. Immanuel Kant, *Kritik der reinen Vernunft* (1781), pp. 367–405; on the "human nature/intentionality" question, see Kant's *Grundlegung*, ch. II (Prussian Academy edition, Berlin), pp. 406–412. Nagel, for example, privately concedes the possibility that the disinterested standpoint of "the universe in general" might just as well answer to Camus's description as his own and that there is no way ultimately to "know" or to justify philosophically the sort of universality in moral reasoning which he recommends.
15. Alan Donagan, *A Theory of Morality* (Chicago: University of Chicago Press, 1977), p. xv.
16. Two human individuals are observed to act in ways that involve selection of strategies, estimation of outcomes, deliberation, and choice. One appar-

ently does so "intuitively," or on the basis of some deep emotional sensitivity. The second can, under cross-examination, elaborate a careful pattern of calculative rationality. On the minimalist and nonexclusivist criteria I am recommending, both activities are evidence of "practical reasoning" and both individuals are agents. More intriguingly, a female bird may feign a broken wing to distract predators from its nest. To dismiss such an act as "mere instinct" seems to me to beg the substantial questions of agency and moral considerability, and indeed to propose an unwarranted judgment in terms of (in this case, the supposed *absence* of) inferred mental states rather than the directly observable features and consequences of the activity of the entity in question. On my minimalist criteria, it is *possible* to allow that such activity is a case of practical reasoning and that the bird is an agent. More importantly, it is not possible to *dismiss* my approach, as is often done with Rawls's or Donagan's, on the grounds that my approach is insensitive to such observations and questions. [I am grateful to Steven F. Sapontzis for a useful discussion of these issues. Cf. his thoughtful analysis "Are Animals Moral Beings?" *American Philosophical Quarterly,* 17, no. 1 (January 1980), pp. 45–52.]

17. Cf. Kant, *Kritik der praktischen Vernunft* (1788); vol. V in the Prussian Academy edition, pp. 4–6, 31–32.

18. Cf. Onora O'Neill, *Acting on Principle* (New York: Columbia University Press, 1975); "Consistency in Action," *New Essays of Ethical Universalizability,* eds. Potter and Timmons (Dordrecht: D. Reidel, 1986).

19. John Rawls has termed this the "CI-procedure": cf. his 1980 Dewey Lectures at Columbia University [*Journal of Philosophy,* 77/9 (September, 1980)]; and more recently "The Fact of Reason: 3 Lectures" [unpublished; given at Harvard University and elsewhere over the past several years].

20. I have deliberately linked Kant's approach with the recent and similar attempts by Alan Gewirth to derive a foundational principle of "generic consistency" on types and systems of agent-constraints that would ground a theory of morality in general – and in particular, a theory of inviolable human rights: cf. *Reason and Morality* (Chicago: University of Chicago Press, 1978); *Human Rights: Essays on Justification and Applications* (Chicago: University of Chicago Press, 1982); and "Economic Rights," *Logos,* 6 (1985).

21. Kant, ch. I of Grundlegung; Sissela Bok, *Lying: Moral Choice in Public and Private Life* (New York: Pantheon Books, 1978).

22. Kant discusses his novel distinction of the public and private sphere in the essay, "What is Enlightenment" (1784).

23. Cf. Whitehead, *Science and the Modern World* (New York: Macmillan, 1925), pp. 228ff.

24. Plato held such views regarding the ontological status of the forms of justice and the summum bonum. Such perspectives infuse medieval realism and many (but by no means all!) religious systems of morality that have been deeply influenced in other ways by Platonism and natural law theory. West Asian religious-moral codes – those of Zoroastrianism, Judaism, Christian-

ity, and Islam – are the most familiar and specific examples of religious traditions that give an ontological grounding to moral law either as an *attribute* of that ultimate reality that is named "God," or even (in Zoroastrianism) as the necessary *ground* of that reality. Taoist critics in essence accuse their Confucianist opponents of an attitude with regard to ritual that is similar to moral Platonism. By contrast, this "ontology of moral principles" is not found, for example, in the Code of Manu, which is the sole test of orthodoxy in Hinduism: For according to Krisna in the *Bhagavand-Gita*, the provisions of this code are in an ultimate sense wholly arbitrary with respect to the true nature of things.

25. Garrett Hardin offers this assessment of altruistic behavior, and, on the grounds of its inevitable consequent elimination, finds no reason to consider it significant in the evaluation of human behavior. See his comments in "Lifeboat Ethics: the Case against Helping the Poor," *Psychology Today* (September, 1974), and also in his more systematic statement of this view "Carrying Capacity as an Ethical Concept," *Lifeboat Ethics*, eds. George R. Lucas and Thomas Ogletree (New York: Harper & Row, 1976), pp. 120–137.

26. Cf. Robert C. Neville, "Hegel and Whitehead on Totality: the Failure of a Conception of System," *Hegel and Whitehead: Contemporary Perspectives on Systematic Philosophy*, ed. George R. Lucas, Jr. (Albany, N.Y.: State University of New York Press, 1985); cf. Neville, *Reconstruction of Thinking* (SUNY Press, 1982), and his essay below. David L. Hall argues for pluralism against universalism in conceptions of human reasoning and cultural order in, *Eros and Irony: A Prelude to Philosophical Anarchism* (SUNY Press, 1982).

27. Cf. Thomas Scanlon, "Contractualism and Utilitarianism," *Utilitarianism and Beyond*, eds. Amartya Sen and Bernard Williams (Cambridge: Cambridge University Press, 1982), pp. 103–128.

28. Kant, *Kritik der reinen Vernunft* (1781), p. 305.

William M. Sullivan

The Civilizing of Enterprise: A. N. Whitehead's Critique of Economic Individualism Reassessed

I. The Revival of the Entrepreneurial Ideal

"Success," according to a cover of *Esquire* magazine in the spring of 1985, "is the religion of the 80s." At the same time, President Reagan announced that this was "the age of the individual," the "age of the entrepreneur." There is little doubt that the past decade in America has been marked by a revival of the old ideal of the entrepreneur, now presented as a moral hero, a selfless benefactor of society at large.[1] Only, unlike the previous great wave of American enthusiasm for entrepreneurship almost exactly a century ago, the current exhortations have a less promotional and more defensive tone about them. To extoll self-reliance and commercial initiative, figures such as George Gilder spend much energy arguing against the moral evil of a large-scale, paternalistic government that saps the initiative of individuals. Yet one of the most popular books of the genre has been Lee Iacocca's *Autobiography*, a story whose context is entirely that of massive corporations and in which timely governmental aid is a necessary means to its happy ending.[2]

The appeal of tales of successful entrepreneurship is akin to the appeal of the Western and the detective story. In both, the courageous, self-reliant individual challenges overwhelming odds and, often, oppressive tyranny to vindicate the value of fair play and initiative. But the hero of the Western, like the great detective, is rarely an ordinary citizen, and typically the story ends with its hero feeling as much an outsider to his society as he was at the beginning. Like these fictional heroes, the great entrepreneurs of legend remain somehow outside many of the usual bonds of social life. The familiar storyline tells us that the heroic traits of the founders of great enterprises, such as Henry Ford, do not survive the first generation, so that the regularizing of a great business, like the taming of the West, is really the beginning of the end of moral virtue. Settled, "civilized" life is viewed with ambivalence. It is the guarantor of safety and comfort, but at the same time its comfort tempts the individual to passivity and dependence on frequently corrupt successors of the founder. Thus the stage is set for the arrival of the next hero who will reinvigorate the moral energy of the frontier, at least for a time. Given this kind of cultural backdrop, it is not surprising that the heroics of business success have until very recently been considered by most an exclusively masculine achievement.

Yet there is something wistful about evocations of this archtypal story of entrepreneurship in the 1980s. After all, the United States is not, and has not for a long time been, a nation of self-reliant business people. Fewer that 16% of Americans are self-employed; the great bulk of our citizens are employed by big businesses, either directly or through myriad franchise chains and affiliates.[3] Besides, none of the leading competitor nations in Europe or East Asia operate on entrepreneurial lines. The economic development of those nations has been heavily directed by central banks and governments rather than by the free-wheeling practices of business entrepreneurs.[4] Thus, in the call to renew our national faith in self-reliant economic individualism one can hear the wish to return America to an idealized vision of a past conceived as prosperous, benign, and free from complex organizations; above all, free of Big Government. Can one not also hear in this call a deep suspicion of the entanglements of social complexity, and so a fear of being engulfed by a world grown too dense and too near?

Trying to reinvigorate American entrepreneurship, then, is a more complex task than some of its proponents may think. It is, after all, a recurrent effort in American history, and one so recurrent across decades as to suggest that it is an articulation of a widespread sentiment. The ideal entrepreneur is both idealistic and practically shrewd, fervor-driven and ingenious. The ideal derives from the venerable Old World wish to acquire an "independency" of sufficient holdings to maintain a dignified and independent household, an ideal that the American Revolution placed at the center of general aspiration.[5] Thus, economic enterprise was invested with republican moral meaning to produce the kind of independent yet community-minded citizens Jefferson hoped for and Alexis de Tocqueville thought he encountered in the nineteenth century rural and small-town United States.

However, that earlier American pattern was changed almost beyond recognition by the stressful transformation of American life that took place in those pivotal decades on both sides of the turn of this century. During most of the nineteenth century, American economic life was small-scale, and the majority of working people – themselves largely white males – were also "businessmen," entrepreneurs in the market for themselves. But the age of the great entrepreneurs changed the nature and scale of business so much that by the century's end most working people had become employees dependent on the "labor market." To date, this change has proven irreversible.

II The Pragmatic Philosopher's Critique of Enterprise

One way to begin recovering the context for the current interest in entrepreneurship is to recall that public discourse in the United States has, since the agitation for independence from Britain, concerned itself with the balance between individual freedom and the general welfare. First, preaching and theology bore the central burden of this effort at public moral argument, partly transformed as well as supplemented by an increasingly secular and scientific educated opinion. Then, about the beginning of this century, with the institutionalizing of the scientific ideal in new research universities, the philosophy of pragmatism entered the public forum, allied with the new social sciences.[6] A chief concern of this new philosophy was to bring together a scientific tone of mind with moral concerns about the great changes in American life then taking place. Thinkers as diverse as Josiah Royce, William James, John Dewey, and the British-born Alfred North Whitehead sought to shape public understanding of practical issues by enlarging the accepted frame of reference. They sought above all to articulate ways to creatively play off the spirit of freedom and innovation against the need for interconnection, community, and loyalty. Perhaps the tone and vision of that era in American philosophy was summed up by Whitehead's admonition that "'The problem is not how to produce great men, but how to produce great societies. The great society will put up the men for the occasions.'"[7]

    In the early decades of the century, John Dewey advocated the application of scientific methods to practical social life. However, he did not speak only from within an academic specialization simply to other specialists. In an important sense, John Dewey was a public philosopher, indeed a public figure, continuing the traditional role of cultural leadership that had been the special calling of the clergy. Moreover, Dewey was of the party of reform before the First World War, and after the national mood turned to embrace the corporate consumer capitalism that had emerged in strength by 1920, Dewey remained its outspoken critic. Dewey's dissent from the postwar settlement in America set the tone for philosophy's public role as essentially constructive criticism, persuading toward "reconstruction," a role that continued until just before the Second World War.

Dewey's analysis of the shortcomings of the American economic order during the 1920s and 1930s sheds useful light on the current revival of the entrepreneurial spirit. Essentially, Dewey argued that the lionizing of business enterprise that ruled the culture of the 1920s was simple-minded and short-sighted. (To many contemporaries, the Depression seemed to vindicate Dewey's analysis.) In *The Public And Its Problems* in 1927, and even more pointedly in *Individualism: Old and New* in 1929, Dewey characterized the American economy as precarious. Pervasive, disruptive technological change guided only by the blind market force of profit maximization spread a pervasive undercurrent of insecurity. This insecurity in turn fed both a wild appetite for consumption and an anxious drive toward competitive self-aggrandisement. As Dewey saw it, the Roaring Twenties were marked by worry and restlessness even for the prosperous.[8] All this was fed by an anachronistic and destructive moral individualism that the industrial order had liberated from its old restraints only to turn loose in a competitive scramble that undercut the aim at "wholeness which is urged as the essence of religion." But for Dewey, "the attempt to cultivate it (wholeness) first in individuals and then extend it to form an organically unified society is fantasy." The only way to bring active individual striving together with a self-sustaining social order would be "membership in a society which had attained a degree of unity."[9] Dewey sought to adapt the methods of natural science to the purposes of a social intelligence conceived as at once moral, aesthetic, and technical. He thought Americans could create a society in which the moral impetus of individual enterprise would be expressed "through personal participation in the development of a shared culture."[10]

It was during the 1920s that Dewey was joined as an exponent of a public philosophy of social and moral reconstruction by the recently transplanted British philosopher, Alfred North Whitehead. Like Dewey, Whitehead was a member of the generation who reached maturity before 1914. As an Englishman, Whitehead was heir to the British tradition of reform associated with the social liberalism of T. H. Green, L. T. Hobhouse, and the pre-war Liberal Party. While Whitehead saw himself primarily as a speculative philosopher in the grand tradition rather than as a social advocate, his lectures and publications during the 1920s were consciously crafted with an approving eye on Dewey. Whitehead announced his own work as allied to Dewey's thought and described himself as trying "to rescue (it) . . . from the charge of anti-intellectualism, which rightly or wrongly has been associated with it."[11] Despite differences in approach, Whitehead's writings embodied and elaborated Dewey's claim that moral theory is "all one with moral insight, and moral insight is the recognition of the relationships at hand."[12] Whitehead and Dewey shared, to different degrees, an Anglo-American liberal spirit of reform that associated the good of the nation with democracy and social justice.

III. Whitehead's Philosophy As Critical Vision

Writing in the economic boom of the 1920s, Alfred North Whitehead concluded his Lowell Lectures with an essay on "Requisites for Social Progress." Revised and expanded as *Science And The Modern World* in 1925, these lectures assessed the larger cultural meaning of what Whitehead called the three-century epoch of modern science. He there put forward the claim that primacy of the notion of "matter" as occupying a uniform space had proven finally inadequate as a way of making sense of the world opened up by twentieth century scientific discovery.

Whitehead argued that as a guiding metaphor for popular understanding the scheme of "scientific materialism" also had deleterious practical effects, particularly in the realm of economic life. The seventeenth century philosophers' separation of active mind from passive matter oversimplified things dangerously. It had passed into popular understanding, where it suggested a legitimating metaphor for purely self-concerned behavior and focused attention exclusively on the utilitarian aspects of the natural and social environment. "The doctrine of minds as independent substances," Whitehead wrote, "leads directly not merely to private worlds of experience but also to private worlds of morals." The cruelty and social destructiveness of nineteenth century industrialization were logical effects of a moral vision in which "self-respect, and the making the most of your own opportunities" occupied the central position.[13]

Thus, the long-term consequences of early modern mechanistic science had been to increase human control over natural processes, but only at the price of ignoring "the true relation of each organism to its environment," while reinforcing "the habit of ignoring the intrinsic worth of the environment."[14] Not surprisingly, Whitehead judged modern business civilization as an instance of these same imbalances, in which the economic actor, the entrepreneur, was conceived as related to the social world only mechanistically through the workings of the market. Indeed, Whitehead saw the moral and social individualism of Adam Smith's political economy as of a piece with the atomistic mechanism of Newton's era. In opposition to that long-dominant cosmology, Whitehead put forward a new synthetic vision, centered on the ideas of organism and interconnection.

Thus, Whitehead's critique of economic individualism is internally related to his overall speculative enterprise. Like Dewey's pragmatism, Whitehead's process philosophy, which he termed "the philosophy of organism," was an effort to rethink the relation of individuals to the social and cultural matrix within which they live. This was an essentially ecological conception of both the natural and the social world. It took as its starting point the historical dissociation, which began with the Enlightenment, between scientific culture and the moral, religious, and aesthetic dimensions of life. Modern social and intellectual life has long been predicated on this dissociation, and yet, Whitehead thought, twentieth century scientific and cultural experience made the reality of interconnection and interdependence undeniable. But once this situation had been understood, the chief intellectual task became reconceiving and redescribing contemporary experience and practice in ways that illuminated interdependence and focused attention on it. In brief, this was the project Whitehead identified as the task of philosophy: to give the best account possible of how things hold together, and to do it in such a way as to stir and guide action.[15]

For this reason, Whitehead's speculative philosophy took the form of a search for a new language to reunite the "two cultures" later described by C. P. Snow. This philosophy was conceived as a general description sensitive to the historical, practical, and aesthetics awareness of "literary intellectuals," yet carefully defined with something of the rigor of scientific discourse. But the very conception of this project means that this kind of philosophy had to break with a key feature of the modern philosophical discourse since Descartes and Locke: the demand that philosophy serve as a cognitive foundation for other "special" scientific disciplines. Instead, Whitehead proposed his philosophy as a speculative, comprehensive hypothesis subject to further revision.[16] Part of the foundationalist enterprise was the further demand that philosophy be intelligible in a self-contained manner, as exemplified in the quest for self-evident truths. But, as Robert Neville has observed, Whitehead's kind of philosophy "cannot be intelligible in a self-contained manner because it necessarily makes external reference to the fields it envisions and unifies, being both informed by them and informing them."[17] Such a conception of philosophy both crucially depends upon a dialogue among a wider range of participants than disciplinary specialists and aims to bring such a public into being.

However, constituting, or perhaps reconstituting, this conception of a literate, actively engaged public was, by the time of Whitehead's writing, a very difficult task. Whitehead's own understanding of the technological society already in place in the United States by the 1920s saw the conditions of modern life as posing a formidable problem. The kind of philosophic vision he was developing had as its practical premise an active public life that the epochal economic and social transformation of modern capitalism had rendered highly problematical.

The crucial determining feature of modern societies, according to Whitehead, has been their capacity for ceaseless scientific and technological innovation. He traced this capacity to a new social formation, "the discovery of the method of training professionals, who specialize in particular regions of thought and thereby progressively add to the sum of knowledge within their respective limitations of subject."[18] The long-term effect of this accelerating rate of progress would be to render "the fixed person, with fixed duties, who in older societies was such a god-send, in the future a public danger."

Certainly this essentially liberal conception of progress through science, while it echoes Condorcet, was also a reading of the importance of the new professional and managerial division of labor in twentieth century industrial society. Whitehead drew attention to the costs this process was exacting from individuals and community life. After all, he noted, the key to this new technical order is thinking methodologically, a habit of mind Whitehead called thinking in a groove. "The groove prevents straying across country . . . But there is no groove of abstractions which is adequate for the comprehension of human life." The danger is that the habits of mind developed by specialized training will overwhelm and distort awareness of the larger, one might say ecological, order of connections and balances, thereby narrowing attention and vision.

Given the cultural climate of individualism strong in a business civilization, the new social forms of technological society seemed to Whitehead to be leading to the belief that there were "not merely private worlds of experience but also private worlds of morals" so that "the moral intuitions can be held to apply only to the strictly private world of psychological experience." Thus, despite the increase of a kind of technical rationality, reason as a feature of social and political life was actually weakening.

The leading intellects lack balance. They see this set of circumstances or that set; but not both sets together. The task of
coordination is left to those who lack either the force or the
character to succeed in some definite career. In short, the
specialized functions of the community are performed better and
more progressively, but the generalized direction lacks vision.[19]

Finally, he concluded that achieving a "directive wisdom" appropriate to
modern societies would be one of the "most useful discoveries for the
immediate future." But, then, what was to be done?

Addressing the Harvard Business School on its twenty-fifth anniver-
sary in 1933, Whitehead told his audience that the Depression showed
the insufficiency of the corporate capitalist organization of society. The
root of the problem was its neglect of the larger concerns of human social
ecology as a whole. His analysis was brief and in outline not very different from Dewey's argument a few years earlier in *Individualism: Old
And New*. Whitehead was strongly critical of both the specialized
organization of work and the tendency of mass production and advertising to "canalize the aesthetic enjoyments of the population," a theme
reminiscent of Aldous Huxley's *Brave New World*.[20] The Depression, said
Whitehead, demanded "economic statesmanship" of a high order to sur-
mount the current breakdown, above all to overcome unemployment.
But this would require that the "great commercial corporations . . .
should enlarge the scope of their activity . . . to interweave in their
organizations individual craftsmanship operating upon the products of
their mass production."[21] Where Whitehead's vision was once again
ecological, with an invocation of John Ruskin's call to the civilizing and
liberating effects of craft and artisanship. Whitehead continued to try to
reintegrate and balance. He acknowledged that his proposals would
"destroy much of the sweet simplicity of modern business policy which
fastens its attention solely on one aspect of our complex human nature,"
but only to achieve a greater degree of social development by "stabilizing
the popular requirements and widening the area of useful occupations."[22]
For despite his criticisms, Whitehead thought that modern society would
remain a technical and specialized one. The issue was how to civilize it.
His answer was largely to appeal eloquently for "statemanship" and
"education." Yet his liberal confidence that somehow good sense would
prevail kept Whitehead from seriously addressing the difficult political
problems raised by both his analysis and his vision.

IV The Limits of Philosophy As Cultural Vision.

The great strength of Whitehead's philosophy of organism was its critique of the assumptions of empiricist science and atomistic individualism. By arguing that these premises no longer made sense of the
world of twentieth century natural science, Whitehead cleared the
ground for his positive statement that both physical and human reality
was better viewed in an "ecological" way. In human affairs, this recovery
of the notion of "internal relations" among entities meant that individuals
were best understood as sharing with others in various matrices of inter-
connectedness. Thus, each of us stands not simply over against others,
as the old individualist culture would have it, but rather with others in
as much as they are part of who we are by virtue of our common participation in shared concerns. Like Dewey and George Herbert Mead,
Whitehead argues for the self as a social entity. The metaphor of
organism and environment, like Aristotelian logic of whole and part,
enabled Whitehead to highlight the overriding dependence of all individual flourishing on the maintenance of a stable, though changing, matrix
of interdependence.

Yet this ecological concern was not opposed to historical change.
Like Dewey, Whitehead believed in progress and wanted to help direct
and humanize the dynamism of modern societies. He hoped that
democracy would serve as the great civilizing ideal in the technological
age in somewhat the same way Christianity had civilized the barbarians
after the collapse of classical culture. Science, the market, and
technology were to be purified of their destructive potentials and given
meaning by an organized effort to bring them into a coherent social and
cultural order. Concretely, Whitehead admired Elton Mayo, on the faculty of the Harvard Business School during the 1920s and 1930s, for his
efforts to reconstitute a moral community under industrial conditions
through reorganizing factories into small production groups. This
counter-Taylorist conception of industrial organization recalled for
Whitehead John Ruskin and William Morris, with their hopes for reconstituting a polity of interdependent artisans.

Thus, Whitehead's criticism of the "rugged individualism" of the nineteenth century entrepreneur was linked to this positive program of
reuniting the scientific, moral, and aesthetic dimensions of modern
experience, the three separate spheres of Kantian philosophy, in a new
aesthetic teleology of the whole. Whitehead looked to the aesthetic order
of whole and part, as in the metaphor of organism, to reunite the scien-

tific and "humanistic" forms of intelligence. In this he resembled contemporaries such as the young Lewis Mumford who, in 1924, wrote that "
. . . our concern with physical utilities and with commercial values is something more than an abstract defect in our philosophy. On the contrary, it seems to inhere in the dominant occupations of the country, and it is less to be overcome by moralizing and exhortation than to be grown out of, by taking pains to provide for the ascendency and renewal of the more humane occupations."[23] In the end, it seems Whitehead looked to the attractive power of his synthetic vision to persuade leaders and "statesmen" in the various specialized fields of modern endeavour, such as Elton Mayo, to work toward weaving the "specialized functions of the community" into a social order of moral and aesthetic coherence.

The ecological conception of self and society certainly gave a sense of direction and comfort to those who felt the attraction of this goal, but according to Whitehead's own theory, persons only come to share understandings by becoming genuine partners in a common concern. American society could have gone in that direction only by deliberate, considered actions, which means that the cultural program could only have been actualized by effectively entering the realm of politics. But in its larger aims, Whitehead's project failed. The two cultures of literary and scientific intellectuals have grown further apart in the decades since his death just after the Second World War, while both "cultures" have developed a great distance from the public at large. Perhaps most tellingly, process philosophy itself, like pragmatism, has become one more subspecialization within the highly professionalized field of academic philosophy. And as to its impact on public discussion about economic life, Whitehead's few essays on the subject never made much lasting impact.

American society has evolved since the 1930s in ways very different from the ways Whitehead or Dewey or Mumford had hoped it would. Whitehead's concern about the suppression of the sense of craftsmanship in work was not so much resolved after the U.S. economy emerged from the Depression via the Second World War, as it was displaced for many by the attractions of a new suburban, consumer society. The new affluence of this society was made available by war-generated technological advances and government-financed social investments that aided a corporate-labor *detente*. As long as the nation maintained its economic and military world preeminence, steady economic growth seemed to obviate the need for more fundamental economic reorganization. Even the great waves of social unrest that broke over the "affluent society" during the 1960s concerned the inclusion of denied minorities in the general prosperity. It took the faltering of the postwar economic arrangements during the 1970s to place the basics of that postwar settlement more or less on the national agenda. Enter, at this point, the entrepreneur *redivives*.

In this historical perspective, the upsurge of entrepreneurial faith appears as an effort at something like revitalizing business culture. The new entrepreneur, whether a Lee Iacocca (or John DeLorean) or a high-tech innovator, is above all a figure who breaks out of the hidebound, overly organized environment of American corporate life to conquer new markets and expand the frontiers of enterprise. Where conventional economic institutions have lost ground to foreign competitors or failed to respond to new challenges, the new entrepreneur proves again the capacity of Yankee ingenuity to succeed competitively. There is in this the Nietzschean tone of human will redeeming itself against dead mechanism. Thus, for George Gilder, the entrepreneur is a generous, fructifying figure, providing needed goods and services for the community, but he is also a paradigm of energetic self-assertion who abashes the lazy herd – and returns women to their proper place!

The case for revived entrepreneurship is, then, couched in old American moral terms much of the time: industry versus sloth, self-reliance versus servile dependence. Yet there is another, far from comforting, side to the entrepreneurial revival, one which has affinities with the Social Darwinian view of nature as struggle for survival that helped justify the deeds of the turn-of-the-century commercial empire builders. Against the tidy, Newtonian equilibrium assumptions of classical and neoclassical economic theory, which is tacitly assumed by much of the entrepreneurial literature, there is the conception of economic development put forward by Joseph Schumpeter and, more recently, by Mancur Olson. According to this view, the logic of market behavior drives in a Hobbesian direction as entrepreneurs struggle to dominate and control markets, a process that ultimately results in oligopoly and rigidity. Economic advance comes in periods of creative destruction when old formations of capital are by-passed and destroyed by new technological advances. These are the moments of the entrepreneurs. But their role is temporary and self-limiting, as they pursue their self-interest in struggling to control, and so rigidify, the new markets. The Nietzschean resonance here is with the theme of the eternal return of the same rather than the triumph of the will.

Only the current entrepreneurial revival is not a return of the same. The structural realities of the world economic system have changed dramatically from the situation of the 1950s, let alone 1900. No national economy, not even our own, can operate independently of the larger environment, and all economies today are heavily dependent upon governmental involvement in the form of subsidy, planning, or direct control. Even President Reagan's favorite success story, the entrepreneurs of Silicon Valley, is the direct result of federal development of the microchip through the space program, and of massive federal spending on scientific education and research. The moral evocation of self-reliant enterprise, by itself, can hardly be expected to resolve the problems of the American economy today. These problems are rooted in the complex reality of the modern world system of international investment and production. But it is precisely the social complexity of interdependence and large-scale institutions that American culture has had great difficulty making moral sense of beyond the evocation of the small community and the self-reliant hero of enterprise.

V. An Opening Toward A New Public Philosophy

One might venture that Whitehead was in large part correct, that the problem is at basis a lack of cultural vision, but that this vision must in turn become embodied in institutional and political life. The problem with the entrepreneurial ideal is its incompleteness. It conceives the self alone as the source of energy and misconceives the ecology of human interconnection as suffocating except when negotiated in terms of self-interest. What is missing is a coherent moral whole that could sustain and give a shared meaning to enterprise. The pathos of the valorization of the entrepreneur, to the exclusion of the larger institutional and social context, is the inability of this project to recover for modern technological life the cognitive and moral coherence necessary for active citizenship. Whitehead's social vision, like Dewey's, helps us see better what has been the cognitive price of progress, but also what needs to be recovered or reconstructed. But if Whitehead and Dewey were correct, the most urgent need is the re-creation amid the economic and social conditions of our time of an active public, together with the institutions and the moral ecology that can sustain it.

To take just one example of what is an enormous task, consider the relation between citizenship and professional specialization, which Whitehead saw as the crux of the modern problem. Particularly as large areas of social life have been brought under the guidance of specialized agencies and business management itself has become increasingly professionalized, the inteconnection between culture and politics has become more apparent.

Part of the story of the fading of Dewey's vision of philosophy was the increasing vogue of the notion that knowledge about social matters could be made technically precise and value-neutral on the model of natural sciences. A version of this notion of technical rationality came after the Second World War to dominate virtually all the areas of professional practice. But since its era of ascendancy in the 1950s and 1960s, confidence in this model of practice has entered a period of increasing crisis, as its claim to "solve" managerial and social problems in a purely technical manner has proven empty.[24] In ways that would have heartened Whitehead and Elton Mayo, the theory and teaching of management has been forced to give conscious attention to the social nexus of managerial practice, which the model of technical rationality had tried to supersede. Not surprisingly, this deflation of the claims of technical expertise has created new problems of self-definition for managers.

The technical model of professional practice defined the manager as an expert in the application of specific techniques to problems of resource and personnel allocation and production within complex organizations. The manager was thought to be a sort of social engineer, deploying value-neutral techniques to facilitate the achievement of agreed-upon ends. The manager as such stood outside discussions of the purposes of the organization he or she served. But the collapse of confidence in the model of technical rationality has broken down the basic assumption of cognitive and moral distance between the manager and the managed, suddenly muddying the clarity of the managerial task by forcing moral terms such as trust and responsibility into discussions of managerial effectiveness. Of course, the force of the bottom line still operates, but the manager now must contend as well with forming consensus, leading a "team," and other activities traditionally more associated with politics than business. Certainly, this recent turn toward the "human," – that is, the moral and political – aspects of organizational life is of a piece with the switch from the economy conceived as a mechanism driven by the anti-heroic consumer to seeing it as the field in which the entrepreneur can exhibit moral courage. Fitfully, American culture seems to be rediscovering the practical basis of its institutions and its techniques, even if as yet only selectively.

In this dramatically changed context, the conception of the professional manager as the detached expert no longer rings true. The result is the blurring of boundaries between the manager's technical competence and his or her moral and political situation. Suddenly, the professional needs to consider responsibility in a wider, more complex context. What is his responsibility to his organization, his subordinates, and what does he contribute to the community as a whole? These are no longer the questions of the technician. They are the animating concerns of the citizen. One consequence of this unsettling situation is the attempt to make the idealized entrepreneur the new role model for the manager. This approach has been proposed by a variety of writers in the business area.[25] The entrepreneurial model implicitly answers the questions of contribution and responsibility by urging the manager to conceive his situation in marketing terms. Yet here the simplistic moral vision of entrepreneurship runs up against the structural realities of modern conditions of work. These more and more demand team work and group loyalty, particularly in the innovative industries, rather than the old entrepreneurial competitiveness or the conformity of the "organization man."[26] The entrepreneurial ideal simply is not adequate, cognitively or morally, to the dimensions of the current managerial crisis. But, then, what is? Recognition of this problem has intensified the long-developing merger of the techniques of therapeutic management of the psyche with managment of "things." Yet that is not the only alternative.

Perhaps this is the first moment in the past half-century when there is an opening in American culture for reconstituting a genuinely democratic public life. The very crisis of technical rationality that has called up the entrepreneurial ideal may also hold the potential for a recovery of the moral dimension of economic life. The ecological metaphor of Whitehead may be our best evocation of that sense.[27] To stay with the example of professional, managerial practice, the breakdown of the division between expertise and conduct is creating a kind of moral vacuum, and might it not be conceivable to fill this vacuum by reappropriating the ethical meaning of professional life? This would mean recovering the notion of a profession as a public trust, with responsibilities for public welfare. In turn, such a reappropriation would mean reorganizing the conduct of, in this instance, management, so that it could play a consciously responsible public role. To do this would be to begin reorienting economic life away from the private corporate form that has been dominant during this century, toward one more consciously responsive to the requirements of an actively democratic society. We might call such a direction economic democracy.[28]

NOTES

1. See George Gilder's *Wealth and Poverty* (New York: Basic Books, 1981). Gilder's book was a big seller in the early 1980's.
2. Lee Iacocca, *Iacocca: An Autobiography* (New York: Bantam Books, 1985).
3. See James Oliver Robertson, *America's Business* (New York: Hill and Wang, 1985), pp. 241–245.

4. See Robert B. Reich, *The Next American Frontier* (New York: Times Books, 1983).
5. Robertson, *America's Business*, pp. 46–47.
6. See Bruce Kuklick, *Churchmen And Philosophers: From Jonathan Edwards To John Dewey* (New Haven: Yale University Press, 1985).
7. Alfred North Whitehead, *Science And The Modern World* (New York: Free Press, Macmillan, 1967, original 1925), p. 205. See also John E. Smith, *The Spirit of American Philosophy* (New York: Oxford University Press, 1963).
8. John Dewey, *Individualism: Old and New* (New York: Capricorn Books, 1962), esp. pp. 51–55.
9. Dewey, *Individualism*, p. 64.
10. Dewey, *Individualism*, p. 34.
11. Alfred North Whitehead, *Process And Reality: An Essay In Cosmology* (New York: Macmillan, 1929), p. vii.
12. John Dewey, "Moral Theory and Practice" in *Early Works Of John Dewey* (Carbondale: Southern Illinois University Press, 1972), Vol. 3, p. 94.
13. Alfred North Whitehead, *Science And The Modern World*, pp. 195–196.
14. Whitehead, *Science*, p. 196.
15. Whitehead's clearest discussions of these ideas are in the final chapter of *Science And The Modern World*, as cited; *Process And Reality*, as cited, Ch. 1; and the last chapter of *Modes Of Thought* (New York: Free Press, 1968; original, Macmillan, 1938).
16. Richard Rorty's *Philosophy And The Mirror of Nature* (Princeton: Princeton University Press, 1979) has argued that the "foundationalist" enterprise of modern philosophy is over, ending "philosophy" as such. However, Rorty, while lionizing Dewey, dismisses Whitehead as a metaphysician. Also see *Consequences Of Pragmatism* (Minneapolis: University of Minnesota Press, 1982), Ch. 4, 5 and 12. By contrast, Franklin I. Gamwell has argued that only a development of something like Whitehead's metaphysics can save Dewey's theory of valuation from fatal inconsistency. See *Beyond Preference: Liberal Theories Of Independent Associations* (Chicago: University of Chicago Press, 1984), pp. 119 ff.
17. Robert C. Neville, "Contributions and Limitations of Process Philosophy," p. 4, Invited Paper, American Philosophical Association, Eastern Division Meeting, Dec., 1984, unpublished.
18. Whitehead, *Science And The Modern World*. This and following quotations are from pp. 282–283.
19. Whitehead, *Science And The Modern World*.
20. Whitehead, "The Study Of The Past – Its Uses And Dangers," in *Science And Philosophy* (Paterson, N.J.: LIttlefield, Adams and Co., 1964), p. 168.
21. Whitehead, "Study," pp. 169–70.
22. Whitehead, "Study," p. 173.
23. Lewis Mumford, *Sticks And Stones: A Study In American Architecture And Civilization* (New York: Dover Publ., 1955, original 1924), p. 109.
24. See Donald Schön, *The Reflective Practitioner: Toward An Epistemology Of Practice* (New York: Basic Books, 1983).

25. See, among others, *In Search Of Excellence*, by Thomas J. Peters and Robert H. Waterman, Jr. (New York: Harper and Row, 1983).

26. See Michael Maccoby's social-psychological study of high-tech management in *The Gamesmen: The New Corporate Leaders* (New York: Simon and Schuster, 1976).

27. I introduced the term "moral ecology" to describe the matrix of human inter-relation ignored yet presupposed by individualistic and instrumental theories of action in *Reconstructing Public Philosophy* (Berkeley: University of California Press, 1982).

28. These themes are developed in more detail in a jointly authored work, *Habits Of The Heart: Individualism And Commitment In American Life*, by Robert N. Bellah, Richard Madsen, William M. Sullivan, Ann Swidler, and Steven M. Tipton (Berkeley: University of California Press, 1985).

Antonio T. de Nicolás

The First Metaphysics: Revisioning Plato

Now, here my dear Glaucon, is the whole risk
for a human being . . . And on this account
each one of us must, to the neglect of other
studies, above all see to it that he is a
seeker and a student of *that study* by which he
might be able to learn and *find out* who will
give him the capacity and the knowledge to
distinguish the good and the bad life, and
so everywhere and always *choose* the better
from among those that are possible . . .

                    Plato/Socrates/*Republic* 618b.

Introduction

Contemporary philosophers, regardless of the "style" of philosophy they
follow or their own personal dislike for metaphysics, have come to two
general agreements. First, some kind of systematization, therefore some
form of metaphysics, is inevitable. Second, this systematization includes
certain "necessary and sufficient" conditions. Besides these two general
agreements, or rather suspicions, about their own activity as
philosophers, there is not much else they agree on when it comes down
to the actual systematization of their own activity. For some, system
equals conceptual taxonomy; for others, contemplation of categories, the
uncovering of essences, the correct formulation of the *factual* information provided by the sciences; for still others, questioning why "there is
something, rather than nothing" (as if history had ever forgotten being,
or Being!). In sum, metaphysics is not only a philosophical problem, but
it is a problem that seems to have appeared in history rather suddenly
and without clear models to guide the philosopher in solving such a

problem. The return to Aristotle as the first metaphysician does not only not solve the problem but compounds it. The name "metaphysics" was added to what he wrote after his physics, and it is certainly problematic to take Aristotle as the finest exemplar of systematic philosophy. Furthermore, by the time Aristotle appeared on the scene, philosophy was already an autonomous activity and therefore already involved with some form of metaphysics or other.

The present paper is a shorter version of a recent study on imagining that I have just finished, which, though focusing on the kind of imagining Ignatius de Loyola practiced in the sixteenth century, paralleled, as an activity, the imaginings Plato describes in the *Republic*.[1] Here, as earlier, I follow the descriptive strategy of focusing on those acts that are "necessary and sufficient" to make decisions with justice, i.e., have the power of affecting a whole community. It is not my intention in this paper to solve the problem of metaphysics: just the contrary. My aim is primarily an invitation to tackle the problem from scratch, for, as I hopefully suggest in abundance, Plato and his whole project of Philosophy has been only partially attended to.

Peiraeus: The Acts Of The Mind

Where do philosophers go to do philosophy?

" I went down to Peiraeus . . ." says Plato, and with these enigmatic words[2] he launches the listener in the *Republic* and the generations of philosophers that followed into one of the most astonishing quests of the human spirit: philosophic wisdom. This philosophic wisdom, however, would be of such a kind as to be able to lead to decisions regarding the good life. The philosopher would be trained in such a manner that he/she could always and everywhere choose the better life from among those that are possible. In short, the general project of philosophic wisdom came down to a training in particular habits that would lead the philosopher to a habitual practice of "virtue." Philosophic wisdom as project meant also the visible aspect of performing "virtue by habit." The intelligible and the visible form the complete project of what philosophy was understood to be in the beginning of Western culture.

"I went down . . ." Socrates says, or even more accurately "down-went-I," and if *then* down-he-went, then *now* he must be "up," or is the writer neither "up" nor "down" but in a third unnamed place?[3] Does writing take place "up," "down," or in neither of the two places? If in neither place, then, where does philosophic writing take place?

"Peiraeus," answers Socrates. In the original Greek, the definitive article is missing. It does not say "the Peiraeus" but "Peiraeus," "the land
beyond," the land beyond the limits, not in Athens and "yet within the
defensive walls of Athens" (Bremer p. 3). "Peiraeus" is both in and not in
Athens, it is the place that gives common interests to the assembled
speakers; it is the writing and the margins, it is the whole page, and the
whole inner landscape of the philosopher.

As the narrative of the *Republic* develops, we find other clues that aid
us in the present study. In Book Five of the Republic we discover that
the young people conspired to hold Socrates with them to make him talk.
Socrates agreed to this "robbery" and in this manner a "community" of
speakers is formed. Polemarchus, Adeimantus, Glaucon, and even
Thrasymachus agree to be part of this community. The same individuals
with such diverse interests as they appeared to have in the earlier Books
of the *Republic*, in particular Book One, by agreeing now, in Book Five
to form a community, bring a new beginning to the discussion of justice.
The new beginning will appear in Book Six with the "divided line," subsequently "the cave," and finally the "journey of Er." But without this community, Socrates' vision "up there" would have never become public
domain.

The spaces of discourse in the *Republic* keep shifting as the "community" moves. Each space provides diverse communication systems,
diverse spectations on the listeners and participants, diverse intellectual
activities, diverse intelligibilities, and diverse visibilities or lack of them.
The spaces of these discourses are all in "Peiraeus," first in what seems
to be Polemarchus's home. This is the space where Polemarchus joins
Socrates in a communal relationship, as later on do the others. Polemarchus is the first to join in community with the project of Socrates
(Bremer p. 14.). He is also the one responsible for initiating the "robbery"
of Socrates through his slave and assumes direct and public responsibility for Socrates' arrest. As the dialogue proceeds, Polemarchus comes
from "far off" to only a "little distance from Socrates," (Bremer p. 14). In
the end, he is even ready to let Socrates go, though Socrates is then ready
to stay.

What begins as the space of "Peiraeus," becomes Polemarchus's
home, the divided line, the cave, Hades, and the journey of Er as the
Republic unfolds. Each space demands a different orientation in the
listener and the participants, each space commands a new language,
each language a new and different technology. Each language and each
technology individually demands a different training for its use. Each
uses a different embodiment in the practitioner. These different embodi-

ments form our human history. This history is the history of that essential activity we recognize as Philosophy, the history of the omnipresent philosophical Greek aorist in action: the action of hermeneutics, the perennial act of interpreting. Ortega y Gasset summarized this vision with his usual eloquence:

> The Universe was not discovered by philosophy, [but rather philosophy] has been a series of trials during twenty-five centuries to deal with the Universe through the mental procedure that is philosophy. In this experiment divers ways of making that instrument function have been tried. Every new try takes advantage of the previous one. Above all it takes advantage of the errors and limitations of the previous ones. In this sense it is proper to talk of the history of philosophy being the description of the progress of philosophizing. This progress may end up by being in the end that some good day we may discover that not only this or that 'way of thinking' philosophically was limited and therefore, wrong, but in absolute terms, to philosophize, any kind of philosophizing, is a limitation, an insufficiency, an error, and that there will be a need to invent another way of intellectually facing the Universe; a way different from any of the previous to philosophy and from philosophy itself.[4]

In trying to introduce into the public domain of philosophic discourse Ignatius de Loyola's use of imagining , I became aware that a description alone was not sufficient. Imagining itself is part of the philosophical activity of hermeneutics from the beginning of Western culture and as such its history needs to be brought out. Communities need to be formed before a project and its success are possible.

The history of philosophy, however is not something we have had from the beginning either. Philosophy is constituted as philosophers "make" philosophy. History appears as history is uncovered. The act of hermeneutics not only interprets but also forms the tradition of philosophy as it interprets. Interpretation is simultaneously a constitution of history that makes itself as it uncovers the history of this same act in history. Philosophy is not just thinking, but rather, thinking-in-community. The same act needs to be at the same time contemporary and historical. Imagining, equally, is not just imagining, but rather imagining-in-community; the same act of imagining must be equally contemporary and historical. The coincidence of these two acts, in the present and in history, constitutes the community and the tradition. It constitutes the justification of what we understand as philosophy. The identification of these acts, however, is not as problematic as it appears if we link this identification to the languages through which they are put into use. Language will take into account not only the *external* tokens of sound, gesture, and word, but also the *internal* tokens of intentionality, conceptualization, and purposive action. In short, the technologies of their use.

This study was started with the seemingly simple task in mind of "reading" several connected and disconnected "texts" from the writings of a mystic, Ignatius de Loyola. Though the main focus of this study was the description of how Ignatius used the act of imagining, I found myself involved very rapidly in developing the technology itself of imagining. Imagining led to those inner orderings of mental life through which imagining takes place. I described imagining by describing how to imagine within the context of Ignatius's writings.

The difficulties surrounding this project accumulated as soon as writing was started. Writing from the center of the page gives out a different "reading" than writing from the margins. The act of imagining, as practiced by Ignatius de Loyola, is of such a variety that it has only seldom been part of the prose of center-page. It can only be "read" from the margins, regardless of the violence to writing/reading this might do to both writer and reader.

Ignatius, as much as Plato, belong to oral-audial cultures, when writing and reading performed other functions than the same acts perform for us today. They were both linked to an orality more fundamental than we make room for today in center-page writing. Today, we are radically biased against orality to the point of denying it the full-fledged citizenship of rationality. For this reason, we are prone to either suppress whatever traits of orality they might show in their writings or translate their orality into intelligible terms by our own criteria of the intelligible. Traits of orality have been labeled "residual orality," as if fully developed humans had suddenly discovered in their less developed ancestors the tail of their atavic irrationality, like an undesirable illness, a weakness to be removed through contemporary models of the rational.

It was only after I finished writing this study on imagining and proceeded to descend to Peiraeus that what had been done "up there" seemed to show its most rational face. It could be possible, after all, to list the different spaces of discourse, the different communities, the technologies in use, and the languages, and to show the inner philosophical orderings of those acts as constituting the contemporary and historical dimensions of philosophical hermeneutics.

Imagining and Western Philosophy

It is not a difficult task to gather a community of speakers from the history of philosophy to gather at Polemarchus's house and talk about imagining. In addition, contrary to all other habits of philosophers to disagree on most things, they all seem to agree that without images there are no judgments of intelligible facts. Outside of this, however, the community seems to disintegrate. The varieties of imaginary acts, how they are performed, which are essential to the common good, which are only individual, which are used for decisions, which to avoid and which used to pass the time, which is the difference between fantasy and imagination, etc., these pass unsaid or unclarified. In short, the history of imagining stands still to be made. A study like the present may aid in that direction.

Plato is the first philosopher from the West to be named as the norm of a general ambivalence towards imagining in this tradition. In the "divided line," the image abstracted from empirical objects is placed almost at the bottom of the line. (Mute within the tradition is the fact that the longer part of the divided line, the epistemic part, is the long journey, Er's journey, of imagining, a journey through cultural frames. This journey may only be undertaken on condition that we drink from the "river of forgetfulness" and cancel the worlds and sensations we are familiar with. But more about this later on.)

It is this image from empirical objects that has held center-page as imagining in the West. Aristotle raised it from the low place in which Plato set it to the lofty realms of epistemology, where thinking "will not exist without images," (*De Anima*, 432a 14) even though "imagination is for the most part false" (*De Anima*, 428a 11). Through the medieval philosophers, Hume accepts the same tradition when on the one hand he calls for a "resolution to reject all the trivial suggestions of the fancy, and to adhere to the understanding" (*A Treatise of Human Nature*, p. 267); but then he defines understanding as "the general and more established properties of the imagination" (*ibid.*). He goes even further by stating that "the memory, senses, and understanding are, therefore, all of them founded on the imagination" (*ibid*, p. 265). Kant distinguishes two types of imaginations: the "visionary" one, which "produces empty figments of the brain," and the "inventive" one, which operates "under the strict surveillance of reason" (*Critique of Pure Reason*, A770, B798). Though for Kant imagination is blind, it turns out that "it is an indispensable function of the soul, without which we should have no knowledge whatsoever," for it provides a synthesis in the understanding and it is such syntheses "that gives rise to knowledge"(*ibid*. A78, B103, A77). In short, without imagination there is no philosophy.

Descartes is perhaps the best classic example of ambivalence about imagining. The *Meditations* would not be possible without a hard dose of imagining, for Descartes has to *imagine* the least doubt" (*Meditations of First Philosophy*, trans. L. J. Lafleur 1961, p.23). Descartes's *Treatise of Man* is again an imaginative exercise on how a mechanistic model for men would "resemble us." Yet he concludes that imagining is "in no way necessary to my nature or essence, that is to say to the essence of my mind" (*Meditations*, p. 69).

Fichte's *Grundlage* of 1794 turns the tables around and proposes a systematic formal analysis of imagining as the transcendental ground of all human acting and human temporality. "All reality . . ." he writes, "is brought forth solely by the imagination . . . . This act of the imagination forms the basis for the possibility of our consciousness, our life, our being ourselves . . . ." (*Grundlage*, 59). Fichte's analysis of the act of imagining is the best formal link phenomenology has to the philosophical past. Some phenomenologists are tapping this forgotten source (Hohler, 1982).

The ambivalence about the varieties of imagining perdures in the tradition, and in no one is the case more evident than in Husserl, and through him in the tradition that followed.

While in many respects Husserl shares with the past the biases of a nonhistorical reconstruction of nature and takes as legitimate the manipulative control over people and things that scientific models hold (and with him Heidegger, Ricoeur, Merleau-Ponty and others of the same tradition), it is at the hands of Husserl that imagining regains a more central foundational role. Phenomenology without imagining is not possible and this on account of two strategies, both philosophical. The first consists in the phenomenological reduction, that is, the technique to bracket objects or even reality. The second is the technique of free variation, that is, the use of actual acts of imagining to let the imagination "have free rein" (*Phanomenologische Psychologie*, p. 71). According to Husserl, "freedom in the investigation of essences necessarily requires that one operate on the plane of the imagination" (*Ideas*, sec. 70).

The tradition that followed Husserl, despite this auspicious send off, has dealt with the imagination and imagining with ambivalent results. Confusion exists as to which description is of imagining and which of fantasy, confusion about daydreaming, reverie, cultural typologies, and how the different uses of imagining operate. But despite these shortcomings, a history of imagining is being built while the dialogue continues.

Notable efforts are those of Edward Casey's *Imagining: A Phenomenological Study* and Robert Neville's *The Reconstruction of Thinking*. Though both take the imagination as the faculty that abstracts from empirical objects, both make substantial contributions to the history of imagining. Casey's study establishes the autonomy of the imagination, while Neville's argues that it is through images that all perception is mediated. Both studies together are an important contribution in line with the present study of Ignatius/Plato in the sense that what we normally call interpretation, or hermeneutics, is originally a basic image that holds together cosmic worlds or empirical objects. In short, the first original human act is that of imagining.

The most remarkable studies on imagination by contemporary philosophers come from Gaston Bachelard and his disciple Gilbert Durand. Though both are different in sensibilities and even projects, both contribute to the dialogue by keeping history opened. Bachelard is the closer to the interests of the present study. "There is," he says, "no phenomenology of passivity. . . . The description of the image requires that we participate actively in the creating imagination" (*The Poetics of Reverie*, p. 4). Like this study, Bachelard focuses on the act of creation itself. But unlike this study, his act of imagining is that of reverie. The images he imagines are those of some poets and some scientists or philosophers. His focus gives us a new variety of imagining through which we learn to do phenomenology. Simultaneously, he introduces a new kinesis, movement, into the phenomenological act that was missing earlier. Through the discovery of the images that created certain worlds, present there, worlds at hand, we discover what it is that we do when we do phenomenology. Furthermore, he has the ability to separate the philosophical act from the psychological act in the same act of phenomenological reduction. "Psychological acts make a man out of a poet, but how to make a poet out of a man, in spite of life?" (*Poetics of Reverie*, p. 10) is Bachelard's challenge as a phenomenologist. Echoes of the same problematic appear in the study of world modellings in science, as may be seen in the recent study by Alex Comfort, *Reality and Empathy*.

Bachelard's disciple Gilbert Duran has aimed for a universal typology of images in his study *Les Structures Anthopoligoques de L'Imaginaire*. This study is closer to Fichte's dream of a transcendental imagination than to a Bachelardian phenomenology. Still, the primacy and autonomy of the imagination is obvious in intent, even when one does not learn its use or one is left wondering if the images one classifies are the same concepts one reads. How does phenomenology deal with the difficult task of translating the image to the public domain? Is it sufficient to translate the image into a concept?

This short list of characters dealing with imagining in our history of philosophy has, at least, helped us to enter into dialogue with the tradition, establish such a tradition, and point out the points of ambivalence about the tradition and the act itself of imagining. How do we proceed from the problem to a continuation of the dialogue, to actually building the tradition in its own historical acts of imagining? Where do we go from Polemarchus's house? Is there any other communal space where the continuation of the dialogue would be possible?

The Intelligible and the Visible

The first five Books of the *Republic* are separated from the remaining five by the "divided line." The community of young men and Socrates have reached a point of communal agreement to talk about "justice." Definitions abound. Every one of the speakers tries a new one. All except Socrates. Socrates refuses to do so because "justice has not yet been seen." Only on condition that "justice be seen" will Socrates define it. Similarly with "imagining." Though the history we have outlined seems to talk about "imagining," the act of "imagining" does not appear anywhere as something seen." The intelligible features of "justice" or of "imagining" are not sufficient if we are to account for "justice" in the *Republic* or for "imagining" in the writings of Ignatius de Loyola or Plato. We are not suggesting a difference of degrees in justice or in imagining, but a difference in kind.

In appearance, the prose of the *Republic* (when focused on the external tokens of language) leads the listener/reader along a smooth and easy pathway; there are changes of direction, delays in the journey, but all in all there appears to be a progressive development and intimation to the listener/reader that he/she is nearly home. But then Socrates takes over, introduces sudden shocks and abrupt discontinuities, and the familiar expectations are set on their heads. These shocks, these discontinuities, draw attention to themselves and force a "new reading," a "new listening" of what now appears totally strange. These shocks, these abrupt discontinuities, are introduced at the end of Book Six with the "divided line," and are followed by the "cave" and the "journey of Er."

The Divided line ought to be a simple exercise in "reading" (509b-511e). How difficult can it be to divide a line into two unequal segments? One must be larger than the other; one must be labelled *intelligible*, the other *visible*.[5] The true problem, at this time, however, is precisely the naming of those parts, which one is the visible and which the intelligible? Are opinions, images from empirical objects, and objects of art and science visible or intelligible? Is the epistemic part, the larger part, visible or intelligible? A decision must be made. Or must it? If the philosopher makes no decision, he has no ground on which to stand. If he does make a decision, his philosophy will suffer.

Every philosopher after Plato has "read" the *Republic* knowing a priori which part of the "divided line" was the visible and which the intelligible. Opinions, images from empirical objects, and objects from science and art all all visible; ideas, models, and theories are intelligible. But here lies the problem and the different kind of philosophy Plato undertakes as a project. Plato does not say which part is which (Bremer, pp. 82-114). It would have been easy for him to do so. But he does not do it. He refuses. A commitment to either side would have ruined his hermeneutical project. It did so for others. The fact that Plato/Socrates continues the dialogue without commitment to such a division and identification presumes that the philosopher has to proceed without such a previous commitment.

As the dialogue continues, it is obvious that Plato/Socrates meant for the philosopher to invert the tables and make the visible the origin of the intelligible, and not vice versa. As we see in the "cave," the intelligible produces only shadows. And the "journey of Er" makes visible a world, several possible worlds, otherwise hidden by the intelligibles. With Plato the memories of the past become visible, are visible, and the origin of the intelligible. With Ignatius de Loyola, Christ and the mysteries are visible and the origin of the intelligible.[6]

The Technologies of the Visible

Before we return to "the cave" and the "journey of Er," we need to make a slight detour. This delay is demanded by the distance of "reading habits" between "texts" like the *Republic* or Ignatius de Loyola's writings and our own. Mixed with those "reading habits," there are a few presuppositions that need clarification to make the "reading" possible.

Natural evolution ends with the appearance of humans. With humans, cultural evolution takes over. The cultural becomes the natural in humans. Hence the need for philosophy. The primary technology of culture is language. Through language, its materiality, its measures, its rhythms, its repeatability, and its orderings of mental life, humans extend themselves as far and as wide and deep as language is able to reach. Language, as much through its internal tokens as its external ones, is a technology. It not only creates the visible and the intelligible aspects of human life but sensitizes individuals to those aspects of the visible and the intelligible it can reach. In this creation of the visible and the intelligible, language and technology become coextensive. The visible and the intelligible adapt to a language and its inner mechanisms, which unfold, repeat, may be taught and learned. The only condition for this human fluidity, for the fluidity of the human body, is that these technologies be kept alive, be remembered. Contemporary studies in several disciplines have lately emphasized the different technologies of languages used by oral and literary cultures. Authors like Parry, Havelock, Lord, Jousse, Goody, Peabody, and particularly Clanchy (1979) and Walter Ong (1967 and 1982), have done an exemplary task in warning contemporary readers of the dangers of "reading" oral cultures by the criteria of contemporary literacy. From Plato (*Seventh Letter*) to Walter Ong, cautionary notes have been issued as to the danger against writing. Writing, printing, and electronics are seen as in some indefinite way *causing* thought to be biased, narrow, arbitrary, and imperialistic. What is not clear, in this criticism, is why writing and not "reading" is the guilty activity of contemporary culture. The written page may be "read" in many ways. The reader makes decisions, not the written page. Furthermore, all "texts," as much from oral as from literary cultures, are written down. We only deal with those that are written down. We cannot blame the only access we have to the past. The dream of an innocent reader using a "natural" language everytime that he/she in his/her innocence feels like it, is still alive. The fact of the matter, however, is that language and technology are coextensive. Language, oral or written, printed or electronic, is an inner technology that organizes mental life, orders its acts, decides by its sheer power and materiality, while extending externally the visible, auditive, tactile, sensuous, and intelligible world of humans. Language is neither natural nor instrumental; language is radically, biologically, and originally a technology organized through cultural habits, needs, and repetitions. Thought is not possible outside of language, imagining is not possible outside of language, fantasizing is not possible outside of language. The intentional ordering of our mental life follows the cultural, human ordering of our linguistic technologies. The fact that there are several such technologies accounts for the shifts in cultural habits, bodily habits, suppression, and forgetfulness of some, and the possible revivification of all.

It was Plato who first conceived of the philosopher as the one to keep alive these multiple technologies. The way to keep them alive was to develop in the philosopher's body itself a sustained habit of recollection in constant exercise, so that when called upon he would be ready and able to make decisions for the rest of us. That is, the philosopher, to be a philosopher, needed as a primary condition to have in himself, not in a written tablet, not in print, not in electronic soft or hardware – hence his opposition to writing – those technologies, plural languages, that need be applied in decision making (*Gorgias, Phaedrus*). All technology can be taught. Language makes that possible; it is repeatable. Repetition makes the possibility an embodied reality. Since we hold historically a plurality of languages, technologies, we also hold a plurality of choices. Depending on how we choose our training, even the best life or virtue can be learned. One may actually learn to perform "virtue by habit," or the philosopher may actually choose "by habit" the best life, as Plato dreamt.

A technology, however, is more than a mere technic. A technology embraces a common system of communication and commerce among the people of a culture. This system of communication is held together by a language interiorized as technology and, therefore, it can be repeated distributively within a common bodily intimacy of understanding and dialogue. Everyone within the communication system knows what is being said, for all order their faculties and linguistic habits to listen to the same things. The external tokens of language, as well as the internal ones of decision, conceptualization, and purposive action, are ordered, included or excluded, in the dialogue according to the technology in use. Any form of conversion, transformation, implies the simultaneous use of a different technology. If the technology is not developed, the greatest vision, the greatest insight, the greatest experience does not reach the public domain as what it originally was, but rather as a condition of the same that already was.

Language as technology, since it is an embodied technology, includes a general, native, background: a biographical immersion of the writer in the technologies he/she describes and a biographical writing where the philosopher shows proficiency in the acts and technologies he/she describes. Language is primarily biographical. It is inner technology, which is primarily transparent, made visible.

The philosopher who is engaged in hermeneutics requires, on the very demand of hermeneutics, that all human possiblities be first held evident, made evident and remembered. This effort of memory by hermeneutics entails that the philosopher practicing it, in order to practice it, must not be committed a priori to any one particular technology. He must be familiar with each one of them, remember them, and repeat them when needed so that the memory remains alive. He cannot be a common mortal, take a philosophical position and "read" the world through that technology. The philosopher must stay in constant exercise, must be a constant reminder.

The knowledgeable reader will by now have anticipated the use of the word "text" throughout this study to be coextensive with language as technology. Antecedents of this use may be found in the large literature of postphenomenological hermeneutics, semiotics, structuralism, deconstruction, etc. Some other readers might find the use of the term to refer to illiterate mystics in illiterate cultures, illiterate cultures, or even contemporary illiterate mystics as inappropriate. They will term my use of the word "text" an example of chirographic bias. By this is meant an opposition between "natural" thought and thought that has built into itself the technology of writing, printing, or electronics.

This present study of imagining addresses both groups of readers in different ways. This study criticizes the use of the word "text" as the ultimate source of reference for analysis and proceeds beyond intelligibility to the embodiment of technology in the human body, the "primary text." This "embodied text" is the referential "text" of all analysis. The present study takes the study of "texts" to be coextensive with the embodied habits of humans found in the human body, and therefore with human history. This is the reason why remembering "texts" in the present is simultaneously building history.

This study also criticizes the belief that we can get outside of language and use it as a tool. Man is language, its use, and the habits accumulated through that use. My own studies about oral cultures (1971, 1976, 1976, and 1982) and those of Ernest McClain (1977, 1978, and 1981), Patrick Heelan (1979 and 1983), Bremer (1984), and Leo Treitler (1984) suggest that language, technology, culture, and "text" are coextensive. Where literary cultures use some logic to map the technology of language, oral cultures used music and the criteria of sound to map the technologies of its use. They used meters of music and their measures as the model, measure of proportion and proportion as experience, and these were coextensive with language and its measures and proportions. Oral language, if it can increase human rationality, needs to be shown as autonomously rational and not simply the victim of literacy and its current technology.

The present study, however, because it takes its stand on hermeneutics, proceeds beyond the issues mentioned above and abandons the common place for a unique place: a place of indeterminateness. In order to be hermeneutical, this study does not take sides on issues; it cannot take sides because of intelligible philosophical principles on the adequate interpretation of "texts." Strategically this study looks for the original acts that makes "texts" visible, thus it is beyond industrial cultures, deconstruction, Marxism, Freudeanism, structuralism, and even phenomenology. This study is simply hermeneutical. Thus it does not issue principles of interpretation, it simply presupposes them. It presupposes them in the "text." Therefore no interpretation is possible, on this hermeneutical stand, unless certain technological embodiments are present in the interpreter and become the guide for "reading." If those technological embodiments are not present, no amount of philosophical principles or descriptions will replace them and do the philosophical job. Hermeneutics works on the assumption that the interpreter is capable of identifying as reader those acts, and no others, that create the "text" in the first place. Since all the material we interpret is written down, printed out, or recorded on electronic screens – even those from oral cultures – the "text" is all we now have. Communication acts, even those from God to the soul, lead only to possible texts. "Texts" become actual only when "written down," and only then do they join the public domain. The interpreter needs to uncover the acts by which the "text" is to be "read" and thereby help the reader reorder the acts of his/her mental life for them to coincide with the "text" and for its interpretation/context to become visible. The task of hermeneutics, as its initial stand, is to bring out the multiplicity of those acts and thus let the plurality of "texts" exemplify the plurality of historical-human-mental-bodily-life.

The Return of the Cave

Plato's *Republic* remains to this day the Primer of hermeneutics. The plurality of "texts" coincides in the *Republic* with the plurality of technologies. Each place of discourse entails a different technology in use. The philosopher is the embodied exemplar of such embodied acts.

After Socrates introduces in the dialogue the "divided line," the house of Polemarchus is transformed into a new "place." It becomes the "cave." The sun is now "up," the "cave" is now "down," and in between there is the mid region of the "fire," where the "intelligible" is *seen* as being the cause of the shadows in the walls. All the previous discourses and speakers are *seen* now waving their "intelligibles" in front of the fire to produce shadows. The prisoners and even the speakers live by them, are sensitized by them, and shortly will feel their emptiness. The region of the sun is obviously the "solitary region," where no one dwells. Life is in the "cave." Prisoners, guardians, and Socrates live there together. The "intelligible" controls the life of the city. Discourse has now a different place: the middle region in front of the fire.

This middle region is the constant place of writing. Socrates not only rewrites "justice" as the community defined it, but he also rewrites Homer as he writes the *Republic*. (The same way Ignatius rewrites Augustine). Homer was a bad poet who took images from discreet objects and made them the prototype of the behavior of the gods. He was also the bad poet that buried the human dead and made them obsolete for posterity. The Hector that Homer buried is not dead in the *Republic* of Socrates/Plato. Hector/Er becomes alive at the hand of Socrates and brings from the dead the history and images – visible – from the past to rebuild the present. Hector does not die, as in Homer, at the hand of Achilles. Plato rewrites the end of the Iliad by not naming Achilles, thus holding back forever the hand that killed memory, and brings Hector/Er back to life from the dead in order to "save the story." Er does not die in the *Republic* and, therefore, never dies (Bremer, pp. 115–152).

No birth, however, takes place without great pain. The joys and over-whelming sensitizations at the sight of the sun are only proportionate to the bereavement and desolation of the familar theory by which we learn our lives were guided, and we see it die in front of our very eyes. The theoretical magicians in front of the fire die hard, for they live in us as living, embodied theory. The bereavement of the customary is much harder to take than the consolation of the sun. A whole range of possible technologies needs to be kept alive from the accumulations of history if we are not to collapse completely. To save humans from the fate that the collapse of a theory like those of Homer or Augustine or Aquinas might inflict in their lives is the primary aim of an education like that of the *Republic*; it insists on a plurality of technological "texts" for human survival.

The model of those technological "texts" is the journey of Er. Once more Socrates/Plato relocates us to another "place" where the dialogue is continued.

Er's place is Hades, a place of total human bereavement. None of the familiar sensations are present. The worlds, as we know them, are forgotten, cancelled. We have drunk from the "river" of forgetfulness, and the only visible things are images through images, total lives through total lives at a glance. Choices are made on the ability to see in this manner. This is the place of the visible only. The place of choice.

Er is a man of "every tribe." He is not a Greek, nor an Athenian, nor a Thracian, nor a Persian. He is a *Pamphylian*, a man who makes his home everywhere. He is every man, He is also Socrates, he is Plato. He is punished alone, alone born again, alone he gives his testimony. He is the warrior for whom every place is all the life there is. He is always in the presence of death, his place is the death of the worlds around him. (He is also the chosen messenger, with no freedom to refuse). It is on Er that Plato/Socrates use a journey of twelve days to describe in detail how the visible is brought to human kind, the "cave," again. Er is systematically dismembered, as witness-to-be, into a plurality of sights, sounds, smells, touch, taste, and movements. This dismemberment is the condition that he will deliver his "message" to those in the "cave." What he tells is the following: What happened to other men is "empirically dead;" that the dead may live again among the living it needs to be remembered by retelling. Homer, the "intelligibles," are wrong burying the dead forever. Plato/Socrates/Er resurrect the dead by turning them first into living memories so that the living may keep alive by the technologies of resurrection. Not to let them be surrendered to something less poetic – such as realism, empiricism, positivism, idealism, to what is "visible" or "intelligible" as dictated by those intelligibles – is the corrective of hermeneutics.

Hermeneutics, however, in its effort to make visibility out of life, is a humble, obedient exercise. The vision of the sun may give us worlds, but not yet communities, societies of cultures. That vision needs to be shared with others, mediated through others, lived in the company of others. The vision needs to be "read" in the company of some other human who has the experience of such "reading" and that of the sun. Plato found Socrates, Socrates found Er, Er found the historical past. Ignatius found other mystics, "reading confessors," the historical past, including the one of Plato. Plato and Ignatius are both exemplars of how to choose the better life from among those that are possible, each within his own historical horizons and the possibilities of his own faith. In either case, the past is the only guide. Though our futures are many, the past is common. There is always that "other" from the past that joins hands with us in the same act of "reading."

Against this project of philosophy as hermeneutics, of which Plato dreamt, the philosophy that followed , given that the past is always made from our present, made a commitment to the intelligible side of the "divided line" as the ground of philosophy. Those secure grounds did not turn out as secure as they seemed. Contemporary efforts at hermeneutics do not find it easy to disengage themselves from past habits of thinking.

The Future of Philosophy

The future of philosophy is necessarily linked to philosophy's origins. Originally, as embodied in Plato's doing of philosophy, philosophy is concerned – motivated in its own activity – with the quality of all the acts it performs. Quality of performance concerns itself with directing the will to select, sort out, those acts that are historically capable of being remembered and therefore executed. The distinctions and divisions leading to the selection of these acts are to be found in the quality itself of the act performed, not in the external properties of objects and their external relations. Thus, we may distinguish between "things" and images, originals and copies, models and fictions (simulacra). Divisions are made for the sake of an inner genealogy that identifies the pure from the impure, the authentic from the inauthentic, and is not at all concerned with classification of genus and species. This is a philosophy primarily concerned with the sorting of gold, as in the *Republic*, or the sorting of claims ("I am the shepherd of men," "I am the possessed, the lover") as in the *Statesman* or the *Phaedrus*.

The selection of the pure act works in Plato under the strict necessity of the model. The model of musical operations performed in Books Eight, Nine, and Ten of the *Republic*, through the marriage myth, the myth of the Tyrant, the myth of Er, and equally in the circulation of souls in the *Phaedrus*, the myth of archaic times in the *Statesman*, or the World-Soul in the *Timaeus*, is the internal criterion of selection itself in the total narrative of foundation according to which selectivity may be applied. The mythical grounds the philosophical; and the philosophical has to deal with the selection of foundation, the object of claims and claimant; in Platonic terms, the unsharable, the shared, the sharer, (the father, the mother, the offspring).

Plato's philosophical corpus divides into those texts that establish the foundations for the claims (authentic claims) and those that hunt down the false claimant (*Timaeus, Critias, Republic, Laws,* and *Phaedrus, Statesman, Sophist*). Plato is as rigorous in establishing the positive path of and for philosophy as he is in predicting the possible false (fictive) path of the same. Plato is aware from the beginning that the fictive is not only the negation of the original but that it has the power to prevent any original from emerging. Philosophy may be done not only as a false copy of philosophical activity but, even more, the false copy may (has the power to) put into question the very notion of copy and of embodied models.

For a copy to be like the original – that is, well grounded in an identity of acts – the copy must retain both the image and the likeness of the original. In the *Sophist*, Plato distinguishes between iconic copies (likenesses) and phantasmic simulacra (semblences) (*Sophist* 236b, 264c). Icons are good images, they are endowed with resemblance, that is, relations and proportions (as in the musical model) that constitute inner performance. The claimant conforms to the real only in so far as the operations through which he/she reaches it conform to the operations modeled by the Idea, the ground and claim of all copies. It is a lineage of qualities on how the derived semblances equal the original modelling.

The similacrum, on the other hand, is not just a copy of a copy, a degraded icon, but rather an image without a resemblance; a fallen angel, or a fallen creature, retaining the image of God while losing the resemblance. This is the state of sin of philosophy. We have internalized a dissimilitude. The simulacrum includes within itself the power to cover and exclude all originality, all history, by forming those constructions that include within them the angle of the observer. This blind center, this decentered self perspective, this point of view occupied by the observer, is the real flight from the original image, a process of progression toward the unbound, a gradual subversion of history, an avoidance of the limit, the Same and the Like. It is also the negation of both original and copies, model and reproduction; it is the birth of *simulation*, the inauthentic, together with no criterion for negating the false claimant. Philosophy has thus entered the Modern Age and the sin of modernism. This study on imagining was undertaken with an alarming sense of urgency. The habits of intelligibility inherited from the past have introduced into practically every area of human education and action fictive – nonhistorical – models of manipulating the cultural. The manipulative control over people and things that scientific models have is taken for granted. The pragmatic goals of science as being the control of natural phenomena are also taken for granted, and this end justifies the means of a fictive reconstruction of nature according to models of science that make this achievement possible. In a recent study entitled *Space-Perception and the Philosophy of Science*, Patrick Heelan (Heelan 83) shows how from the beginnings of Western culture with Aristotle, and later on with Augustine, Aquinas, Galileo, Spinoza, and, in our times, Einstein, there has been the belief that nature is a book "written" from the start in its complete form, final and original, and that science – be it theology, as the science of the past, or the natural sciences of the present – is the actual form of that "reading." Heelan shows in his exemplary study that hermeneutics are performed on embodied technologies that make visible the transparencies of intelligible technologies. We hope his model may stimulate others to do hermeneutics rather than talk about them.

Similarly, the external technologies created by science are taking over a human form that is being denied to humans by the criterion that all technology is expected to be only an external extension of the human body. External technologies have a way of interiorizing themselves and become the software of inner mechanisms in humans. Eventually software may become hardware and form a cultural loop the way printing created reading. Through external technology man is displaced as the bearer of thought, imagination, and other mental operations; he is being displaced by the machine, which by now not only 'thinks,' 'counts,' or imagines," but in certain cases may also decide. A hormone made through genetic engineering, for example, brings science and technology so close that they are indistinguishable. Learning how a foreign protein can be made by bacteria (science) and the production of a functional hormone (its application, its technology) were realized simultaneously. Science and technology are in this case inseparable. How can technology not escape detection when it masquerades as science? Who is there to supervise? If humans are deprived of their legitimate operations that constitute them as humans, expecially their will, what kind of humans are we educating? Inner technologies are linked to the human will. If we deprive humans of the exercise of these technologies, we deprive our population of those exercises. The problem, obviously is not the machine. The problem is the models we humans select as those of our training.

No other voice from the recent past has been more eloquent than that of Ortega y Gasset to turn hermeneutics into a program of education.

Whoever aspires to understand man – that eternal tramp, a thing essentially on the road – must throw overboard all immobile concepts and learn to think in ever shifting terms.[7]

This inner mobility is the way of hermeneutics:

If primitive humanity had not possessed this ability to inflame itself with far off things in order to struggle against obstacles it encountered close at hand, humanity would continue to be static.[8]

But according to Ortega this task is impossible unless we change our habits: "We need a new technique of invention."[9] Ortega understood this need in the fact that man is bodily linked to his past. Man and history are the accumulation of those internalized habits: "The historical past is not just a simple past because it is not the present . . . but because it has happened to other men of whom we have a memory and, therefore, it keeps on happening to us who are constantly remembering it."[10] Ortega aimed at returning philosophy to its hermeneutical origins, its own history. Intelligibility has not always been full and immutable; it has also been empty and deficient. Knowing has not been the exercise of a faculty that produced knowledge when used. To know is mediated through multiple technologies that men and women may use as their birth right, it is not permanent. To know, rather, is an historical form humans reached in view of certain failures in their own lives. Ortega's reformulation of hermeneutics is closer to our own interests in this study, and I bring it in here to separate it from the formulations of hermeneutics of Dilthey (1958), Gadamer (1975), Ricoeur (1981), and Heidegger (1962). Different from Dilthey, Ortega would focus on the primary *decisions* of history rather than its ideas. As against Gadamer, Ricoeur, Heidegger, and others, Ortega would insist on the primary condition of embodied technologies, habits of thought, linquistic habits of the "text," etc., before the "text" may be analysed. It is only *after* this technological embodiment that philosophical reflection is possible. Otherwise, what we call hermeneutics is only a bridge of passage for foreign texts to migrate into our own hospitable but imperialistic soil. As philosophers, we need to keep the conversation alive.

NOTES

1. *Powers of Imagining: Ignatius de Loyola.* (Albany: State Univ. of New York Press, 1985).
2. John Bremer's *On Plato's Polity.* This book is close in the most pertinent way for this study. This little monograph and Ernest McClain's *The Pythagorean Plato* are the most insightful studies to come out recently on Plato. Both studies complement each other and also verify each other's insights. From both I use several themes and verifications. I recommend the reader to study both authors diligently. See, on the first words of the Republic, *On Plato's Polity*, pp. 18–32.
3. *On Plato's Polity*, p. 20.
4. Ortega Gasset, Obras Completas, Abrev. *O. C.*, Vol. 8 p. 260. (All the translations from the Spanish are my own.)
5. Kant, *Critique of Pure Reason* A 313/B 384 writes: Plato made use of the expression 'idea' in such a way as quite evidently to have meant by it something which not only can never be borrowed from the senses but far surpasses even the concepts of the understanding. Plato's ideas are archetypes of the things themselves, and not, in the manner of categories, merely keys to possible experiences. In this view they have issued from highest reason, and from that source have come to be shared in by human reason.
6. *Spiritual Exercises* (47): . . ." on a visible object, for example, contemplating Christ Our Lord during his life time, for He is visible . . ." It is easy to see the coincidences with Plato's world of Er and its visibility.
7. *O. C.*, vol. 3 p. 500.
8. *O. C.*, vol. 9 p. 361.
9. *O. C.*, vol. 5 pp. 532–533.
10. *O. C.*, vol. 9 p. 361.

BIBLIOGRAPHY ON HERMENEUTICS

Aristotle (1941) *The Basics Works Of.* trans. W. C. Ross. Ed. Richard McKeon. New York: Random House.

Bachelard, Gaston (1960) *The Poetics of Reverie.* Trans. Daniel Russell. Boston: Beacon Press.

Barthes, Roland (1976) *Sade, Fourier, Loyola.* Trans. Richard Miller. New York: Hill & Wang.

Bataillon, Marcel (1950) *Erasmo y España.* Trans. Antonio Alatorre. Mexico: Fondo de Cultura Económica.

Bremer, John (1984) *The Polity,* Houston: Institute of Philosophy.

Casey, Edward (1976) *Imagining: A Phenomenological Study.* Bloomington, Ind.: Indiana University Press.

Clanchy, E. (1979) *From Memory to Written Record.* Cambridge, Mass.: Harvard.

Comfort, Alex (1984) *Reality and Empathy.* Albany: State University of New York Press.

de Nicolás, Antonio T. (1971) *Four-Dimensional Man.* Bangalore: Dharmaram College.

(1976) Meditations through the Rg Veda. Maine: Nicolas, Hays.

(1976) *Avatāra: The Humanization of Philosophy through the Bhagavad Gītā.*

(1980) "Notes on the Biology of Religion." *Journal of Social and Biological Structures* 3:219–225.

Descartes, Rene (1961) *Meditations on First Philosophy.* Trans. L. J. Laffleur. New York: Bobbs-Merrill.

Durand, Gilbert (1969) *Les Structures Anthorpologique de L'Imaginaire.* Paris: Bordas.

Fichte, Johann Gottlieb (1971) *Fichtes Werke.* Berlin: Walter de Gruyter & Co.

Gadamer, Hans-Georg (1976) Philosophical Hermeneutics. Trans. David E. Linge. Berkeley: University of California Press.

(1975) *Truth and Method.* Trans. Garret Barden, John Cumming. New York: Seabury Press.

Hall, David (1981) "Antonio de Nicolás and Ortega y Gasset." *Philosophy Today.* Vol. 25, n 1/4 pp. 63–67.

(1973) *The Civilization of Experience.* New York: Fordham University Press.

Havelock, Eric (1963) *Preface to Plato.* Cambridge: Harvard University.

Heelan, Patrick (1983) *Space-Perception and the Philosophy of Science.* Berkeley: University of California Press.

(1979) "Music as Basic Metaphor and Deep Structure in Plato and in Ancient Cultures." *Journal of Social and Biological Structures* 3:279–91.

Heidegger, M. (1962) *Being and Time.* Trans. J. Macquarrie and E. Robinson. New York: Harper & Row.

(1977) *The Question Concerning Technology and Other Essays.* New York: Harper Colophon.

Hohler, T. P. (1982) *Imagination and Reflection: Intersubjectivity.* Fichte's Grundlage of 1794. The Hague: Nijoff.

Hume, David (1955) *An Inquiry Concerning Human Understanding.* New York: Bobbs-Merrill.

(1967) *A Treatise of Human Nature.* Oxford: Clarendon Press.

Husserl, E. (1931) *Ideas.* London: Allen and Unwin.

(1970a) *Logical Investigations,* 2 vols. Trans. J. N. Findlay. London: Routledge & Kegan Paul.

(1970b) *The Crisis of European Science and Transcendental Philosophy.* Evanston: Northwestern University Press.

Kant, Immanuel (1781) *Critique of Pure Reason* Trans. Norman Kemp Smith. London: Macmillan & Co. 1956.

Locke, J. (1689) *Essay Concerning Human Understanding.* El. Peter Niddich. Oxford: Clarendon Press 1975.

Neville, Robert (1974) *The Cosmology of Freedom.* New Haven: Yale University Press.

(1980) *Creativity and God.* New York: Seabury Press.

(1981) *Reconstruction of Thinking.* Albany: State University of New York Press.

Ong, Walter (1967) *The Presence of the Word.* New Haven: Yale University Press.

(1982) *Orality and Literacy:* The Technologizing of the Word. London: Methuen.

Ortega y Gasset, José (1946) *Obras Completas,* 12 vols. Madrid: Revista de Occidente.

Plato (1961) *The Collected Dialogues Of.* Various Trans. Ed. Edith Hamilton, Huntington Cairns. New York: Bollengen Foundation.

Ricoeur, P. (1967) *The Symbolism of Evil.* Trans. E. Buchanan. New York: Harper & Row.

Spitzer, Leo (1963) *Classical and Christian Ideas of World Harmony.* Baltimore: The Johns Hopkins Press.

Treitler, Leo (1984) "Orality and Literacy in the Music of the Middle Ages." *In Parergon.* Australia.

Turchetto, Gerald (1983) *Plato's Musical Imagination.* Michigan: Ann Arbor. University Microfilms.

Turner, F. (1983) "The Neural Lyre: Poetic Meter, The Brain and Time." *Journal of Social and Biological Structures* 8:277–307.

Lewis S. Ford

Creativity in a Future Key

Alfred North Whitehead introduced the term "creativity" to designate that activity whereby actualities (conceived as individual instances of self-creation) come into being. Creativity is Whitehead's word for that generic activity intrinsic to every instance of becoming. He appears to have coined this neologism, which has been adopted into common parlance. [1] In ordinary usage, creativity now is used evaluatively to mark those processes that bring forth noteworthy novelty,[2] but Whitehead intended it in a purely metaphysical sense to apply to all occasions. Though we will want to consider creativity in a future mode, Whitehead conceived it to be exclusively present. This includes even such creativity as will become active later when that later moment finally becomes active, because its activity can only be exercised in the present. It will require a modification of Whitehead's concepts to consider creativity as active in a future mode.

Now, there are many kinds of future. Since we will be examining one kind that is seldom explored, we need to specify some of the alternative kinds we do not intend to consider.

The future we have in mind is not principally that which will be. Such a future is the mirror image of the determinate past. It is not yet, but when it comes into being later it will be as determinate as that that has already been. At present, such implicit determinateness is somehow implicit, becoming then explicit. It is (now) what will be, but later it will be revealed for what it had (now) been. If ths is so, then the being of what will be remains unaffected by its temporal modality. This ignores the ontological character of the temporal modality of being, whereby future indeterminate possibility is transformed into the determinate actuality of the past by means of the process of present determination.

The future we intend to consider is not what will be, but primarily what might be, since this alone is open to transformation and determination by present activity.

Because it is indeterminate, the future as yet does not (at least formally) contain any determinate actualities. For this reason, we are apt to think of it as populated exclusively by the plans we propose for it and by the possibilities we project upon it. Then, the future may primarily mean all those appointments for subsequent times we have agreed to. All these derive their being from our own mental activity in some form or other. Other anticipations derive their possible being from trends already discernible in the actual world; there might be nuclear holocaust, or ecological disaster, or mass starvation. In whatever case, actuality is prior, possibility derivative.

For Whitehead some possibility, at least, is prior to past actuality, which we shall term "novel possibility." Originally, in the philosophy of nature, (eternal) objects functioned solely as the immanent characteristics of events. Once Whitehead adopted temporal atomism (Spring, 1925), he conceived of eternal objects as also functioning transcendently as the possibilities for actualization, some of which would not be finally realized. This formed the basis for a new conception of the nature of God. If God were the sole creator of the actual occasions, there would be a divine determinism in this event ontology. A substance can be created to act freely on its own. But an event is its own activity, such that whatever creates it also determines that activity. Determinism would also result if God were the sole source of order, as Stephen Lee Ely suggests in "The Religious Availability of Whitehead's God" (EWP 170–211).[3] But if God were to order only novel possibilities, determining the metaphysical and cosmic limits of what can and what cannot be actualized, leaving actualization up to the free activity of actual occasions, then there could be room for God as the Principle of Limitation, functioning as a cosmic orderer, without this undercutting finite freedom (EWM ch. 5). By *Process and Reality* this becomes an activity of divine persuasion, whereby God provides each nascent occasion with its initial aim. As Ely observes, both approaches are "based on a fundamental postulate of Whitehead's – that the possible is prior to the actual, not only logically but metaphysically" (EWP 178).[4]

Such novel possibility is what we are primarily concerned with, particularly that which generates it. We experience some, at least, of what might be derived from a source not our own. This novel possibility cannot be merely the result of our projections or the product of past trends. Whitehead derived novel possibility from God, the source of novelty for the world, conceived as a present everlasting concrescence or act of becoming. Since novel possibilities are created as future lures for the world, as the way God expresses himself toward the world, we can conceive of them as the manifestation of God's own act of self-creation. If so, divine self-creation can be conceived to be itself future, such that the novel possibilities are created in the future, satisfying the ontological principle by being grounded in this future activity. Along these lines we wish to modify Whitehead's conceptuality by conceiving God as future activity,[5] which is also the source of creativity for present occasions.

Since this proposal initially may seem quite outrageous to many, we should be clear as to why the other ways of accounting for finite creativity will not work.

I. Alternative Sources of Creativity

First of all, the creativity sustaining particular concrescences cannot be derived from prehensions of past actualities. For one thing, creativity lacks the unity of a datum, which it must have in order to be prehended. (This is why creativity is not an entity, to be classified among the categories of existence.) For another, prehending depends on the very creative activity to be derived from such prehension. Without creativity, an actuality could not prehend, while without prehending, it could not derive the creativity it needs in order to prehend.

For these reasons Whitehead (at least in *Process and Reality*) treats creativity as underived; it comes "from nowhere." Becoming just wells up from within any concrescing occasion. Each particular instance of creativity is a unification of the many past conditions into one present unity. Why? "It lies in the nature of things that the many enter into complex unity" (PR31). If we try to find a reason why that is so, Whitehead can only reply: "The sole appeal is to intuition; (PR32).

This answer may be sufficient, depending on our requirements for explanation. To be sure, creative unification could initially appear quite counterintuitive to those accustomed to thinking in terms of traditional causation; but then Newton's inertial motion was radically counterintuitive for old-fashioned Aristotelians. Just as sufficient immersion in Newtonian mechanics makes intertial motion seem very matter-of-course, so creative unification becomes quite intuitive to the process thinker. Creativity is a necessary feature of all occasions. Since it cannot either come from the past or from God, it seems it *must* come from within.

Our "intuition" about creativity, however, may be facilitated by some dubious considerations. While every individual instance of creativity is understood in terms of concrescence in the final stages of Whitehead's theory (principally found in Part III of *Process and Reality* (EWM, ch. 9), creativity as a more generalized notion tends to be understood in terms of his earlier notion of an underlying substantial activity that flows from earlier to later loci, always forming the present of the creative advance. Generalized creativity appears to flow from the occasions that are now past to the present, whereas individualized creativity draws past actualities drained of creativity into an active present. The present instance of creativity is a new unifying activity, discontinuous from that of preceding occasions, yet there seems to be a continuous flow in terms of generalized creativity.

The notion of such generalized creativity could be challenged by a stricter application of the ontological principle whereby creativity, like all entities that are nonactual, exists only as instanced in particular actual entities. It is nothing in and of itself, except as expressed by these actual entities. In one sense, to be sure, creativity is more fundamental than the acutal entities – it is that by which these actual entities exist – but that does not preclude creativity from existing only as ingredient in specific actualities (PR 10f). If so, it is difficult to conceive how there could be any continuity of activity from the past, for the creativity of a past occasion is completely exhausted in its "perishing." The activity of unification ceases in the attainment of the unity or the being to be subsequently prehended.

In his general description of creativity, we are told that "the many become one, and are increased by one" (PR 31). This statement is most plausible as a generalization of the creative rhythm whereby the many past occasions are unified in each new occasion, which then contributes its being to a new many. Yet it is subtly ambiguous, insofar as it suggests that it is the many that actively bring about the unification. If so, this activity could carry over into the nascent occasion. Yet, it is very difficult to conceive how the many could unite. It is possible to unite around a person, or a symbol, or a cause, but how can the many unite to form an occasion that does not yet exist? How plausible is it to claim that this uniting takes place in each and every instance?

Whitehead's original theory of concrescence, to be sure, attempted just such an approach. This theory, found in large portions of Part II of *Process and Reality* (EWM, ch 8), postulated two species of process, transition and concrescence (PR 320, 326f).[6] Here the creativity of transition was thought to enable the many past actualities to cause the initial datum to exist, from which concrescence as subjective appropriation could proceed. But Whitehead found that he could not articulate the precise conceptuality whereby the many could bring about unity, and he silently abandoned this separate species of process in favor of a more comprehensive theory of concrescence in Part III. Transition now becomes the succession of occasions effected by the rhythm of concrescence. If so, the many do not actively achieve their own unifications, but are unified by the emergent occasion.

Later, in *Adventures of Ideas*, Whitehead evidently became troubled by the implications of his perfected theory of concrescence. At least, he sought to correct the impression left by *Process and Reality* that "an occasion of experiencing arises out of a passive situation which is a mere welter of many data" (AI 230). He emphasized the continuity of experience, which "balances and limits the doctrine of the absolute individuality of each occasion of experience" (AI 235), so clearly articulated in the earlier 1929 book. Nancy Frankenberry draws her interpretaiton of creativity principally from these later texts in *Adventures of Ideas*:

> The language Whitehead uses there makes it clear that the creativity of the past is far from being passive or static as though only inertly 'given' to the present. Rather, Whitehead speaks of "the throbbing emotion of the past *hurling itself* into a new transcendent fact," "a flying dart hurled at the future, *provoking* some special activity of the occasion in question," "*energizing* in the present," "*imposing* . . . on the novel particular in process of creation. (AI 227, 226, 241, 242)[7]

Despite the rhetoric, it is just barely possible to interpret all this activity on the part of the past in terms of the systematic position of *Process and Reality* by making the tenth paragraph of "Objects and Subjects" the controlling text. There Whitehead notes that the "initial situation includes a factor of activity which is the reason for the origin of that occasion of experience," which is creativity. Yet where does this factor come from? "The initial situation can be termed the initial phase of the new occasion. It can equally be termed the 'actual world' relative to that occasion" (AI 230). Interpreting this passage simply in terms of the immediate context, Whitehead can be seen as insisting upon a continuity between the past as a multiplicity of concreta suffused with creativity and the initial situation of the present occasion. But if we were to adopt the systematic interpretation inspired by *Process and Reality*, then the actual world with its creativity would simply become an alternative way of describing the initial phase of concrescence, whose data are derived by simple physical feeling but whose creativity would be purely and simply inherent within that occasion itself. In other words, Whitehead here would be accommodating himself to the ordinary intuition of the

transference of energetic activity from the past, while managing to interpret the intuition in terms of a systematic doctrine he had espoused
earlier.

There are thus two interpretations of Whitehead's theory of creativity in *Adventures of Ideas*, and there seems so far to be no clear way to
decide between them. There is at least one text, however, that may be
decisive, since it is very difficult to account for in terms of the *Process
and Reality* interpretation. In speaking of Lucretius's dart, hurled beyond
the bounds of the world, Whitehead might have spoken of energy hurled
into a new occasion. Energy, a favorite term in *Adventures of Ideas*, could
then have been interpreted in terms of the transference of a form characterizing the inherent creativity of the new occasion. However, Whitehead chooses to emphasize that it is precisely "the *creativity* of the world
[which] is the throbbing emotion of the past hurling itself into a new
transcendent fact" (AI 227, italics added).

Frankenberry's interpretation of creativity is convincing with respect
to *Adventures of Ideas*, but it becomes very strained when applied to *Process and Reality*, just as the traditional interpretation based on the earlier
book becomes strained with respect to the later. It appears that
Whitehead changed the direction of his thinking between 1929 and 1933,
which is not surprising in light of the many shifts in Whitehead's thinking since 1925 (EWM). The later sense of the continuity of creativity and
its derivation from beyond the immediate occasion fits better perhaps
with our intuitions, but tensions remain. How can it possibly be derived
from the past? Creativity cannot be prehended, for only unified data can
be, and precisely because they lack all creativity.

Prehended data and creativity by the later theory are both earlier
than the immediate occasion and form its initial situation. Yet they are
very different: The one is what is to be prehended and the other is the
power of prehension. Frankenberry terms the latter "the power of the
past," yet it is not past in the same sense as are the objectified data,
themselves lacking all creativity. Whitehead also conceives of the antecedent creativity as past. Both make the very common assumption that
what is earlier than a given occasion must lie in its past (even though
Whitehead did not make that assumption with respect to earlier phases
of concrescence). Later we will have reason for questioning this assumption. Thus there are differenct senses in which past concreta and
creativity are earlier than the present concrescence. Since concreta are
definitely regarded as past, we will use a different temporal modality to
describe the earlier status of creativity. Although we can hardly justify
the claim at this point in our argument, Frankenberry's "power of the
past" turns out on our terms to be "the power of the future."

So far I have argued that creativity can neither be inherent in the present occasion nor derived from the past. We have not yet considered whether God could be its source. Robert C. Neville proposes that it is nontemporally created. He analyzes each present moment of coming-to-be into the past facts providing the raw data to be unified, the ideals directing the process of unification, and the "spontaneous features arising within the occasion" that cannot be derived from the past (SSS 106). "Without the spontaneous features there would be no process; things would remain as they were given at the initial stage. If there were only past facts and ideals, there would be no subjective decisive process of adopting the ideals as definitive of one's own development" (SSS 106). These spontaneous features are then precisely the creative elements within becoming.

> "Regarding the private acts of coming-to-be, God creates the spontaneous features of the moment. He gives rise to the decisive acts of the subjective process. Viewed from the causal commitments of the past, those features do appear spontaneous; there is no reason for them. Viewed from within the private subjective process, God's contributions simply *are* the present decisive acts by which the process exists as something over and above its past conditions. God is closer to us than we are to ourselves" (SSS 106).

In this formulation, the phrase "spontaneous features" is subtly ambiguous. I may mean all those factors of the resultant being not derivable from the past. These could be derived from God; for Whitehead these are contained in the aim God provides to initiate the act of unification or concrescence. But if they are derived from God in such a way that God alone creates all these features, then God determines the outcome and there is no room for creaturely freedom.

On the other hand, these "spontaneous features" may refer to the spontaneity of the concrescence itself. It could refer to the becoming and not to aspects of the resultant being. In that case, spontaneity cannot be created, whether by God or by another. To create is to bring into being that which had no being. Pure creativity is not something that could be brought into being. Every being has unity, but becoming, because it is sheer unification, lacks definite unity. In acquiring unity, the unification ceases. Just so does becoming perish in the attainment of being. We may speak of becoming as creating, since it is the bringing of being into being, but because it lacks both being and unity, becoming cannot be created.[8]

All this means that an occasion's own creativity cannot be accounted for in terms of nontemporal creation. We have also seen that it cannot be accounted for in terms of the past, and any claim that it is simply intrinsic to the occasion seems inadequate to the situation. Faced with this impasse, some would minimize the problem by conceiving of creativity as a very abstract formal property, even as a complex eternal object.[9]

It is difficult to see how something so dynamic could be conceived as purely formal, particularly since the two are contrasting formative elements (RM 90), yet one statement by Whitehead may have led some to tht conclusion: "Creativity" is the universal of universals characterizing ultimate matter of fact" (PR 31). What is universal is necessarily abstract, but it need not be a form. In hylomorphic theories, matter is also universal as ingredient in every thing. Creativity is universal as that purely formless activity capable of absorbing and unifying every form. As Whitehead says in another place, creativity is only capable of characterization through its accidental embodiments, and apart from these accidents is devoid of actuality" (PR 10f). If we compare Whitehead's philosophy to Thomism, creativity is akin to the *esse* or act of existing that provides the "thatness" of each actuality; it is not a feature of its essence or "whatness." Creativity is just as universal as *esse*, for both provide the balancing factor to form. Just as *esse* requires an extrinsic source in the case of finite actualities, so does creativity.

II. The Future as the Source of Creativity

Now if the derivation of creativity is a serious problem, and it can be derived neither from the past nor the present (from itself) nor from a nontemporal creator, how can it be derived? What other source is there than the future? Therefore, I propose that we extend Whitehead's creativity into a future mode. The future is usually conceived to be quite inert, containing only those necessities the past lays down on that which comes after it, together with any real possibilities the present may project forward. If the future also contains its own mode of creativity, as I propose, then it is very active. Indeed, it is God conceived as a single everlasting concrescencce or unifactory activity, forever future, forever unifying, never terminating in any past determinate actuality, yet forever generating novel possibilities.

This future creativity values each occasion's particular past conditions in terms of all the ways they can possibly be unified, and then passes on this individualized valuational activity to the occasion for its determination. (In this way, God functions both as the source of creativity and the source of that which functions as "subjective aim.") Determination, resulting in *this* rather than *that*, is a finite activity intrinsic to the occasion itself, but the present creativity receives its impetus from future creativity. This single future creativity thus pluralizes itself into many individual acts of present creativity. Instead of prehending God as one actuality among the past actualities of the world, we acquire the power of prehending the world from God's own power of prehending. The way creativity is derived from the future is not by prehension. Prehension is the way the present (and future) is derived from the past and the atemporal, but there are other modes of derivation. Thus, the past concretum is derived from what had been a present concrescence, yet no prehensions are involved, since the past lacks all subjectivity. In the transition from future to present, there could well be a continuity between the creative activity whereby God prehends the particular actual world for an occasion-to-be and that occasion's concrescence. As purely future activity, God's prehensions are cosmic, without specific standpoint and its attendant perspectival elimination, and unified only in terms of possibility; the present activity, on the other hand, is individualized by its particular standpoint, separate from other contemporary activities of unification, and driving towards concrete, determinate unity. These two types of creative activity are ontologically distinct, yet the present activity of finite occasions constitute many pluralized modes of the creativity flowing from the one future source.

By conceiving of the future as creative activity, we are identifying God with future creativity but not with all creativity. This speaks to a problem that has troubled many theists about Whitehead: Which is ultimate, creativity or God? To be sure, this problem is not as severe as might first appear. In perhaps an excess of rhetoric, Whitehead once described God and the World as both "in the grip of the ultimate metaphysical ground, the creative advance into novelty" (PR 529). This can easily give the impression that creativity is some sort of impersonal substratum creating all actualities, God included.[10] But Whitehead emphatically rejects *any* sort of external creation; the whole theory is designed to prevent that. Creativity simply names that activity of self-creation whereby each actuality creates itself. As an actuality among other actualities, God also creates himself. As the chief exemplification of the metaphysical principles (PR 521), God is in no way only created by another. Both God and finite actual occasions are only "in the grip of . . . the creative advance" as instances of self-creation.

In another place, Whitehead expressed the relationship between God and creativity in this manner: "In all philosophic theory there is an ultimate which is actual in virtue of its accidents. . . . In the philosophy of organism this ultimate is termed 'creativity'; and God is its primordial,

non-temporal accident" (PR 10f).[11] Again, this cannot mean that creativity creates God, since it lacks any independent actuality. But it does
say that creativity is *metaphysically* ultimate as this feature that is universally ingredient in all actualities.

For theists, creativity, as metaphysically ultimate, is generally not
identified with God, the source of all values, who is *axiologically* ultimate.
Which is religiously ultimate depends on our final persuasion. Jews and
Christians confess God to be so. The relation of these two ultimates
proves troublesome if kept distinct, as John B. Cobb, Jr., has indicated in
his sensitive essay on "Buddhist Emptiness and the Christian God."[12]
If we identify God with future creativity, such that present creativity
flows from the future, then the cosmic future creativity is pluralized into
particular present occasions. As the activity valuing the novel
possibilities for each occasion, God is the source of all values and
transcends the world the way the future transcends the past. In no situation is God's exercise of creativity coincident with ours, so no pantheism
is involved. Theists are oriented towards this future creativity, Buddhists
towards present creativity, and the two are definitely related by
temporality.

Hopefully this notion of future creativity will become clearer as we
proceed, but one insistent objection needs to be answered immediately.
In the order of being, it is always the earlier that influences the later and
never vice versa. This must be so, for when the earlier was coming into
being, the later did not yet exist. This same principle should apply to the
order of becoming, since the earlier does not presuppose the existence
of the later. Now, if the future is later than the present, how would it be
possible for future creativity to pass over into the present? How can the
later pass over into the earlier?

It cannot. There is no way the future can pass over into the present
as long as we restrict ourselves to the order of being. For many philosophies, that is all there is. For Whitehead, however, there is not only the
realm of being, constituted by the many natural events or occurrences
of the world, but there is also the realm of becoming, whereby these
natural events come into being. Besides concreta there are concrescences. The order of succession for being in terms of what is earlier
and what is later turns out to be the opposite of what it is for becoming.
The order for being is the succession of determinate actualities, the latest
of which verges on the present. In contrast, the order for becoming is the
succession of phases of determination, the latest of which, being the
most determinate, verges on the past. The earliest phase of determination or concrescence, being the least determinate, verges on the future.
What our proposed modification does is extend Whitehead's concept of

the order of succession within becoming to apply to the future outside the concrescent occasion. Being earlier, that future can influence the later present.

III. Temporal Atomicity and Nontemporal Concresence

My proposal clearly runs counter to a widespread interpretation of Whitehead's analysis of becoming, whose "phases are *not* ordered temporally in terms of earlier or later phases," as Bowman L. Clarke (for one) has claimed (JAAR 48:570, italics added). Clarke assumes that what is earlier necessarily lies in the past of the later. Yet, if it is part of the past, it must be wholly determinate. Such cannot be true of genetic phases. Whitehead has a broader meaning of "earlier" that any simple identification with the past would permit, although he fails to complete the distinction by holding, as we do, that the orders of succession for being and becoming are opposite to each other with respect to "earlier" and "later." Clarke's insistence on the strict identification of "earlier" with "past" stands in tension with Whitehead's concern for the increasing complexity and determinateness that takes place within concrescence. Whitehead notes that the contents of "one phase of concrescence control the specific integrations of prehensions in later phases of that concrescence" (PR 132), so that certain highly complex prehensions "can arise only in a late phase of the process of the prehending subject" because "it requires, in earlier phases," very specific factors that are then synthesized (PR 397). [13]

This is an ordering in terms of "earlier" and "later," yet Clarke insists that it is not *temporal*, even though it pertains to the successive phases of a dynamic process. He gives three reasons: 1. It is impossible to interpret concrescence in terms of the temporality of being; 2. Whitehead repeatedly denies temporality to concrescence; and 3. Whitehead's doctrine of temporal atomicity precludes temporal succession within concrescence.

We accept the first reason, as rephrased for clarity's sake in terms of our own framework. Rather that being an objection, however, we see it as grounds why becoming should be analyzed in terms of a different, even opposite, order of succession. The second objection is not strictly true. Feeling the force of the first objection, Whitehead evades the question as to the temporality of concrescence. What he is certain of is that the "genetic passage from phase to phase is not in *physical* time" (PR 434, italics added). Physical time is the time of physics: the division into earlier and later that pertains to the being of determinate events. Analysis by this means is inappropriate to becoming since becoming concerns the process of determination, none of whose phases (save the last) is wholly determinate. In Whitehead's terms, coordinate division is inappropriate to genetic analysis. The dynamic succession of increasingly determinate phases calls for its own kind of time. To be sure, Whitehead never names an alternative to physical time, but only physical time is denied of concrescence.[14]

The third objection follows from a common interpretation of the conclusion to Whitehead's discussion of Zeno's paradoxes, which disregards the following careful qualification with which that statement ends: "'The conclusion is that in every act of becoming there is the becoming of something with temporal extension; but that the act itself is not extensive, in the sense that it is divisible into earlier and later acts of becoming which correspond to the extensive divisibility of what has become" (PR 107). A single process of determination cannot be divided into smaller acts of determination because then the larger process would be punctuated by completely determinate phases (the final phases of these smaller acts of determination) at times when the process must still be indeterminate. But surely the statement is compatible with there being another division of this process into more or less determinate phases.[15] Some take this statement to reject *any* kind of division other than coordinate, but at the time Whitehead wrote this statement he spoke only of coordinate division, contrasting it to genetic *analysis*. The acknowledgement of "genetic division" comes much later, in the last chapter to be written (PR IV.1M: EWM 239f).

It is true that the being or the occurring of an occasion happens all at once, although the occasion can be distinguished retrospectively by coordinate division in terms of determinate subevents. For the act of becoming results in one occasion, not in a series of smaller beings, each requiring its own act of becoming. With respect to events, however, talk of becoming is apt to be confusing, since we ordinarily use "becoming" with respect to the coming into being of enduring substances. In that context, an enduring substance comes into being by means of some initiating event, such as the event of manufacturing producing an automobile or a box of cereal. In our terms, the event of manufacturing occurs or has being, and the question of the origin of its being becomes a second-order one: How does the being or occurring of an event itself come into being? The flux or dynamic succession of occasions in the world is not the becoming by which these occasions come into being. Each occasion begins its being all at once, if we attend strictly to its status as being. Its process of becoming, however, is genetically divisible into earlier and later phases of determination, none of which, except the final one, have determinate being.[16]

Clarke does not see it this way, to be sure. Once having established to his satisfaction that the act of becoming is in no wise temporal, it is but a short step to regard it as "nontemporal." Thus he says that God's prehensions of the temporal occasions of the world constitute a single "nontemporal everlasting actual entity" (JAAR 48:574). This is contrary to Whitehead's own usage, which restricts the nontemporal exclusively to God's primordial nature. "Nontemporal" never characterizes concrescence in general, nor is it applied to the unification of God's temporal prehensions.[17] Whitehead has in mind solely the primordial envisagement of all eternal objects, whereby they are valued and ordered together, in total abstraction from the temporal world. Because they are devoid of time, God's subjective unification of them is thought to be also.[18]

Clarke also seeks to explain how God could have any causal influence upon the world. First, "there is no reason in *Process and Reality* to deny that temporal transition is in the satisfaction of a nontemporal everlasting actual entity. It is in the satisfaction of all actual entities" (JAAR 48:570). Second, while transition requires perishing in the temporal world, there is no categorical requirement that all objectification needs perishing. Third, God never perishes, but objectification is possible since his is an imperishing transition (JAAR 48:574–76).

The key to this argument is the interpretation of transition. The primary meaning of transition is the temporal shift from one occasion to the next. As one occasion becomes a being, it is then prehended by a supervening one. In this process, the "satisfaction," or attained unity, is taken up as a whole into the next concrescence. For Clarke, however, transition is primarily a process *within* the satisfaction. This comes about, apparently, from investing all temporal meaning in the process of transition and denying it totally to the other kind of process, concrescence. For Whitehead, transition emerges from the rhythmic processes of concrescence, as the rhythm proceeds from one concrescence to the next. By draining all temporality from this rhythmic process, Clarke is constrained to find temporality exclusively in the spatiotemporal extensiveness or coordinate divisibility of the determinate beings that are the results of these concrescences.

Perishing, however, at least the sort Whitehead speaks of, is essential to transition. There is no transition without objectification. An actuality becomes prehensible only when it achieves determinate unity. *Pace* Clarke, perishing is the perishing of becoming in the attainment of being. The act of becoming is a unification of all past conditions into a unity;

once that final unity has been achieved, there can be no further unification; it ceases. Or again, concrescence is a process of determination whereby an initial indeterminate state is transformed into a complete state of determinate being. Once determinateness has been achieved, all process of determination must cease. Time is a perpetual perishing, as the rhythmic perishing of all these successive acts of becoming.

If God is continually prehending the entire world as each actuality begins to be, God never achieves a final unity encompassing all beings whatsoever. It is in that sense that the divine everlasting concrescence or process of creative unification never perishes. God is always in becoming, never in being. But if so, God is not prehensible.

Whitehead himself saw this as a real problem, not to be resolved by close textual interpretations of the twenty-second category of explanation (JAAR 48:576). In 1936, some seven years after the publication of *Process and Reality,* A. H. Johnson asked him: "If God never 'perishes,' how can he provide data for other actual entities? Whitehead replied: "This is a genuine problem. I have not attempted to solve it" (EWP 9f).

If Whitehead's conception of God were revised in terms of future creativity, we might be able to solve the problem. God is not prehensible, but he influences us in bequeathing to us the power of prehending. By prehending and valuing our past in every possible way it can be unified, we can acquire and be influenced by those novel possibilities in taking over God's prehending for us.

IV. Other Difficulties

Some may raise this objection to our proposal: "Creativity is activity, yet we expect all activity to take place in the present. How can there be 'future activity?'" Relativity physics might have taught us otherwise, since contemporary occasions are also in "unison of becoming" with our present immediacy. We continue to think of contemporaries as somehow "present," yet we can have no present interaction with them. These actualities affect us only as past, from which we can calculate back to what would have been contemporary activity. As an everlasting concrescence, God is also in unison of becoming with us. For this we have assumed that God is contemporary with us, but for this there is no clear warrant. We have no way of calculating God's contemporary status on the basis of past effects, for God is "always in concrescence and never in the past" (PR 47). We propose to regard any actuality as active relative to our own concrescent becoming if it enjoys unison of becoming with us, and to locate that activity according as it comes to affect us. By this criterion, other actual occasions in unison of becoming with us turn out to be contemporaries, while the activity of God embraces the whole of the future.

A present occasion "perishes *and* is immortal" (PR126). That is to say, it loses its own subjective immediacy and becomes an objective datum to be prehended by supervening occasions. Looked at from this perspective, perishing is the shift from present immediacy to pastness. Yet God never perishes, being forever future. To be sure, the future becomes present, but what this means is that the unificatory activity generating possible means of unification divides itself into the many contemporary activities of actualization. The present is the self-diremption of the future. The one cosmic activity of the future breaks up into the many activities of the present, each finally achieving its own particular concrete unity, thereby perishing. Thus there are derivative processes of determination emergent from the one cosmic activity of unification, each bearing the creaturely stamp of the present. God is always ahead of the present; when any particular activity becomes present, it is no longer part of the divine activity.

While God's activity is always in our future, valuing what we receive, this activity is in unison of becoming with ours. In the same way as we respond in prehensive unification to the determinate actualities that have just become past, God also responds to the immediate past we determine. But the reponses have different results. Creaturely responses add further determinate actualities to the world, whereas the divine response values how particular determinations will be possible. Since what God creates is future for us, and since God is active in intimate association with the region now future, according to the creative advance, it seems best to think of God as future creativity or as the activity of the future.

In my view, future activity generates novel possibility that is then received from the future, while Whitehead's analysis limits possibility solely to its nontemporal aspects. By means of his primordial envisagement, God orders all the eternal objects together, thus determining what is metaphysically possible or impossible. In this sense he determines what is *purely* possible. That, however, is not enough to determine what is *really* possible in the sense of being actualizable. What is actualizable depends on more than purely formal conditions alone; it also requires enabling conditions, i.e., past occasions to be unified by those formal conditions.

The lures God provides for each nascent occasion must be both relevant and valued. They must be capable of being realized in that particular situation. Whitehead tells us that God is the agent of such relevance (PR 46), but not how relevance is temporally achieved. Somehow God must provide the range of valued alternatives that can be actualized in any given particular situation. In themselves, eternal objects are neither good nor evil, for value is dependent upon the circumstances of actualization. Hydrogen fusion is a destructive evil should atomic bombs ever be rained upon the cities of the earth, but it is the source of life-giving warmth and light as it occurs in the interior of the sun. It is the attempted conjunction of many past conditions by means of some particular form that can be valued as either good or evil. Since the lures God provides are indeed valued, they must pertain to the real possibilities confronting each nascent occasion.

If God is the source of lures that cannot simply be explained in terms of a primordial, nontemporal ordering, there must be some sort of divine temporal activity explaining their relevance and value.[19] It cannot be past, since possibilities are not determinate, nor can it be present, if God is to have any influence on present activities. It can only be future.

If so, God's creative activity must be one and undivided, since the realm of the possible is nonexclusionary. Nuclear war next year is perfectly compatible with peaceful world government, as long as we dwell in the realm of what *might be.* Just as actualization brings about the atomization of the extensive continuum, it also disrupts the continuity of divine unification. The one single divine activity of unification of the past in terms of possible lures is then pluralized into the many present activities of unification producing determinate beings.

Creativity as the means for bringing about unification is shared by God and the occasion. This cannot be a concurrent sharing. The occasion must retain the sole inherent power of actualization whereby it unifies past causal influences in terms of those possibilites provided it by God. It is the sole agency of determination. Initially the creative process is exercised by God on behalf of the nascent occasion, then it is taken over by the creature as it seeks to create itself determinately. Finite determination is exclusionary and irreducibly plural, unlike the monistic activity that preceded it. Yet it is God who has bequeathed to each occasion its measure of creative unification.

The transference of creativity from the one, infinite, inexhaustible activity of future creativity to each finite instance of present creativity bears important affinities with the Thomistic notion of the divine communication of *esse,* the act of existence, to the creatures. In the first place, creativity and *esse* function similarly in these two philosophical systems. Moreover, this essay agrees with Father W. Norris Clarke, S. J.: Present creativity needs a source, and that source is in God.[20] One analogy with the efficient causality that God exercises in communicating *esse,* Father

Clarke proposes that the Whiteheadian God should transmit creativity by efficient causality as well, But as we have seen, newly concrescent occasions cannot prehend their own power of prehending, which is what such a proposal would entail.[21] But this power of prehending the past can be bequeathed to the present by a retreating future, which is not exhausted thereby, since God is always creating himself anew, concrescing further into the future.

There is an important difference from Thomism, however. *Esse*, as the act of existence, brings each actuality into being, so that by communicating to the actuality its *esse* God creates that actuality. This is the core of Thomas Aquinas's creationist revision of Aristotle. For Whitehead, however, the communication of creativity in no way creates the actuality, since the actuality does not acquire its being by that single action. Creation is a double action that requires the conjoint activity of God and the actuality. God is the source of the becoming, which the occasion then transforms into being. But in both philosophies, the basic communicative power of God is similar.

NOTES

1. "Creativity" is not mentioned in the *Oxford English Dictionary* (published 1933), although "concrescence" (1614) and "prehension" (1843) are. Paul Oskar Kristeller traces "creativity" to Whitehead's *Religion in the Making* (New York: Macmillan, 1926), following a suggestion by Paul G. Kuntz. See Kristeller's essay in the *Journal of the History of Ideas* 44/1 (January 1983), 105–113.
   The *Oxford English Dictionary Supplement* (1972) does list one stray citation for 1875 besides two from Whitehead (RM 90, 152). A. W. Ward speaks of "the spontaneous flow of his [Shakespeare's] creativity."
2. See Carl Hausman, "Criteria of Creativity," *Philosophy and Phenomenological Research* 40/2 (December, 1978), 237–249, at 23f.
3. References to the following books will simply be given in the body of the text by these sigla: EWP = *Explorations in Whiteheads Philosophy*, ed. Lewis S. Ford and George L. Kline (New York: Fordham University Press, 1983); EWM = *The Emergence of Whitehead's Metaphysics*, by Lewis S. Ford (Albany: State University of New York Press, 1984), SSS = *Soldier Sage, Saint* by Robert C. Neville (New York: Fordham University Press, 1978); RM = *Religion in the Making*, PR = *Process and Reality*, and AI = *Adventures of Ideas*, all three by A. N. Whitehead (New York: Macmillan, 1926, 1929 and 1933, respectively). JAAR 48 will indicate *The Journal of the American*

Academy of Religion 48/4 (December, 1980), for the essay by Bowman L. Clarke, "God and Time in Whitehead."

4. In the final analysis unrealized eternal objects are located within God's primordial nature to satisfy the general Aristotelian principle that only actualities are primary existents, but these eternal objects are still prior to finite occasions.

5. For the justification of this modification, see my essay on "The Divine Activity of the Future," *Process Studies* 11/3 (Fall, 1981), 169–179.

6. Jorge Luis Nobo calls attention to this earlier understanding of transition in "Transition in Whitehead: A Creative Process Distinct from Concrescence," *International Philosophical Quarterly* 19/3 (September, 1979), 265–283. Where he seeks to reconcile this theory with the theory of concrescence in part III, I find the two theories incompatible, with the second superseding the first.

7. Nancy Frankenberry, "The Power of the Past," *Process Studies* 13/2 (Summer, 1983), 133. See also George L. Kline's discussion of these texts in "Form, Concrescence, and Concretum" (EWP 125f). We will use his term "concretum" for a past occasion as the concrete outcome of concrescence.

8. See also my essay, "Can Freedom Be Created?" *Horizons* 4/2 (Fall, 1977), 183–188.

9. R. J. Connelly, *Whitehead vs. Hartshorne: Basic Metaphysical Issues* (Washington: University Press of America, 1981), pp. 7–31.

10. See, e.g., Laurence E. Wilmot, *Whitehead and God* (Waterloo, Ontario: Wilfrid Laurier University Press, 1979).

11. From the way Whitehead has formulated this, he probably had not yet anticipated the consequent or temporal nature of God (EWM 183).

12. John B. Cobb, Jr., "Buddhist Emptiness and the Christian God," *Journal of the American Academy of Religion* 45/1 (1977), 11–25. See also his book *Beyond Dialogue: Toward a Mutual Transformation of Christianity and Buddhism* (Philadelphia: Fortress Press, 1982).

13. This text comes from a fairly late stage in the composition of *Process and Reality* indicating that Whitehead did not abandon talk of earlier and later phases in his mature theory of concrescence. Among other passages using similar expressions, see PR 38f, 179, 184, 243, 255, 261, and 324, and related use of such phrases as "successive phases," "initial phases," "intermediate phases," and "final phases."

14. The next paragraph does say that "the genetic process is not the temporal succession" (PR 434), but in the context this could be simply an abbreviated way of referring to physical time.

15. See also my essay "On Genetic Successiveness: A Third Alternative," *Southern Journal of Philosophy* 7/4 (Winter, 1969–1970), 421–425.

16. This theme is further developed in my essay on "The Duration of the Present," *Philosophy and Phenomenological Research* 35/1 (September, 1974), 100–106.

17. Some may interpret "the everlasting nature of God, which is in a sense nontemporal and in another sense temporal" (AI 267) to mean that God

might nontemporally unify his temporal feelings, but I take this state to be simply a rather vague way of referring to the primordial and the consequent natures respectively. The primordial nature alone unifies the nontemporal feelings.

18. See my essay on "The Non-Temporality of Whitehead's God," *International Philosophical Quarterly* 13/3 (September, 1973), 347–376. That essay sought to assimilate the temporal as much as possible to the nontemporal within God, whereas I now think that by means of an enriched understanding of the future it might be possible to assimilate the nontemporal to the temporal.

19. Though we approach these issues somewhat differently, I now agree with Father Felt that God's freedom is temporally emergent in specific acts of evaluation. See James W. Felt, S. J., "The Temporality of Divine Freedom," *Process Studies* 4/4 (Winter, 1974), 252–262.

20. W. Norris Clarke, S. J., *The Philosophical Approach to God: A Neo-Thomist Perspective* (Winston-Salem, N. C.: Wake Forest University, 1979), chapter 3. This chapter is also summarized in "Christian Theism and Whiteheadian Process Philosophy," *Logos: Philosophical Issues in Christian Perspective* 1 (1980). 9–44. (*Logos*, edited by James W. Felt, S. J., is available from the Philosophy Department of the University of Santa Clara.)

21. See my critique of Father Clarke's proposal in "The Search for the Source of Creativity," *Logos* 1 (1980), 45–52.

Elizabeth M. Kraus

God the Savior

The problem of evil – its nature, source and transmission, as well as the manner in which it relates to and is overcome by a loving, compassionate God – has long been a central issue in Christian moral and theological speculation. The purpose of this essay is to transpose that discussion to a level of higher generality in order to explore the cosmological grounding of that paradoxical portion of the Easter Proclamation that exults, "O happy fault, O necessary sin of Adam, which gained for us so great a Redeemer!"

I will define evil in the cosmological order as the loss of aesthetic intensity – "aesthetic destruction" in the words of *Adventures of Ideas* (AI 256).[1] It is immediately obvious that the evil of which I speak is neither the brutal, obstructive selfishness found in human sin (moral evil) nor the tragedy of the extinction of a life or a species or an ecological system that follows from the "blind running" of the laws of nature (physical evil). Rather, I address my inquiry to that more general evil, that "sin," that "death," of which human sin and biological destruction are further specifications. My thesis shall be that evil, the loss of aesthetic intensity, is an essential component in finite process, and that a complex divine activity overcoming that evil is equally essential. Thus, for the purposes of this essay, I will use the terms "evil," death," "sin," "selfishness," "redemption," "sanctification," and other such words, normally restricted to the moral sphere, in a cosmological sense, removing from them the limited or at times pejorative connotations they have in the moral sphere, and will explore (1) the role of these now generalized phenomena in the cosmos and (2) the divine activity they elicit in a process cosmology.

First of all, it is to be noted that the existence and presence of cosmic evil and the corresponding necessity for some form or forms of cosmic redemption are not accidents befalling an innocent world. By the very nature of the self-creative process, the cosmos and all its creatures are the bearers and executors of cosmic evil in its two-fold manifestation:

death and sin. Any and all finite processes culminate in death, because the achievements of new moments of subjective immediacy entails the perishing of achieved moments. Death is the necessary evil manifest in the suicidal urge that drives the accomplishments of the present, lemming-like, into the sea of the past, so that new presents can be nourished by their decomposing riches. Finite process likewise bears the responsibility for sin, because the achievement of self-value in the present both accomplishes the disintegration of past values and inhibits the intensity of value achievable in the future. As I will demonstrate, sin is an equally necessary consequence of the finitude (i.e., determinateness) of the self-creating creature, a finitude rendering multiple immediacies mutually obstructive. Such obstructiveness mandates the fragmentation and exploitation of past achievements, be they peak human experiences or minerals hidden in the base of mountains; at the same time, it tends to spill over into the future in an attempt to coerce its repetition, thereby inhibiting the creative urge driving the universe on to the achievement of new value intensities in experience.

The cosmic evil I term death is a fairly straightforward rendering of Whitehead's enunciation of the necessity, in his cosmological scheme, for the perpetual perishing of subjectivity. Likewise, one of the forms of cosmic sin — the type I will later call "sin against the past" — is fairly traditional Whiteheadian doctrine: It represents the activity whereby an emergent entity selectively objectifies the fully determinate entities in its past and admits those aspects selected into its emerging viewpoint as revalued from the perspective of that viewpoint. However, the second form of cosmic sin — "sin against the future" — may not seem to be a direct consequence of Whitehead's thought. In fact, it might be argued that the more aesthetic importance achieved in the present, the *greater* are the riches bequeathed to the future, and hence that this talk of present value achievement inhibiting future value achievement (and thus being sinful) is erroneous.

A brief digression in response to such an objection is in order, therefore, before I proceed to the main body of my exposition, where the topic will be pursued in greater detail. The point I wish to make is that the more important the value achieved in the present, the more it pressures its continuance or reiteration in the future and (unless this pressure is compensated for) the more it inhibits the emergence of novel forms of value in the future.

If I may use an illustration from the history of human creation, every artistic genius, in taking art forward a step by his or her novel creation, spawns a school: a generation of imitators or commentators so impressed by the achievement of the genius as to wish only to continue in his or her aesthetic footsteps by further explicating the implications of the creation. It is obvious that the solution cannot be the repression of genius in favor of a mediocrity that does not tend so powerfully to perpetuate itself. Nor can it be a refusal to be influenced by great value achievement. Both mediocrity and value-rejection are themselves evil in an aesthetic or cosmic context. What I term "sin against the future" is a cosmic necessity if value achievements are to survive beyond their fleeting moment of presentness. This sin is an integral part of the cosmological scheme; it is the affirmation of the "this myselfness" of value importance.

Since all creatures in Whitehead's process universe must die and must sin against both past and future because of the very nature of the self-creative process, it is imperative that we probe more deeply into this metaphysics of sin that I have postulated, for only after a full exploration of the nature of creaturely evil can the overcoming of that primal fault be understood. If I may take a cue from C. S. Peirce, the evil, the sinful of which I speak, is not to be counterposed to the good, to the virtuous, for the dyadic opposition between good and evil, between virtue and vice, appears only in the moral realm, where sin in the strict sense of the term is an ugly reality. In a Platonic cosmology such as Whitehead's, where the aesthetic takes logical primacy over the moral, the good (defined as harmony: the immediate "fit" of the parts comprising a whole) has no opposite. Thus, in an aesthetic context, evil *qua* the totally inharmonious has no reality, for to be real is to incarnate a harmony. Therefore, in such a context, every variety of evil is good.

However, to identify the good with the harmonious is to express only part of the Platonic understanding of the good – that part that is teachable, that part that is graspable by theoretical understanding. This grasp of the good is radically incomplete unless supplemented by a dialectical vision of its normative aspect. Such a vision of the good reveals not merely the harmony of the parts in a whole (i.e., its structure) but, more importantly, the appropriateness of that harmony to components it conjoins. It is through an examination of the dimension of appropriateness that the aesthetic sense of sin is revealed, as well as sin's cosmic necessity.

The key issue is prefigured in the curious bivalence of the term "appropriateness" itself. As an adjective, "appropriate" signifies suitable, fit, proper; while as a verb it connotes "to take exclusive possession of," "to make peculiarly one's own." A similar bivalence can be seen in Whitehead's examination of value in *Modes of Thought*, where he sees value manifested phenomenologically, "at the base of our existence, [as] a sense of worth: . . . the sense of existence for its own sake, of existence which is its own justification, of existence with its own character" (MT 149) as a "this myself." Yet, at the same time, the "this myselfness" aimed at and achieved in self-creative process is accomplished through the appropriation of "others" who were selves in their own right, and is contributed to future "others" for their appropriation in their self-creative processes.

In the former sense, objectifications of past selves (which is to say, of past values) achieve the immediate unity of a present self-value. In the latter sense, the present value is a datum provoking future revaluation as it is taken up into future self-creative processes aimed at future value achievements. Thus, in the words of *Modes of Thought*:

> Everything has some value for itself, for the others, and for the whole . . . No unit can separate itself from the others and from the whole. And each unit exists for itself, and this involves sharing value intensity with the universe. Anything that in any sense exists has two sides, namely its individual self and its significance in the universe. Also, either of these aspects is a factor in the other (MT 150–151).

It is in the necessary conflict between these "two sides" of existence, between these two aspects of the appropriate, that the necessity of cosmic sin is rooted.

The conflict is necessary as an aspect of the order of the cosmos for a number of reasons that can only be elaborated on the basis of a further examination of Whitehead's construal of value. Since the root metaphor of his cosmology is "experience," value must be grasped in experiential terms; it must be seen as a subjective characteristic of experience. Yet, since experience is always "experience of . . .," value must likewise have an objective aspect.

Both faces are hinted at in the *Modes of Thought* quotation, for the "individual self" aimed at is an *enjoyment* of individuality, the subjective intensity of the experience of being "this myself;" whereas what is significant "for the others and for the whole" is not the intensity of an experience as once enjoyed but the pragmatic after-effects brought about by that experience as an entity, – i.e., as a determinate structural unity functioning objectively in subsequent acts of experience. Thus, borrowing language from Teilhard, value has a within – the intensity of subjective experience aimed at in subjective process – and a without – the determinate structure of the being that emerges from the self-creative process of becoming.

Each aspect is a function of the other, in the sense that a loose or simplistic structure is the external sign of a low intensity experience, whereas if high intensity experience is aimed at, the aim will crystallize a structure characterizable as elegant in the mathematical sense of the term. In both cases, the intensity attainable and the complexity achievable are a function of the order present in the actual world out of which the experience arises and whose unification is accomplished in the experience.

The operative term in the process creative of value is "unification" – the fitting together of the objects of experience (1) into the unity of an experience, (2) into the unity of a fitting (intensely enjoyed) experience, and (3) into the unity of an intensely enjoyed experience that will be a datum for future intensely enjoyed experiences. Thus, both the structure and future functioning of an act of experience, of an actual entity, derive from its subjective aim at intensity, as also does the way in which it objectifies the past.

It is this aim at intensity that lies at the root of the necessary evil of the cosmos, for it both demands the fragmentation, the "depersonalization," of the self-values achieved by past entities and opens up the possibility of inhibiting intense value experience for future entities. The activity achieving both of these ends is cosmic sin, for it involves a trivialization, a manipulation, a self-centered appropriation of past others. and their self-values as well as a coercive attitude toward future others. Thus, "appropriate," when construed normatively, signifies the maximum intensity of experience, the maximum elegance of structure, achievable by a self arising out of its private appropriation of its actual world. This is equivalent to saying that to become is to sin, in as much as becoming a self necessarily involves a self-ish relation to past and future selves.

The paradigmatic instance of this cosmic sin in Whitehead's philosophy of organism is the antisocial nature of a "living occasion," an occasion characterized by its immersion in the present and by the intensity of its grasp at immediate novelty. Such an occasion is so centered in its present that (1) the past of its organic host is grasped as though created solely for its private enjoyment and (2) the future of the host is totally irrelevant. As Whitehead points out in *Process and Reality*, the activites of living occasions within the "animal body" have such a destructive influence upon that body, in the form of chemical dissociations, imbalances, etc., that the host organism must steal from its environment in order to repair its internal damages.

In the course of evolutionary history, living occasions have had to become both "socialized" and "civilized" in order to avoid the negative consequences of the piracy they provoke. In one sense, they have had to acquire a concern for the personally ordered threads of which they are a part. But more importantly, they have had to develop some degree of sensitivity regarding their potentially detrimental effects upon the "animal body" harboring them and upon the environment supporting that animal body. Without such concern, it would be impossible for complex organisms classifiable as living because of the dominance of living occasions within them to develop a "life span" sufficient for them to adapt to environmental change and hence survive by evolving.

It might be said that in this fashion the cosmos has initiated its own redemptive process by introducing the germ of concern for the others, a concern that is both selfish and unselfish, both erotic and agapistic. But this redemptive germ is incapable of overcoming the inherent self-centeredness of finite process to any significant extent, for the evolutionary path opened by it is, in our cosmic epoch at least, a path in the direction of more complex organisms with a consequently higher degree of individuality and autonomy (i.e., self-centeredness) resulting from the emergence of historical threads of living occasions within the organic lattice, threads even more concerned with self-perpetuation.

In the words of the *Function of Reason*, the thrust of life is "to live, to live well and to live better" (FR 18). In the low grade organisms in which they first arise, these threads, these "living persons," interrelate in a democratic fashion; but as life ascends the evolutionary ladder, the democracy evidenced in the protistan and plant kingdoms gives way to the increasing monarchical control of a central thread of occasions – a central living "person" or "personality" that directs the organism for the sake of the continuance of its (the regnant person's) occasions of self-enjoyment. Thus, interest in the past, present, and future is intensified, but it is the past, present, and future of the regnant person and (secondarily) of the organism harboring the regnant person, not necessarily of the other organisms in the environing cosmos. These "others" are perforce merely *used* to ensure survival, used only in so far as they have literal or figurative "food-value" for the living organism.

The social structures that appear within species of higher grade living organisms, as well as the ecological relations among species in an environment, are further attempts on the part of the cosmos to redeem itself from its aboriginal "fault," for they seek to replace the self-interest of individual organisms with an interest in the survival of the group. Yet the success is only partial, for as long as the aim at intense enjoyment is the central thrust of experience, and so long as enjoyment is a private event confined within a subject, complete altruism is a cosmological impossibility. Far from disappearing in a social context, exploitation merely becomes the exploitation of lower status individuals within the society or of individuals outside the society in question.

The emergence of the human being and of human civilization increases the possibility of exploitation and gross selfishness because of the heightened intensity of experience possible for human consciousness and the consequent heightened lure for enjoyment. At the same time, however, it opens the path toward genuine altruism, inasmuch as a human has at least the germinal capacity to grasp values more general than private self-values, which more general values transcend the good-for-THIS-self toward the goodness of self-hood. However, even on the human plane, the good is, to use Plato's words, "seen but hardly seen" (*Republic* 517c); hence, the life history of a human is best characterized as a journey *toward* the vision of the good, a journey that can never entirely escape the relativistic confines of its finite perspective, a journey always partly evil because it is only partly good, partly selfish because the ego and its interests (the limitations imposed by its perspective) can never be totally overcome.

In point of fact, the ego and its interests *should* not be overcome, for in the context of Whitehead's cosmology, self-value and value-for-the-others cannot be torn apart. Each is what the other makes it to be: hence, if significant self-value is *not* sought, no value of any significance can be contributed to the others. The purpose of human societies, of human political and constitutional creations, is to harmonize, to fit together appropriately, the two faces of value in the human realm in such ways that each is given its due importance.

Yet this harmonization is always inadequate. Value conflicts, conflicts of interest, conflicts of "rights to enjoyment," are inescapable road-signs on any path to the future, for if the human or cosmic future is to be more than a mere reenaction of the past inevitably generating staleness of experience, it must create itself in an opposition to the past that nevertheless retains an analogy with the more general contours of the past it opposes. As Whitehead has said, "the art of progress is to achieve order amid change and change amid order" (PR 339).

This art entails the exploitation of the past for those of its elements that are susceptible to novel syntheses. These novel syntheses perforce disturb the social lattice and diminish the intensity of experience for the more tradition-bound members of the society, inasmuch as the traditionalists cannot integrate the novel elements into their experience by means of traditional categories. Ostrich-like, they must ignore the new, dismiss it to the vague, chaotic background against which their now impoverished experience is set, and suffer either the mists of confusion or the self-destroying, impotent rage of the reactionary. By the same token, the novelty created cannot destroy the social order completely without at the same time destroying itself. It must be a "change amid order," a novelty synthesizable into a new social order that is more of a generalization of the old than its replacement.

Thus, children oppose parents; each generation takes a stand against its progenitor; "each new epoch enters upon its career by waging unrelenting war upon the aesthetic gods [i.e., values] of the immediate predecessor" (PR 340). The war, be it that of a child, a generation, or an epoch, culminates when successful in a period of adjustment, of adaptation, of generalization, of integration of the old into the new, and reaches senescence when the new order has solidified into a tradition merely passed on. At this point, intensity of experience diminishes, life is pervaded with ennui, and an era begins its fruitless pursuit of perversely novel "pleasures" in the hope that by means of them it may revivify itself while still retaining the deadening tradition.

As has been seen in this phenomenology of cosmic evolution, unredeemed cosmic sin results in a manifold loss of value-intensity in the future. On the one hand, there is the suffering produced in the bearers of tradition (be they human or inorganic reactionaries) by the forces of creation, as well as that produced in the same traditionalists by the senescence of the tradition. In both cases, the effects of sin are suffered by the "inorganic" members of society: those shaping their lives by inherited behavior patterns. On the other hand, the living members, those refusing to be bound by tradition, must themselves undergo a two-fold suffering: that produced by the creative enterprise itself (the agony that accompanies the ecstasy), as well as that produced by the rejection of the created product by traditionalists.

Thus, in the more aesthetically complex areas of the cosmos, we find a two-fold sin producing a two-fold suffering for the future. The creators are guilty of the Nietszchean sin. Having passed beyond good and evil as defined by the past, they diminish the lives of those who must bear the consequences of creation. The creators come, as Christ said, not to bring peace but to bring a sword. The traditionalists, on the other hand, commit the reactionary sin of attempting to inhibit future creation by the massive weight of the tradition they pass on; again, diminishing future others. In both instances, the root of sin is foundationally the same: The process of value achievement in the present tends to inhibit the advance of value achievement in the future.

In the preceding exposition, the two modalities of sin stand revealed: 1. sin against the past, which brings about the exploitation of past for the sake of the present; and 2. sin against the future, which brings about the perpetuation of present achievement at the possible expense of future novel achievement. Both are intimate and essential aspects of creative process, which weaves relevant fragments of past creations into the unity of a newly emergent self, which self then adds itself to the many with the demand that it be taken into account by being reiterated.

Therefore, cosmic sin, the necessary sin calling for a necessary redemption, is at base the sin of selfishness, and that which must be redeemed, i.e., bought back, is not the sinning self but the past and future selves sinned against. If finite process in its temporal, historical form is not to be brought to a halt by the self-centeredness of the present, then the fullness of past self-achievement must be ransomed from the fragmentation produced by the present's exploitative appropriation of it, and the possibilities for novel, creative self-realization in the future must be the object of a special providence that protects them from being overwhelmed by the dominant selves achieved at the present. Without the inclusion of a two-fold divine activity of this sort, an activity safeguarding both past and future, the Whiteheadian cosmological scheme falls apart.

The scheme demands, therefore, the postulation of an actual entity capable of physically overcoming the disjunction of past achievements by conjoining them in a unity that does not entail loss, and of conceptually overcoming both the pompous oppressiveness of tradition and the insolent disruptiveness of novelty (1) by providing *relevant*, alternative possibilities, and (2) by introducing self-transcending values into the world.

To be more specific, the exigencies of the scheme demand the postulation of a divine entity whose physical feelings bring the manifold of realized selves into a unity that does not destroy the unity of the realizations unified. Because realized selves are not mutually obstructive from the more general, divine standpoint, their unification can be achieved without the fragmentation and exploitation that are an essential aspect of the process of selective objectification. The scheme likewise demands that this same entity's conceptual feelings order possibility in such ways that despite (or rather because of) the selves that have been achieved, further possibilities for further self-achievement are realized, and further self-realization processes are shielded from the overwhelmng pressure of the past.

Moreover, the scheme demands the conquering of the other modality of cosmic evil: death. This entails that perishing be overcome, that the haunting "terror at the loss of the past" (PR 340) be mitigated by a divine act that gives everlasting being within divine experience to the self-values that have become in finite process. The same divine act that brings about the progressive unification of the cosmos in divine experience (and therefore creates the cosmos *as a cosmos*) "creates" the unitary beings within that cosmos, not by an act of efficient causality that summons their being into being, but by an act that captures, and establishes as permanent and unfading actualities the unitary self-values aimed at and accomplished in all finite becoming. The creature may be self-creative in its becoming, but its being is "created" in this nontraditional yet not antitraditional sense of the term when that self-value is absorbed into God.

The divine entity has, therefore, a complex, two-fold function in the scheme: to be (from one point of view) Redeemer of the past and Creator of the future, and, from another viewpoint, to be Creator of the past and Redeemer of the future. Furthermore, this function must be exercised in such a way that it does not introduce a more profound, irredeemable "divine sin" into the cosmos, a sin of infinitely selfish appropriation of the past and infinitely coercive closing off of the possibility of novelty in the future.

Inasmuch as finite selfishness is a direct consequence of the limited character of creaturely acts of experience, of the fact that they are of necessity views from a viewpoint, the perspective of divine experience must overcome the limitations of a viewpoint. Yet, at the same time, it cannot be a view from no viewpoint without falling into the nonentity of the totally indeterminate. This is to say, therefore, that the divine subjective aim, the value aided at and progressively realized in divine experience must be general enough to subsume all finite subjective aims as further specifications of itself, and yet not so general as to be infinite in the sense of totally indeterminate. Only if the divine aim has the requisite generality can the divine appropriation of actual finite achievement and the divine envisagement of the possibilities for future achievement avoid the double sin of appropriation and coercion.

The divine aim must therefore be at the good of which all other goods are further specifications; it must be at the value of values, at the appropriateness of the appropriate, at the form of forms – itself a form (i.e., a determinate harmony, itself and not other) and yet the condition for the possibility of all less general forms, grounding both their possibility and their mutual harmony. It must be an aim that both defines and establishes the good as authentic selfhood.

This divine subjective aim is granted no dispensation from the laws of metaphysics; it is a self-centered aim at intensity of experience. Because of the polarity of intensity and complexity, however, it is also an aim at the realization of the most elegant structure possible given the available components to be structured, an aim at a structure capable of integrating all other structures, an aim at self-overcoming the mutual obstructiveness of all lesser selves.

It is this aim that guides the divine physical activity of "saving" the world by preserving the full unity and identity of achieved finite values (or finite selves) in the immediacy of the experience of the divine self, thereby giving them the everlasting permanence of being. The physical redemptive act is therefore one of overcoming the perishing and fragmentation of the past produced by the obstructure character of finite achievement, and of mitigating the consequent cosmological necessity of objective immortality via *selective* objectification as the sole fate of finite self-value.

The divine salvific act, however, must be more than an overcoming of the present's sin against the past, for, as has been detailed *supra*, the cosmic sin of selfishness affects the future as well. Important self-achievement pressures reenactments of itself. As is seen most clearly in inorganic societies, the force of social tradition inhibits the arising of future selves whose self-hood is more than an inherited repetition of the defining character of a present self and whose self-enjoyment can transcend the intensity of self-enjoyment experienced by that present self. Since cosmic sin affects the future, the divine overcoming of it must extend to the future as well.

The cosmos, as a creature of the creativity, is an active agent in this second modality of world salvation. Its successive instances of primal creative energy combine and recombine into more and more complex social organizations, which provide more and more order in the actual worlds of their included members and hence more and more intensity and complexity in the experience of those members (despite the fact that the structural complexity of their experience is inherited and not subjectively generated). At the threshold of life, the inherited data are susceptible to nonimitative integrations (i.e., integrations structured by forms not exemplified in the data to be integrated) because of the complexity of the social order contained in the data. At this point, it becomes possible for an emerging entity to overcome the pressure of the past and achieve novelty without at the same time isolating itself from the past. Thus, J. S. Bachs can ultimately be followed by Beethovens and not merely by C. P. E. Bachs.

Such finite self-redemption is impossible, however, without divine assistance, for unless values unexemplified in the past are nevertheless relevant to that past, they can never become the object of finite conceptual feelings. God's conceptual feelings, the valuation or ideal realization of the eternal objects, is therefore more than merely the ground of possibility-as-such; it is as well the ground for novel possibilities *and* for the possibility of their ingression into the actual. Only if the eternal objects are together in the "mind of God," together in an ideally realized unity of mutual and graded interrelations, can physically unrealized potentialities bear a real relatedness to the realized potential of the cosmos. Thus, God's providence for the future is, in a strange way, the creating of that future, for it is the source of the possibility for living, nonimitative, "free" occasions of experience. The same providence achieves the overcoming of the future-directed effects of present selfishness. As Whitehead put it, God "does not create the world [in the sense of producing it through the exercise of an act of efficient causality], he saves it," and saves it by " the overpowering rationality of his conceptual realization" (PR 346).

Even given both the emergence of life as a "bid for freedom" (PR 104) from the pressure of inheritance and the divine creative providence for that freedom, the cosmic sin of selfishness is not completely overcome; for, as described earlier, while life may achieve creative autonomy in its drive at self-realization, it can still fall guilty of indifference to the future consequences of that realization. Despite the various attempts of the cosmos to overcome the anarchy of living occasions through varying forms of socialization, the basic problem, the foundational evil, is unresolved. Each attempt, by restricting life in historically ordered channels (thus giving it historical sensitivity), deepens the intensity of self-realization a living occasion can achieve in its self-creative process and, in consequence, increases both its potential for selfishness and its possibly adverse effect upon future selves.

The imbalance, the loss of intensity and harmony in some areas of the future that can result from the robberies of living occasions, calls for final divine activity that will inhibit the thief's potentially detrimental effects without at the same time inhibiting the thief. As Whitehead has aptly phrased it, the action of God in the world cannot "combat destructive force with destructive force" or even "productive force with productive force" (PR 346).

For the Divine actual entity to engage in physical combat with the world, thereby preventing thievery, would entail a violation of the primordial thrust of the creativity, of which God is the first instance – a thrust toward novelty, toward intensity of experience, towards freedom. Again, God does not forcibly create the world but saves it through "a tender care that nothing be lost" (PR 346).

We have already seen that the cosmic evil termed death (the perishing of immediacy) is overcome by the absorption of all finite value achievement into the ever-growing aesthetic creation that is the burgeoning divine experience. We have already seen that this same divine function overcomes the sin of the present against the past (the exploitative fragmentation of value achieved) by preserving achieved values in their integrity. We have already seen that (at least in part) the sin of the present against the future (the coercion that leads to value-repetition rather than value-innovation) is overcome by a divine providence that makes novel future values possible and relevant despite the power of important present values. What has not been explored is the final divine salvific act, that which enables every value achieved to be a value not only "in itself" and "for the others" but "for the totality" as well. With this exploration, God's saving function will stand revealed as a trivalent activity: creation, redemption, and sanctifiction.

Central to Whitehead's cosmology is the insight that the achievement of novel, determinate, significant self-hood is the primal thrust of cosmic creativity. However, as the preceding pages have attempted to show, the lure of this self-achievement is like that of the apple whose symbolic attractiveness destroyed Eden and forever threatens to inhibit the creation of Eden II. The tragedy buried in the Whiteheadian cosmology is the fact that the glory of individuality (or, to put it another way, the ecstasy of intense experience), is the primal source of evil in the universe, its Satanic vice. This is not to fault the Whiteheadian scheme; rather it underlines the fact that no element in the system is such that it could be called primary; not even individuality. Each element is organically interfused with all others; hence the glory and the ecstasy of individual achievement are genuinely glorious and ecstatic *only* when overcome by the divine saving function. The final divine task is a civilization of individual value-experience whereby individuality may be transcended without tarnish to the glory of individual autonomy. How is this to be done?

Clues are scattered throughout Whitehead's later works, particularly *Modes of Thought* and *Adventures of Ideas*. In the latter, he speaks of "our sense of the value *for its own sake,* of the *totality* of historic fact in respect to its essential unity" (MT 164, emphasis added). The extract is significant enough to be quoted *in toto*.

> There is a unity in the universe, enjoying value and (by its immanence) sharing value. For example, take the subtle beauty of a flower in some isolated glade of a primeval forest. No animal has ever had the subtlety of experience to enjoy its full beauty. And yet this beauty is a grand fact in the universe. When we survey nature and think however flitting and superficial has been the animal enjoyment of its wonders, and when we realize how incapable the separate cells and pulsations of each flower are of enjoying the total effect – then our sense of the value of details for the totally dawns upon our consciousness. This is the intui-

tion of holiness, an intuition of the sacred, which is at the foundation of all religion (ibid.).
What is this holiness, this sacredness intuited?

Whitehead responds:

> Finally there is Deity, which is that factor *in the universe* whereby there is importance, value, and ideal beyond the actual. It is by reference of the spatial immediacies to the ideals of Deity that the sense of worth beyond ourselves arises. The unity of a transcendent universe, and the multiplicity of realized actualities both enter into our experience by this sense of Deity . . . . We owe to the sense of Deity the obviousness of the many actualities of the world, and the obviousness of the unity of the world for the preservation of the values realized and for the transitions to ideals beyond realized fact (MT 140, emphasis added).

Whitehead's answer seems to be that the necessary and essential selfishness of individual actualities, particularly high-order actualities, is overcome, is saved from its potentially destructive consequences, by an intuition of the sacredness of the cosmos -*as-one*: as one which was, and is becoming, and will become.

Whence comes this past, present, and future sanctification; Whence this holiness, this wholeness, of the has-sinned, is-sinning, and will-sin multiplicity of self-creating actualities? From the fact that all actualities, despite their discord and mutual obstructiveness, have been, are being, and will be taken up into the unity of divine experience, where perfect harmony is attained. But this divinely created holiness of the universe does not accomplish the final salvation of that universe, for the universe attains wholeness only from the standpoint of God: within divine experience. Without a final divine function, the many actualities of the world remain locked in their mutually obstructive aloneness, unaware of their divinely accomplished unity. As alone in this fashion, they are blind, without a vision of altruistic goals and of the value of a unity transcending self-unity, which vision would enable them to adventure in their self-realization processes without the mutual destruction that results from their drive at personal rather than collective unity.

The first extract from *Modes of Thought* is explicit in its insistence on the presence of an *intuition* of holiness within the experience of a high-order actuality. *Process and Reality* vaguely hints at the same sort of intuition in its tantalizing, suggestive penultimate paragraph.

The Principle of Relativity is not to be stopped at the Consequent Nature of God. This nature itself passes into the temporal world according to its gradation of relevance to the various occasions. . . . For the perfected actuality passes back into the temporal world, and qualifies this world so that each temporal actuality includes it as an immediate fact of relevant experience. For the kingdom of heaven is with us today. . . . What is done in the world is transformed into a reality in heaven, and the reality in heaven passes back into the world (PR 350–351).

In *The Metaphysics of Experience,* I have styled this passing back into the world of the heaven-transformed reality the Superject Nature of God, the divine activity of expressing the divinely created holiness of the world to and in the world. In light of the *Modes of Thought* extracts, it becomes possible to see that the holiness intuited is the aesthetic unity of the world, "the value of the details for the totality" (MT 164), and that the intuition of this holiness can enable a self to transcend its private self-value in its self-creative process. The terminal chapters of *Adventures of Ideas,* with their magnificent exposition of Beauty and Tragic Peace, take the insight to fulfillment and flesh out what I am styling the third "saving" function of God vis-à-vis the world: santification.

Like *Modes of Thought, Adventures of Ideas* appeals to an experience: "a positive feeling which crowns the 'life and motion' of the soul"; "a broadening of feeling due to the emergence of some deep metaphysical insight, unverbalized [i.e., not compressible into rational categories] and yet momentous in its coordination of values"; "a trust in the efficacy of Beauty"; "a sense that fineness of achievement is as it were a key unlocking treasure that the narrow nature of things [i.e., the limitations of finite selfhood] would keep remote"; "a grasp of infinitude, an appeal beyond boundaries" (AI 285). When a component in the complexity of a high-order entity, such an experience brings about the altruism needed to finally overcome the essential selfishness of the self-creative process, to finally put to rest its "restless egotism" (ibid.).

Calling this the experience of Peace, Whitehead makes it an essential element in the civilization of experience. I maintain tht the "Peace" of *Adventures of Ideas,* the "holiness" of *Modes of Thought,* and the "kingdom of heaven" of *Process and Reality* are all perspectival accounts of the same divine function – world sanctification – as announced to and in the world. As a revelation of the holiness of the past, a holiness brought about by the absorption of the multiplicity of past achievements into the ever-growing unity of divine experience, it reveals the fact that the fullness of self-achievement is attained only when the self-achieved is such that it can transcend selfish goals and become an integral part of a cosmos whose unity is divinely created and hence sacred. The revelation, when it enters present experience, inspires the broadening of selfish goals and makes possible the attainment of maximum holiness in the future.

The modality of the revelation is critical, however, Whitehead is careful to note that the experience comes "as a gift" that is "largely beyond the control of purpose" (AI 285). I see this as implying that the intuition does not come about through cosmological or epistemological necessity, as would be the case if the datum experienced were a fact in the past of the experiencer. The wholeness of the cosmos is a wholeness becoming, not a wholeness already become. The gift, the giver, and the giving (which are merely different perspectives on the same reality) are not past from the temporal vantage point of the recipient but rather contemporaneous – in unison of becoming – with the self experiencing.

In addition, the language of "gift" suggests that the experience is not somehow "earned" by the experiencing subject as wages for previous episodes in its self-functioning. It is offered in the *Matthew* 11:15 sense of "He who has ears to hear, let him hear," where "having ears to hear" could be interpreted as having reached a level of intensity of experience where aesthetic sensitivity is possible, and "let him hear" would represent an invitation to aesthetic receptivity, not an imposition of aesthetic fact.

One might borrow language from another philosophico-theological tradition and call the gift sanctifying grace, for it opens the hearts of those ready for it, making them capable of acts whose value and efficacy is "supernatural." In an intriguing manner, this vision of the holiness of the past (the past as being-redeemed-in-God) sanctifies and quasi-divinizes the present by making it capable of escaping the sinful limits of finite selfhood and of cooperating with God in the creation of a future to be itself assimilated to God.

Like sanctifying grace, the vision does not coerce its acceptance. In fact, from within a Whiteheadian context the medieval disputes concerning the noncompelling yet efficacious power of grace can be seen as wrongheaded. The vision cannot compel, because the holiness seen is not a created fact in the past of the visionary but a creation-in-process: partially complete, partially incomplete, yet nevertheless pervaded by the divine subject. It is this pervasion of the past by a God becoming definite through that past, it is this immanence of the divine subject in every phase of its becoming, that is vaguely glimpsed in the intuition of holiness. Since the subject grasped in the intuition is not fully determinate, the intuition can be admitted into experience only via a free leap of faith, a "trust in the efficacy of Beauty" (AI 285) without which subjective despair of savage selfishness are only other alternatives.

But the trust, the faith, the leap are neither blind nor reasonless. The vision is efficacious because despite the unfinished character of the epic in the process of composition by "the poet of the world" (PR 346, 526), its initial stanzas can be recognized as poetry. That the past is being redeemed, that the evils of death and sin are not triumphant, can be vaguely glimpsed in the whispered testimony of history that good eventually emerges out of even the most hideous barbarism. This testimony, albeit incomplete and faint, is nevertheless factual and can ground faith if the potential believer does not deliberately turn away from it or has not been temporarily deadened by the force of recent evil. But what the vision grounds is still faith, not knowledge. Hence it must be said that it is faith which makes us whole.

However, faith without works is dead. The vision is not given for the private contemplation and enjoyment of the visionary. It is given in order to be translated into a self-functioning at the present that cooperates with God (1) in bringing about the holiness of the past and (2) in making possible the holiness of the future. This faith in a sacred cosmos whose being is being created by loving redemption inspires a trust in the operation of the same divine functions in the future, thereby evoking a love that transforms present selves who have "heard" into finite cocreators, coredeemers, and cosanctifiers of the cosmos: *adjutores Dei.*

NOTES

1. Citations will be made in the text through abbreviations listed in the bibliography.

BIBLIOGRAPHY

AI   Alfred North Whitehead. *Adventures of Ideas.* New York: Macmillan, 1933.
MT Alfred North Whitehead. *Modes of Thought.* New York: Macmillan, 1938.
PR   Alfred North Whitehead. *Process and Reality,* Corrected Edition, (edited by David Ray Griffin and Donald W. Sherburne). New York: The Free Press, 1978.
ME Elizabeth M. Kraus. *The Metaphysics of Experience.* New York: Fordham University Press, 1979.
FR   Alfred North Whitehead. *Function of Reason.* Princeton, N.J.: Princeton University Press, 1929.

Carl G. Vaught

Metaphor, Analogy, and the Nature of Truth

In philosophical discussions about the nature of truth, a distinction is often drawn between claims that are true and the meaning of truth, and for those who are familiar with the history of the problem, a further contrast sometimes emerges between the meaning of truth and the concept of the highest truth. Truths, truth, and the highest truth can therefore be distinguished from the outset as separate contexts in which the problem of truth arises for reflective consideration. In the light of these distinctions, the approach to the problem of truth also appears to have a three-fold focus: at first approximation, truths are said to be the preoccupation of scientific inquiry; the meaning of truth becomes the special province of the philosopher; and the highest truth becomes the subject matter of theological speculation. Thus, just as there are three domains in which the problem of truth arises, so there are three approaches to the problem as it presents itself within each separate region. Of course, these approaches overlap, for every theory of the meaning of truth purports to be true; most of us wonder whether it is true that there is a highest truth; and truth and the highest truth come together for those traditional views that hold that the nature and the existence of the highest being are identical. If the highest being knows what is true because of its own nature, and if the essence of this being is identical with its existence, then the truth that it knows is the truth that it is, which is in turn to be identified with truth itself.

In this essay I will begin with the philosophical concern with the nature of truth and with the traditional philosophical theories that have attempted to explicate its meaning. In the process I will attempt to connect these theories with their scientific and theological counterparts, seeking in particular to do justice to the scientific attempt to find the truth and to the theological concern with the highest truth. However, my ultimate aim is to develop an account of the nature of truth which is not only related to these other regions but will also give us access to the ground of truth. As I will attempt to indicate, this ground lies beyond the scientific, the philosophical, and the theological enterprises as they are ordinarily construed, and is to be explicated in terms of the crucial role of metaphorical and analogical discourse in human experience. Our fundamental purpose, then, is to locate the ground in the light of which the three-fold nature of the problem of truth can be understood and to articulate its significance in metaphorical and analogical terms.

I

The most familiar place to begin our discussion is with the correspondence theory and with the definition of truth as the adequation of the intellect and the real order. According to the traditional Aristotelian formulation:

> To say of what is that it is not, or of what is not that it is, is false, while to say of what is that it is, and of what is not that it is not, is true; so that he who says of anything that it is, or that it is not, will say either what is true or what is false . . . [1]

It has often been suggested that the "is" of Aristotle's definition can be translated in either an existential or a predicative fashion, and that depending on the translation, the real-order correlate of what is thought or said can be either a thing or a fact. According to the existential formulation, what is spoken about is "what is," while on the predictive version of the definition, what is thought or said is "what is so."[2] This point is important for our later discussion, for according to most modern versions of the correspondence theory, what corresponds with thoughts or statements is a fact about a thing rather than the thing itself. By contrast, Aristotle's definition leaves open the possibility that the objective term of the correspondence relation can be either a fact or a thing, depending on the philosophical intentions of the one who makes the original statement.

It is also important to notice what is perhaps a less familiar fact: Thomistic versions of the correspondence theory not only emphasize the adequation of intellect and thing but also the adequation of a thing to its own nature and its adequation to the divine idea in accord with which it was created.[3] In fact, the order of adequation on the Thomistic theory reverses the directionality of the original Aristotelian definition. According to the Thomistic account, the first level of correspondence is between thing and idea; the second is between a thing and its own nature; and the third is between the intellect and the thing as a created being in the real order. On this view, to be true is first to correspond with God's ideas; then to be true to one's own nature; and finally, to be true in the more familiar sense of a correspondence relation between the intellect and the fact or object about which judgments are made. Of course, we must not overlook the fact that this reversal of direction is canceled in the modern period, where the first two senses of correspondence drop away and where the real-order object of correspondence at the third level is transformed into a fact understood as an object of consciousness. From Descartes onward, with only a few notable exceptions, the objects to which thoughts correspond are facts about those objects, which are in turn modeled after the thoughts that appear within the original correspondence relation.[4] According to this view, it is senseless to say that a judgment corresponds with an object rather than a fact, while it is tempting to assume that the facts to which judgments correspond are simply pale reflections of the conceptual order in terms of which their structure is made accessible to the cognitive consciousness. The history of the correspondence theory thus takes us from the world, to God, to consciousness as the fundamental term in the correspondence relation, which in turn tempts us to embrace the philosophical standpoint of transcendental idealism.

Most contemporary criticisms of the correspondence theory presuppose that the objective pole of the correspondence relation is a fact rather than a thing, but most of them also move beyond their Kantian ancestors by quickly assimilating facts to the linguistic order. For example, in the most well-known debate about the correspondence theory in contemporary philosophy, P. F. Strawson insists that facts are at bottom linguistic entities and that their obvious kinship with "that-clauses" is a clear reflection of their linguistic origins.[5] In particular, it is a fact that the "indestructible" Titanic once sank into the ocean, and it is also a fact that its builders and designers were amazed when this occurred. Yet in this case, what they were amazed about was the sad but verifiable truth that the oceanliner sank from view. This truth is formulated in the statement that the Titanic was destroyed, and one might wonder what this truth could be other than the true statement that this episode occurred. Of course, the transition from facts to truths by means of "that-clauses," and the further transition from a truth to a true statement, would scarcely be plausible unless the transformation of consciousness precipitated by the transcendental turn lay behind each step of these transitions. In the final analysis, it is due to the conviction that only objects are in the world and that our cognitive access to them is mediated by judgment that facts are deprived of their real-order status and are transformed into objects of consciousness.[6] But when this occurs, and when we notice the analogy between the fact that S is P and the statement that this is the case, what could be more tempting than the suggestion that facts simply are true statements masquerading as objective entities? The fate of the correspondence theory, with its robust sense of reality, is thus a paradox of philosophical transformation. What began as a doctrine about the distinction between the mind and the world, and about the relationship between the real and the logical orders, becomes in the end a domesticated offshoot of the modern triumph of subjectivity.

There was of course another voice in the contemporary debate about the correspondence theory, and in his paper, "Unfair to Facts," J. L. Austin attempts to show that facts are not linguistic entities but are instead items in the world by analogy with things.[7] Thus he says that just as targets can be what correct signals signal, so facts can be what true statements state. In both cases, he claims that the subject term is in the world and that there is no reason to reduce either of them to its linguistic counterpart.[8] However, what Austin overlooks in comparing facts with objects is that a fact can easily be understood as *a true statement in use* rather than as a special kind of object. Thus, the contrast between "What we state is always a fact" and "What we state is always a statement" need not point to the distinction between a fact and the corresponding statement that picks it out, but simply to the distinction between a true statement *in use* and this same statement as merely *mentioned*. When we state a fact, we make a true statement, and when we "state" a statement, what we do is mention what has or might be stated of another occasion. But in neither case are we required to refer to facts as objects in the real order. Now at this point, Austin attempts to buttress his argument by reminding us that the original meaning of the word "fact" connects it with a deed or an action, and that there is no etymological justification for assimilating facts to the "that-clauses" in which they are typically expressed.[9] In this way, he insists once more that facts are in the world and that they never should have been reduced to their linguistic counterparts. However, even if we understand a fact as either an act or a deed, assimilating facts to things or events within the world, the correspondence between fact and statement is apparently undermined by this very reconstruction. The statement that S is P scarcely seems to correspond with a thing or an event, and to reconstrue facts in these terms would seem to deprive the correspondence relation of its objective correlate. Of course, Austin says that to deny that facts are in the world is to flirt with idealism, for he clearly sees the implications of the history of the correspondence theory as it has been subjected to modern transformations.[10] However, Austin never considers the possibility that the best way to resist linguistic idealism is not only to insist that facts are special kinds of objects or events but also to claim that it is statements *reconstrued as natural objects* that ultimately correspond with them. In this case, structured object would correspond with structured object, and there would no longer be any transcategorical tension in the claim that statements mirror their objective counterparts in the real order.[11]

How this reconstructed correspondence relation can obtain will be considered at a later stage of our argument, but at this juncture, the important point to notice is that this proposal takes us back to the existential version of Aristotle's original definition. Moreover, it preserves the radical otherness of the real order to which the correspondence theory has always attempted to call our attention. According to this account, the essential mark of truth is the real distinction between subject and object, and it is this contrast that must be acknowledged if the meaning of truth as correspondence is to be preserved as a primordial relation. Perhaps a stronger way to make this point is to suggest that there is no truth without *radical otherness*, and that otherwise truth as correspondence will be reduced to a pale linguistic surrogate of a real-order relation. However justified the reduction of facts to statements might be, the real otherness of things within the world must be acknowledged unless truth itself is to vanish into a set of merely conceptual relations.

II

It is a sad but undeniable fact that the correspondence theory of truth lies buried beneath the wreckage wrought by the modern preoccupation with subjectivity. There is perhaps no clearer evidence for this than the repudiation of the correspondence theory by other theories of truth that reject the value of radical externality as a necessary condition for truth. For example, proponents of the coherence theory turn away from the concept of truth as adequation, claiming that truth is finally a relationship among epistemic and conceptual elements, and that there is no justification for a theory of truth that attempts to bind the real and the logical orders together by a merely external relation. It is true that the core of this theory is to be found in its commitment to the notion of approximation. However, what is approximated in this case is not an object related externally to a subject but a system of truths in which every claim to truth must find its place as a constituent element. As a result, truth ceases to be a relation of adequation and becomes the systematic Whole within which every individual truth can be included. As Brand Blanshard formulates the point in *The Nature of Thought:*

> Truth is the approximation of thought to reality. It is thought on its way home. Its measure is the distance thought has travelled, under guidance of its inner compass, toward that intelligible system which unites its ultimate object with its ultimate end. Hence at any given time the degree of truth in our experience as a whole is the degree of system it has achieved. The degree of truth of a particular proposition is to be judged in the first instance by its coherence with experience as a whole, ultimately by its coherence with that further whole, all-comprehensive and fully articulated, in which thought can come to rest.[12]

In laying the foundation for the pragmatic tradition, Peirce expresses a similar view about truth and approximation when he claims that if belief "were to tend indefinitely toward absolute fixity,"[13] we would have truth, and when he adds that "the opinion which is fated to be ultimately agreed to by all who investigate, is what we mean by truth . . ."[14] Of course, the Peircean pragmatist is not simply an idealist, for he insists that the final opinion is infinitely distant from any finite stage of inquiry and that it displays the real externality of a regulative ideal.[15] Nevertheless, both idealism and pragmatism are committed to the view that there is a conceptual commensurability between the truth of an individual judgment and the final opinion or system. As a result, both positions maintain that the approximation relation is not merely external, since every judgment is either a partial embodiment of the system it presupposes or is conceptually related to the final opinion with which it is to be compared. These accounts of approximation are also formulated in terms of an organic metaphor that replaces the external relation of the correspondence theory with the internal relation among the stages of an unfolding system of truth or inquiry. As Blanshard suggests in echoing the earlier remarks of Hegel:

> If we want analogies for the relation of our thought to the system that forms its end, we should leave aside such things as mirrors and number systems and their ways of conforming to objects, and think of the relation between seed and flower, or between the sapling and the tree.[16]

In both examples, the seed and the sapling simply are their ends realized imperfectly. Thus, Blanshard suggests that a thought is its object in the organic process of developing toward systematic completion, while Peirce's pragmatic definition implies that thought is the process of inquiry that will always attempt to come to rest in the truth of a final opinion.

One of the consequences of this organic metaphor and of the theory of approximation it reflects is that it enables the idealist to repudiate the spatial otherness of the correspondence theory and to transform it into the temporal expectation that truth will one day appear as a completed system. In this way, the original contrast between subject and object is transposed into a distinction between two stages of an unfolding process, the end of which is present at the beginning as an implicit element. Moreover, the Peircean suggestion that the final opinion can be approximated only by a community of inquirers enables the pragmatic tradition to accommodate the scientific demand that truth be achieved within the framework of a philosophical definition of truth. In this case, the very meaning of truth as a final opinion that is destined to be achieved becomes the goal of the scientific quest for truth and the foundation for the scientific enterprise understood as a process of inquiry. Finally, the idealistic commitment to a systematic whole in which truth can be found and the pragmatic suggestion that this system can be approximated only in an indefinite series of stages imply that openness to the process of inquiry is a necessary condition for the emergence of truth in systematic form. If radical otherness is a necessary condition for truth according to the correspondence theory, and if the spatial otherness of objects is transformed by the coherence and by the pragmatic theories into a series of temporal stages in which the end of the process is approximated progressively, this goal is accessible to us only if we are open to it in the act of scientific inquiry. As a result, *openness* to truth becomes a necessary condition for its complete realization. However, it is equally important to notice that in transforming the otherness of objects into a sequence of stages that are related internally to the goal of inquiry, the coherence and pragmatic theories also seek to acknowledge the concept of otherness as a constituent element in their unfolding conception of truth. According to both accounts, the concept of otherness points to the cognitive separation between part and Whole and between beginning and end that makes the process of inquiry necessary, while the concept of openness points to the stages of approximation that make the goal of inquiry accessible to the cognitive consciousness. As a result, both theories involve both openness and otherness as necessary conditions under which truth can be achieved in systematic terms.

In more traditional terms, I have been suggesting that the long-run dimension of the pragmatic theory[17] and the degree of truth dimension of the coherence theory[18] presuppose the concept of openness, while the separation between subject and object of the correspondence theory points to the concept of radical otherness. In addition, I have suggested that a transformed conception of otherness is an integral element of the idealistic and pragmatic attempts to understand the nature of truth, and that both openness and otherness are presupposed in the attempt to say what is true within the scientific context of cognition. However, when openness and otherness are taken together, and when their nature as epistemic conditions of truth is taken into account, we must not overlook the fact that the concept of the highest truth also becomes a crucial element in the attempt to define the nature of truth. Because they are oriented either toward a larger Whole or toward a final opinion, the idealistic and pragmatic theories point to a highest truth that must be taken into account if truth is to be possible within a finite context. Of course, this highest truth is not a highest being, but simply a cognitive ideal that is to be approximated progressively as truth itself unfolds. However, what must be emphasized at this point is that the definitions of truth in terms of systematic completeness or of a final opinion are simply modern ways of identifying the nature of truth with an ontological condition that is not to be reduced to any finite stage in the process of inquiry. As a result, the radical otherness of the correspondence theory with which we began and the openness and otherness of the idealistic and pragmatic theories into which it was transformed finally call our attention to an ultimate truth in terms of which particular claims to truth are to be appraised.

In evaluating these traditional accounts of the nature of truth, it is important to emphasize the fact that the concepts of openness and otherness are irreducible elements in any attempt to understand the nature of truth and that these concepts must be preserved if we are to give an adequate account of its nature in philosophical terms. However, it is also clear that these conceptions can easily degenerate and can thus become inadequate modes of access to the truth they attempt to articulate. In traditional criticisms of the correspondence theory, we have already observed that the objective pole of the correspondence relation often vanishes into a tissue of linguistic entities. Facts that are first said to be present in the real order are identified with truths about a set of objects, and these truths, in turn, are easily transformed into statements that are to be located in the conceptual domain. In light of criticisms of this kind, it might appear that all that survives of the correspondence relation is an unmediated contrast between subject and object that is related only tangentially to the intelligible correspondence between statement and fact that the original correspondence theory attempts to articulate. It is of course just this problem that the idealistic theory attempts to remedy by transforming the radical otherness of correspondence into the epistemic otherness of an unfolding sequence of cognitions.

Yet we must also notice that just as an unmediated and unintelligible otherness is all that seems to survive of the correspondence theory, so a dimension of absolute openness that fails to issue in a final truth is all that remains when the idealistic theory's conception of the Whole is subjected to serious scrutiny. The Whole is not to be identified with an infinite collection of truths, for such a Whole is self-contradictory, and if the Whole is said to be what allows us to understand a collection of items *taken as a whole*, the concept of wholeness itself is partially indeterminate. The collection in question is always numerically indefinite, which entails that the concept of the Whole shifts its meaning, depending on the number and the character of the constituents it orders. But this means that the Whole is an open-ended context that is not fully bounded by absolutely determinate limits. Other contents can always be added to any collection that the Whole must then attempt to harmonize, and we can never be certain that the relationships among these elements will not present new configurations that will require holistic modifications. It thus appears that the concept of the Whole explodes into an open-ended context that requires perpetual modification, and as a result, openness alone seems to survive as a mark of that version of the truth that seeks systematic completion.

Finally, absolute openness and external opposition are all that remain, even when radical otherness is taken up into the pragmatic modification of traditional idealistic theories. If truth is a regulative ideal, as the Peircean pragmatist suggests, and if the end toward which the quest for truth is directed is infinitely distant from any stage within the quest itself, as this suggestion implies, openness to it becomes the quest for a mystery that can never be revealed, even in principle. But in this case, the quest for truth as an infinite process is reduced once more to openness itself, which in turn is indistinguishable from the mystery of the end toward which the quest for truth is always directed. Moreover, if the externality of the end that stands in contrast with us cannot be understood as a determinate cluster of truths, but is simply identified with a goal that lures the process of inquiry, this goal becomes an external principle that can never be fully accessible to the finite consiousness. The radical externality between subject and object to which the correspondence theory has been reduced is thus transposed into the radical dyad of the pragmatic long-run, and the existential separation between process and telos becomes a chasm that can never be mediated in cognitive terms. As a result, even the Peircean pragmatist must face the fact that according to the implications of his own system, there is no truth, but at best an absolutely open-ended framework of otherness that requires more determinate specification.

III

If openness and otherness are necessary conditions for truth, but if these conditions as they are understood by the traditional theories are subject to a radical degeneration, questions quite naturally arise about how these concepts can be reinterpreted in order to avoid the defects of earlier accounts. For example, we might wonder how the openness and otherness characteristic of idealistic and pragmatic theories can be preserved without reducing them to the mystery of absolute openness or to the cognitive inaccessibility of a regulative ideal that can never be achieved. Further, we might ask how the robust sense of reality to which the correspondence theory calls our attention can be recaptured without the subject-object relation it presupposes degenerating into an unmediated opposition. In what follows, I will argue that at least one way of answering these questions is to transform the openness and otherness of idealistic and pragmatic theories into a special kind of discourse that exhibits an openness and otherness of its own, and to understand the radical otherness of the correspondence theory in terms of a second kind of language that transcends literal discourse. The open-ended kind of language I have in mind is metaphorical in structure and will allow us to preserve the commitments of the idealistic and the pragmatic theories to openness and otherness in an intelligible fashion. By contrast, the second kind of language involves analogical predication and is an extension of customary theories of analogy into a vehicle for the re-definition of truth in metaphorical and analogical terms. Of course, just what metaphorical and analogical discourse are, whether they are indeed special or distinct forms of discourse, and if so, how these different kinds of language are to be related are difficult questions that ought to be examined in their own right. However, since I cannot deal with all of these questions here, I must simply presuppose a view of metaphor and analogy that is at least like that of others who have defended the view that they are both autonomous modes of discourse.[19] Thus, in what follows I will assume that metaphors and analogies are not reducible to literal statements or to one another, and on this basis I will attempt to show that both kinds of language have distinct roles to play in giving us access to a conception of truth that avoids the defects of the earlier accounts.

There are three dimensions of metaphorical discourse that have a bearing on the problem of truth as we have begun to understand it. In the first place, a metaphor contains structural elements that can be understood as intelligible units and that allow the metaphor as a whole to be identified with a complex interaction of determinate constituents. For example, the "rosy fingered dawn" contains a set of terms that can be distinguished from one another and that allow us to identify the metaphor in which they occur in terms of an antecedent set of intelligible elements. In the second place, a metaphor combines its structural elements in a unique and unexpected fashion, generating an open-ended product that can issue in a potentially infinite series of interpretations. As a result, the structural dimension of a metaphor is supplemented by an inherent indeterminacy that allows metaphorical discourse to transcend any finite sequence of determinate responses. Finally, the structural elements of a metaphor often stand in tension with one another, and it is this tensional element that accounts for the uniqueness of the metaphor and that drives the process of interpretation forward from stage to stage. To return to our original example, the "rosy fingered dawn" is not only a unique combination of familiar elements, but is also a tensional unity that can produce an endless cluster of interpretative responses. Thus, a metaphor is a complex mixture of structural determinations, radical indeterminacy, and a tensional dimension, all appearing in a linguistic expression that is accessible to the finite consciousness as a tensional unity.[20]

Though it is often assumed that metaphorical discourse is merely a linguistic ornament, and that as a result, metaphor and truth can never be related in positive terms, the features of metaphorical language we have just considered can in fact be brought into relation with our earlier discussion of the openness and otherness characteristic of idealistic and pragmatic theories. First, the open-ended richness of metaphorical discourse can be correlated with the temporal openness of idealism and pragmatism, not only in the sense that the sequence of interpretations generated by a metaphor constitutes a temporal series of cognitive elements, but also in the sense that this sequence can never exhaust the metaphor itself, understood as a regulative ideal to which every interpretation must finally be related. In both cases, the indeterminate dimension of a metaphor reflects the inherent indeterminacy of earlier theories, pointing simultaneously to the openness and inexhaustibility of truth as it is understood within these more traditional accounts. In the second place, the structural dimension of metaphorical discourse serves to give us access to the kind of intelligible content that the quest for truth always attempts to make accessible, without suggesting that truth can ever be exhausted by any finite set of structural determinations. It is the special merit of idealistic and pragmatic theories that they refuse to reduce the quest for truth to structural terms alone, even though neither theory ever succeeds in binding together the determinate and indeterminate dimensions that a metaphor displays as characteristics of its own nature. The relevance of metaphorical discourse to the problem of truth is thus to be found in the fact that a metaphor is an intersection of indeterminacy and determination, allowing a metaphor to hold together the open-endedness of the quest for truth with the determinate structures that are required if truth itself is to be given a determinate content. Finally, the tensional element to be found in metaphorical discourse reflects the tension displayed in the process of inquiry as it moves from stage to stage within the scientific context of cognition. Even though it is an epistemic process, the stages of the process of inquiry are partially external to one another, and there is resistance to be encountered as this process unfolds toward the cognitive unity it attempts to achieve. In fact, it is this moment of resistance between stages of the process, which is reflected in its most extreme form in the externality of the Whole or of the pragmatic long-run to any finite stage in the process of inquiry, that allows both idealism and pragmatism to incorporate a dimension of otherness into their own conception of the meaning of truth. However, what is most important to notice is that metaphorical discourse not only exhibits this same kind of tension, but that it does so in a fashion that allows both the tension and the structural elements that produce it to be accessible to the cognitive consciousness in the metaphor itself, understood as an open-ended unity. In the end, the superiority of metaphorical discourse as a mode of access to truth lies in the fact that it can become a microcosm in which determinacy, indeterminacy, and tension are bound together as a unified phenomenon. In this way, all the elements that are necessary for truth as the idealist and pragmatist understand it are contained within a metaphor and are made accessible to the cognitive consciousness as a tensional unity.

The principle defect of both idealism and pragmatism is that neither theory is able to unify the intelligible structure, the open-endedness, and the dimension of otherness required to make truth accessible within the context of cognitive inquiry. This is suggested most forcefully by the fact that idealism easily degenerates into absolute openness and that Peircean pragmatism seems to commit itself to an external and unmediated opposition between the end toward which it is directed and any finite stage in its own quest for absolute comprehension. By contrast, I have claimed that metaphorical discourse avoids these degenerations by binding together the openness, the otherness, and the intelligible structure that the quest for truth presupposes. In fact, it can even be argued persuasively that both idealism and pragmatism are rooted in crucial metaphors, and that in the end, it is these metaphors that make truth possible within either of these more traditional accounts. For example, the concept of the Whole is a metaphorical extension from finite contexts where bounded totalitites occur, and the concept of the pragmatic long-run is a metaphor for bounded contexts in which a limit is posited in contrast with a determinate sequence of developing stages. In both cases, the strength and the suggestiveness of the positions in question depend on the fact that these metaphors unify all the elements necessary for framing an adequate account of the nature of truth. The corresponding defects of these theories result from the fact that they do not understand these metaphors for what they are, consequently allowing them to degenerate into only one or two of the elements that make truth possible in metaphorical terms. On the other hand, perhaps the strongest claim that can be made for the role of metaphor in giving us access to truth is that the traditional accounts we have rejected are theoretical degenerations from the crucial metaphors on which they are founded.[21]

The positive suggestion that both idealism and pragmatism rest upon a metaphorical foundation should not be surprising, for the linguistic character of a metaphor is perfectly commensurable with the conceptual dimension that dominates both of these traditional accounts. The idealist and the pragmatist both attempt to define truth in essentially conceptual terms, incorporating otherness only in the guise of opposition between one conceptual stage and another, or in the contrast between all of these stages and the end toward which the quest for truth is directed. However, even if the predominance of conceptual elements in these earlier accounts encourages us to reconstruct the positive insights of both theories in metaphorical terms, questions will no doubt arise about which metaphors are most fruitful in giving us access to truth, and about how metaphorical discourse can be embraced without imprisoning us within a linguistic idealism that cuts us off from the real order. Must we not finally face the fact that otherness of a merely intralinguistic kind is not sufficient to anchor our account of the nature of truth in the real order? In addition, must we not incorporate a stronger sense of otherness into our discussion if our position is not to degenerate into a tissue of merely linguistic entities? I believe that the answer to these questions is clear and that the only way to avoid linguistic idealism is to return to the positive insight of the correspondence theory about the real externality between subject and object, grafting this stronger concept of otherness onto the metaphorical dimension of our own constructive account.

As I have indicated, I believe that this can be done by introducing a second kind of language that transcends literal discourse but that also stands in contrast with the metaphorical language that lies at the foundation of the idealistic and pragmatic positions. This mode of discourse is analogical in structure and is intended to do justice to the real externality between subject and object that the correspondence theory presupposes. The crucial point can be suggested in the following way. Even if facts within the world are reduced to truths, and these truths are in turn transformed into linguistic entities, it is still possible to claim that subject and object can be bound together in a truth relation by a set of analogies, all of which are elements of the real order. These analogies would hold between utterance and object rather than between statement and fact, and would in this respect preserve the dimension of difference to which our earlier discussion of the correspondence theory has called our attention. As the same time, the analogies in question would preserve the structural dimension of the relation between structured utterance and the structured object without which truth would vanish into the unintelligibility of sheer externality. In the following section, I will elaborate this concept of analogy and attempt to show how it can be conjoined with our earlier discussion of metaphorical discourse in order to yield a revised conception of the nature of truth. In the process, I will also attempt to show how the apparently linguistic character of metaphor can be transcended and how it can be brought into a positive analogical connection with the real order so that truth can be redefined in objective terms.

IV

In the previous section, I suggested that the use of metaphorical and analogical discourse will allow us to preserve the positive insights of traditional theories of truth, and that both kinds of language have a crucial role to play in giving us access to a revised conception of truth that avoids the defects of the earlier accounts. The openness and otherness of idealism and pragmatism are present in the open-ended structure of a metaphor, and the intelligible otherness of the correspondence relation can be reinterpreted as an analogical relation in the real order between subject and object. However, when both considerations are taken into account, two obvious difficulties arise about how these two quite different modes of discourse can be brought together. On the one hand, the linguistic character of a metaphor seems to imply that truth can only be defined in intralinguistic terms and that to move in this direction is finally to be imprisoned in a web of words. On the other hand, the characterization of analogy as a real order relation suggests that truth transcends language and that it has nothing to do with the openness and otherness that can be incorporated in a metaphorical context. However, in spite of these apparent difficulties, perhaps we should consider the possibility that the metaphorical dimension of language can be brought into an analogical relation with the real order and that the openness and otherness of idealism and pragmatism can be connected with the more radical conception of otherness characteristic of the correspondence theory. In this way, a metaphorical utterance could be brought into an analolocal relation with a structured object, allowing both the openness and the otherness of previous theories to be bound together in an intelligible relation. In what follows, I will develop some of the implications of this paradoxical suggestion, attempting to show how the object of cognition and the analogical relation in which it stands are to be understood, and how analogy itself must be reinterpreted if it is to bind a metaphorical utterance and a structured object together in an intelligible relation.

The first step in developing this account of the nature of truth is to notice that the analogies that bind a subject and an object together are analogies between developing and partially indeterminate contents rather than between static substances that merely stand apart in radical opposition. Both the subject and the object of a truth relation are spatio-temporal entities that are never fully determinate, and as a result, both the language and the objects of cognition must be understood as open-ended contents subject to change and development. However, this suggests as a second stage of our argument that metaphorical language is not only required from the standpoint of the subject who is engaged in a process of inquiry, but is also necessary to describe the objects of inquiry as they are presented to the cognitive consciousness. As I have claimed in a previous paper about Aristotle's metaphysics, there is a sense in which metaphors are not only to be found in language but also in the world, for the spatio-temporal objects to which metaphorical utterances are to be related are themselves both structured and open-ended by analogy with the metaphors that give us access to them. [22] Of course, metaphors are in the world in an extended sense of this expression, and in this respect, the objective use of the term "metaphor" is a metaphorical extension of its usual signification. However, this does not cancel the fact that the structured objects to which metaphorical utterances are related are structured in such a way that they reflect the partial indeterminacy of the metaphors that serve to make them cognitively accessible. Perhaps this crucial point can be made in a more traditional way by claiming that just as there is both an analogy of language and an analogy of being in the philosophical tradition, so the metaphorical dimension of language has its objective counterpart in a metaphor of being. The purpose of this second kind of metaphor is to call our attention to the fact that objects can be understood as metaphorical extensions of the metaphorical language that gives us access to them, even though these objects exist independently of our attempts to know them in metaphorical terms. In this respect, our recognition of a metaphor of being merely recapitulates the familiar Aristotelian and Thomistic thesis that the order of being and the order of knowing develop in different directions.

As a final step in this philosophical reconstruction, it is important to notice that when objects are reinterpreted in metaphorical terms, the analogies that connect utterance and object will not simply be structural similarities between absolutely determinate elements but analogical relations between contents that are both determinate and indeterminate as subjects and objects of the process of inquiry. Analogy itself must therefore be reconstrued as a relation between the openness, the otherness, and the intelligibility of objects and the corresponding openness, otherness, and intelligibility of the language used to make them accessible. To be sure, analogy is usually understood in merely mathematical or structural terms, suggesting that analogies can obtain only between one set of structures and another, bound together in an isomorphic relation. However, the root analogies that make truth possible are the much richer relations between cognitive contents that display both determinate and indeterminate dimensions. Formulated in a somewhat different way, what is represented in an analogical relation between subject and object is not merely lifeless and schematic, but the concrete content of living experience. It is this living dimension of the object to which metaphorical discourse gives us access, while the analogies that bind metaphorical utterance and "metaphorical" object together serve to anchor what would otherwise be a merely linguistic episode in the real order to which the quest for truth must be related. The most accurate formulation of this revised conception of truth can therefore be summarized as follows: *Truth is an analogical relation of conformity between metaphorical utterance and "metaphorical" object, where the relation in question transcends the usual restriction of analogy to merely structural elements, and where this relation binds the metaphorical dimension of the utterance and the determinate and indeterminate dimensions of the object together in an epistemic nexus.*

Perhaps this account of the nature of truth can be expressed more concretely in terms of an example. Consider the metaphorical statement "John is a fox" and the state of affairs to which this statement is intended to call our attention (*that* John is a fox). If the correspondence relation between these two terms is understood in the traditional way, the state of affairs to which the statement corresponds might easily be reduced by way of that-clauses to the statement itself, and this statement would in turn reimprison us within the conceptual framework that the idealistic and pragmatic theories have attempted to explicate. However, if the statement "John is a fox" were transformed into the metaphorical utterance "John-the-fox," and if the state of affairs to which this statement calls our attention were transformed into the structured object, John *qua* fox or John's being a fox, the analogical relation that binds them together would become a real order relation that both preserves the otherness of the object and also brings it into an intelligible relation with the subject. Thus, the correspondence theory and the otherness to which it points need not degenerate into the kind of linguistic idealism that has often accompanied the reduction of facts to truths and of truths to a tissue of merely linguistic entities. On the account of truth I am proposing, both metaphor and analogy are crucial elements for introducing an intelligible dimension into a truth context that would otherwise remain opaque. The first of these elements allows us to preserve the openness and otherness of the coherence and pragmatic theories; the second permits us to do justice to the more radical concept of otherness that underlies the correspondence theory; and both proposals attempt to accommodate the intelligible dimension to which any theory of truth must ultimately be connected. The metaphorical dimension of a linguistic utterance allows it to be both determinate and indeterminate as well as to point to an open-ended set of future interpretations that will serve to develop its cognitive content, while the analogical conformity between utterance and object allows them to maintain their radical otherness as they are bound together in the intelligibility of a structural relation.

In developing this account of the nature of truth in relation to the other theories we have considered, we should emphasize the fact that analogy as a relation between metaphorical utterance and "metaphorical" object is a way of unifying the spatial and temporal dimensions of our earlier discussion and a way of holding together the openness and the otherness to which these dimensions call our attention. The openness and otherness of the idealistic and pragmatic traditions point to the primacy of time as the fundamental condition that allows truth to emerge, while the radical otherness of the correspondence theory suggests that a spatial element is also involved in the cognitive attempt to bring utterance and object together. According to our own account, truth itself is a complex interplay of space and time, openness and otherness, structural and nonstructural dimensions, and is a way of binding all of these elements together in a metaphorical and analogical nexus. Temporality appears on both sides of the subject-object dichotomy as the ten-

sional and open-ended dimension that allows truth to transcend conceptual obstacles as it unfolds in the process of inquiry. Moreover, spatiality
in the traditional sense appears as a relation between utterance and
object that allows their otherness to be preserved while binding their
structural dimensions together in an intelligible connection. Finally,
analogy as a relation between open-ended and developing contents appears as the fundamental concept that brings both the determinate and
indeterminate sides of the object into relation with the corresponding
sides of the knowing subject. In this respect, this analogical relation
between "metaphorical" elements is the locus of truth, for it is within this
context that space and time, determinacy and indeterminacy, openness
and otherness, come together at a point beyond the conflict among traditional accounts.

Having begun our discussion by mentioning the relations among the
concept of truth, particular truths, and the concept of the highest truth,
it is now possible to return to these themes by noticing that the analogical locus to which we have been led is not a place in any ordinary sense,
but is instead the Place of places within which truth occurs on particular
occasions.[23] The truth of a particular occasion is established by an
analogical relation between "metaphorical" object and the metaphorical
utterance, and it is this condition that must obtain if truths are to be
discovered in the course of scientific inquiry. Of course, the claim that
this is the case is a philosophical thesis, which has as its focus the meaning of truth rather than the particular contexts in which truth itself is to
be found. It is in this sense that the account to which we have been led
is a Place of places, or perhaps more accurately, the ground of truth as
it is to be apprehended on particular occasions. However, there is also
a sense in which the ground of truth is to be equated with the highest
truth. The metaphorical and analogical nexus that makes truth possible
is not simply a transcendental condition for the emergence of truth but
is also a network of connections between utterance and object that
actually obtains. It is for this reason that our discussion has not been confined to the distinction between truth and truths but has also focused on
the concept of the highest truth. The Place of places is the truth that
makes truth possible, and it is the actually existing condition that serves
to bind the utterance and object together in every context where truth
is discovered. It is in this sense that the ground of truth is both the transcendental condition for truth and the highest truth that these particular
contexts always presuppose.

In conclusion, we should notice that when truth as a metaphorical
and analogical nexus is regarded as the highest truth, the temptation
finally vanishes to transform the concept of truth into an overarching

unity that subsumes all other truths within itself. The analogical relation between subject and object presupposes both the openness and the otherness of its metaphorical terms, but because this relation holds these two dimensions apart, it also preserves its own integrity in contrast with the terms that find a place within it. One way to acknowledge this fact is to insist that the nexus in question is not a Whole, but is the Place in which the subject and the object can be brought together in cognitive interaction. As I have indicated, this Place is as much like a highest truth as it is like a transcendental condition, and it is this fundamental fact that finally undermines the holistic quest for complete comprehension. When subject and object stand in contrast with one another, the object moves "metaphorically" from its original determination toward an open-ended future, while the subject moves from its original indeterminacy to a more determinate grasp of the nature of the thing unfolding before it. It is this mirror-image relationship between subject and object that both binds them together and holds them apart and that constitutes the truth to be discovered in their cognitive interaction. In the final analysis, Truth is a middle ground conception to be found between absolute opacity and absolute completeness, and it is the Place of places where the highest truth makes the truth of the image possible on particular occasions.

NOTES

1. *Metaphysics*, trans. W. D. Ross, Vol. VIII of *The Works of Aristotle*, ed. W. D. Ross (Oxford: Clarendon Press, 1908-1931, II Vols.), 1011b25-28.
2. A. N. Prior, "Correspondence Theory of Truth," in *The Encyclopedia of Philosophy*, Vol. II, ed. Paul Edwards (New York: Crowell, Collier, and Macmillan, Inc., 1967), p. 224.
3. Saint Thomas Aquinas, *On the Truth of the Catholic Faith: Summa contra Gentiles*, Bk. I, trans, Anton C. Pegis (Garden City, New York: Doubleday and Company, Inc., 1955), pp. 204-205, 208.
4. Descartes himself is responsible for this transformation, identifying truth with clear and distinct conception in Meditation III and implying in Meditation VI that the real-order existence of objects is a matter of probability rather than absolute certainty. The most notable exception to this subjective transformation is the Locke of the *Essay*, however much his original position was undermined by the criticisms of his British successors.
5. P. F. Strawson, "Truth," in *Truth*, ed. George Pitcher (Englewood Cliffs, New Jersey: Prentice-Hall, Inc., 1964), pp. 37-38.
6. *Ibid.*, pp 36-37.
7. J. L. Austin, "Unfair to Facts," in *Philosophical Papers* (Oxford: Clarendon Press, 1961), pp. 104-105.

8. *Ibid.*, pp. 120–122.
9. *ibid.*, pp. 111–112.
10. *Ibid.*, p. 109.
11. A position of this sort is defended with great subtlety by Wilfrid Sellars in "'Truth and 'Correspondence', "*Science, Perception, and Reality* (New York: The Humanities Press, 1963), pp. 197–224, and in *Science and Metaphysics: Variations on Kantian Themes* (New York: The Humanities Press, 1968), pp. 116–150. However, the position that I will sketch in sections III and IV is a modification of this original view in a number of important respects.
12. Brand Blanshard, *The Nature of Thought*, Vol. II (London: George Allen and Unwin Ltd and New York: The Macmillan Company, 1939), p. 264.
13. *Collected Papers of Charles Sanders Peirce*, Vol. V, ed. Charles Harshorne and Paul Weiss (Cambridge, Mass.: Harvard University Press, 1960), 416.
14. *Ibid.*, 407.
15. *Ibid.*, 408.
16. Blanshard, *The Nature of Thought*, Vol. II, p. 273.
17. *Collected Papers of Charles Sanders Peirce*, Vol. V, 408–409.
18. Blanshard, *The Nature of Thought*, Vol. II, pp. 304–311.
19. See Max Black, "Metaphor," in *Models and Metaphors* (Ithaca, N. Y.: Cornell University Press, 1962), and Paul Ricoeur, *The Rule of Metaphor*, trans. Robert Czerny (Toronto: The University of Toronto Press, 1977).
20. This view is a blending of an interactionist view as developed by Max Black in "Metaphor" and the verbal opposition theory defended by Monroe Beardsley in "The Metaphorical Twist," *Philosophy and Phenomenological Research*, Vol. XXII (1962), 293–307. In this form, this view is approximated by Paul Ricoeur in *The Rule of Metaphor* and is developed explicitly by my colleague Carl R. Hausman in *A Discourse on Novelty and Creation* (The Hague: Martinus Nijhoff, 1975), pp. 99–110.
21. For a detailed discussion of the view that philosophical theories are founded upon root metaphors, see Stephen C. Pepper, *World Hypotheses* (Berkeley and Los Angeles: The University of California Press, 1942).
22. Carl G. Vaught, "Categories and the Real Order: Sellar's Interpretation of Aristotle's Metaphysics," *The Monist*, Vol. LXIII (1983), 438–449.
23. For a more detailed discussion of this concept, see my recent book, *The Quest for Wholeness* (Albany, New York: The State University of New York Press, 1982), pp. 182–197, and Carl G. Vaught, "The Quest for Wholeness and Its Crucial Metaphor and Analogy: The Place of Places," *Ultimate Reality and Meaning*, Vol. 7 (1984), 157–165.

Brian John Martine

Relations, Indeterminacy, and Intelligibility

Le bon sens est la chose du monde la
mieux partagée: car chacun pense en être
si bien pourvu que ceux même qui sont les
plus difficiles à contenter en toute autre
chose n'ont point coutume d'en desirer plus
qu'ils en ont.

Descartes.

It was in reflecting on the nature of the individual that I first became interested in the status of relations in ordinary experience. As I tried to come to a clearer understanding of the relation between individuals and universals, it became increasingly evident that I had originally been attending to the wrong things altogether. That is, I had been attending to *things*. I started off, in a manner typical of the modern tradition, assuming that some of the things in our experience are universals, other particulars – or more full-bodied forms of the particular, individuals – and that in order to describe the relation between these two primary entities it would be necessary to detail something like their most fundamental characteristics. Here, of course, the underlying assumption was that they *had* some fundamental characteristics that could be described independently of their relations to one another. The relations that stand between the individual and the universal could then, and only then, be completely explored.

The problem I confronted was the same problem that every thinker has had to come to terms with at some point; that is, no sooner do we try to describe the individual independently of the universal than we run into an apparently insurmountable problem. The words – any words – that are the basic tools of the task that we have outlined are themselves entities of a certain sort, or at least signs that point to entities of some sort, and the entities that they are or to which they point appear to be things that stand in direct logical contrast to the entities one is trying to describe as independent. The only tools available to description appear to be structured in accord with one of the two entities one has set out to describe, and that seems to leave only a couple of alternatives open: one, that the thing that had originally been taken as having a fundamental character of its own really does not, or, two, that it is something that stands outside the reach of discursive language and thought.

The reasons that neither of these alternatives seems acceptable are detailed in the first chapter of *Individuals and Individuality*, and the search for some third alternative is the primary concern of the rest of the book.[1] Allow me to quickly retrace the steps that led to my suggestions concerning such an alternative. It is clear enough that, short of treating individuals as inaccessible to discursive thought, we are forced to admit that we cannot *think* about them independently of their relation to universals. The possibility that they cannot *be* independently of that relation arises quite naturally then as the ontological correlate of the logical point. Nor does this come as a surprise. To modify Whitehead's claim, it is certainly true that one branch of the western tradition can be understood as a series of footnotes to Plato, or at any rate as variations on an essentially Platonic theme; and while that lends a certain air of respectability to our ontological correlate, it provides at least as much reason for pause. We have been down that road before only to find that it can lead to a position just as unattractive as consigning the individual to the logical wasteland of bare particularity. Here, instead, the individual turns out on reflective consideration to amount to a sort of logical mistake, a function of the failure of naive consciousness to recognize the essentially universal structure that undergirds that which at first presented itself as self-contained.

We seem at this stage to be confronted by the most serious sort of dilemma. The course of our reflection has bifurcated, issuing in two quite different but equally unacceptable alternatives. Moreover, given our historical vantage point, it seems unlikely that much would be gained by some further exploration of these alternatives in the hope of discovering some solution that had eluded the finest minds of our tradition. (At this juncture, the thinly veiled intellectual despair represented by deconstructionism becomes understandable, if no more palatable.) The most reasonable response, then, is a return to the point at which we began and a reassessment of the presuppositions that guided our movement away from that point. As I mentioned at the outset, in thinking about the relation between individuals and universals, I assumed that each introduced its own character into the subsequent structure of the relation and, as a result, that the relation between the two could only be understood after having come to an undestanding of those fundamental characters. It finally occured to me that quite different conclusions might issue from taking the relation (or relations) between the two as prior, as giving rise to the "fundamental characters" we think to have indentified when we speak of "individuals" and "universals."

For centuries now, we have been accustomed to assume that *things* occupy a status prior to that of *relations among things* in both the logical and ontological sense. If it is possible to speak intelligibly of relations per se, it has seemed reasonable to suppose that there must first be things that stand in relations, and which at least from a logical point of view can be considered the causes of the relations we are trying to describe. We move from relations like "being next to," "on top of," or "between," to being "similar to," "different from," "identical with," and so on. The things that are seen as standing in such relations are taken to be self-identical givens that the relations simply help to describe. But when we examine this sort of description, we encounter a difficulty logically similar to that which arises when we try to describe individuals using universal terms. Everything that we say about the objects that we had taken to be prior a moment ago calls our attention to the relations in which those objects stand to the other objects around them. We find ourselves having to describe these "prior" *things* by means of relational frameworks of one kind or another, and in the process, the possibility of seeing the relations themselves as prior emerges as a serious one.

What would it mean to think of relations as prior? At first the suggestion seems counterintuitive, and while many of the "givens" of common sense expose themselves on closer examination to lead to unacceptable logical consequences, there are others that appear so fundamental to our ordinary modes of thought that calling them into question seems tantamount to calling intelligibility itself into question. If, for example, we tried to suggest that the spatial relations of direct experience occupy a position either logically or ontologically prior to the things we are accustomed to think of as sustaining those relations, we would end in making some very curious claims. Surely, my typewriter and the table on which it rests are prior to the relation between the two. (Now we are not speaking of the sort of self-sustaining individuals with which we began; but by beginning with individuals in the sense of individual objects in ordinary experience, it will become possible eventually to show how some simple claims made in this context hold even more clearly in the case of such complex and full-bodied individuals as, say, works of art.) We naturally think of the typewriter and the table as prior to the ordinary spatial relation "on top of" in the sense that the typewriter and the table do not stand in any necessary relation to one another. That is, the typewriter would obviously be what it is if put in other places — on top of other tables, in the closet, on the floor, etc. It would still be the same object in the sense that it could be placed on a table and used in the way that it is being used now. To assign a certain independence to the thing, then, means at least that it has a meaning independent of the particular place in which it is situated at the moment. And, of course, it is true that its relation to *this* table is coincidental. The same sort of thing can obviously be said of the table, and it seems to follow that the relation between the two is something, far from being that on which they depend in any important sense, that depends on the objects for its meaning.

But if we continue to reflect on the apparent independence of the objects, it turns out that while *this* relation may be coincidental to what they are, it is not in the least clear that it would be possible to hold intelligibly that they are what they are *independent of any relation whatever*. It is this that we often take ourselves to mean when we assert that the objects are prior to their relations to one another and to whatever else there may be. It is certainly true that most of the things we confront in ordinary experience (though not all) are independent of this or that set of relations, but can we really hold that they are ever independent of — here in the sense of being the sort of thing that can be thought separately from — relations in the more general sense? Think again of the assertion of the independent meaning of the typewriter. Are we really saying anything more than that it is possible to think of the object in terms of some set of relations other than the ones that currently apply to it? Well, if the only relations we consider are those that describe its connection with the other physical objects around it, of course we are. But review the other possibilities. Suppose we were to describe it as a unique collection of molecules. No matter how one tries to think of molecules, it is impossible to do so without becoming involved once again in a framework of relations, both internal and external to the structure of the entities. In fact, here the framework becomes even more complex in that it necessarily entails a reflective assessment of experience to the extent that molecules are obviously not a part of direct experience, and such an assessment carries along with it the usual set of presuppositions, categorical structures, and so on. When we turn from the theoretical back to the experiential, and try to describe the typewriter in terms of the colours, shapes, textures etc., that seem to apply to it, we find ourselves once again confronted by a series of relations. Attending to its function will lead us, if anything, more directly down the same path. While in terms of its function, it is possible to distinguish it from some objects, we do so only by drawing it into relation with others: paper, human hands, needs, abilities, and so on.

In order to be known as a this or a that, the typewriter has to be considered in terms of this or that set of relations. After only a brief reflection of this sort, one becomes less and less inclined to see those sets of relations as coincidental to the meaning of the object, but the notion that the object *is* something prior to all of them lingers still. What then? Perhaps an individual. That is, while all of the things that we think about the object entail its relation to things that it is not, isn't there still some sort of thing about which we are thinking, and which is independent of the things we think about it? The typewriter is not only *a* typewriter, it is also, and importantly, *this* typewriter. To say this, however, turns out to mean simply to point to another of the relations in which it stands to other things. This relation, as I have shown elsewhere, stands significantly apart from relations of the sort described above, in that its foundation is negation as opposed to difference, but it is a relation all the same.[2] What I am more interested in at the moment, though, is the way that the apparently determinate relations that detail the universal dimensions of our ordinary experience of the typewriter are connected to the indeterminate ground out of which they arise, and what that means with respect to the relation between indeterminacy and intelligibility in more general terms. Using the term "ground" may be misleading. I should like to make it clear at the outset that in doing so, I do not mean to present indeterminacy as having a more fundamental status than determinacy. However, I do want to insist that a certain indeterminacy surfaces in any reflection on determinately structured relations as something without which they would not make sense.

Imagine describing the typewriter to someone unfamiliar with objects of this sort, but familiar enough with the culture of which it is a part to make sense out of the various determinations (spatial location, molecular structure, physical characteristics, function) mentioned above. The relation between those determinations and what I have just characterized as their "indeterminate ground" might be drawn into better focus by considering the mistakes such a person might make if left to his own devices. Say we choose to develop our description of the typewriter primarily in terms of its function. To do so successfully, we should have to separate from all the possible uses to which one might imagine such an object being put, the use to which it actually is put. That is, we should have to take into account, either implicitly or explicitly, the various mistakes that might be made concerning its use. Doing so, however, does not eliminate the other possibilities in either a practical or a theoretical sense. The typewriter could conceivably be used in a variety of other

ways (for making designs, stopping a door, etc.), or, to put the point
(which is hardly a new one) more broadly in practical terms and more
directly in logical terms, its definition depends as much on what it is not
as it does on what it is. It is in this sense that the rationalists are right.
The thing is tied to a larger set of things than it appears to be from the
point of view of sense-certainty; and even if we deny the claim that it can
ultimately be resolved into some determinate set of such relations, we
cannot deny the importance of the discovery that we have made. It
depends on what it is not in a fundamental way. But the rationalistic
tradition has consistently neglected the extent to which the *indeterminacy*
of what it is not enters into the determinate characterizations that we
ordinarily provide in our attempt to come to an understanding of the
thing.

The point I mean to emphasize is that when we examine the determinations that seemed from the point of view of naive consciousness to
isolate the object in the sense of uncovering a meaning that it has for
itself (i.e., that is independent of our reflection on it), we find that those
determinations, far from separating the object from the larger context of
which it is a part, draw it into closer and closer connection with it. So
far we seem to be with the rationalists, and one of the possible conclusions available at the stage we've reached is theirs. That is to say, we
could expand our original notion of the determinations of the typewriter
by assuming that they point to a larger set of determinations that structure not only the object in question but any object whatever, as they
structure the Whole. But to do so involves an unsatisfactory reduction
of the experience with which we began just to the extent that none of
the possible descriptions mentioned above, theoretical or experiential,
can be seen as in and of itself determinate. Even if we are willing to make
the difficult move toward accepting the notion that the relations that
emerge as the primary meanings of those descriptions are more fundamental than the relata appropriate to the respective contexts, various
conflicts appear that seem to refuse the completely determinate
character of a rationalistic superstructure.

There is real difference, for example, between describing the
typewriter as a collection of molecules on the one hand, and in terms of
its function in a human world on the other. For one thing, the first sort
of description presupposes an analytical approach to the world of ordinary experience, whereas the other certainly need not rest on such a
presupposition and on some accounts might be seen as standing insistently against analysis. (If the typewriter *is* its use, etc., to think of the
thing in terms of a collection of molecules is to think of something other
than the typewriter.) Ignoring for the moment the wide variety of

disputes that might arise within the camps of adherents to either view, imagine an argument between a committed materialist (or eliminative physicalist, if you must) and a committed phenomenologist. While such people seem ready to claim that the opposing view is *wrong*, one wonders what they could possibly mean by doing so. The problem appears, of course, when one or the other insists that he has identified what the object *really* is. If the object is really (i.e., at the most fundamental level) a collection of molecules, then its place in a world of intersubjective meanings and activities takes on a secondary role with respect to an understanding of the thing. Bugles sound, and the other camp is up in arms. What do you mean by suggesting that . . . ? But isn't it equally as unreasonable to try to hold that the typewriter is not really a collection of molecules as that it is? Or that one or the other of the two possibilities we are considering must be seen as secondary? That the physical objects of ordinary experience can be described in terms of their molecular structure is obvious. We do so. Moreover, we have been doing so with extremely impressive results for some centuries now. To argue that it is a *mistake* to describe the thing in these terms is simply ludicrous. But it is just as ludicrous to insist that on offering such a description we have come somehow closer to the *real* meaning or being of the thing than we do when we think of its place in ordinary human experience. If a child walked into my office just now, pointed to my typewriter, and asked "What's that?" I should scarcely respond by telling him about its molecular structure. Nor, on describing its operations and functions, would I understand myself to be reserving the real truth about the thing until he was old enough to understand it. In fact, it seems to me that to tell him that it is a collection of molecules *would* be to make a mistake. That is not the sort of thing he was asking me about. To genuinely understand the object is not only to understand that both of these descriptions apply to it, but also to understand the context within which each becomes useful and meaningful. Each description can, from a certain point of view, be seen to conflict with what the object *means* and *is* when considered from other points of view. (Its place in the world of intersubjective human experience does not quite come apart into discretely meaningful pieces in the way that its molecular structure does.) And to assume that there *must* be some complete and thorough resolution to such conflicts is to ignore the indeterminacy that enters the picture with the contextual variety that has emerged as fundamental to the meaning of the object. Not only is it the case that some of those contexts are themselves indeterminate, but likewise that the relations between those that are determinate and those that are indeterminate must remain itself indeterminate. But this is a sort of indeterminacy with which we are ordinarily inclined to deal quite happily. That is, it seems to me that it never occurs to us to think that the indeterminacy of our experience stands in conflict with the claim that the world is intelligible until we start doing philosophy. In fact, indeterminacy figures strikingly in a variety of experiences that we should never dream of characterizing as unintelligible. Let me try to develop this claim by turning to a context in which it is not only difficult to hold that intelligibility is fundamentally tied to determinacy, but clearly a mistake to do so.

Not long ago, while still searching for a context particularly appropriate to an exploration of the relation between indeterminacy and intelligibility, I appealed to a friend who is a professor emeritus of English literature. It seemed a good idea to settle on some single literary example as a method of attack, and she suggested Yeats's familiar poem, "Among School Children." Of course, this is not an example that came to mind entirely without reason. In the poem, Yeats is clearly reflecting on his own experience, thinking about the relation between youth and age, what it means to have come to a new way of seeing the world, comparing it to ways in which he had once seen it. The poem has to do with just the sort of issue we had been talking about. That is, its images awaken in the reader a sense of returning to a beginning, considering its shape and texture not only in terms of the end that has in fact issued from it, but likewise in terms of those alternative ends that might have done. But the primary reason for considering this poem would apply just as well to any other good piece of poetry. That is, we are presented with something that must be seen as indeterminate in that it can be interpreted in not one but several perfectly reasonable ways. Furthermore, while the range of available interpretations is not without limits (since it is certainly possible to make mistakes), neither are its boundaries determinate in the usual philosophical sense of the term. What is particularly to the point here is that this is ordinarily seen as strengthening rather than weakening the claim that the poem is meaningful.

With that much said, let us take a more direct look at "Among School Children" itself. I hope that the poem is familiar enough that quoting the last stanza will be sufficient to recall its tone and imagery to mind.

> Labour is blossoming or dancing where
> Body is not bruised to pleasure soul,
> Nor beauty born out of its own despair,
> Nor blear-eyed wisdom out of midnight oil.
> O chestnut tree, great-rooted blossomer,
> Are you the leaf, the blossom, or the bole?
> O body swayed to music, o brightening glance,
> How can we know the dancer from the dance?

At the opening of the poem, Yeats finds himself in a schoolroom sur-
rounded by a group of children involved in the elementary stages of
education. He is naturally drawn to some reflection on the relation
between his own youthful experience and the developed perspective of
"a sixty year old smiling public man." Out of that reflection emerges a
series of ideas concerning the passage from youth to age, the consideration of the early stages from the point of view of the later, the relative
weight of this influence or that as it is considered from either the beginning or the end. Depending on the reader's focus, the meaning of the
poem might be seen to move in either direction or in both. Consider the
lines quoted above. One might interpret the last two lines as meaning
that the dancer is actually identical to the dance. For the "scarecrow"
whose dance is nearly completed, the return to a schoolroom calls to
mind the progress from youth to age, conjuring up images and relations
that have become part of him in an internally necessary sense. He *is* his
relationship with Maud Gonne (who is usually taken to be the woman
of stanzas two through four), he *is* his early fascination with and later
departure from the world-view of the classical Greeks, he *is* the
spirituality both sacred and secular that enshrouds the images of the
"nuns and mothers" of the seventh stanza. At the same time, he remains
in some sense identical to the infant on the mother's lap, full of potential
crying out for realization, though not necessarily for the particular
realization that was to come. For the dance is not yet complete, and the
dancer not after all identical to the dance. In fact, if he were, there could
be neither dancer nor dance, and the image would collapse into
meaninglessness.

But the emphasis to be placed on the one view or the other remains
open to question. Is Yeats telling us that the view from the perspective
of the nearly completed whole is to be taken more seriously than the
view from the mother's lap? Less? A reasonable argument might be made
in either direction. Or perhaps the most reasonable interpretation of the
poem lies somewhere in between. Not "between" in the sense of a diffi-
dent vacillation between the two possibilities mentioned, but firmly between, where the meaning of the two directions is to be found in the
curious relation between the indeterminacy of the one and the discrete
determinations of the other. Perhaps we see the poem most clearly when
we allow our focus of attention free rein, looking from end to beginning
and beginning to end, recognizing that the play between the two draws
us nearer to the truth than a narrowed focus in either direction could do
on its own.

Or we might follow some other path altogether. It would not be
wholly unreasonable, for example, to interpret the poem as a critique of
a certain kind of formal education. There is some evidence supporting

such an interpretation in the poem itself – the description of the children learning "to be neat in everything in the best modern way," the characterization of Plato, Aristotle, and "golden-thighed" Pythagoras as "old clothes upon old sticks to scare a bird." Further support for such a view appears on discovering that Yeats was at the time interested in Gentile's ideas concerning education reform; and still other variations on both themes seem reasonable in light of the note concerning the topic of the poem that Yeats jotted down about three months before the completion of the final draft: "School children and the thought that life will waste them perhaps that no possible can fulfill our dreams or even their teacher's hope. Bring in the old thought that life prepares for what never happens."[3]

We might account for variations within the range of possible interpretations in a number of ways, but the primary reason for such a range seems fairly obvious: The poem can be and is assessed from a variety of significantly different perspectives. If we cast our understanding of the poem in the mold formed by what we know of the poet and his experience prior to and contemporaneous with the writing of the poem, certain interpretations will seem more reasonable than others, but it would be odd to insist that those interpretations are more accurate than others. Further, even on narrowing our focus by choosing to adopt this perspective rather than others, we find that while some interpretations are excluded (at least from immediate consideration), there is no single interpretation that emerges as the only reasonable possibility. Imagine the course our reflection would take if we were, say, to approach "Among School Children" using the note quoted above as a point of departure. Because the note itself is open to a number of interpretations, we would first have to choose from among those possibilities the one that seems best suited in terms of what we know of Yeats's background, related interests, etc. That is, we should have to engage in a sort of second-order interpretive activity before it became possible to apply the note and our interpretation of it to the poem itself. Once having done so, we would find ourselves faced with still another series of decisions concerning the most reasonable application of the interpretation we have elected. Moreover, as many artists have pointed out, there comes a moment in the making of a work of art when the work seems to take on a life of its own, thereafter making demands on the artist that he might or might not have anticipated. To the extent that this is true of at least some works of art, (Croce et al. notwithstanding), and might well be true of the particular piece under consideration, it is perfectly reasonable to suppose that by the time "Among School Children" was completed, Yeats had departed in large or small ways from his original plan. In short, even after having adopted one of the various perspectives from which the poem might be considered, we still find ourselves ultimately offering an interpretation that no amount of argument could show to be the single best interpretation of the poem from that perspective, let alone others.

So far, in thinking about the poem from the perspective of the ideas and experiences brought to the work by the poet, we have seen that such reflection would eventually produce a range of interpretations including some that conflict with one another. Should we turn our attention to the various experience of the poem's audience, that range would obviously broaden enormously. Where the average college student might be inclined to focus on the romantic imagery in the center of the poem, allowing it to color his understanding of the beginning and end, his teacher, who has perhaps become a "sixty year old smiling public man" will have strikingly different notions about the poem's core. Enough. It is clearly possible to propose a wide range of reasonable and nevertheless significantly different interpretations of a poem like "Among School Children." Likewise, in the case of a genuinely important poem, that is to say one that will "last" and develop a history of its own, that range of interpretations will undergo constant change. That it provides a framework within which this can occur is one of the things ordinarily taken as grounds for referring to it as "genuinely important."

Now, the poem is certainly intelligible in the ordinary sense of the term. It is open to meaningful interpretation. Its meaning, however, remains indeterminate at least to the extent that a variety of interpretations are available and choosing among them involves further interpretation. It is equally important to note how strange it would be to suggest that we approach the poem with a determinately formulated goal in mind. If we think of ourselves as seeking the "truth" about the poem at all, it is certainly not in the sense of hoping to ultimately identify the most clear and distinct of all the possible interpretations that might be offered. We seek, if anything, to constantly enrich our understanding of the poem by considering new ways of thinking about it in relation to the poet himself, his audience, the complex relation between the two, the history of its imagery, the extent to which its metaphors reshape ordinary conceptual links of this sort or that, the peculiar perspective it affords for a reconsideration of the past out of which it has emerged and the future at which it hints. At the same time, none of this is to suggest that any interpretation whatever would do. It is quite possible to make mistakes. In fact, one of the most obvious ways to do so would be to attempt to treat the poem in an overly determinate fashion, as if, for example, it were made out of parts in the way that a machine is. One imagines (if only with a shudder) some hard-bitten analyst zeroing in on the lines

O chestnut tree, great-rooted blossomer,
Are you the leaf, the blossom, or the bole?

and taking it as his task to figure out which one it is. To attempt a formal analysis of the poem would be as silly – and a silliness of the same sort – as telling the child in section one that the typewriter is a collection of molecules.

The poem then can reasonably be seen as *both* meaningful and indeterminate. I should like to turn finally to a preliminary sketch of the bearing this seems to have on modern presuppositions concerning the structure of intelligibility.

In the first section, I suggested that we would do well to reconsider the prior logical and ontological status we have been accustomed to accord to "things," on the grounds that some of the most perplexing problems with which we have struggled throughout the history of the western tradition, and in particular during the modern period, appear to discover their logical roots in this presupposition. When we try to consider "things" while neglecting the significance of the relations in terms of which we describe them and by which they are structured, we doom ourselves to an unnecessarily restricted view of our own experience. At the same time, certain uncomfortable consequences seem to appear as soon as we shift the balance between *things* and *relations* in favour of relations. For it is not possible to raise doubts concerning the fundamental logical and ontological status of "things" without at the same time raising doubts about the fundamental logical status of determinacy. Furthermore, the notion that determinacy should be taken to have such a status is so firmly lodged in the tradition that it seldom occurs to us even to raise questions of this kind, let alone to take them seriously. Yet, as I tried to show in general terms at the end of the first section and in particular terms in the second, it turns out that intelligibility is by no means necessarily linked to determinacy. It is quite possible to reflect seriously, that is, to make intelligible claims, within and about contexts that are fundamentally indeterminate. And if this is the case, still another reassessment is called for. Something is amiss vis-à-vis the criteria we have been applying in making judgments concerning what is and what is not intelligible. Allow me to conclude, then, with some general observations concerning the relation between determinacy and indeterminacy, and the importance of that relation for the structure of intelligibility itself.

Several months ago, a colleague asked me to make some remarks about the development of the scientific method as an introduction to her seminar in physiological psychology. Describing the roots of the method in primarily Cartesian terms, I was stuck by the curious tension between determinacy and indeterminacy to be discovered within the method itself. There is scarcely any need to draw attention to the extraordinary success that we have had in learning more of the world and of ourselves as we have drawn this method into play in contexts both theoretical and practical. At the same time, I found myself anxious to convince my audience that while I had no interest in debasing the theoretical structure or the practical efficacy of the method, it was of equal importance to be chary of its hidden presuppositions. To the extent that it is a method whose core is analysis, it is one that leads toward a view of human experience that can generate any number of significant misconceptions. For one, if we assume that we can learn most about things by analyzing them, we have to assume at the same time that the things about which we can learn are things that give themselves over to analysis; we must assume that they are things that come apart into pieces. Now of course, in ordinary experience, we confront almost nothing that can't be broken into pieces, but the further and more important underlying assumption here is that the pieces that are the necessary byproducts of analysis have independent meanings. Whether the pieces in question are molecules or natural laws, sense-data or logical principles, they are invested with discrete meanings understood to stand independent of our experience. Nor is this in the least an unreasonable view when one considers the general character of our day-to-day experience. The things around me in the room as I write are things that certainly have meanings independent of those I am inclined to attach to them, and it is reasonable to suppose that they are made of smaller bits of which the same thing can be said. Here the move toward reflection on *my* world and the ways in which these objects have special meanings for me – my grandmother's violin, my friend's book, my parents' gift – seems to be beside the point. One thinks of learning to ask "But what is it really?" where of course the question directs one's attention away from the world of idiosyncratic tastes, familial sentiment, even some larger sense that grows out of a kind of general human sympathy, toward a world that has some meaning of "its own." This is the world of the "things" we considered in the first section. It is a world that we imagine transcending the merely personal, and which, in becoming universal, becomes likewise more complete, more true, more real.

A hunger for that meaning that stands independent of oneself is typical of the whole tradition of western philosophy. First gods, then natural phenomena, then ideal constructions, then God, then back to a combination of God, natural phenomena, and ideal constructions; round and round the search goes, always, it seems, with Thales's primary notion in mind: There must be something out of which everything else is made, there must be some fundamental meaning behind the appearances, if we are not to surrender ourselves to the more than just mildly disconcerting thought that the world we confront and try to come to terms with is merely whimsical. It is simply not acceptable. There must be a meaning. That this search is worthy of our time and effort, respect and sympathy, surely stands, if anything does, without argument. However, it cannot be carried out intelligently without a constant reappraisal of the extent to which the character of the search itself affects what we find.

When we treat analysis as the single most significant method of investigation, presuppposing as we must that the world is made up of discretely meaningful bits and pieces, the general structures in terms of which we articulate the relations among those pieces (principles, laws, meanings, etc.) are predestined to take on the same character as the pieces that we set out to look for in the first place. That is, they must be determinate. When determination is seen as the primary model for thought, and likewise for being, that which appears indeterminate is taken to be intelligible (or, in an extreme view to be at all) only to the extent that it might approach (whether actually or ideally) some ultimate moment identified in terms of the articulation of a determinate structure. When Descartes speaks of clarity and distinctness, he means to refer to just such a structure, and the frustration with which he repeatedly meets grows out of the sense that little or nothing in direct experience can be characterized in such terms. The indeterminate is seen here as an incompletely articulated version of the determinate. There is nothing inherently unreasonable in making such a suggestion. Its origins are in fact readily apparent. In both practical and theoretical contexts, it is often the case that success depends on becoming increasingly determinate in our understanding of various situations. Determinate forms emerge as the building nears completion, as the machine is further developed, as the mathematical proof is knitted together, even from a certain point of view, as the work of art coalesces, and in each case, the notion of accomplishing the task one has set for himself appears to involve more and more thoroughly defined structures. When we turn to reflection on such activities, isn't it reasonable to generalize, reaching the conclusion that human activity broadly defined involves a making-determinate?

But when we think of such activities from a slightly different angle, the apparently central character of this "making-determinate" can be seen to stand in a certain conflict with the notion that the determinations characteristic of the end-products have been "discovered" rather than created. If for no other reason than that in each case some other end is at least in principle possible, the claim that the determinations we have come upon at the end of the process are not really ideal structures that were undergirding the process (together with everything else) from the outset seems more and more reasonable. Even in those contexts that seem most highly refined, a sense of the indeterminate lingers stubbornly. We can choose, of course, to put this aside as a function of not having enough control over our procedures, etc., but in the case of direct experience that won't do simply because of the problem with sense experience that has troubled us since the pre-Socratics. Even in the case of the mathematical system, it lingers penumbrally around the imaginary and transfinite numbers that seems necessary to the making-determinate of real numbers. (Or, one might just as well point to the existence of and relation between alternative systems, as specifically in the case of Euclidean and non-Euclidean geometries.)

The point in all of this is that if we shift our focus away from an insistence on the primacy of the determinate in both orders toward an inspection of the pervasive character of indeterminacy, it becomes possible to see the determinate as an inadequately articulated form of the potential represented by the indeterminate dimensions of experience. From this point of view, the indeterminate comes to the fore as the ground out of which the determinate systematic account has arisen in the first place, and into which it will in a sense recede on having outlived its usefulness. In fact, now the determinate is seen as incomplete. That which stood as the model for and the goal of the complete account is itself as incomplete as a single interpretation of a work of art.

I hope that it is clear that in saying this I do not mean to suggest that indeterminacy should be accorded a more fundamental status than determinacy. Depending on the context within which we are working, one or the other may come to the fore as more fundamental to the character of our procedures and our conclusions. What seems true of every context, however, is that the *relation* between the two is as logically necessary to the meaning of both as it is fundamental to the structure of intelligibility itself. That structure, then, is neither completely determinate nor completely indeterminate, but a function of the relational framework out of which these notion originally emerge and on which they continue to depend for their meaning.

NOTES

1. Brian John Martine, *Individuals and Individuality* (Albany: The State University of New York Press, 1984).
2. Ibid., see especially pp. 31–39.
3. A. Norman Jeffares, *A Commentary on the Collected Poems of W. B. Yeats* (Stanford: Stanford University Press, 1968), p. 299.

Robert C. Neville

Sketch of a System

Systematic philosophy is the critical attempt to comprehend everything in one discursive reflective view, marking out connectives and relations of value or importance. In this general sense, it is as essential for cultural self-consciousness as a sense of self is for personal self-consciousness. That systematic philosophy is discursive means that it needn't have a vision of things "all at once" but only that it can move with critical reflection from anything to anything else. That it is reflective means that it involves both an interpretive grasp of its subject matter and an interpretation of the conditions, categories, purposes, and strategies of the first-level interpretation. Reflective levels can back up indefinitely toward conditions of conditions, categories of categories, higher level purposes, and more general strategies. And since nearly all philosophically significant subject matters already are shot through with selective abstractions, reflection can move to more concrete conditions from which the moment's starting point already was an abstraction: Reflection moves as much toward greater concrete embodiment as toward greater abstraction.

That systematic philosophy is critical means that it steadily examines its own vulnerability.[1] With regard to moving between poles of the more and less concrete, it identifies and assesses what of the relatively concrete is left out by a move to a certain abstraction, and what would happen with alternate abstractions; good abstractions carry along the relatively valuable and leave behind the relatively trivial. Since there may be many ways of selectively abstracting from a situation, each with its own merits and perhaps not commensurable with the others, there are even higher level abstractions that allow the incommensurables to be identified. Critical philosophy also requires a dialectical examination of alternate categories organized as systems, which in turn requires an historical self-consciousness. The critical part of systematic philosophy really amounts to a persistent attempt to discover whether anything has been left out of the considerations that organize experience, and to assess and cope with what has been left out, thereby bringing it in. This does not presuppose that reality or a philosophic view is a totality, only that systematic philosophy cannot rest if something is unconsidered.

A philosophical system, in contrast to a systematic philosophy, is a complex set of abstract categories and principles that are proposed as the basic guiding suppositions of a systematic philosophy, true to the extent that the philosophy is worthy. In principle, there could be many such systems with theoretical plausibility at any one time because there can be many systematic ways of thinking discursively, reflectively, and critically. Systematic philosophy is an interpretive art, and, in a sense, the systems that can be created as suppositions are like works of different composers; we don't have to choose between Schumann and Schubert but can enjoy the worlds of both. It is the same with appropriating both Platonic and Aristotelian ways of taking reality. But because a systematic philosophy has a critical need to come to terms with alternatives to itself, incorporating the others' values and finessing their drawbacks, any system at least intends to be internally related to its alternatives, unlike most art works.

A philosophic system is only a part of the larger practice of systematic philosophy. It presents itself as an hypothesis about the basic, worthwhile guiding suppositions of systematic philosophy, preferable, according to its lights, to other systems construed as alternate hypotheses, and struggling to find as its own lights those that illumine the arena of public discussion. As the warranted suppositions of systematic philosophy, the categories of a system are presented as expressing the most basic, pervasive, and metaphysically important truths. They are hypothesized as expressions of the most important values of reality as carried over into the discourse of the systematic philosophy, subject to the qualifications of that philosophy.

The situation of our own time is not a competing plurality of well-developed systems but a dearth.[2] Some philosophies, such as Deconstructionism, argue that the nature of language makes any philosophic system fraudulent by virtue of imposing a univocal meaning across a varying realm of discourses. Looked at positively, this opinion is a version of Charles Peirce's observation in the last century that general signs tend to generalize further and therefore change. The negative part of the Deconstructionist attack of philosophical system comes from its Heideggerian assumption, which assimilates metaphysics or philosophical system to the special kinds of systems he found in the "onto-theological" tradition. There are other kinds of system, an example of which is below, to which this attack is irrelevant.[3]

Other thinkers, often not philosophers, argue that even if a system were possible it would be a bad thing because it reduces the concrete individuality and uniqueness of things to abstract principles that don't express the values of haecceities. This is a valid criticism of all systems that take their abstract categories to be concrete, failing to recognize that their abstractions selectively have lost something as well as gained in formal clarity. Systems should never be taken out of the context of the systematic philosophy that uses the rest of reality to criticize them. Not all systems are intrinsically related to the rest of reality from which they are abstractions, and this makes them subject to the charge of reductionism. But where a system requires that its categories be made specific in more concrete terms before being applied to objects, the reductionist charge has no force.[4]

The greatest challenge to the project of developing a philosophical system is not the argument that it is impossible in principle, or that it would be bad in any case, but the fundamental practical difficulty of thinking up good abstractions and systematizing them. Most philosophers in the first half of this century, reflecting on the history of modern philosophy, despaired of both system and systematic philosophy, lamenting or celebrating (depending on whether they were German or French) the end of The Tradition.[5] Whitehead, almost alone among his contemporaries, believed that the difficulty was a failure to think up and properly understand enough good ideas. Whether he was correct is a difficult matter to judge at this close range, but it surely is the simpler hypothesis. Now that the age of modernism is about over, the need to delimit the tradition in order to close it down has diminished. We are in a position not only to reassess the tradition but to enrich our philosophic heritage with traditions from China and India, as well as from nonelite cultures. A crucial difficulty for good philosophic ideas today is being able to conceive of fragmentation. It seems that there are very few philosophically interesting orders extending uniformly over much of reality. How dull, though fundamental, for art or for the struggle for distributive justice that e = mc². Rather, there are pockets of interesting order, apparently only minimally related to one another under most circumstances. A contemporary system must recognize the fragmentation of orders into pockets. David Hall rightly conceives of systematic philosophy's subject matter as the sum of all orders, though his identification of this with chaos is only part of the story.[6]

What follows is a sketch of a system put forward as a tentative hypothesis. Although it may be nothing more that what I understand to be the core suppositions of my own systematic practice, it is offered for public examination. As a sketch, many of its parts have been explored in more detail elsewhere and others of its parts are just hunches.[7]

1. Identity as Harmony

To be something rather than nothing, and to have a determinate identity in relation to and over against other determinate things, I propose we conceive a thing to be a harmony of essential and conditional features (*GC*, ch. 2; *CF*, ch. 2; *SSS* pp. 106–109; *RT*, ch. 3; *TD*, pp. 30–39, 52–55). "Harmony," "essential," and "conditional" are notions to be understood in terms of one another and in reference to the problem of the nature of identity.

Conditional features are those a thing has by virtue of which it relates to other things. They constitute its situational, logical, and causal relativity. Essential features are those a thing has unique to itself by virtue of which it orders the conditional features in a definite way defining its identity. Without conditional features the thing would not be determinate with reference to anything else. Of course a thing can be partially determinate with respect to some things, and wholly indeterminate with respect to some things, but if it is wholly indeterminate with respect to all things it has no determinate identity. Furthermore, without conditional features, the essential features themselves would be indeterminate, since they would relate to nothing.

Without essential features a thing would be a mere function of the other things to which it is conditionally related. Worse than that, without essential features its functional relations would not be integrated and the thing would have no identity of its own over against the other things. In fact, if there were no essential features there could be no conditional features, since there would be no focal point for the other things to condition or be conditioned by. Therefore, there must be both essential and conditional features harmonized together for there to be either essential or conditional features.

If to be determiante is to be a harmony of essential and conditional features, then each of the features must itself be a harmony of essential and conditional features, and so on down. A harmony itself, however, is not a third kind of feature over and above the essential and conditional ones. For if it were, it would have to be either indeterminate or determinate. (*GC*, pp. 24–28). If it were indeterminate, it would add nothing to the essential and conditional features unharmonized. If it were determinate, it would need essential and conditional features relating it to its own essential and conditional features, thus generating a fruitless infinite regress.

That a thing's essential and conditional features are harmonized is simply the fact of their togetherness. Harmonies are de facto. What is achieved in the fact of their togetherness, however, is the value of having them together that way. As will be explained below, a harmony is the achievement of value. So we can say on this systematic hypothesis that to be a thing is to be the achievement of this essential value here in the context of these conditions. To be is to be or express a value.

The metaphysics of harmony, essential, and conditional features is extraordinarily abstract; abstract in the sense Peirce defined as "vagueness." To give any examples, we need to fill in the kinds of essential and conditional features involved. As the discussion stands, it applies to the determinateness of logical forms, of biological organisms, of cloud formations, social situations, memories, and purposes. Suppose we specify this vague cluster of categories by talking about physical reality in space-time, as interpreted, for instance, by the cosmology of process philosophy.[8] The prehensions would be the conditional features, the contributions of subjective form would be the essential features, and the objectified datum would be the harmony of both. With regard to this kind of thing, as Charles Hartshorne has emphasized, there is an asymmetry to conditional features. Past things enter as conditions to an emerging thing, but there are no special conditional features relative to the future save for the subject-superject; rather, future things take up the whole of the emerged harmony as a condition. If one prefers an Aristotelian to a Whiteheadian interpretation of physical reality, we can say that formal and final causes are essential features, and that efficient and material causes, along with specifications of time, place, relation, etc., are conditional. The point is that the vague categories need to be specified with some middle range set of abstractive interpretations that have some standing on their own.

The notions of essential and conditional features have utility in many kinds of analysis. They call for discovering the factors that impinge upon a situation and understanding how the situation relates and structures those factors. The distinction between essential and conditional features is a functional one. A feature that functions essentially in one thing, or in one way of looking at a thing, can function conditionally in another thing or in another way of looking at the same thing. The functions of essential and conditional features are to provide different aspects of identity or determinateness. The study of determinateness is the beginning of metaphysics.

II. One, Many and Divine Creativity

The theory of things as harmonies of essential and conditional features directly addresses the problem of the one and the many. Atomistic theories have a fine many but only ad hoc unities. Field theories have fine unity but only an artificial or conventional many. Idealistic theories suppose that any two different things are united by a third term; but if the third term is different from the first two, it only compounds the problem by needing fourth and fifth terms to relate it to what it is supposed to unite. Other theories believe that separateness is overcome by a unifying action; but then the integrity of the many is lost.

In the theory of harmony, a thing is necessarily related to some other things by virtue of its conditional features. It has essential features of its own unique to itself, so that, as a harmony of conditional and essential features, it maintains its own integrity while in relation to other things. Further, because a thing may lack any conditional features relating it to some other particular things, it can be indeterminate with reference to them even though in the same world with them from the standpoint of yet other things conditionally related to both. This theory provides a powerful tool for defining things relationally without exhausting them in relations that themselves then collapse.

The theory of things as harmonies also formulates a deep sense of ontological concern that is nigh universal across cultures and that has frequently marked the link between philosophical reflection and religion (*TD*, ch. 6). In facing another person, or thing, the sheer fact of difference suggests a deeper unity than that composed of all the mutual conditionings. The theoretical structure is this. If A has essential features of its own and conditional features with respect to B, and B has conditional features with respect to A and also its own essential features, how are the essential features of A related to the essential features of B? The essential features of A are not determinate except as harmonized with A's conditional features, and the conditional features are impossible except through B, which itself is a harmony of its own conditional and essential features. The relation between the two sets of essential features thus cannot be constituted by the conditional features as mediators but must be primordial on a par with the conditional features themselves. I say, therefore, that the two harmonies with their essential and conditional features must be in an ontological context of mutual relevance, of which their cosmological context constituted by conditional features is a subset and specification.

What is the character of the ontological context of mutual relevance (*GC*, especially p. 59; *TD*, pp. 50–57, 189–92)? It cannot be determinate on its own, for that would involve an infinite regress of relations with the other determinate things. Yet it is that upon which the very being or existence of the determinate things depends. Without that ontological context of mutual relevance, the separate sets of essential features could not be together; and so the harmonies could not be together, nor could there be the conditioning of one thing by another.

In deference to Western religious traditions, I call the ontological context of mutual relevance "divine creativity" or "God," but with warnings about theistic misinterpretations (*GC*, chs. 3–4). The ontological context is the mutual making of harmonies together. But there is no determinate maker apart from the making, no singer apart from the song. The structure of divine creativity is trinitarian, namely, the act of creating, the resultant harmonies created, and the creating as source without which there would be nothing determinate (*TD*, ch. 3). Since the creative act is immediate and has no steps, its only character comes from its results, the harmonies, or in Western religious terms, Sophia or the logos. Without the actual creating, the creator as source would be wholly indeterminate – not even a potential creator – and hence would be indistinguishable from nothing, or would be the creative abyss to which the mystical traditions have pointed. The metaphor of creativity resonates not only in Western religions but in the Chinese traditions of the nameless and then the named tao, and in the Indian traditions of the playing and dancing gods. In traditions such as Vedanta and Buddhism, which do not emphasize creativity, there still are profound symbols for the ultimate context in which things are unified in ways deeper than their connections.

I cite these authorities in order to forestall the accusation that the need for an ontological context of mutual relevance merely comes from the inadequate conceptuality of harmonies of essential and conditional features. My claim is that things are unique integrities in relation to one another and that this itself rests on a profound ontological base of contingent-existence-making, and that both of these factors are deep elements of human experience to be articulated but not explained away.

III. Harmony as Value

Recall the claim made above that to be a harmony is to be an achievement of value. How is that to be analyzed? The first point to discuss is the formal aspect of harmony?

In a harmony, the various component features are integrated in patterns that cohere in one definite overall pattern. A pattern's harmony exhibits both complexity and simplicity (*CF*, ch. 3; *RT* ch 3). Complexity refers to the different things involved as components, including the patterns of components. Simplicity refers to the economy with which the components are harmonized, such that higher levels contain relatively

little complexity but encompass great variety in the components of components, etc. Every harmony thus has both complexity and simplicity,
and the degree of harmony is dependent on maximizing both complexity
and simplicity. It is easy to gain simplicity by sacrificing complexity; this
happens as one approaches homogeneity. Equally, one can maximize
complexity at the expense of simplicity by levelling off the harmony and
having the components related by mere conjunctions. Harmony is
increased in value as both complexity and simplicity are increased. Since
these are two variables, both of which might be subject to increase, there
are many possible ways in which a harmony might be increased in value.

   In moral deliberation, is it not the case that the main reflection is to
vary complexity and simplicity in imagination and then assess the imagined outcomes? Most moral dilemmas could be solved easily if we could
cut down on the complexity, that is, just will to leave certain factors, people, or interests out of account. The bite in morality is that we can't often
vary the complexity downward, only upward by making things more
complicated. Most moral deliberation concerns comparing alternate
paths of action or patterns for integrating all the factors with a moral
claim. Moral ingenuity is finding a solution so simple that one can have
the cake and eat it too. The greatest ingenuity is in finding a solution so
simple that everything falls into place and all the relevant factors are
improved by virtue of being together with each other in the resultant
pattern.

   The creation of a work of art differs from solving a moral dilemma
in many ways, the most formal of which is that there is great latitude in
the choice of complexity. A painter can use whatever colors, textures, or
other compositional elements that serve the purpose. The great limitation in art is that the forms of simplicity must be high to begin with and
are difficult to lower. There has to be an overall compositional design,
a "conception," and the artist can choose the complexity best to bring it
off. In moral situations, we can be satisfied if all the claims are met one
way or another, however inelegant and uninteresting. In art, the work
must first of all be interesting, and that is a function of the simplicity of
the patterns. Of course, in art we also may look for satisfaction in the
sense of wanting the painting to have a good use of color, a painterly
brush stroke, and so forth; art work can be valuable if it is interesting but
not very satisfying from the standpoint of antecedent expectations about
the work's components.

   I cite the imaginative variations employed in moral deliberation and
in the creative artistic process to make plausible the claim that maximizing complexity and simplicity is what is at stake in increasing value. We
could also discuss the mathematician's preference for the elegant proof

even when several proofs validly derive the result; or our efforts to develop a life style that holds together the various facets of our lives; or the strategies by which a general directs a campaign or a university president allocates a budget.

The argument is that since varying complexity and simplicity is what we do in assessing alternate patterns of value, complexity and simplicity are the crucial elements in value, or among the crucial elements. Since maximizing them leads to more intense or greater harmony, alterations in the patterns involved in a harmony are alterations in the value achieved in that thing. And at bottom, none of this would make sense unless harmonies as such are valuable.

If a harmony as such has some value, then the components of a harmony are all achievements of value of some sort. The meaning of a harmony's value is thus intensified. It first of all has the value that is the sum of the values of all its components; this is the value it achieves just by holding them all together, the "complexity value." Then there is the "simplicity value" achieved by the special ways in which the harmony integrates its components, the value that shows up when the components are enhanced by being together that way rather than some other ways.

How do we know something's value? I suggest that it is by a kind of educated intuition that simply grasps in an appreciative way the value in the harmony. The intuition is educated because it must bring to the situation an interpretive readiness to recognize all the components and understand how they work together. The hard work in moral deliberation and artistic creativity is in educating our grasp of things so that our intuition can appreciate how they fall into place. One of the penalties of poor education is that people leap to judgment before understanding what's going on. To claim that we appreciate experience valuationally through appropriate intuitions is not simply to appeal to the reader's intuition. Rather, I am presenting a theory, and its plausibility will be determined by its capacity to clarify experience and speak to the relevant experiences.

Before pressing on to a more sophisticated analysis of formal value, an important disclaimer must be made. It is frequently assumed that if everything is a valuable harmony, then there is no evil, and one should always pursue greater harmony. Quite to the contrary, evil is very real and conflict is often a virtue, morally obligatory. A harmony always must be judged for its proper placement and timeliness. Cancerous tissue and totalitarian social orders are out of place, and one should seek the conflicts that destroy them, not the orders by which they prosper. In moral deliberation, the form of actions decided upon should be harmonious, cognizant of all the claims; but the content of the actions might be obligatory destruction. Conflict, empirically described, is a species of harmony, and whether it is justified depends on whether the harmony it upsets ought to be upset. The reasons for this disclaimer will be more apparent in Sections IV and V below.

Returning to the formal analysis of harmony as value, the conditional features of a harmony are those that contribute to its complexity, and the essential features are those that contribute to its simplicity. The concrete thing is the de facto harmony of all the features. Each of the component features is itself a de facto harmony. There is a pattern of the features harmonized that can be abstracted from each harmony. We change this pattern in imaginative variation by altering the complexity or the simplifying elements, and then assess whether the imagined altered pattern is better or worse than the original pattern, and at what price. This suggests that the patterns are all determinate specifications of a true normative measure, or set of normative measures, for how the components are to be mixed. "Normative measure" is Plato's term in the *Statesman* for that to which the statesman appeals in attempting to find the proper mix of elements, the due proportion. The "Form of the Good," or normative measure, has no determinate character of its own and hence cannot be an object of knowledge like other objects.[9] But relative to a given set of components to be harmonized, reality (or the Good) has it that there are better and worse ways of harmonizing those components. We cannot know these ideal values except by imagining schemata that relate them to the candidate components. The imagined patterns, and the given pattern if there is one, are such schema-images (*RT*, pp. 223–235). The schemata of which the schema-images are images are the normative measures or Form of the Good relative to the components at hand. The fact that we can construct schema-images and assess their relative merits indicates that there are indeed schemata, and the simplest hypothesis is to suppose that they are normative.[10]

What is the character of the value-filled pattern or form ingredient in a harmony? I suggest, following Whitehead, that form is the particular togetherness, the unmediated harmonious fit, of certain components so as to arrange all the components with triviality, vagueness, narrowness, and breadth.[11] Triviality means that the form of the harmony holds most of the vast and infinite array of components at a distance so that none stands out as more important than the others, or even as different; this is the first strategy for handling complexity. Vagueness means that there are certain components that play a representative function for the trivially distanced components so as to give them a general orientation within the harmony; the vague orienting components refer to or contain the trivial mass, but not specifically with reference to any one trivial item; this is the second strategy for handling complexity and, together with the first, guarantees that the whole world is present in any harmony to the extent that there is any determinate connection at all. Narrowness means that certain components are given great clarity and reinforcement by other components so as to stand in a sharp, focused contrast; the narrow components are what we think of in identifying a harmony in the first place. Breadth means the bearing that the narrow components have on the vague and trivial field so as to achieve overall unity of the harmony. Narrowness and breadth are special strategies for achieving simplicity. When harmony appears as world for an experiencer, triviality and vagueness constitute the organization of background, whereas narrowness and breadth constitute the focal center of the Gestalt (*RT,* especially pp. 162–66).

It should be apparent now that a harmony is in itself a way of focusing or containing in perspective its whole world of components. Two harmonies determinately over against one another are alternate focusings, each dependent for its independence on its own essential features – that is, those components making for narrowness and breadth in simplicity. This gives expression to the ancient intuition that somehow the whole world is contained in each thing. The limitation to this intuition is that a thing can contain only those other things to which it is ordered: Where orders are not congruent, there is indeterminate relation.

Return to the claim made above, that the ontological context of mutual relevance is the ground of the togetherness of related but different harmonies. This may be spelled out in a much richer way than before. The co-creation of many different and determinately related harmonies, each with essential and conditional features, requires two converging creative modes, the normative and the chaotic.

A de facto created harmony is a normative achievement of some good way of having its components together. It may be far from the best way, and it may in context be a positively evil way in the sense that its good is misplaced or destructive to greater possible goods. In this metaphysics, a harmony cannot fail to embody some good. This is true of each of the harmonic parts of a harmony; that is, of all the rest of the world as focally harmonized from this standpoint. The ontological creator thus functions as the Good, indeterminate in itself (as required by the metaphysics of harmony as well as by Plato's observation in the *Republic*) but schematically related to the harmony's components as the specifically relevant normative measure. As schematic normative measure, it is imaginatively available in the schema-images we might invent, and it normatively measures the harmony as to whether it might be better. To use other philosophic metaphors, creation takes place through the creation of orders, normative orders, according to which the welter of potential components of things are mixed. This metaphysics does not ascribe existence to orders apart from embodiment or imagination, but it does recognize that they are normative whether or not perfectly embodied or imagined; that is, orders have normative reality relative to orderable components. This is as true of mathematical orders as of moral ones. Creation in the normative mode has been a dominant theme of the Western tradition.

Creation in the chaotic mode is the production of diversity, the multiplication of plenitude. A finite harmony cannot be created without its components, and the components' components. Without the otherness of other harmonies of conditional and alien essential features, no harmony could be determinate with respect to other things. Nor would it be possible for there to be other things with respect to which a harmony is partially or wholly indeterminate did creation not function as a principle of plenitude. In practical experience, a particular order might vanish and the situation dissolve into the now unordered components. Each remaining thing, of course, is a mixture of its order and its components, and thus is in jeopardy of dissolution. The fundamental apprehension of creative fecundity that transgresses and disposes of orders, which produces swarms that cannot be grasped or comprehended by established order, is a deep religious vision, a story of Pan and Dionysus. This side of creation has been suppressed in the dominant Western tradition, only to be recovered with a new mythology by Freud and Jung. But it has remained at the forefront of Chinese sensibilities since the ancient roots of Taoism and Confucianism. The religious apprehension of this side to creation is intoxicated, immediate revelry in spontaneous diversity and more-ness, coupled with deep terror at the potential loss of the orders that give recognized value to life.

Definite existence requires both diversity and order if existence is that of harmony. A harmony is a mixture and thus contains the negativity of diffusion along with the positivity of order. Descartes's conception that the created world is wholly positive, and thus wholly knowable through representations, is inadequate to the quality of mixing chaos and order. Yet the contingent, created world as a bunch of mixtures is concretely real, and the moves away from the concrete harmony to higher level orders or contrary-to-fact unrelated components are abstractions. If one were to break up orders and move down to components, then to their components, and so on indefinitely, the last component would still have its order. Likewise, if one were imaginatively to ascend to higher levels of order, more vaguely structured while more broadly normative, one still must find components to be ordered lest the order slip into total indeterminateness. Purely unordered chaos and purely indeterminate goodness might be said to be divine potentialities wholly apart from actual creation. But apart from actual creation the divine ground is not even divine ground, and must be wholly indeterminate; hence, it is nonsense to call that ground pure chaos or pure goodness. It is rather nothing except as creating the harmonies through normative and chaotic modes.

Plato suggested an ontology something like this in the *Philebus* when he put forward the following categories. The concrete world of finite, changing things is Mixture. It is a mixture of the Indefinite (chaos) and Limit (order); the Indefinite and Limit do not exist apart from each other but only as mixed. The fourth category is the Cause of Mixture, which the dialogue proceeds to explore as the good, beautiful, proportioned, the source of measure. What Plato failed to give metaphoric stress is the sense of contingency in both chaos and order with the resultant need for creativity, or for employing chaos and order modally in creating mixtures. But he did argue that the forms or orders are not definite without some plurality to measure, and that the chaotic indefinite has no finite existence without some order.

IV. Cosmos

The above discussion has been general in the sense that it might apply to any state of this or any other world (if other worlds are possible). Let us now turn from metaphysics (the study of determinateness) and ontology (the study of being) to cosmology, and specify the previous categories to a characterization of our world.

The harmonies implicated in space and time are changing and discursive, as Plato knew. Let us catch the rough drift of Whitehead's cosmology and say that a harmony in space and time is an occasion in which past harmonies are taken up as conditions to be integrated into a completely definite harmony, which is the emerging occasion's full nature. All of the past harmonies are themselves occasions with their own values, and part of the normative process in the emergence of the new occasion is to bring the greatest value out of the welter of values making claim for recognition (*CF*, chs. 2-6; 1 *RT*, chs. 3-4). The essential features of the emerging occasion are those that perform the integration, bringing in novel patterns, possibly, and achieving essential as well as conditional values. The completed nature of the emerged occasion thus has a composite value that must be taken into account by subsequent occasions into which it enters as a condition. That completed nature is a mixture of the conditioning components and the orders by which they are brought together, and it displays an arrangement of the conditions and essential integrating elements so as to exhibit triviality, vagueness, narrowness, and breadth.

All the harmonies that directly can condition the emerging harmony are in the past; and since some of those are conditions for others of them, that past itself is temporally ordered. All harmonies for which the emerging occasion, when completed, can be a condition are in its future, and they similarly are related as conditions-conditioned so that the future has some kind of temporal structure. Other harmonies that neither condition nor are conditioned by the emerging harmony can share all, some, or none of its past conditions. Likewise, they can be conditions for all, some, or none of the same future occasions. To the extent occasions do not condition one another either way, and share all the same past and all the same future, they are congruently ordered contemporaries. If they shared none of the same past and none of the same future, they would be wholly indeterminate with respect to one another in temporality. In between these poles, sharing some past and some future, or all past and some future, or some past and all future, things are in partially overlapping but not fully congruent pockets of temporal order. Within a single pocket of temporal order there is a strict layout of past and future, with specifiable contemporaries, for any occasion within it.

The temporal pulse of creation thus involves both the chaotic drive of the diverse past harmonies to evoke a new harmony of which they are conditions, and the normative drive of emergence in the new occasion to contain the conditions together with their values and to add the essential value of putting them together with the most intense harmony. Chaotic and normative creativity are modes of the same temporal creation, or creation of temporal things temporally related. This is how the ontological context of mutual relevance "works" regarding temporal things.

Not all beings in our cosmos are momentary occasions, although all may contain them. Just about anything we can think of is at least an event of many occasions, and the substances of our world, especially living things, have an even tighter unity. Some enduring objects may be merely many occasions, all with the same or similar overall pattern. Many enduring objects are events containing many occasions but structured to play related different roles in a temporally extended pattern of harmonic change; e.g., notes in a piece of music that play roles in the harmonic whole of the piece. Many enduring things, however, are discursive individuals whose very essential individuality involves encompassing an expanse of time, and perhaps developing through a career in which new structures and values are achieved; for instance, an animal growing through a life. Whereas the score for a piece of music expresses a static pattern for a series of changes, a discursive individual might be free at any moment to change or develop its overall pattern, so long as it takes into account its past and future as essential components in its momentary actions.

A discursive individual harmonizes an organised group of occasions each of which has essential features deriving not only from its present, which function to integrate the conditions, but also from its past and future occasions (*CF*, pp. 104–110; *CG*, pp. 54–57). Essential features from past occasions are those entering as conditions that mark those conditions as the individual's own past states (in contrast to the states of other things in the past). The present occasion of the individual's life is thus committed essentially to respect the values of the individual's own past in forming up its present integration. The individual's own past occasions thus function both conditionally and essentially in the harmony of the present occasion.

Essential features from future occasions, similarly, are anticipations of future occasions as the individual's own. Dumb animals may have projective feelings for only a short future. People have complicated symbolic capacities for representing themselves in far distant states. It should be remembered that the function of essential features is to integrate the conditions so as to preserve their values and to enhance them in the harmony. For momentary occasions involving only the essential features arising from the spontaneous task of achieving momentary harmony, the relevant normative measure has an aesthetic momentary quality. For occasions in discursive individuals, however, with essential features from the individual's past and future, the relevant normative measure has a moral dimension, coping with bringing the best result out of things done in the past, and doing things now with which the individual in the future can do well. Put in moral language, the normative task of essential harmonization in a given moment of a discursive individual's life includes obligations stemming from other moments in that individual's life.

Although a discursive individual's temporal existence changes moment by moment, the individual's structures are temporally enduring, cumulative, growing, and hierarchically built on one another. That is, the normative obligation to maintain organic integrity in a changing environment, for instance, once achieved, makes it possible to engage in social relationships, which once achieved make it possible to nurture offspring out of the mother's body, offspring which (with other factors of course) make possible the transmission of culture. Each of these structures becomes normative as previously achieved structures make it possible. A discursive individual is a complex hierarchy of achieved structures and plays roles in complex social hierarchies.

We may image our cosmos as a welter of pockets of order, each with a temporal thrust. These pockets interweave and overlap. When they overlap, new and sometimes more valuable kinds of harmony are possible. What fortune when the right conditions of earthly chemicals and solar radiation made it possible for life to emerge! Or when social life allowed leisure for the invention of the arts and philosophy. But the pockets of order when harmonized together still have lives of their own and may cease to overlap. The higher dependent harmonies are thus threatened. The chaotic mode of creation may in fact undermine the finer achievements of the normative mode – gods are terrible before they are tame. Within this image, any being with the power to act upon things stands under a kind of ontological obligation: to affect the weaving of pockets of order to bring about the greatest value. Since things are always in movement, life is coping as well as suffering and enjoyment.

V. Persons and Society

A discursive individual is a very tight pocket of order and exists within larger pockets of order. An individual, even a momentary individual, however, can be a point of congruence of several pockets of order that only partially overlap. As a person, for instance, I exist in my family order, in the order of my university and its social structure, in the order of my career as a scholar and writer, and in a host of other partially overlapping orders (e.g., the neighborhood, regional, national, political economic, and religious). All these orders are fully congruent with encompassing temporal and spatial orders, so far as I know, but not necessarily with each other. In fact, the norms for my behavior in my family are directly in competition with those for behavior at the university, and those for my scholarship compete with both. The orders overlap partially; some colleagues are family friends and are partners in scholarship, and our neighborhood, counting the airport, is the place that allows all the activities to take place. There is no way, however, in which I can measure the worth of an evening with my family over against attendance at an important meeting over against revising the draft of a paper one more time; the value of each of these is univocal and commensurable only within its own order. What I do as a person is balance out the orders, keeping each one going, and sculpting particular shape to my life by the style with which I balance them, giving now one priority, now another.

Let me suggest that a person is a discursive individual with highly developed biological and social structures, with a capacity to represent normative behavior through time in each of the orders or ecosystems in which he or she is involved, and also with a capability to represent himself or herself as harmonizing all these orders, responding to norms in each case. This is a fancy way of saying that a person is a being that represents itself to itself and responds to that representation in terms of norms (not that the reponse need be the right or normative one).

Suppose that at least some of a person's relevant orders are tightly systematic, like ecosystems. A person's metabolism and economic systems are overlapping ecosystems. Family relations, certain social relations, participation in the political system, in the legal system, in an organized religion – all are memberships in overlapping if not congruent ecosystems. How an individual fits together some participation in each of these (and others like them) constitutes his or her style. Less systematically organized orders, such as historically unique events, chance infections, climatic oddities, all must be responded to, and for each potential action there are relevant normative measures. A basic conundrum of life is that most actions are measured by norms for more than one order, and sometimes the norms are in conflict. Richness consists in resources to do most of what we are obliged to; poverty is having to fail at basic obligations. A person is one who not only participates in all these orders, balancing them willy-nilly, but also who has the capacity, and hence the obligation, to represent himself or herself as doing this, and to respond normatively to that representation.[12] Normative response to that representation is acknowledgement of virtue or guilt. Good or bad behavior in an individual who cannot represent himself or herself as good or bad cannot be virtuous or guilty in the full sense, as the M'Naughton Rule has sought to express; it is less than full personhood. Being moral, of which being rational is a subcase, involves the capacity to represent oneself as being in a situation bound by normative measures that would measure any moral or rational person in that situation. As Paul Weiss says, being a personal self involves taking ourselves to be representative of all such moral or rational selves.

The distinction between nature and society is an artificial one. We play roles in natural ecosystems without knowing it. Perhaps a social system can be defined as one in which we cannot play a role without recognizing (through some symbols or other) that it is a role, e.g., that of a speaker of a public language, a participant in an economic transaction. At any rate, the metaphysics of value, or axiology, developed above suggests that the proper study of social systems should be the study of how values are transferred around the system, how they are transferred to the individuals participating in them, how the individuals in which they overlap transfer values from one system to another, how the choices and stresses in an individual can transfer values back to a system, and how values are transformed in all these transfers. The analysis of the structures of social systems, and of their mutual interest, coherence, and overlap, would follow from an analysis of the transfer of value, since value is a function of form in harmonies. The whole study of societies should be genetic or historical; but the history should be a following out of the development of each of the pockets of order, not the imposition of a super-story on the whole. There may be no super-story beyond mere chronology and geography. Even space and time may not be universal baseline orders for micro and macro pockets of events ordered in additional ways.

A society is a group of people causally interacting by means of assorted social systems and nonsystematic structures. That loose kind of harmony, tolerating much indeterminateness among the relations between its components, still is measured by norms, and usually fails the ideal. Injustice, oppression, needless poverty, ignorance, disguised opportunities – many social conditions call for amendment. These constitute social obligations about which something ought to be done. But how do these social obligations become the personal responsibility of particular people? According to the liberal polity, public obligations become personal reponsibilities when the person plays a role which the social contract defines as liable; the basic role is citizenship, and public offices define more specific roles with public responsibility. But because liberalism conceives of individuals as rather externally related to these contractual roles, people can foreswear public obligations by willing to abandon the roles, abandoning citizenship in the extreme case. Perhaps then the obligation would be no one's personal responsibility. According to the system described here, the public obligations would be everyone's personal responsibility to the extent each person can make a difference. The task of political polity is to delimit and channel the fulfillment of responsibility so that certain people can represent the others in fulfilling the reponsibilities of all. A politically organized society works so long as the responsibilities are fulfilled; where they are not, however, the primary responsibility devolves back on those who were represented, and new efficient structures must be sought. Whereas in the liberal ideology everyone is private unless contractually made public, in the axiological ideology everyone is personally responsible for public obligations unless contractually permitted a suspended level of responsibility.

In general, the axiology within the system presented here urges a very practical understanding of personal and social life, recognizing that there are no norms branching across diverse pockets of order except where they overlap in persons and their local situations.

VI. Conclusion

The sketch of the system has moved from very abstract considerations to slightly less abstract ones. It would be hard to continue the discussion of persons and society, however, without dealing specifically with particular societies, analyzed particular ways, and with particular analyses of people. That would go beyond the sketch of the system.

A parenthetical word might be added about epistemology. A theory of knowledge ought to be able to show how we know what one's metaphysical system says there is to know. In the modern period, epistemology has been thought foundational to metaphysics, and metaphysics has been thought to be justified to the extent a plausible epistemology shows it warranted. Epistemology has not been successful, and so metaphysics has been thought by many to be unjustified. It is difficult in the long run to give either metaphysics or epistemology priority over the other.

The axiological metaphysical system does, however, suggest ideas for the development of an axiological reconstruction of epistemology. Most modern work in epistemology has accepted the European Renaissance invention of mathematical science as legitimately integrating qualitative and quantitative modes of thought, but at the price of delegitimating valuative thinking (*RT*, ch.1). An axiological epistemology would reconstruct the models of thinking, not denying the achievements of the mathematical-scientific model but setting them in the context of valuative thinking. Four kinds of thinking need to be rethought in this way, I believe: imagination, interpretation, theorizing, and the pursuit of responsibility. The analysis of imagination would show how experience begins with the causal impingements on people being systhesized according to forms that organize a "world," namely those exhibiting triviality, vagueness, narrowness, and breadth. The analysis of interpretation would show how truth is both triadically a function of the interpretation of signs and dyadically a function of the carryover of the value of the objects interpreted into the experience of the interpretation, properly qualified by the structures of the interpretation. The analysis of theory would show how theoretical forms allow the importance of things to be appreciated according to the structures relating things in the subject matter to one another. Pursuit of responsibility is the intelligent behavior of dialectically examining and reassessing the goals and directions of life, including intellectual life.

The contribution of the system sketched here is its axiology, its thematising of value. This sets it off from the systems of Whitehead, Hartshorne, Weiss, Buchler, and those of my colleagues in the present volume for whom value plays a less central role. I have tried in this sketch to depict the basic categories of harmony, essential and conditional features, and to show how value emerges as the central theme in dealing with such rock bottom issues as the one and the many, the nature of concrete harmonies, individuality, and obligation. Whether the system sketched is fruitful in the long run will depend on ramifying it beyond a sketch.

NOTES

1. This use of "critical philosophy" differs from Kant's by being internal to systematic philosophy or metaphysics itself. Critical philosophy for Kant is something outside the conception of system that violently makes the system vulnerable. Kant was led to this view by construing the internal form of system as architectonical. Rather, it should be viewed as discursive and dialectical, with the process of criticism built in. If there is an alternative to one's architectonic, then the alternative should be considered internal to the system. On the conception of systematic philosophy I am defending, even in the system the categories one uses are not ordered formally by architectonic but rather dialectically by their usefulness in being employed systematically.

2. Although the creation of systems seems relatively unpopular in academic philosophy, the twentieth century actually has been a heyday for systems. Among the more notable are those of Whitehead, Hartshorne, Blanshard, Findlay, Weiss, Buchler, and the late Leonard Feldstein; the authors in the current volume are engaged in system building, each in his or her own way; and there are others not represented here. For a review of the situation, see my "Metaphysics," in *Social Research*, 47/4 (Winter, 1980), pp. 696–703.

3. One must be careful that the control over the use of names does not fall into the hands of those who wish ill to some applications of those names. It is absurd that all systematic philosophy or metaphysics be condemned because certain systems are flawed. Since each system contains its own conception of system, it is highly unlikely that valid arguments against one system would apply mutatis mutandis to very different systems. The public discourse of philosophy needs to allow each position to define its genealogy and therefore claim its right to a name. The rhetorical function of names, of course, is to lay claim to the legitimating weight of a genealogy.

4. The mention of philosophic categories being made specific is a reference to a theory of logical vagueness in systematic philosophy, developed in my *Reconstruction of Thinking* (Albany: State University of New York Press, 1981), chapter 2. The idea, of course, comes from Charles Peirce's distinction between general and vague abstractions.

5. The German ones that come to mind are Husserl, Wittgenstein, and Heidegger; the positivists just went on to something other than philosophy in the grand tradition. The French ones are Sartre, Foucault, and Derrida. Merleau-Ponty, I believe, was working toward a more systematic view, abandoning the phenomenological subjectivism of his early work.

6. See his *Eros and Irony* (Albany: State University of New York Press, 1982) and our debate in *Process Studies* 14/1, Spring, 1984. See also Chapter 1 above.

7. Where certain of the discussions below reflect more complete argumentation in my books, I will give the citation in the line according to the following abbreviations: *GC* for *God the Creator* (Chicago: University of Chicago Press, 1968); *CF* for *The Cosmology of Freedom* (New Haven: Yale University Press, 1974); *SSS* for *Soldier, Sage, Saint* (New York: Fordham University Press, 1978); *CG* for*Creativity and God* (New York: The Seabury Press, 1980); *RT* for *Reconstruction of Thinking* and *TD* for *The Tao and the Daimon* (Albany: State University of New York Press, 1982). I apologize for the self-citations, but that's how systematic philosophy goes.

8. The basic text of process philosophy is Whitehead's *Process and Reality* (New York: Macmillan, 1929). I have related essential and conditional features to this model in *CF,* chs. 2–3, and in *RT,* ch. 3. The current essay makes far less use of process categories than either of those references.

9. Some commentators say that Plato abandoned his *Republic* notion of the Form of the Good, which claims that it is the ground for the distinction between knowers and objects, and that it in itself is not an object of knowledge. In the Analogy of the Sun, Plato says the Form of the Good creates the world. Although the language changes, I believe Plato continued this theory of normativeness, particularly in the *Statesman* and *Philebus;* moreover, I think he refuted the critics of the participation theory of the Form of the Good in *Parmenides.* See *CF,* ch. 3.

10. The discussion of schemata and schema-images comes from Kant's chapter of the "Schematism" in the *Critique of Pure Reason.* But the use made here of the language derives from *RT,* especially pp. 223–235.

11. See *Process and Reality,* Part II, ch. 4. Whitehead used the term "width" rather than "breadth." The first two sections of that chapter are among the most pregnant in recent philosophic literature.

12. The connection of personhood with the capacity for viewing oneself as a representative of humankind was first brought to my attention by Paul Weiss, in *Man's Freedom* (New Haven: Yale University Press, 1950), and developed in masterly fashion in his *Privacy* (Carbondale: Southern Illinois University Press, 1983).

David Weissman

The Spiral of Reflection

What is metaphysical thinking? What are its subject matters; and how is it related to, but different from the rest of thought? Philosophers who were once embarrassed by the word now describe themselves as "metaphysicians." Is there a consensus among them regarding these issues; or is the word invoked only for the suggestion that this part of philosophy is subtle and profound? Can we identify tasks and a method which might be accepted all around as metaphysical? This paper speaks to these unsettled questions. It makes some provisional but firm declarations about the character and pursuit of metaphysical inquiry.

I suppose that thought moves in a spiral turning from the plans and projects of everyday life through scientific hypotheses and theories to the speculations of metaphysics. Only the aims, generality, and standards of verification are different. Thought's subject matters are transformed in a parallel way, from the particularities of science to nature's categorial form and conditions. Why say that thinking moves in a spiral? Because our focus is steady as it turns about the particularities of each thinker's life, advancing from immediacy and contingency to mediating, constraining universals, from his singularity to all of being. This progression is my first concern. Second are three obstacles to metaphysical thinking. They Are: its speculative character, its too frequent emphasis on subjectivity as the paradigm for claims about reality, and the requirement that metaphysical hypotheses be applicable to matters of fact. Whitehead is often said to be the boldest metaphysician of our century. I will demur, saying that his views are defective in all three regards.

I.

Consider the man set down in an unfamiliar but spacious house. He will need to pass thorough several rooms, looking out the windows and climbing the stairs if he is to have even a partial idea of the house's design. The metaphysician's situation is like that; he cannot hope to discover the world's categorial form and conditions, or his position within the world until he has moved through and studied some parts of it. Metaphysics is late or last in the order of inquiry. Only as we know particulars and some intermediate generalities can we speculate successfully about nature's most general differentiations and constraints. This does not imply that nothing metaphysical is thought or said until every other inquiry is completed. We often step back from practice and science to formulate more general hypotheses about the categorial form of things, to evaluate our human nature and our place within the world, or to look beyond nature to its conditions. We speculate, for example, that our actual world presupposes a domain of possible worlds, each of them having a certain least degree of complexity, without our knowing altogether which possibility is actualized here. Still, metaphysics is late in the order of knowledge, however fundamental to the order of being.

Descartes's *Meditations* is the emphatic challenge to this view. Metaphysics is first not last, Descartes insists, because "I am, I exist" is prior in knowledge and being to every claim except the one affirming God's existence. His *cogito* is the unqualified foundation for every truth when Descartes's successors have dispensed with God. For they believe that mind controls or creates all the conditions for intelligibility. Nothing is or can be, they say, if it is not thinkable, so that mind's power for certifying the ideas, words, or rules to be used for thinking about the world is also a power for deciding what differences and relations may exist there. Thoughts or sentences that are thinkable and true will be those that satisfy some criterion internal to the mind; e.g., they are either consistent and coherent or deducible from other thoughts or sentences chosen as axioms. Mind will be, as Protagoras urged, the measure of all that is and is not. This is a protean view, one having many expressions. They go from Descartes's clear and distinct ideas through the concepts of the transcendental ego to the logical geography of ordinary language, Husserl's eidetic reduction and Carnap's semantical frameworks. Mind is first through all these variations as it lays down the conditions for intelligibility, hence existence, where nothing inconceivable can exist. It is merely ironic that Descartes should be celebrated for announcing that metaphysics is defunct. He is instead the clearest proponent of a different metaphysics, one that cripples the spiral of reflection while reducing all thought to the survey or construction of mind's ideas, or to mind's reflection on itself.

There would be no reason to speculate about the world if we could learn about it merely by turning on ourselves. Suppose we were to find a system of ideas implanted in us and representing all the differences and orders within nature; or that we should discover the rules or ideas that mind uses for synthesizing experience, hence all of nature that we can know; or that we might successfully imitate Leibniz in regarding mind's structure as paradigmatic for every other entity. These are strategies calculated to save us the difficulty of testing our claims against the world. For each of these strategies affirms that mind or something within it supplies all the evidence that is required for certifying our beliefs about the world. They save us from having to make, test and revise hypotheses about states of affairs whose existence and character are independent of what we think and say of them. Self-inspection, or the survey of thoughts, words, sentences, or theories, is to provide immediate and assured access to every differentiation and relation, whether specific or general, that might be thought and known.

This a priorist outcome should be easily averted. Don't most of us agree that mind is not the measure? We have only to test our claims about the world against the empirical evidence, where Hume not Descartes is our standard. There are two things to notice.

First is a deep affinity between Descartes and Hume: Both of them are *intuitionists*. Both agree that something qualifies as real only if it can be set before our inspecting minds. God is the one exception to this rule for Descartes. The rule has no exception for Hume. Nothing is, he argues, if we have no impression of it. The existence of things is only the force and vivacity of our impressions. Consequently, the fact that Hume will not have mind prescribe what we may think about the world, waiting for perception to reveal what is present there, should not incline us to say that Hume locates reality in states of affairs having an existence independent of our minds. To the contrary, Hume shrinks reality to the ambit of inspecting mind. Hypotheses tested against the phenomena reach no farther than the impressions inspected.

Second is the fact that subsequent empiricists, including some of those best known in our century, distrust the clarity that Hume ascribed to percepts. On the one side are phenomenologists who say with Husserl that impressions are obscure in themselves and that mind cannot discern them without using the concepts or ideas that signify, or exhibit and project, the relevant differences. On the other side are philosophers such as Carnap who say that mind is baffled by the richness of perception until it introduces those thoughts, concepts, words, or ideas that differentiate among the myriad percepts. Both sides agree that the intelligibility of perceptual data is founded, partly or absolutely, in mind: we have or make the concepts with which to think the data. But then it follows that every difference credited to the world, however specific and empirical, is founded in thought or language, not in the data themselves. Impressions are opaque, too obscure or profuse for thought, until mind has introduced the concepts that make them discernible.

This is the progression as empiricist intuitionism is reclaimed for Cartesian a priorism. It is contingent that the flash I see is red; though *red* is an a priori difference, one that I project onto the sensation occuring within me. More abstract notions – e.g., dog and cat, gene and boson, property, number and law – all the more plainly are notions that mind has introduced for differentiating and organizing experience. We are to know these concepts by self-inspection, in the style of ordinary language analysis or Husserl's eidetic reduction. They are not in any way the product of inquiries that carry past mind into the world. Scientific and metaphysical theories will have this same origin and function. All of them will be devices certified by the mind as it uses them to introduce those differences and relations that make experience thinkable. We will decide both the qualities and relations that the world may be thought to exhibit, and the rules to be used for evaluating the consistency and coherence of our theories. Only one fact, and its corresponding metaphysical claim, will be pretheoretical: Mind creates these theories, and a thinkable world, while affirming itself. The spiral of reflection is aborted now. Thought does rise from particulars to generalities, but it never moves beyond the arena of inspectable images and ideas. It never turns into a world whose existence and character are independent of our ways of thinking so that hypotheses might be tested there. Nothing is better known to mind than mind and its constructions. Nothing else is or can be known.

What could justify the autonomy here claimed for mind? Only the intuitionist demand that nothing is to be alleged of the world unless thought can certify both the meaning and truth of every claim by inspecting first that claim and then the evidence for its truth. "I am, I exist" is paradigmatic, for what this means – i.e., what it signifies – is founded in my self-perception, where this same evidence is also sufficient to confirm the truth of what I say. Mind would like to exploit this autonomy to ever greater effect by taking responsibility for both the meaning and truth of the conceptual systems with which it thinks the world. Notice however that the parallel to "I am, I exist" is lost because the truth conditions for what we think and say exceed the fact of our thinking and saying it. There are norms for evaluating our hypotheses and theories as there are rules for playing chess; but the satisfaction of those rules is not a sufficient condition for truth: It is only a well-founded theory, not a well-played game, that may be true. Truth is more than the consistency and coherencce to which inspecting mind can testify. Truth requires, additionally, that there be matters of fact satisfying our claims. Thought merely formulates and projects hypotheses that might be true because they are meaningful. Thought alone does not create the states of affairs that satisfy these hypotheses. Thinking is not making. Thought's autonomy is circumscribed: Thought creates meaning, not material truth.

The spiral of reflection is thought's trajectory as it formulates hypotheses of ascending generality while probing for the evidence of their truth. The spiral begins as we make the plans that direct behavior. Some plans are successful if a need or desire, such as hunger is satisfied and reduced. Other plans have aims more enduring, as every equilibriating state – e.g., health – endures. Plans of both kinds have these two aspects: A succession of behaviors is prescribed and a map represents the domain where the plan is to be enacted. These two, the prescribed sequence and the map, are mutually conditioning: the prescribed behaviors invoke the map of that region where the plan directs behavior, while success in using the plan is evidence for the accuracy of the map. This is thought as it turns on the world, thought as it directs the behaviors that will satisfy and sustain us. There is a balance here among three interests: life, speculation, and confirmation.

First is the demand that thought should serve life by enhancing and securing it. This guarantees that thought will have a steady focus, forever grounding thought's spiral in the particularities of need and practice. What are the circumstances where plans are made, enacted, and revised? What do we need? How do we cope? These are some initial questions for an existential phenomenology, one that observes from the standpoint of the actor who is engaged by his circumstances. The emphasis on participation is all-important because it clarifies the difference between plans made and enacted, and those interpretations that "make sense" of the world without having to direct us as we make a difference there. Interpretations are maps of a kind, but they are not plans. Interpretations represent salient features of the world, though more fundamentally they are projections of value, where the matters selected for representation express the values and priorities of the interpretor. These interpretations, with their typically unreflected confusion of fact and value, represent our circumstances while expressing our attitudes. They are, therefore, a reasonable starting point as we choose what to do, how and where to do it. Yet, interpretation is a stage in the development of thought, not its objective. For thought must distinguish its values and intentions from the truth of its hypotheses and the efficacy of its plans. Phenomenologists sometimes ignore these differences. They suppose that thought has fulfilled itself by representing some part of the world in this evaluating way.

Consider for example those phenomenologists who start from

Heidegger's lived world. They imagine the engineer in his locomotive, describing him as he accommodates himself to levers and gauges, isolation, power and speed. The man is "thrown." He is quixotically here in his cab, not there behind a merchant's counter or sitting at a desk. Their interpretations express the distinguishing aesthetic of this man's experience; though carelessly, they falsify experience by forgetting that this man's interpretation of his circumstances is one for which appreciation is secondary to understanding, action, and control. His interpretations are tested at every moment by the rigors of driving the locomotive. He runs it best when his interpretation of the controls at hand extends to testable hypotheses about the linkages to engine and wheels. His interpretations do express the conflation of a map representing his circumstances and his values. but his principal value, his objective, is a performance. These phenomenologists care too much for the Heideggerian injunction regarding things as they exist "alongside" us: Let nothing be concealed; let these things be revealed and seen as they are. There is too little regard for this other fact: Our every encounter with the world is mediated by those symbolic structures – i.e., hypotheses – that represent our circumstances in ways that are appropriate to the uses we would make of them. Every interpretation that distracts the agent from thought-directed performance by reminding him (or us) of noise, smell, exhilaration, or boredom is merely aesthetic and precious. It ignores intelligence and interpretation as they serve life.

The second of the three interests mentioned above is speculation. Speculation is complex, with several aspects that are significant for practice. Most conspicuous is the fact that we make and act on plans without being able to guarantee the outcome. This is a world we cannot altogether control, a future we cannot fully anticipate. Speculation is the prediction that the plan will work. It is the conviction that we have power and means sufficient to make it work.

Two additional aspects are more subtle. One is the speculative character of thought as it uses words and ideas. For thought is more than the entertaining of words or ideas set before the mind and more than the derivation or construction of ideas, sentences, or theories. Descartes could emphasize these two kinds of thought because he relied on God to secure the objective reference of clear and distinct ideas. Mind could attend to the ideas themselves, all the while forgetting or ignoring the fact that ideas are signs having objects distinct from themselves. Most of us no longer suppose that God renders this service. We are left to explain the relation of words and ideas to the things they signify. We say that thought is speculative, meaning that words and thoughts are construed as the signs of possible properties or states of affairs. Construal is speculative because it regards the sentence, word, or thought as the sign of its object. The plan for hunting might have a map with an entry for centaurs even though this possible beast is not actual. So is every entry speculative when it may happen that none of the possibles signified is actual.

The second of these two aspects is the over-determination of evidence by theory; *viz.*, our claims about the world exceed the empirical evidence. No matter that these are hypotheses about the most effective sequencing of behaviors, or the maps representing the region where a plan is to be enacted; hypotheses of both sorts project a world before us, always saying or implying more about it than the evidence confirms. Thought anticipates a richer network of differentiations and relations that perception alone can justify.

Speculation in all its aspects shows thought reaching beyond itself as we estimate what the world is and can be made to be. This is speculation as it dissolves the isolating membrane of individual or social consciousness. Denunciations of speculation are usually a not-so-veiled defence of this isolation. They express the intuitionist demand that nothing be said about the world unless inspecting mind has immediate access to the matters signified, hence to evidence sufficient for proving our claims about them. All of this ignores the circumstances where animals of every sort satisfy their internal needs while acommodating themselves to the world about them. We cannot have a priori guarantees for the truth of our maps or the success of our plans. With only death as the alternative, we act upon these plans, moving into the world about us in order that we may live. Speculation is the ineliminable risk that falls to thought as it directs the behaviors that secure us within the world.

Speculation is a bad word only if we forget that the overreaching side of thought is joined to its practical, experimental side, Thus, confirmation, with life and speculation, is the third of the interests founded in practices. For we often say more than we can prove, though we regularly act upon our hypotheses in ways that confirm a fair part of what is said and planned. Action and experiment in pursuit of an aim or defence of an hypothesis are the essential but ordinary complements to speculation. They supply the evidence that confirms that our speculations do have application. Is anything green? Can anyone catch fish with a straw hat? Are there fewer accidents when speed limits are reduced? These are hypotheses – i.e., speculations – expressed as questions. None of them flaps loosely in the speculative breeze because each one signifies a possibility. There will be factual differences confirmed by experiment if one or another of those possibles does obtain. Not speculation, but untestable, undecidable hypotheses are the issue. For thought is correctly and irretrievably speculative. The problem is confirmation, i.e., the formulation of meaningful and testable hypotheses.

Confirmation is urgent where reflection begins, because thought makes plans that satisfy or relieve some need or desire. Errant speculation is quickly exposed: The plan is too obscure, or wrong; we can't determine what it prescribes, or we are frustrated, wet and hungry when it misdirects us. This practical emphasis is and will always be the necessary starting point for human reflection. Yet all the while, practice itself liberates thought from narrowly practical objectives. Behavior is successful only as we look beyond personal and social concerns to things in themselves.

This objectivist interest is apparent already in the maps that are coupled to our plans. The earliest of these maps contains very little that is general, as the infant knows the shape of his crib without generalizing to all rectangles. The child does eventually generalize, and then maps that were based on his partial survey of a particular place or thing begin to incorporate various orders of generality. He generalizes about kinds and relations – e.g., any dog, every circle – and also about the constancy of things, the connectedness of space and time, and the regularity of changes occuring about him. He knows his own efficacy, and also that causality that is apparently a universal feature of our world. His maps represent these several kinds of generality, with the result that his plans are more accurate and flexible, his behaviors more successful.

This regard for objectivity may become our premier interest. Rather than map some part of the world for the purposes of need or desire, we may consider it in the more neutral interests of science. We speculate now about the entities, variables, and relations of various domains, some like astronomy that extend well beyond us, some others like biology that include us. We test these hypotheses by acting on them, though action now serves as a test of thought, whereas before thought and action were the instruments of desire. Certainly, this objectivist bend does enhance social and self-interest by providing more accurate maps and greater control of nature; human action and experience extend themselves to fill a larger part of the world. Yet this objectivism never reduces to merely utilitarian value. We come to accept the truth of our hypotheses and theories as an intrinsic value. The practice of science becomes a right: We wish to know about things in themselves, with nothing beyond that wish to justify the practice. We demand only that scientific speculation be responsible. Granting that hypotheses will imply more than experiment could ever confirm, we insist that hypotheses be testable, i.e., that there be some empirical criterion for choosing among the various claims about nature. This over-determination of evidence by theory does embarrass us when two or more quite different theories are certified by the evidence. That happens when neurologists cite different evidence when supporting the contrary claims that brain functions are localized or global. There are also competing theories that rely on the same evidence, as all the data confirming Newton's theory of gravity also confirm the one of Einstein. This irresolution delays the choice of theories without forever thwarting it. For there are two considerations that facilitate choice: First, there are very few competing theories because of the difficulty of formulating a theory that is adequate to all the significant theoretical and empirical considerations; second, we do inevitably, so far, discover phenomena that one or another of competing theories cannot explain. The choice among theories is plain, though not always final, when the theory confirmed by some critical datum is also the one that explains the largest array of phenomena while best cohering with other theories.

The product of theory and experiment is a complex network of more or less integrated theories, each of them confirmed to some least acceptable strength within its domain. Some of the hypotheses and theories are weak because they are merely descriptive, as psychoanalysis may be more adept at describing pathology than explaining it. Other hypotheses are stronger because they identify those variables that generate the observed behaviors. Still others, quantum physics is an example, make a virtue of anomalies that require that we revise either this theory or our assumptions about certain categorical features of nature. Unevenly and still problematically, we resolve our uncertainties about nature. Every particular does seem to exhibit the more general and constant features of nature even as it is distinguished by its complexity and functions. Thought does achieve a good if still partial representation of nature's constitutive and organizing features.

This is the place, still within science, where reflection turns metaphysical. It is not that responsible thought suddenly gives way to fantasy, rather that thought's subject matters have achieved the generality of *categorical form.* Maps that represent the circumstances of our locale, and the dynamic relations important to science and practice, have been elaborated to the point where they represent nature's most general features. Diverse things are represented and explained by clusters of variables, where it is the values of these variables and their functional relations that explain the differences. Even matter and energy have come to be understood as the two expressions for something more fundamental. Matter and energy, motion and especially space and time; these several factors seem to be the basis for every difference and change.

Science speculates that diversity in nature may be the expression of these elementary factors, and then it establishes, partly by observation partly by experiments that imitate natural processes, that the compounding of these factors does produce those differences. These most pervasive features of our world are some considerable part of categorical form.

There is more. Practice and science will have formulated their plans and hypotheses under the direction of certain regulative principles, i.e., that effects have causes, that nature endures, that changes are regular not chaotic. Reflection will have moved repeatedly between its scientific and metaphysical attitudes so that we might consider the meaning of these principles and the evidence for their truth. Now, with all the substance of categorical form articulated by scientific theory, there is still the task of embedding these scientific claims within the framework of whatever is fundamental to nature, and not merely conventional. One response will be that these regulative principles have no significance beyond their utility as leading principles, as though principles that organize and direct inquiry need have no application to the character and relations of things in the world. That is plainly false. The principle of cause and effect prescribes that we should look for causes sufficient to produce whatever events do occur; we do regularly discover particular causes and kinds of cause for typical effects. Quantum physics seems to refute the generality of this principle; but then we are or ought to be all the more impelled to determine where and why the principle does apply, and where it does not. The status of the other, most general regulative principles is similar: Changes are regular, nature endures with its categorical form apparently unchanged. How shall we establish the basis for these principles within nature? Hypotheses have been formulated and successfully tested by using these principles. Can we now regard the hypotheses in another way, surveying them to discover a basis for the truth of the regulative principles in the facts represented by the hypotheses?

There is, for example, this convergence. One regulative principle affirms that actuality presupposes potentiality, where potencies are founded somehow in antecedent actualities; e.g., no one sits unless he can, though the power for sitting is founded in the actual structure of his body. One physical theory having the generality of categorial form supposes that matter is the expression of gravitational forces, where gravity originates in the geometry of a dynamic space-time. We explain the natural basis for the regulative principle by way of this theory, saying that potentialities are founded in the geometrical-structural properties of things. So, the key's potential for opening a lock derives from the complementarity of their shapes. Is this an empirical test of this categorial claim? Yes it is, though confirmation is only partial because there are many dispositional properties – i.e., many potentialities – that do not seem reducible to geometrical-structural properties, just as petulance, humor, and every other psychological and moral dispostion is not currently reducible. Ultimate success at identifying the geometrical basis for these psychological and moral dispositions is, of course, a vital condition for the generality of this reduction, hence for establishing that we have located the material basis for this regulative principle. The example is imperfect because the result is provisional. It does show, however, that we may turn back on the hypotheses that were formulated and tested under the direction of regulative principles in order to determine the material basis for those principles. There are other examples more familiar than this one, as we use the causal principle when searching for a thief, and then learn some things about causality as the thief tells how he cracked the safe. Still, this example is not so deep as the one before; this one is ad hoc, so that this example, like every one of its kind, leaves us grasping for some more general consideration common to every instance where causes are changed as they interact. The previous example is deeper because it locates the basis for all potentiality within the geometrical-structural properties of the things that act and change.

Let us suppose that metaphysicians have successfully identified the material basis for at least some of the regulative principles used in science and practice. Thought's spiral has moved beyond science as the responsibility for categorial form passes from scientists to metaphysicians. It is metaphysics that will supply the comprehensive representation of categorial form, somewhat as an architect's schematic drawing represents a building. Why leave this task to metaphysicians? Because scientists are usually too busy with their special interests to care about the whole. This might seem to be a temporary incapacity, one that would pass if physics were to establish that certain least variables and relations are the necessary and sufficient constituents of all phenomena. The laws representing these relationships would have application throughout nature, so that their statement would seem to be the best possible schematic representation of it. But that cannot be so, for a reason which is apparent. Consider the status of laws. One regulative principle affirms that all natural phenomena are explicable, i.e., they fall under laws. We are left to determine how these laws regulate natural processes while being immanent within nature. Philosophy typically obscures this issue by conflating natural laws with the law sentences of scientific theories: We take advantage of the fact that these sentences represent the laws without telling how the laws operate within nature. We may correct this failing by telling how the laws secure a footing within nature; but then

it is too late to regard the law statements as a comprehensive schematization of nature, because those sentences represent only factors that are
constitutive of and responsible for variation and change. They do not
represent, in any explicit way, the considerations that make laws immanent within nature. Therefore, no set of law sentences is or can be an
adequate representation of categorial form.

It also follows that the task of formulating this schematic representation falls to metaphysics, not to science. This is an insignificant difference if we remember that science and metaphysics are only two
moments in the spiral of generalizing thought. The difference is important if we care to emphasize that thought moves beyond the generalities
of science. We should be explicit in formulating and sometimes testing
the principles and notions that science has assumed and applied. We can
hope to identify the natural origins for those laws, dispositions, and
causal relations that science exploits without explaining.

Are there examples of these categorial schemas? The one best known
is still Aristotle's metaphysics. His views about substance and the four
causes seemed for a long time to be as good a précis as we might formulate. There were several considerations, each independent of the
others, to confirm it. Most of them were factual; one was dialectical. The
factual evidence included perception. It seemed to reveal a world of
things and their properties. It showed things being created and
destroyed, or retaining their identity through the alteration of their properties. So did grammar divide the things represented into subjects and
predicates. No wonder that Aristotle described primary substances as the
elementary realities, where the four causes signify the principles of
stability and change within them, and sometimes the manner of relatedness among them. The dialectical evidence was equally confirming.
Aristotle was determined to save Plato's Forms from reification. Matter
was to be the instrument for doing that, because matters are particular
and stable. A Form instantiated – i.e., a form enmattered – could be
designated, perceived and relied on to hold its form.

These are some of the considerations that seemed to justify Aristotle's emphasis on primary substance. It is this preference for free-
standing, usually inert, matter that is no longer defensible. In its place
goes a schematization that acknowledges some of Aristotle's concerns
while it satisfies them in this other way. Rather than individual,
aggregated substances, we speak of a protean space-time, one having an
immanent geometry and dynamics where matter derives from the
combination of motion and form. This space-time is the One. It has
four powers.

1. The One is self-differentiating, in three respects:
   a. It is self-diversifying, resulting in the generation of myriad properties.
   b. It is self-dividing, resulting in a diversity of particulars.
   c. It is self-stratifying, using configuration and aggregation to produce systems that are dominant or subordinate to one another.
2. Space-time achieves self-differentiation — i.e., it is self-transforming — because its dynamics are causal. Further properties, particulars, and stratifications are produced by the reciprocal effects of differences already current within space-time. This acknowledges that space-time must already be differentiated in order that it may transform itself.
3. This complex is self-coordinating, implying that each differentiation has value or disvalue for one or more others. The patterns of these values and disvalues are expressed as the harmonies and disharmonies that pervade a region, connected regions, or all of space-time.
4. Space-time is self-perpetuating, though only in such a manner and form as is determined by its internal dynamics.

These powers have a product. For nature, as the self-differentiating, geometrized, and enmattered space-time is comprised of overlapping and nested *stabilities*. Each stability is a system of properties having persistent organization and cohesion. It has some degree of resistance to external, intrusive forces, and a measure of self-regulation; i.e., it has an outside and an inside. Each stability is faced, metaphorically, with a permeable membrane; *vis.*, it extracts energy or information from its environment while sustaining its own organization and processes. This resistant perimeter, with its powers for self-regulation, qualifies the stability for a degree of internality. It can behave as a monad, developing in ways that are determined by its internal constituents and organization. A human being is a stability, but so is a rain storm, a solar system, a government, and a spade. The persistence and organization of stabilities, their resistance to external influences, and their self-regulation explain their relative autonomy. Every stability may have a developmental history that is exempt from changes within other possibly contiguous but independent or overlapping stabilities. Nevertheless, stabilities are coordinated and subordinated to one another; none is perfectly autonomous because each is generated within and is nourished by those others that constitute its environment. These dependencies are confirmed whenever radical changes in one stability affect some other ones. The one fully autonomous and externally unconditioned stability is the whole; though the evidence for a single, all-embracing stabiity is more speculative than established. It is equally likely that the many separate, overlapping, and stratified stabilities cohere with one another in a way that is imperfectly harmonious, with only space-time and the laws deriving from its geometry to unify the whole.

This schema provides for categorial factors such as cause and law by locating them within the structures just described. It proposes that laws of motion and the force laws − i.e., laws having application within more restricted domains − are founded in the geometry of space-time. We speculate, without sufficient confirmation, that other laws are also founded in the geometry of phenomena generated within space-time, thus embodying its geometry. This is plainly inadequate for the law correlating guilt with sin, so that the schema is incomplete. The notion of causality required by this schema is flawed in a parallel way. It reform-ulates Aristotle's four causes, with the following revisions. Formal cause is the geometry of space-time, hence of every system embodying that geometry. Material cause derives from motion and form. Efficient cause is the motion that produces and then impels matter in space-time. Every stable system persists; it achieves, if only for a while, a sustainable equilibrium within itself. Final causes are the least energy principles that sustain these systems, when the quantity of energy required to disrupt them is greater than the energy required for sustaining them. These final causes too are grounded in geometry as it limits the magnitude and direction of motion. The four causes are suitable, when elaborated, to the dynamics of physical systems. They are inadequate or irrelevant to the fact that an increase in lending rates causes inflation. Here too the sche-matic account is too spare for the representation of all categorial form.

An example does not have to be a finished theory; and this one, a generalized description of self-sustaining and self-equilibriating thermo-dynamical systems,[1] is not. It is, however, more plausible and more powerful than Aristotle's schema; and it does illustrate the schematic representations with which metaphysics is to integrate and interpret the combination of scientific theories and regulative principles. This is more-over a viable schema, one that is applicable to at least some of the phenomena to which it might seem incidental.

Consider intentionality. There is no way known to me of showing that this or any mental activity is explicable in the terms of space-time and its geometry. We can, however, go some way to understanding inten-tionality in terms of the stable systems that are generated within space-time, for they are constituted of matter produced in the gravitational warps of space-time, and they are established and sustained in accord with its constraining geometry. A satisfactory rendering of whatever is intentional within these systems goes some way to showing that intentionality is not exclusively mental, and that it can be explicated in terms more elementary.

A stable system may be "intentional" in one or more of the following four ways.

First, it intends its own persistence, though this intending is not usually or necessarily conscious. Stones and the chassis of old cars are intentional in this way, because of a least energy principle; *viz.*, things persist because the energy required for altering them is greater than the energy that sustains them. The "intention" to persist reduces to the fact that things do persist, for this reason.

A second kind of intentionality, one still relevant to the conditions for survival, is exhibited in a system's behaviors as it accomodates to its environment. So, Chesapeake Bay is tidal but not as salty as the Atlantic Ocean or as sweet as the fresh water rivers that empty into it; it accommodates to them while having a sustainable integrity of its own. Someone who is set in his ways but threatened by a new boss acts in a parallel way; he alters his behavior just enough to satisfy that new supervisor's expectations. Common sense denies that there is anything intentional in the behaviors of the Bay, while agreeing that the man's behaviors are intentional. Yet both are intentional in this respect: Each one accommodates to its circumstances in ways that concede some least alteration of its own behaviors, organization, or constituents while sustaining its integrity as a stable system.

A third kind of intentionality also promotes the system's ability for sustaining itself. This time, the objective is utilization or incorporation, i.e., the system extracts information or energy from its environment; the one so that it may act more effectively on its surroundings and within itself, the other so that it may nourish itself. Behaviors of this third sort often satisfy our common sense notions of intentionality, as someone going to school or the grocery is acting purposively. Yet sharks and hurricanes do something comparable when they take some part of the world about them in order to sustain themselves.

Only the fourth kind of intentionality plainly distinguishes intelligent behavior from the other kinds of intentionality; *viz.*, we use signs to represent some remote or prospective state of affairs. These signs are the maps and plans that direct our behaviors in regard to this objective. No matter then if the medical student is not yet a doctor. He can symbolize that outcome and direct himself for years at a time under the regulative force of his objective and its instrumentalities. Intentionality of this fourth kind is the use of these mediating thoughts or words. We construe them as signs of the objective desired. This last sentence is the difficult one, because it marks out construal and desire as the two intentional notions requiring elaboration. But neither of them is problematic. Construal is association, i.e., words or thoughts are organized and associated with appropriate behaviors or other thoughts and words. Desire is already anticipated when systems accommodate to, or incorporate some part of, the world – desire being a state of need, hence a provocation to those behaviors that will satisfy or reduce the need. Finally, notice that this last sort of intentionality is not exclusively human. We may be unique for our use of signs. Still, this kind of intentionality does not require anything so elaborate as human thought or language. It is satisfied wherever the relation between a system's behaviors and its internal condition is mediated by some third thing. These mediators are precepts in the case of lower animals. They may also be uninspectable electro-chemical changes, as when the body's immune system "interprets" these changes by acting to suppress or eliminate some alien thing. These are cases where the mediator is more than a link in a complex causal sequence. It is a causal link, but with these two differences: This link has a certain autonomy; and the linkage from this to subsequent moments in the causal sequence is variable, even loose and unreliable. So, the percept must be interpreted, its autonomy; and it does not guarantee that the thing desired will have the property it is perceived as having, its unreliability. There is more autonomy and more tolerance for unreliability as we move from these examples toward the intentionality of intelligent creatures using signs. For protoza and rats may have little or none of our freedom for witholding a reaction to mediating signs while considering the likely effects of our behaviors. Nor can they invent the words that will need construing. Still, these differences are less important here than the generic affinities among stable systems whose accommodating or incorporating responses are mediated by signs or other relatively autonomous processes or events. That is so because our commitment just now is to categorial form. We are concerned to identify nature's pervasive features. They are the point at issue when we say that a striking difference – e.g., human as compared to every other sort of intentionality – is only a specific difference.

It is not necessary or even desirable that every specific difference be prefigured within the schema representing categorial form. It is obligatory that we formulate this schema in a way that is sensitive to each of these differences. For this is a summary statement of those categorial features that were discovered by practice and science as they moved from particularities to the generalities they express. The metaphysics of categorial form abstracts from these particulars without forgetting that its rendering of categorial form must be applicable to all of them.

This demand for applicability is sure to make us cautious when saying that any proposed representation of categorial form is universally applicable. We are reminded that this metaphysical hypothesis is like all the hypotheses of science and practice because it is provisional and fallible. That fallibility does not demonstrate or even imply that there is no categorial form, or that categorial form is too complex ever to be represented. That might have been true; we might have lived in a world that is endlessly complex, one whose categorial features change in apparently irrational ways. That is not the way it is, or seems to be, in our world. Codes, including some that are very complex, do ultimately prove to have generating principles. Our speculations about categorial form are justified by successive confirmations of the hypothesis that our world does have a certain fixed and discriminable form.

The schematic rendering of categorial form is a well-marked place in thought's spiral, because it is the highest reach of empirical confirmation. This is not however the end of the spiral, the place to which thought should rise, then rest. Reflection has two more tasks, both of them metaphysical.

One task requires that we should descend the spiral. We who have moved beyond experience in order to identify nature's categorial form must return to it so that we may locate human beings and our experience within a larger, articulate world. Our earlier attitudes were practical, interpretive, and phenomenological. We planned and acted, created, interpreted and described. We transformed an alien world into a system of familiar differences, relations, and meanings. Scientific and metaphysical theorizing have identified the constituents and conditions for experience, so that we return to it with these antithetic but still complementary attitudes: We think and act while understanding what we do and why we do it.

Suppose for example that nature has the categorial form described above. It is comprised of systems that are stabilized in two ways: Their parts are reciprocally related, with these relations sustained by least energy principles; and the system is nourished by its relations to the other systems of its environment. Human beings are stable systems of this kind, like ink wells, oceans, city governments, planetary systems, and stones. We are complex, self-sustaining systems of reciprocally related parts. Like those other stabilities, we overlap and are nested within the larger scale systems that limit our freedom while supporting us. Stable systems differ among themselves, however, in regard to the complexity and efficacy of their internal, reciprocal relations. They differ too in respect to the efficacy of their external relations, as some are better able to establish and sustain their sources of energy and information.

Human action should have certain predictable variations if these generalities apply to us. Activities internal to the body should sustain and renew its several parts and their relations. Activities performed by the body as it affects other systems should express a diversity of interests. So, we nourish ourselves by destroying other stable systems; but we also bond ourselves to other people and things in order to create stable systems of larger scale. Every stability "knows" something of its environment and itself, where "knows" signifies that its responses to internal and external stimulation are appropriately inflected, however gross and unconsidered or precise and self-controlled. Human knowledge is different from these lower adaptations in principally six ways.

1. Symbols mediate between the facts represented and the changes impelled by the facts themselves or our evaluation of them.

2. The symbols are compounded, by a grammar, so that they are well-formed or not.

3. The symbols allow for various degrees of precision and complexity in representing the matters at issue.

4. The symbols are general, as "red" applies throughout a domain.

5. The symbols hold the impelling circumstances by representing them, i.e., they enable us to defer action while considering alternative plans for action.

6. We demand justifying reasons for affirming that some part of the world has the character prefigured by a particular complex of symbols, and we demand reasons for choosing one of the alternative plans.

The differences between this human knowing and lower forms of "knowing" do not annul the commonalities. For thought is the activity with which we enhance our adaptive, accommodating responses to the events within and without us. The tuning fork can only vibrate when struck. We represent the intrusion and then reflect on the possible responses. These are specific differences against a backdrop of family identity. Evaluation is pervasive in the same way; viz., every stable system evaluates and then accepts or rejects the things it may incorporate and the other systems to which it may engage itself. The point is trivial if we ignore the differences between a girl choosing among her suitors, and the paper clips on my desk, each one rejecting all the others. But there are also some similarities to remark. Systems at every level of complexity respond differentially to the things about and within them. Every system is more or less able to defend itself from intrusions, and more or less selective as it rejects, incorporates or bonds itself to others.

I suppose that our ability to show the immanence of categorial form within the particularities of human life is one test of our claims about categorial form. Human beings are, presumably, natural creatures. The form immanent within nature would also, therefore, have application to us. We humans could not avoid subjection to this form, unless some part of us exceeds nature. That is possible, though science and metaphysics will have established our exclusively natural origins if it is shown that every aspect of our activity and experience is an application of their generalities about nature.

This descent from the higher orders of thought's spiral is a test of our theory's applicability. This return is speculative, but only in the way that applying a generality to some new particualr is speculative. There is one further task for metaphysics, and this one is speculative in all the ways that positivists deplore. Thought about nature's form is the highest reach of empirically testable generalizations. Thought about nature's conditions exceeds empirical testability. Why? Because testability requires the interaction of individual thinkers with the things they percieve. These are transactions occuring in space-time. They are altogether natural. Nature's conditions would be inaccessible to them. Why bother to speculate about nature's conditions? Because there is no alternative to speculation if we discover that some well-confirmed hypothesis suggests that nature alone is incomplete.

There is, for example, the highly confirmed hypothesis that words and sentences are meaningful. A sentence is meaningful if it is syntactically correct, meaning well-formed, and if the conjunction of its descriptive words is semantically correct, as "It is raining numbers" is one but not the other. Both conditions must be satisfied if a sentence is to be meaningful. Yet, these are necessary, not sufficient, conditions for meaning. That is so because words and sentences are the signs for extra-linguistic matters of fact. Words are representations, with two other conditions to be satisfied if they are to be used in that way. First is the requirement that the words be construed as signs. Imagine a sentence in English, then a different one in a language we do not read, where both sentences satisfy the syntactic and semantic combination rules of their respective languages. Is the apparent familiarity of the English sentence merely a symptom that we recognize it as satisfying these rules? This is one of the relevant considerations, but not the only one. The English sentence is meaningful because it is construed as signifying a possible state of affairs. The possibility signified is the second condition for meaning; *viz.*, a word or sentence is meaningful if it is construed as the sign of some possible property or state of affairs. Material truth is definable now as the relation between a sentence and that actuality that instantiates the possibility signified by the sentence.

Remember the first lines of Wittgenstein's *Tractatus*: "The world is all that is the case" (paragraph 1), and "The facts in logical space are the world" (paragraph 1.13). The facts in logical space are the possible states of affairs represented by meaningful sentences, logical space being just the aggregate of these possibilities. The world that " . . . is determined by the facts, and by their being all the facts" (paragraph 1.11) is the world of instantiated possibles, the world of actual states of affairs. Wittgenstein has supposed that every possibility in logical space is independent of every other one; but in this, I believe he is mistaken. Possibilities are organized in various ways, and a possible world is one satisfying a certain least degree of complexity.[2] These least organizing features are common to all possible worlds. Our world instantiates one of those possibilities, so that is differentiations and relations, together with the least complexity required of all possible worlds, are conditions for our actual world, i.e., for nature.

This is one example of the conditions about which thought speculates as it exceeds the reach of empirical confirmation. We might bar every hypothesis of this sort, claiming that no one of them can be true if there cannot be empirical evidence for it. But that would cripple inquiry in the name of a principle that wrongly describes the evidence for some truths as a necessary condition for every truth. Why should we suppose that nothing is a fact if it cannot affect our sense organs? This might be true; but assuming that it must be so is only dogmatism. Why not allow reflection to proceed? Let us speculate about nature's conditions wherever there is reason for believing that nature need have conditions. Then too, let metaphysicians give reasons for whatever hypotheses they affirm.

This is not a prayer for tolerance, or the plea for an exercise that might be pointless. There is a principle that demands that reflection should move beyond nature to its conditions, whether or not our hypotheses are empirically testable. That principle is completeness. Everything partial, dangling, and conditional unsettles us. We invoke the principle of sufficient reason as we look for the missing cause or ground. We do very often find these reasons and causes, thereby justifying this instinct. This empirical test might seem insufficient. We might want to demonstrate this principle, finding it contradictory that something should exist without conditions sufficient for its being as it is. That demonstration would be most important for our understanding of nature and all of being; but we do not require a demonstration of this principle for any inquiry, metaphysical or otherwise, because we may use the principle of sufficient reason as a leading principle. Apply the principle wherever possible, we may argue, because its application is frequently justified by the reasons and causes that we discover. Completeness is an expression of this principle, and a case in point. Noticing something for which sufficient conditions are unknown, we may reasonably speculate about them. If the conditions are discovered, our good sense in using this leading principle is confirmed. If conditions are not discovered, we are forced to choose: Sufficient reason applies, and there are undetermined conditions; or it does not apply, as we confirm when no conditions are identified. This choice is most disturbing, though happily we are saved from having to choose wherever this leading principle vindicates itself as we discover anticipated conditions. We do not have to prove that everything, nature included, must be complete because of having conditions. We need only liberate ourselves to ask if anything, nature included, might have conditions. It is only this provisional attitude that is required, even as we acknowledge that completeness operates regulatively throughout our thinking but especially in metaphysics. Indeed, the formulation of a theory adequate to the unconditioned totality of being is traditionally one defining obligation of metaphysical reflection. We can acknowledge and respect this motive, all the while proceeding in the experimental way just suggested: Nature may have conditions; we should try to identify them wherever inquiry establishes that nature is incomplete in some respect. We should proceed in this way even when the search for these conditions passes beyond the limits of empirical verification. For there is no reason to suppose that such conditions as there are, especially conditions for nature itself, must be perceivable.

Is there, perhaps, some other kind of verification still available to us? There is. Without demonstrating that completeness itself is necessary, we may establish that the negations of hypotheses about particular conditions claimed for nature are contradictions. Hypotheses confirmed in this way would be necessary truths; e.g., they would be true in every world where the conditions cited by the hypotheses do obtain. Only one hypothesis known to me has this force. It affirms that every property and complex of properties exists in the first instance as a possibility, where possibility is prior to actuality as our world presupposes a possible world. The argument is this: Whatever property or complex of properties is not contradictory is possible; hence properties and their complexes are either contradictory or possible, so that noncontradictory sets of properties are, by the law of excluded middle, possible. What is more, their possibility is necessary; they cannot be other or less than possible in the two-valued world where they are not contradictory. Further characterizations of possibility as a mode of being for properties, and claims about the least complexity demanded of all possible worlds, are a speculative embellishment of this argument. Still, the argument by itself justifies our saying that nature, meaning our actual world, is conditioned by a possible world. Nature does have conditions. Here is one that reflection does confirm.

Notice that this demonstration helps to satisfy two notions of completeness. On the one side, metaphysics would be complete because it identifies all the terms of a relationship, e.g., nature and its conditions. On the other side, metaphysics would be complete because it is comprehensively applicable and systematic. Metaphysics is comprehensive if our theory has application to every differentiable aspect of being. The theory is systematic in a bookkeeping way if it marks out its assumptions, shows their relations, and argues for its conclusions. It is systematic in a more important, substantive way if it marks the deep affinities of the things within its domain. There is a convergence of that sort in these claims about possibilities. For here beyond the limits of nature, we see the conditions for actuality merging with the conditions for meaning; the possibilities signified by our sentences, words, and thoughts are the possibilities from which our world is instantiated. True sentences represent a subset of all these possibles, i.e., our actual world. We should expect many of these convergences if being is arranged economically, though what they may be is left to theory and discovery.

We have ascended to the final turns of thought's spiral. Consider the hypothesis that our actual world is conditioned by the many possible worlds, and especially by that possible world that prefigures this actual one. How shall we explain the instantiation of possible worlds? Is there a *telos* within one possible world driving it into actuality? Is there a God to actualize one possible world for reasons apparent only to it? Could it be true that every possible world is actual, perhaps in a space and time disconnected from the space and time of every other actual world? This is the place where speculation exceeds our ability to test its hypotheses, whether logically or empirically. Here, but only here, does metaphysics risk confusion with religious myth. For now the evocative character of our hypotheses displaces our concern for their truth. We lose the discipline that is founded in practice and carried through to science and all the previous orders of metaphysical speculation. All of them have required that imagination be constrained by the rigors of truth or possible truth. Myth and poetry may ignore that rule. Metaphysics should not. Yet imagination is and ought to be liberated for speculating at the borders and foundations of reality. Ideas that satisfy our taste for significance may yet prove to be testable, even in the standard modes of empirical verification and demonstration. All of this speaks to the impulse of thought. None of it is rightly deplored if we distinguish those speculations that are testable and those that are not, those that satisfy a craving for mystery and those that are true.

Thought's spiral has carried on responsibly through many turns, from practice through science to metaphysics. The danger of irresponsibility at these farthest reaches of speculation cannot obscure thought's efficacy and discipline over this extended span. No one occupied with a practical project is offended by the derision to which thought is subject at those other, more remote frontiers of speculation. Responsible metaphysics, like science, may be equally oblivious. The greater threat to metaphysics lies elsewhere. It lies with those habits that subvert the spiral of relection at its source. There are three of these habits to consider now: first is a debilitated kind of speculation; second is the refusal to extend speculation beyond the circle of human experience; third is the formulation of generalities without an equal concern for their application. Whitehead is my example.

II.

All of us believe in change, and we are to that extent process philosophers. Yet some of us are not Whiteheadians. We fault Whitehead for irresolutions internal to his system; or we object that his method and views conflict with our own. My criticisms have this external bias. I will say that Whitehead's views are flawed irreparably because of his views about speculation and subjectivity, and because of his failure to establish that his metaphysical claims are applicable to matters of fact. None of this detracts from the audacity of Whitehead's thinking. It does substantially reduce his value as a model for our thinking.

Whitehead is remarkable for affirming hypotheses that reach beyond human experience to all of being. A phrase that he uses for some of his categories is appropriate to all of them: Whitehead's hypotheses are "categoreal obligations"; they are regulative principles laying down certain least conditions for anything that exists. Whitehead never apologizes for this unabashedly speculative turn. To the contrary, philosophy betrays itself if it does not formulate hypotheses that are adequate to the pervading forms of our world.

> Philosophy will not regain its proper status until the gradual elaboration of categoreal schemes, definitely stated at each stage of progress, is recognized as its proper objective. There may be

rival schemes, inconsistent among themselves, each with its own merits and its own failures. It will then be the purpose of research to conciliate the differences. Metaphysical categories are not dogmatic statements of the obvious; they are tentative formulations of the ultimate generalities.[3]

One may endorse all of this while objecting that speculation still has a rigor of its own, a rigor from which Whitehead turns.

Let Plato be our example of good speculation. Acknowledging both change and the fixity of thought's objects, he explains that which is prior in experience – i.e., perceptual flux – by reference to that which is prior in being, namely the Forms. This is an instance where speculation is daring; it specifies the generating condition or ground for the phenomenon at issue, as Forms are the source for whatever is differentiable within our perceivings. Starting from something observed or alleged, thought speculates about a generating condition that may be unobserved. That we may confirm the hypothesis by searching for and observing this condition, with the eye or the mind's eye, is important to verifying hypotheses but incidental to their speculative character. The point decisive for speculation is different; *viz.*, Plato's hypothesis *explains* the intelligibility of our perceivings by identifying, however fallibly, those conditions that have been necessary or sufficient to make our precepts thinkable.

Whitehead's speculative style is weaker. His hypotheses are generalized descriptions, not explanations. As Whitehead describes his method:

> The conclusion of this discussion is . . . the assertion that empirically the development of self-justifying thoughts has been achieved by the complex process of generalizing from particular topics, of imaginatively schematizing the generalizations, and finally by renewed comparison of the imagined scheme with the direct experience to which it should apply.[4]

This says that hypotheses are to be speculative in the way that every inductive generalization is speculative: will the next swan resemble the last one? Whitehead's hypotheses are never speculative in the manner of Plato's explanation; he does not try to identify the generating conditions for those phenomena that he regards as paradigmatic for all being.

But surely Whitehead knew the difference between explanation and description, so that his preference for description was reasonably motivated. What could that motive have been? Whitehead tells us in this other passage from *Process and Reality*.

Descartes modified traditional philosophy in two opposite ways. He increased the metaphysical emphasis of the substance-quality forms of thought. The actual things 'required nothing but themselves in order to exist,' and were to be thought of in terms of their qualities, some of them essential attributes, and other accidental modes. He also laid down the principle, that those substances which are the subjects enjoying conscious experiences, provide the primary data for philosophy, namely, themselves as in the enjoyment of such experience. This is the famous subjectivist bias which entered into modern philosophy through Descartes. In this doctrine, Descartes undoubtedly made the greatest philosophical discovery since the age of Plato and Aristotle.[5]

This passage comes several pages after the paragraph where Whitehead lists Descartes's assumptions.

The subjectivist principle follows from these premises: (I.) The acceptance of the 'substance-quality' concept as expressing the ultimate ontological principle. (II.) The acceptance of Aristotle's definition of a primary substance, as always a subject and never a predicate. (III.) The assumption that the experient subject is a primary substance."[6]

This third assumption is the decisive one for Whitehead's own ontological views: He ". . . fully accepts Descartes' discovery that subjective experiencing is the primary metaphysical situation which is presented to metaphysics for analysis.[7] Whitehead reformulates Descartes's subjectivist principle, eliminating many of the features that identify it as an exclusively human perspective. It is nevertheless this Cartesian notion that is paradigmatic when Whitehead writes that

'actual entities' – also termed 'actual occasions' – are the final real things of which the world is made up. There is no going behind actual entities to find anything more real . . . . The final facts are, all alike, actual entities; and these actual entities are drops of experience, complex and interdependent.[8]

Whitehead could not be plainer: Subjectivity, however purified, is the elementary stuff of which all the world is made.

These are passages where description is emphasized and explanation ignored. Why? Because "subjective experiencing" is the primary datum for metaphysics. This is a datum available to us as we turn self-consciously upon it. Analysis describes this datum without explaining it, because explanation would require that we specify constituents or grounds more fundamental than the datum itself. That we cannot do, for subjective experiencing is like the Sun of Plato's *Republic*: It is the creative source for everything existing, and the source of that light that makes all its creatures visible. Subjectivity has no elements or grounds more fundamental than itself, when God and eternal objects are discounted. There is nothing ulterior to which we might refer in explaining it, not even those two things just now set aside. Subjectivity is ground and cause of itself. Its analysis could only be descriptive. Turning upon ourselves, we are to discern those essential and organizing differences that are constitutive of any possible reality. This emphasis on description, coupled to his subjectivist principle, decides the content and bias of Whitehead's metaphysics. He supposes, after Leibniz in the *Monadology*, that subjective experience is the paradigm for all of being: Everything that exists, eternal objects apart, is a subjective experience, i.e., an actual occasion. Every issue regarding substance and change is to be resolved with only the resources that are available as we examine the elements, structures, attitudes, and aims of these momentary experiences.

Whitehead's notion of cause is a familiar example of notions that are reformulated so that they may accord with his subjectivist principle. Aristotle has said that causes produce effects. Effects are, as we reformulate this, changes occurring in one or more of the interacting causes. Effects are dependent on their causes in regard to both their character and existence. So the kind of change occurring depends on the character of the causes and the manner of their interaction. Effects are existentially dependent on their causes because the very occurrence of the effect presupposes the altered cause, as sunburn presupposes the face that's burnt. Whitehead's emphasis is different in three ways: first as the existence of every actual occasion owes nothing to the existence of any occasion antecedent to it; second as the character of the effect is thereby severed from the character of its antecedents; third as the activity of interacting causes is denied in favor of activity in that integrating occasion where the effect is "prehended."[9] It is only current actual occasions that are active, as they register, then integrate these effects within themselves.

My characterization of Whitehead's views about causality, and especially the three implications just cited, may seem mistaken. For Whitehead does say that every actual entity is connected to its antecedents by its prehendings of them.

> The philosophy of organism is a cell-theory of actuality . . . . In the genetic theory, the cell is exhibited as appropriating, for the

foundation of its own existence, the various elements of the universe out of which it arises. Each process of appropriation of a particular element is termed a prehension.[10]

Shouldn't remarks like this one preclude my saying that the existence and character of every actual occasion owe nothing to its antecedents? The language of "prehension" and "appropriation" does seem to imply a dynamic relatedness between every actual occasion and its antecedents. Yet this implied connection is only the effect of Whitehead's evocative language. For there is nothing in the way of theory to support these words. To the contrary, Whitehead elaborates on his claim that reality is cell-like.

The physical field is, in this way, atomized with definite divisions: it becomes a 'nexus' of actualities. Such a quantum (i.e. each actual division) of the extensive continuum is the primary phase of a creature. This quantum is constituted by its totality of relationships and cannot move. Also the creature cannot have any external adventures, but only the internal adventure of becoming. Its birth is its end.[11]

All the dynamics of Whitehead's ontology is restricted to the internal lives of his actual occasions, with nothing left over for the relations among the many actual occasions: " . . . [A]n actual entity never moves."[12]

There are, therefore, these three things to consider as we interpret Whitehead: 1. the views suggested when Whitehead says that actual occasions are related to their antecedents when one is "prehended" and "appropriated" by the other; 2. Whitehead's justification for this figurative language; and 3. those consequences entrained when Whitehead's own, very careful specifications of his views are taken as the measure for those other, more evocative characterizations. My three point summary of Whitehead's views about causality is an instance of this third point. Whitehead does often write as if actual occasions are windows into the past. But then his own formulations subvert that claim, however, much he may intend it. Accordingly, we may deny the very claim first intimated by the words "prehension" and "appropriation." Nothing is or could be prehended or appropriated, because there is no action connecting any actual occasion to any other one. All the burden that Whitehead assigns to causality falls instead within the many actual occasions.

Self-realization is the ultimate fact of facts. An actuality is self-realizing, and whatever is self-realizing is an actuality. An actual entity is at once the subject of self-realization, and the superject which is self-realized.[13]

It is here in subjectivity, not in the external relations of things, that Whitehead applies his notion of cause. Every actual occasion is self-integrating, self-sustaining, and self-caused.

This model of causality is nicely suited to Whitehead's views about knowledge. For every actual occasion, however self-concerned, is more or less obscurely a mirror of its place within the universe. It acknowledges all of its past, ranking and integrating its affections in ways that are appropriate to its aims. So does an English professor interpret the evidence of Tudor literature in ways appropriate to his interests and aesthetics. Thomas More and the others are dead, with no power over him. He is left with their books. They live only as he uses them. Mind will be the measure, and everything that is, eternal objects apart, will be a splinter of mind. Every splinter will mirror the universe, distinguishing itself by its perspective on the rest; i.e. by what it prehends, and how these prehendings are organized.

This model of causality is appropriate to a theory of interpretation, but not to a theory of nature or action – which requires a notion of causal efficacy and an ontology compatible with that efficacy. Rather than monads related to one another by way of the information available to each one as it prehends its antecedents, we require the idea that nature is constituted of agents or systems related spatially, temporally, and dynamically. Whitehead's subjectivist principle disables him for the task of speculating about the dynamics of change because he has no notion of efficacy or interaction. Nor is there an ontological theory adequate to the agents that effect other things while sustaining a dynamic equilibrium within themselves. There is, finally, no place within Whitehead for the spiral of reflection, no realization that we are alternately engaged within the world while pursuing our aims, then withdrawn as we formulate and revise the maps and plans that direct our behaviors there. Whitehead is the Cartesian for whom thought never exceeds the limits of subjectivity. We never can locate ourselves within the world in which we participate. We are to know the world in a different way, by decreeing that all of it is like us. If the spiral of reflection is the record of thought at work, of thought as it finds itself within the world, then Whitehead's speculations have this different effect: Thought is turned only upon itself; subjectivity is exaggerated and generalized rather than explained; we are falsely secured in our isolation from one another and the world.

Whitehead's pan-psychism implies that all the world is available to knowledge, as like is intelligible to like. This assumption underlines the assurance of Whiteheadians as they remark the comprehensive applicability of Whitehead's theory. Science, politics, religion, art, history, and practical affairs will all be comprehensible to occasions having our human powers for symbolic representation and sympathy. Yet this optimism properly turns to alarm if it cannot be established that each of these subject matters is constituted only of actual occasions. This, Whitehead hardly bothers to prove. For his theorizing carries on at a microlevel, never rising to that complexity that would enable us to establish that a human body, let alone a society of bodies, is an organized system of actual occasions.

Whitehead's speculations fail the test of applicability, i.e., they are not testable. There is no reason to believe that his hypotheses do have application to any single aspect of being. This finding may appear excessive when Whitehead has established that his notion of *actual occasion* does apply to those moments of human experience that are its paradigm. But is that so? Does experience divide into atoms of the sort Whitehead describes? The archetypes for Whitehead's actual occasions are those momentary experiences that William James described as the "specious present." Yet James left the precise status of these moments uncertain. Is experience an aggregate of them, or is it true instead that experience is continuous, while the specious present is the smallest continuous span revealed to introspection? Should we assume, either way, that everything significant for the specious present, including all its conditions, is discernible within this momentary experience? Might some of its organizing, sustaining conditions by uninspectable, as the activities described by cognitive psychologists and Kant are not inspectable within the experiences they condition or create? Whitehead never establishes that his subjectivist paradigm is exempt from these questions and conditions. We are left to suspect that his analysis of this starting point, hence his descriptive generalization from it, is a erroneous description of that experience. For Whitehead favors the intuitionist claim that nothing is better known to mind than the mind itself, where everything pertinent to these momentary experiences should be visible within those moments. There may be uninspectable conditions for the differentiation and coherence of experience, implying that the very reference point for Whitehead's speculations wobbles under foot. His theory may not be applicable to even this favored subjectivist beginning.

This is one very general reason for doubting that Whitehead's hypotheses are applicable to any single matter of fact. We reinforce the point by considering some particular case, where applicability is as much a test of subtlety as of truth. Consider this example. Robert Neville has suggested in the previous essay that norms, meaning values having the force of regulative principles, are a basis for personal identity. This suggestion speaks to the fact that each of us, and every association among us, has a more or less abiding and articulate moral identity. Individually and within societies, we have a source for our identity, or the moral part of it, in our adherence to certain values. So, our Constitution is a set of norms, and a basis for our national moral identity.

Suppose that Whitehead were to endorse this point, where values are the standards applied within each actual occasion as it prehends its antecedents, then integrates these affects. A person will be a society of contemporaneous occasions, each of them prehending its antecedents. A person's moral identity will devolve upon these three considerations: the character of norms applied within particular occasions, the similarity or diversity of norms applied within concurrent occasions, and the persistence of norms through the several constituent sequences of occasions. The aggregate result will be the moral man or woman. We who observe him or her may infer from the apparent consistency of this person's attitudes that only one or a few norms direct the integration of these many occasions. The inner reality might be different, for each of the constituent occasions might be applying norms that are peculiar to itself, each one revising in its own way the norms prehended in its antecedents. The observer's estimate of one or a few norms being applied might be only the statistical average of the many norms actually being applied.

This formulation of mine is only the gloss of a Whiteheadian view. Yet we can see already that Whitehead's ontology deprives Neville's idea of its power. Consider what we expect from that idea as it might be amplified. First is the demand that someone having moral identity should reveal himself in what he does. Each of us has an efficacy, and we show our moral qualities in what we do and the way of our doing it. Whitehead's actual occasions pass away when their prehendings have been integrated, i.e., when their focus is turned from antecedents to a subjective aim. They have no efficacy, and a fortiori no way of exhibiting their values in what they do. Second, we are responsible for what we do, as we are praise- or blameworthy. Yet, Whitehead's actual occasions do not survive to be the subjects of praise or blame. Third, moral identity presupposes moral development. Whiteheadians have two choices: They may reduce this development to the span of a single occasion, or they may describe a succession of occasions showing that some moral quality is sustained or developed through it. Both alternatives are crippling for moral development, because each one restricts the influences on development to those occuring within an actual occasion, or within that sequence and society of occasions that are the person. This ignores the fact that moral development is very often the response to demands made on us by circumstances or other persons. Each of us develops morally because of his interactions with those others. They have expectations, and they make demands. We respond, learning their rules, making them our own. Imagine a child in the company of family, teachers, and friends. What is it that socializes the child: the prehendings of an amoral past or his response to their expectations?

One imagines the Whiteheadian analysis. The child is at every moment a society of occasions, each one prehending all the world before it while integrating its prehensions in ways appropriate to its values. There may be a great diversity of norms applied at the microlevel, where each norm is prehended in a single occasion's antecedents, then rejected or espoused, sometimes revised and finally applied within the prehending occasion. The norms credited to the society at large – i.e., to the child – will likely be as suggested above the statistical average of these diverse norms. Even more significant, the only norms relevant to this child's development and history are the ones inherited and revised within those sequences that are constitutive of the child's history. Every moral value and condition falling outside this society and history are incidental to the child's identity.

This imagined response is unsatisfactory as an account of moral identity. There are three things to notice. First, it ignores the demand that the child show his moral values in what he does, where moral identity is exhibited in the doing and not merely in the prehending and integrating of antecedent occasions. Second, this account obliterates all traces of that interaction that is the crucible of moral education. The child is not his own moral teacher, as he is never the only judge of what he has done or should do. He acts and then survives the doing in order to learn that his behavior is approved or not. He revises his habits and norms under the pressure of that regularizing social persuasion. He will experiment all along with values of his own; but moral development firmly locates the child within a world to which he regularly accommodates himself.

A third deficiency is more complex. Moral identity is to be the distinguishing feature of a complex but unitary agent. He or she is more or less reliable over a range of circumstances and through a span of time. He or she is, and possibly feels, virtuous or guilty for what was done. He or she perceives other people with a more or less consistent moral persuasion. There is the one person who is a focus for a moral identity, for himself and for others, now and over a lifetime. Does the Whiteheadian ontology provide a subject for moral identity? It does not, because Whitehead cannot distinguish one complex thing from others – i.e., one society from others – within the aggregate of concurrent occasions. There is only this aggregate, and no way is implied by the ontology for differentiating the many systems of occasions from one another. Each occasion does grade all of its antecedents, but it is equally near or far to its contemporaries. Each monad's appraisal of its antecedents may produce, miraculously, a harmony among the contemporaries; but this is no substitute for the missing principle of differentiation. Without it, Whitehead cannot distinguish any man from his overcoat.

We expect that moral identity will be a differentiating principle, as the honest man is different from one who is not; however, we also assume that other bases for differentiation are already secured, as there is a living child that might learn to be moral. What are these prior conditions for differentiation? Describing them is easier if we first renounce Whitehead's ontology of actual occasions and their aggregates. We talk instead of stable, self-equilibriating systems. These are the systems described earlier. They have parts and a history, where the character and existence of the parts are mutually conditioning. It is the reciprocal relations of the parts that establish their persisting, collective identity. Thus, there is nothing adventitious about the harmony of heart and lungs; each sustains the other. I suppose that the constituents of these stable systems are either smaller-scale systems or the elementary forms of matter. We need to emphasize this material grounding, because the only clear notion of reciprocal causation is the one of material things linked dynamically to one another. So, talk regulates and sustains our relations to one another, where the mutual efficacy of our talking is explicable in spare materialist claims about the character and activity of the interacting systems. Equally vital to us is the fact that a material system enables us to locate those boundaries and constraints that differentiate one stable system from another. At the crudest level, we are distinguished from one another by our skin and bones. More subtlely, the Rosicrucians among us are distinguished from the others by propensities and mutually supporting behaviors that are unknown to the rest of us. Their behaviors are those of physical systems who generate and sustain a still higher-order physical system. The material character of the most elementary parts and all their relations enables us to account for the generation of nested systems having any number of hierarchical elaborations. For all of those relations will likely resolve to the ones occurring in any simple feedback relation. We understand the differentiating basis for these complex systems, as we identify their reciprocally sustaining causal conditions.

Moral identity is cogent just here. A physical system embodying reciprocal causal relations already exhibits certain constraining norms, first within itself, second as it effects the other systems within its environment, whether nested, overlapping, or independent. Moral norms are merely constraints of a special kind; namely, they are learned self-directives. These moral constraints are similar to constraints of every sort, for all of them direct and limit the manner of our engagement with other things or within ourselves.

There is one last point to emphasize as we describe an ontology adequate to moral identity. Consider the societies of Whiteheadian occasions. They are reminiscent of the NBC Symphony after Toscanini's death; they played for a time without a conductor, each musician seeming to play coherently with the rest because of a preestablished harmony. Whitehead might have been delighted by the Symphony of the Air, regarding it as paradigmatic for the harmonized parts of every society. But there are no stable systems harmonized within or without in this apparently miraculous way. Certainly these musicians reject that interpretation, for each of them had adjusted his playing while accommodating to the other over many years. Then too, each one remembered the instructions of that conductor who had dominated them. There is, therefore, no satisfaction in this example for those who believe that norms might be satisfied and harmony achieved without the reciprocity of mutually engaged parts. Here additionally, there is the problem of a dominant part. Some of Whitehead's actual occasions are more self-conscious than others; but none of them has the power for coordinating and directing its contemporaries. We need to acknowledge that some stable systems are dominated by a part, be it the conductor or a brain. This dominant part enforces norms; however, we allow that there are degrees of internal domination, as humans have more of it and jelly fish less. A dominant part may not be necessary for every coherent behavior, as a music box is rhythmic without having a musician inside it. There are, however, some aspects of moral identity for which a dominant part is indispensable. This part is an intelligence, hence a power for setting moral standards and giving moral reasons, a power for revising its principles and habits as argument and experience prescribe. Through all of this, moral identity may be centered or diffuse, not because the individual is constructed like a jelly fish but because his style of accommodation and incorporation encourages him to behave as one.

Consider then these requirements of metaphysical inquiry. Does our theory have application to the facts, e.g., to moral identity? Is it adequate to the phenomena it would describe and explain, i.e., does it specify all the pertinent categorial factors and their relations? Whitehead's ontology does neither. It does not prove its applicability, because it fails to establish that moral identity is or could be the expression of concrescent actual occasions. A fortiori, it cannot be an adequate — i.e., exhaustive — survey of those categorial features that are constitutive of this phenomenon.

Why does Whitehead's theory fail to prove itself? Because of that failure of speculative nerve mentioned above. Whitehead endorses the easiest and most accessible paradigm of modern philosophic thought; he redescribes the *cogito* and then generalizes his revision. Whitehead would deter us from believing what seems to be true – that self-experience is only one of many clues about the reality of things, not the single best expression of that reality. Why does Whitehead believe otherwise? For two reasons, both of them fundamental to the traditions of metaphysical thinking. One is intuitionism: Whitehead's allegiance to the view that nothing can be real if it is not visible to inspecting mind. What is left to reality? Only mind, and the ideas, norms, and impressions that are set before or created by it. Descartes is the exemplary intuitionist of modern thought. Whitehead is outspokenly pre-Kantian but loyally Cartesian.

The other reason is Whitehead's constricted notion of applicability. Applicability is like a two-barreled gun, each barrel splayed to an opposing side. One barrel aims at other theories; the theory is applicable to the extent that it speaks to and solves their problems. The other barrel is aimed at possible states of affairs. The theory is applicable if these possibles are actual, i.e., if it represents things as they are. Whitehead, like most philosophers, is satisfied to answer the dialectical questions, all the while ignoring the requirement that metaphysical theories be applicable to matters of fact. It is enough that Aristotle distinguished substances from their qualities and laid down the requirment that we locate a primary substance that is always a subject and never a predicate. Descartes had responded to these same dictates when he described the *cogito*. Whitehead is satisfied that his reformulated subjectivist principle is an even better solution to their dialectical questions. Yet how could Whitehead or anyone suppose that a solution to these problems is sufficient when no theory is worth the time used to formulate it if the theory could not be applicable to matters of fact? One answer is that theory, and especially metaphysical theory, has an autonomous history that makes it oblivious to the facts; *viz.*, we needn't care about the world as it is, because we theorize in response to the dialectic sustained within that history. Some of philosophy's indifference to fact might be explained in this way. Some additional component might be explained by the bias against testable theory and for interpretation, as we say that a theory is adequate if it provides a coherent and useful way of regarding the facts. Yet neither of these explanations is sufficient, because Whitehead like Descartes does so plainly intend that his theory should be applicable to matters of fact. Why then is Whitehead so careless in establishing that his theory is applicable to the world? One reason is that he cannot; the theory is deficient in the ways described above. Yet Whitehead is persuaded to the contrary: The theory does apply; it must apply. This is, I suggest, the reason and justification for Whitehead's carelessness. His theory says that everything, eternal objects apart, is a moment of consciousness. But consciousness is known to itself, as nothing is better known to the mind than mind itself. Self-inspection should confirm the truth of theory's paradigm. Sympathetic generalization should confirm that everything else is like us, i.e., one or a society of momentary experiences. Even the reality of eternal objects will be confirmed, as we discover them ingredient within experience. Here is the reason for Whitehead's allegiance to Descartes: His *cogito* is so fundamental in being and so available to inspection that every metaphysics founded upon it is unproblematically testable and confirmed. Familiar already with ourselves, we suppose that everything else is knowable because of being like us. This is parochialism reborn as messianic universalism. It has many applications in morals, politics, religion, and manners, and is the stoutest defence for being as I suppose myself to be, wishing that others could be it too. Whitehead has smiled on the universe, extending reality throughout by redescribing everything as one or a society of momentary experiences. Applicability is guaranteed by our self-inspected starting point, by this universalizing act of charity, and by our determination to think of the world as his theory represents it. Never mind that this point of view is resolutely blind to the facts that other things are different from us and that we ourselves are not the self-transparent objects of intuitionist myth.

It is not so implausible now that Whitehead should be the chosen nemesis to my own views about the content and conduct of metaphysical inquiry. Whitehead is like Descartes where both insist that metaphysics is first in the order of knowledge and being. I suggest, with Aristotle, Hegel, and Peirce as my authorities, that metaphysics is last or late in the order of inquiry. Thought tends to the interests of life before turning beyond these exigencies to tell who and where we are. From practice through science to metaphysics, we use signs to speculate about things that are separate and different from us. We use logic and experiment to confirm that some of these hypotheses are true. In the end, we brace ourselves more firmly, knowing what to do and what not to do, what to be and what not to be, because these testable hypotheses have illumined some large part of being and our place within it.

Philosophy may ignore the opportunities for metaphysics as thinkers of other times and places have ignored the ones for science. Retreating from Whitehead's already constricting views, we may reduce philosophy to the critique of prejudice, comparing and grading the many conceptual frameworks, all the while emphasizing that mind has created each of them. This is mind near the origins of thought's spiral, mind self-adoring as it enjoys the power for making culture and the "life-world." This is mind at the back of the cave, hostile to philosophy, out of touch with the world. We have a better past, and prospects for a better future.

NOTES

1. Also see Justus Buchler, *Metaphysics of Natural Complexes* (New York: Columbia University Press, 1966).
2. David Weissman, *Eternal Possibilities* (Carbondale: Southern Illinois University Press, 1977), pp. 109–140.
3. Alfred North Whitehead, *Process and Reality* (Corrected Edition; New York: The Free Press, 1978), p. 8.
4. *Ibid.*, p. 16.
5. *Ibid.*, p. 159.
6. *Ibid.*, p. 157.
7. *Ibid.*, p. 160.
8. *Ibid.*, p. 18.
9. *Ibid.*, pp. 19, 22, pp. 219, 280.
10. *Ibid.*, p. 219.
11. *Ibid.*, p. 80.
12. *Ibid.*, p. 73.
13. *Ibid.*, p. 222.

Index